MALORY: THE CRITICAL HERITAGE

THE CRITICAL HERITAGE SERIES

GENERAL EDITOR: B. C. SOUTHAM, M.A., B.LITT. (OXON.)
Formerly Department of English, Westfield College, University of London

For a list of books in the series see the back end paper

MALORY

THE CRITICAL HERITAGE

Edited by

MARYLYN JACKSON PARINS

Associate Professor of English
University of Arkansas at Little Rock

ROUTLEDGE
LONDON AND NEW YORK

First published in 1988 by
Routledge
a division of Routledge, Chapman and Hall,
11 New Fetter Lane, London EC4P 4EE

Published in the USA by
Routledge
a division of Routledge, Chapman and Hall, Inc.
29 West 35th Street, New York, NY 10001

Set in 10/12 Bembo by
Thomson Press (India) Ltd., New Delhi
and printed in Great Britain
by T J Press (Padstow) Ltd
Padstow, Cornwall

British Library Cataloging in Publication Data

Parins, Marylyn Jackson
Malory: the critical heritage—
(Critical heritage series)
1. Fiction in English. Malory, Sir Thomas. Morte d' Arthur
—Critical studies
I. Title II. Series III. Series 8'.232

ISBN 0–415–00223–0

General Editor's Preface

The reception given to a writer by his contemporaries and near-contemporaries is evidence of considerable value to the student of literature. On one side we learn a great deal about the state of criticism at large and in particular about the development of critical attitudes towards a single writer; at the same time, through private comments in letters, journals or marginalia, we gain an insight upon the tastes and literary thought of individual readers of the period. Evidence of this kind helps us to understand the writer's historical situation, the nature of his immediate reading-public, and his response to these pressures.

The separate volumes in the *Critical Heritage Series* present a record of this early criticism. Clearly, for many of the highly productive and lengthily reviewed nineteenth- and twentieth-century writers, there exists an enormous body of material; and in these cases the volume editors have made a selection of the most important views, significant for their intrinsic critical worth or for their representative quality—perhaps even registering incomprehension!

For earlier writers, notably pre-eighteenth century, the materials are much scarcer and the historical period has been extended, sometimes far beyond the writer's lifetime, in order to show the inception and growth of critical views which were initially slow to appear.

In each volume the documents are headed by an Introduction, discussing the material assembled and relating the early stages of the author's reception to what we have come to identify as the critical tradition. The volumes will make available much material which would otherwise be difficult of access and it is hoped that the modern reader will be thereby helped towards an informed understanding of the ways in which literature has been read and judged.

B.C.S.

For my parents, Arline and Ewing Jackson,
and for A. F. House

Contents

Acknowledgments

I am grateful to the publishers listed below for permission to include passages essential to this book and for their prompt responses to my inquiries: Boydell & Brewer for the excerpt from Professor Derek Brewer's introduction to *Aspects of Malory*; Cambridge University Press for the passages from *The English Works of Roger Ascham*, ed. William Aldis Wright, and for extracts from *The Complete Works of Sir Philip Sidney*, ed. Albert Feuillerat; Columbia University Press for a passage from the *New Letters of Robert Southey*, ed. Kenneth Curry; J. M. Dent & Sons Ltd and Everyman's Library for the use of Caxton's Preface to the *Morte Darthur*; the Early English Text Society for excerpts from Richard Robinson's translation of Leland's *Assertion of Arthur* which appeared in *Chinon of England*, ed. W. E. Mead; Ginn & Company for the extensive use of W. E. Mead's introduction to *Selections from Sir Thomas Malory's Morte Darthur*; Macmillan, London and Basingstoke, for introductory material from the *Morte d'Arthur*, ed. A. W. Pollard; and Yale University Press for the passages from the Yale Edition of the Works of Samuel Johnson, *Johnson on Shakespeare*, ed. Arthur Sherbo.

This book owes a great deal to the work of other scholars in the field. In addition to specialized books and articles, I am particularly indebted to three more comprehensive works, James Merriman's *The Flower of Kings*, Beverly Taylor's and Elisabeth Brewer's *The Return of King Arthur*, and Page West Life's *Sir Thomas Malory and the Morte Darthur: An Annotated Bibliography and Survey of Scholarship*. (Complete citations appear in the notes to the Introduction.)

I am also indebted to those who generously gave time and assistance to this project. In particular, I wish to thank Professors Barry Gaines and Toshiyuki Takamiya for their very helpful comments and suggestions on the lists of Malory editions. Professor Takamiya kindly read the Introduction as well and provided additional information at several points. I am grateful for errors prevented; for any that remain, I am, of course, responsible.

Finally, I owe special thanks to Frank Kenney of the Department of Philosophy and Religious Studies, University of Arkansas at Little Rock, for the translation of John Bale's Latin and to my friend Mary Ann Littlefield for her invaluable assistance with the translations from Gaston Paris's introduction to the Huth *Merlin* and parts of his *Romania* article included in the text.

Note on the Text

In order to avoid a long string of end-notes in the Introduction, I have much abbreviated references through Section VII, the brief survey of twentieth-century criticism, and have incorporated most of these references into the text.

Through the collection of commentary from Caxton to Saintsbury, all notes are those provided by the authors except in the case of Leland (No. 3A) and H. Oskar Sommer (No. 41), where I wrote the explanatory notes.

For the convenience of the student, I have usually cited more easily accessible twentieth-century reprints of older texts where such reprints or new editions are available.

Introduction

Whether it is considered as a single unified work or as a collection of several loosely connected romances, Sir Thomas Malory's *Morte Darthur*[1] has exerted a unique shaping influence on other literary works and on the popular consciousness. That influence is with us today in the classroom, in films, in best-selling novels, in re-creations of medieval jousts, even perhaps in the modern quest for the historical Arthur.

It is not the purpose of the present volume, however, to provide evidence of the far-reaching and pervasive influence of the *Morte Darthur* by tracing every allusion to it over five centuries, nor to assess the degree and nature of its influence on the numerous poets, novelists, and playwrights who have turned for inspiration to its pages. While influence and popularity are aspects of the literary reputation here considered, particularly in its early stages, the bulk of the record presented here is drawn from nineteenth-century critical assessments of the *Morte Darthur* itself. It is to the nineteenth century that we owe the Arthurian revival, with its demonstrable effects on Malory scholarship, as well as the very editions of the *Morte Darthur* through which many a twentieth-century critic was first introduced to Malory. In addition, the nineteenth-century material anticipates the concerns of twentieth-century critics in its discussion of style, structure and unity, characterization, theme, and sources.

For the earlier period, selection of material was not difficult, and indeed so sparse is the 'critical' record that comments indicating mere familiarity with the *Morte Darthur* have been included. From the end of the eighteenth century on, discussions of Malory grow more frequent, showing markedly higher evaluations as the nineteenth century advanced. Selections from this material, more abundant and more positive especially after about 1860, have been chosen to reflect these general trends, though not ignoring negative evaluations as late as the 1890s. To sum up previous attitudes and to point the way toward twentieth-century work on Malory, an appropriate point was available in the work of George Saintsbury, where three selections, from 1885, 1898, and 1912, provide increasingly appreciative, increasingly serious, and increasingly detailed studies of the *Morte Darthur*.

The *Morte Darthur*'s popularity and its consequent influence were in part the result of its accessibility and its comprehensiveness. William Caxton printed Malory's work in 1485 precisely because it did reduce into English the 'many noble volumes... which be not had in our maternal tongue' and because it met the requirements he claimed on the part of divers gentlemen that the work include the history of King Arthur and of his knights, the history of the Sangreal, and the death and ending of Arthur. With the medieval revival of the nineteenth century, the *Morte Darthur* proved the single most important source of new considerations of the legend for the same reasons. Unlike medieval French and German romances, or even 'Sir Gawain and the Green Knight', it could be read and appreciated without translation or extensive glossing, and it presented the whole and essential Arthurian story from its beginning, through a loosely constructed middle, to the end. And, with only a slight shift in emphasis, the very elements which made the *Morte Darthur* popular and influential made it, finally, a critical success. Over the past two hundred years, increasingly higher evaluation of Malory's stature has evolved from consideration of his language and his treatment of the Arthurian legend.

To examine the critical record, it will be convenient to separate several strands for individual consideration. First to be discussed is the publication record and its relationship to the popularity of Arthurian romance in general. Another broad area of commentary from the beginning was the theme and morality of the *Morte Darthur*; included here also are considerations of the book's proper audience. Structure and style are remarked upon (often in the same sentence) from the later eighteenth century and will be considered in one section. A fourth element, source studies, dependent upon the accessibility of earlier material, did not develop until well into the nineteenth century, but became increasingly detailed and important to the recognition of Malory's achievement. Finally, a brief bibliographic survey of twentieth-century scholarship in these areas will be followed by an account of the biographical record, which was not significantly developed until late in the nineteenth century.

II PUBLICATION HISTORY

The publication history of the *Morte Darthur* is closely linked to the distribution of commentary on the work and thus to the selections in this volume; many, in fact, are drawn from the prefaces provided by Malory's numerous editors. (A list of complete editions up to 1983 appears at the end of this Introduction.) This publication history also reflects the rising or waning of interest in Arthurian romance in general in any given portion of the period covered here. As James Merriman has pointed out, 'There is no exaggeration... in saying that interest in Arthurian matter closely parallels interest in Malory.'[2]

Which way the influence worked is harder to determine. The initial publication of the *Morte Darthur* must have itself aroused new interest in material thitherto difficult of access, as did its reappearance in the early nineteenth century, although larger societal, political, or literary influences might determine the book's prestige at any given point.

The only fifteenth-century comments on Malory come from his editors and printers, Caxton and Wynkyn de Worde, but the fact that de Worde reprinted the work only thirteen years after initial publication and again in 1529 points to a very favorable reception. The sixteenth-century editions published by Copland (1557) and East (c. 1578) suggest continued demand; also, around the time of these editions there appears a cluster of comments on the work, and there is additional evidence of influence on literary productions of the period.

Caxton tells us that he finished printing the *Morte Darthur* on the last day of July 1485.[3] In less than a month Henry of Richmond, born in Wales and claiming descent through Cadwallader from Arthur himself, would become Henry VII at Bosworth Field. His victory there had been preceded by a virtual triumphal march through Wales as well as a failed attempt on the throne in 1483. Whether Thomas Malory was Yorkist or Lancastrian in his sympathies has been much debated, and the choice usually depends on which of three persons by this name is being proposed as the author of the *Morte Darthur* (see below, 'Biography'). Malory completed his work, he tells us, during the reign of Edward IV, a monarch who had also claimed descent from Arthur, and it has been suggested that Caxton was furnished Malory's manuscript by the queen's brother, Anthony Wydville.[4] However, Henry VII's Tudor ancestry was more dramatically Welsh and more to the point by August of 1485.

In the first flush of victory, the *Morte Darthur* could serve to advance the cause and the heritage of the Tudors, but during the sixteenth century new forces would arise to affect its influence. One was the questioning of Arthur's historic authenticity, a threat to the Tudor claim of restoring his glory in the sixteenth-century present. Another was later Renaissance humanism with its classical and Protestant affinities. The first led to John Leland's defence (No.3A) and John Bale's qualifications (No.3B), and finally to the replacement of Malory the historian by Malory the writer of chivalric romance, a role in which he was more useful to later writers. The second led to Roger Ascham's denunciation (No.4A), although he was not the first to castigate romance,[5] and to the attack by Nathaniel Baxter (No.4C), who was irritated by a recent publication of the *Morte Darthur*.

Ascham chose the *Morte Darthur* for attack precisely because it was being read at court. Although the prince he refers to is Henry VIII, the editions of Copland and East were published in the reigns of Mary and Elizabeth respectively, and certainly, in Elizabeth's time, Malory was in vogue. The entertainment for her at Kenilworth in 1575, written by George Gascoigne and others, shows use of the *Morte Darthur*,[6] and the references in Robert Laneham's letter (No.4B) indicate familiarity with the book. An interesting text of the second half of the sixteenth century has recently come to light; it is an·autograph manuscript by John Grinkin, 'King Arthur and the Knights of the Round Table, a compilation of the principal deeds of the King and his Knights as they appear in Malory's *Morte Darthur*', a sort of catalogue of knights and their deeds accompanied by many illustrations of their armorial bearings.[7]

It has been suggested that Shakespeare was acquainted with at least portions of the *Morte Darthur*, but the evidence is far from conclusive.[8] Sir Philip Sidney did know Malory's work. Ben Jonson is quoted by Drummond of Hawthornden as saying that Sidney had intended 'to turn all the stories of Arcadia into the admired legend of Arthur'. As some scholars believe, Sidney had already drawn on the *Morte Darthur* when composing the *Arcadia*, and in fact Marcus Goldman has said that 'Malory was one of the truly great influences that wrought to form the perfect and chivalric unity of Sidney's life and writings.'[9]

In Edmund Spenser's writing of the *Faerie Queene*, the *Morte Darthur* was not the shaping influence it apparently had been for Sidney, but Spenser was indebted to it, if not to the degree that Thomas Warton would later maintain. Spenser died in 1599, and in the new century the fortunes of Arthurian matter began to decline; there was a longish gap between the edition of the *Morte Darthur* published around 1578 and the next one, printed by William Stansby in 1634, and this latter would be the last issue of the *Morte Darthur* for nearly two hundred years.

The 1634 publication can be viewed in either of two ways. One is that there was still considerable demand for Malory's work well into the seventeenth century. At an opposite extreme is the view that Malory was almost entirely abandoned in the first Stuart reign and completely ignored after it. Certainly there was interest in the *Morte Darthur* in the early part of the century. Ben Jonson contemplated an epic poem based presumably on Malory; he is quoted as having said, 'for a Heroik poeme... there was no such ground as King Arthur's fiction.'[10] But Jonson's occasional references to Arthur and his knights of romance belittle the genre. Milton in his youth read romance and considered using the Arthurian story as an epic subject, but abandoned the idea. He rejected the possibility that Arthur was an historical person, and the brief references to the *Morte Darthur* in *Paradise Lost* and *Paradise Regained* are merely echoes evoking the realm of romance.[11] In the last decade of the seventeenth century, John Dryden produced an opera, *King Arthur*, and Richard Blackmore wrote two epic poems, *Prince Arthur* and *King Arthur*, but none of these works owed anything to Malory.

The preface to the 1634 edition (No. 5A), presumably written by Jacob Blome, announced that the *Morte Darthur* had been rescued 'almost from the gulph of oblivion', a phrasing which suggests that the earlier editions had become scarce. But this edition itself seems to have produced no revival of interest; it is apparently the version referred to by William Nicolson in the *English Historical Library* (No. 5B), but Nicolson's comments give no indication that he had read the work, and he notes merely that its matter is often the subject of popular ballads.

The editor of the 1634 edition announced his intention of

expurgating the older text, especially in passages where Arthur or his knights 'were declared in their communications to sweare prophane, and use superstitious speeches'. A later editor, Sir Edward Strachey, noted some 20,000 variations (including printers' errors, misreadings, etc.) between the original Caxton and this edition of 1634.

There were no new editions of the *Morte Darthur* in the eighteenth century, nor was there any notice of the work until nearly mid-century, when William Oldys included a brief account of the work in his discussion of Caxton's publications (No.6). Oldys knew of more than one edition and must in fact have seen a copy of one as he describes 'a large thick volume' and paraphrases from Caxton's introduction. By the 1760s, although publication of a new edition was still some fifty years away, growing antiquarian interest in the older literature resulted in increased attention to Malory's work. Thomas Warton's *Observations on the Fairy Queen* clearly showed his close familiarity with the *Morte Darthur* and brought to attention Malory's work—its matter, and its previous popularity and influence. Collections of older ballads and then of longer poems began to appear, and their editors often used Malory's version of the Arthurian story to explain or amplify the Arthurian parts of this material; examples are Percy's *Reliques*, Joseph Ritson's *Ancient Engleish Metrical Romanceës*, and George Ellis's *Specimens of Early English Metrical Romances*.

Sir Walter Scott noted in his *Sir Tristrem* that the *Morte Darthur* 'is in the hands of most antiquaries and collectors', indicating its rarity by this time, and by 1807 he felt the time was ripe for a new edition. Scott planned initially to use the 1634 edition, but as he was aware of its expurgations, he wished to restore altered portions of the text by collation with an earlier edition. At this time Scott did not know of the survival of any Caxton text. There are, in fact, only two known copies of Caxton's original edition, one complete, the other lacking eleven leaves. By 1809, Scott had learned of the existence of the perfect copy, in the Osterley Park library of Lady Jersey. By this time, however, his project had been forestalled by Robert Southey's announcement (in late 1807) that he planned to bring out a new edition of Malory, one in his series of 'Ancient Romances' for Longman, a series which already included *Amadis de Gaul* and *Palermin of England*. Southey knew less about available editions than Scott did, and through 1807 he wrote to Richard

Heber and other collector friends requesting editions of Malory and related romances; 'were there an Academy of the Round Table,' he wrote, 'I believe myself worthy of a seat there in point of knowledge, but my Round Table library is very poor.'[12]

However ready Scott and Southey were to see a new edition of the *Morte Darthur* in print, Southey's publishers were apparently not so eager and Southey's project languished. By late 1809 he had given up the plan and in fact relinquished the project to Scott, urging him again in 1810 to take up the work and offering his notes. Scott by this time wanted to make use of Lady Jersey's Caxton, but after 1810 no more is heard about his proposed edition. The Caxton at Osterley Park was, however, examined and described by Thomas Dibdin (No. 10D) in 1810, and in 1815 Dibdin, librarian to Lord Spencer and his extensive collection at Althorp, announced that Longman & Company planned to publish a limited edition of the *Morte Darthur* from Spencer's unique copy of Wynkyn de Worde's 1498 edition. Before this plan was carried out, a previously unknown second copy of Caxton turned up in the sale of the John Lloyd library in 1816. This copy was purchased by Lord Spencer, and Longman & Company decided to have it printed even though, like the Wynkyn de Worde, it was incomplete. When the editor Longman had hired for the proposed reprint 'decamped with another man's wife, leaving Longman and the subscribers in the lurch',[13] the publishers turned once again to Southey, who wrote the introduction and notes while the text was edited by William Upcott. This text was regarded as an accurate reprint for years, although in fact Upcott had ingeniously drawn from later editions to make up the missing eleven leaves of his original. The new two-volume edition, handsome and rather expensive, came out in 1817.

Scott had said in 1807 that he thought a reprint of Malory would sell, and the thought presently occurred to others as well, for the 1817 edition was not the first to be published in the nineteenth century. In fact, the preceding year had seen the publication of two other editions of the *Morte Darthur*, both inexpensive, both showing evidence of hasty editing, and both based on the more accessible edition of 1634. The first of these, a two-volume edition, was published by J. Walker & Company in its series Walker's British Classics. The second differs from the first in being a three-volume set and, according to its editor, in being expurgated 'to render the text fit for the eye of youth; and that it might be no longer secreted from the fair sex'.[14]

Thus, after a long hiatus, the *Morte Darthur* was thrice printed in a two-year period, and it was through these editions that Malory's work became accessible not only to a popular audience but to poets and artists whose use of it would in turn engender re-reading and reconsideration of the *Morte Darthur* itself. Edward Strachey, whose Globe edition of the *Morte Darthur* (1868) was very influential, said that the 1816 editions were 'probably the volumes through which most of my own generation made their first acquaintance with King Arthur and his knights'. As Barry Gaines has pointed out, Keats owned the Walker 1816 edition, and Wordsworth noted his own use of that edition. Tennyson owned both 1816 editions, both 'much used by the poet' according to his son's *Memoir*.[15]

Edward Burne-Jones and William Morris treasured a copy of Southey's 1817 edition which Morris had had bound in white vellum, and their interest in the book radiated through the Pre-Raphaelite brotherhood. The same edition provided Swinburne's introduction to Malory, and he apparently borrowed Southey's edition from Burne-Jones when he was planning his own version of the Tristram story.[16]

After this flurry of publication, forty years elapsed before the *Morte Darthur* was again reprinted. In the interval, several forces were working to increase the reading of Malory and to produce critical evaluation of his work. One was the proliferation of book clubs and literary and publishing societies. Such groups as the Roxburghe Club, the Bannatyne, the Maitland, the Abbotsford, the Surtees and Camden Societies, and the Society of Antiquaries issued a number of Arthurian romances including Layamon's *Brut*, *Syr Gawayne*, *The Awntyrs of Arthur*, and the stanzaic *Morte Arthur*. Also published during the period were Lady Charlotte Guest's *Mabinogion* and the alliterative *Morte Arthure*. Editors of these texts frequently referred to the *Morte Darthur* and often used extracts from it as explanatory reference points. Several of these publications, and later in the century editions of the English prose *Merlin*, the French Huth *Merlin*, the French *Queste*, and other romances, would of course make it possible to study Malory's work against his sources.

A second factor was the increasingly acceptable idea that

medieval chivalry could provide an appropriate guide to conduct in the shaping of a nineteenth-century gentleman.[17] A now curious but once widely read example of this approach is *The Broad Stone of Honour* by Kenelm Henry Digby, first published in 1822 and then enlarged into four volumes, 1828–9. The first edition carried the subtitle 'Rules for the Gentlemen of England', changed in later editions to 'The True Sense and Practice of Chivalry'. Here, on page after page, Malory is quoted and his king and knights used as exemplars.

A third force operating during this period and well beyond was the rise of English studies in the schools and a corresponding increase in the publication of literary histories, manuals, and guides to English literature. Examples of remarks on Malory drawn from such sources are those of Dunlop, Hallam, and Craik (No. 14); David Masson's longer commentary (No. 18) exemplifies the increasingly important place given to Malory in English studies.

Finally, of course, the period following the first three nineteenth-century editions was rich in new literary treatments of Arthurian material, much of it drawn from or inspired by the *Morte Darthur*. Less well-remembered treatments include works by Peacock, Reginald Heber, Emerson, and Bulwer-Lytton. But by 1842 Tennyson had published his 'Morte d'Arthur', 'Sir Launcelot and Queen Guinevere', 'The Lady of Shalott', and 'Sir Galahad'; in 1852 came Arnold's 'Tristram and Iseult' and in 1858 Morris's *Defence of Guenevere and other Poems*.

1858 was also the year in which Thomas Wright brought out a new edition of the *Morte Darthur*. Wright (No. 16) considered the 1817 edition of Caxton 'useless to the general reader'; in addition, he said, the two popular editions of 1816 had both become rare, and 'the want of a good edition of this romance has been felt generally.' Wright chose to use the 1634 edition for its more accessible language.

From 1858 on, editions and critical commentary proliferated. Between 1862 and 1900 there were six complete editions (although Strachey's and Rhys's were expurgated) and some thirteen books of selections or adaptations of the *Morte Darthur* (see 'Editions' following the Introduction). Beginning with Wright's edition, major new editions were regularly reviewed in the periodical press both in England and in America.

In 1859 Tennyson's first group of *Idylls* had appeared, and through succeeding decades reviews and other discussions of Tennyson's continuing additions to the work naturally involved comparison with the *Morte Darthur*. Another effect of the *Idylls* was the publication of a number of popular editions that were expurgated, modernized in spelling, and usually abridged. When H. Oskar Sommer in 1889 published a complete scholarly edition of Caxton's text, it was the first unexpurgated edition to have appeared since 1817 and the first unaltered Caxton since Caxton. Sommer's edition of the text, along with his two volumes of commentary, in turn led to new considerations of Malory's achievement by reviewers and scholars and to the publication of several new editions of his work, unexpurgated, though modernized in spelling, in the final decade of the nineteenth century. W. E. Mead and A. T. Martin produced volumes of selections, and complete editions included those of Israel Gollancz, A. W. Pollard, and the Dent edition with an introduction by John Rhys and illustrations by Aubrey Beardsley. Frequent reprints of these popular editions as well as others such as Sidney Lanier's *The Boy's King Arthur*, and numerous new adaptations and retellings, supplied the scholarly and the popular markets for several decades.

III THEME, MORALITY, AUDIENCE

William Caxton's preface to the *Morte Darthur* (No. 1) advertised the book as providing an example of noble chivalry in which the good gained honour and the vicious were punished. His catalogue of the work's various features included murder, hate, and sin as well as courtesy and virtue, and his admonition to follow the good and leave the evil would be often repeated through the nineteenth century as writers found it necessary to defend Malory's moral tone. Wynkyn de Worde's interpolation (No. 2)—long thought to be Malory's (or Caxton's) interjectory warning to 'mighty and pompous lords' on the *Morte Darthur*'s depiction of transitory glory—echoes Caxton's sentiments.

Both publishers assume an aristocratic audience for the book, though Caxton the businessman includes 'other estates' along with the lords and ladies who could afford to own the book. For this contemporary audience, it is possible that Caxton and de Worde (and Malory himself) intended the *Morte Darthur* to serve as a nostalgic evocation, or as reassertion, of the value of feudal and chivalric ideals in an age which seemed to be abandoning them.[18] Certainly the book's emphasis on loyalty to the rightful sovereign would be later associated with the divisiveness of the Wars of the Roses.

For Roger Ascham, the portrayal of murder, hate, and sin in Malory's book rendered it entirely immoral, although not quite as pernicious as the contemporary Italian influence (No.4A). This response, as suggested above, is linked to the devaluing of products of the barbarous, non-classical, and Catholic Middle Ages. Even the Grail story—the moralistic mainstay of many a nineteenth-century critic—is dismissed by Nathaniel Baxter as 'vile and stinking', presumably because it represents monkish and supersti-tious fanaticism.

That literature in order to be acceptable must also be morally improving was not a new concept in the sixteenth century, nor was it exclusive to classical or neoclassical theorists. The notion is as evident in Caxton's preface as in the remarks of Ascham and Baxter, although its application is not quite yet as a standard of literature. The standards by which literature was to be judged from the sixteenth century on, best-known perhaps through Sir Philip Sidney's *Defence of Poesie*, differed essentially from those of the earlier period. Derek Brewer has shown how the shift in values from 'Gothic' to neoclassical values affected evaluation of Malory's work as well as that of Chaucer; the introductions noted provide useful discussion of this topic.[19] The term 'neoclassical' is broadly used here to indicate a nexus of values applied to literary criticism: among these are the appreciation of symmetry, clarity, and a logically consistent structure, and the idea that serious art imitates nature and therefore portrays what is real but at the same time what is elevating. Neoclassical standards applied to the *Morte Darthur* would have their greatest effect on evaluation of the book's structure, as will be seen below. But Malory's mixture of vice and virtue and the absence of overt didacticism created equally mixed responses, especially among Victorians.

Sidney's *Defence* was influential in its articulation and application of neoclassical standards to literature. But, as noted earlier, Sidney's own literary work was influenced by the *Morte Darthur*, and in the *Defence* he insists on the power of chivalric romance to move men to virtuous action (No.4D). Although Sidney does not apply neoclassical criteria to the *Morte Darthur*, his expressed dislike of mixed modes (low/high, comic/tragic) and his view of the poet/maker as responsible for the moral improvement of readers would contribute to some negative evaluations of Malory's work through the eighteenth century and well beyond.

Through much of the seventeenth and eighteenth centuries, there is so little comment on the *Morte Darthur* that questions of its morality (or of anything else) do not arise, although the absence of interest in the book implies a negative response.[20] The next comment is from William Oldys (No. 6), who, at mid-eighteenth century, seems to think Caxton was misguided in believing that the book would inspire a spirit of valour in the gentry. His remarks that Malory had neither made his heroes 'commanders of their passions' nor 'rigorously confined them to honour and decorum' are but an eighteenth-century adaptation of Ascham's comments, and the cause-and-effect logic of the sentence in which they occur suggests an eighteenth-century gentleman-scholar's deploring of the ill-judged exemplars chosen by 'persons of the highest distinction' (presumably Henry VIII) in an earlier, less decorous age. Even after Ascham's condemnation of it, Oldys says, the book remained in print into the seventeenth century, but only for 'the entertainment of the lighter and more insolid readers'.

Samuel Johnson's attitude toward romance cannot be simply categorized. Like Warton, he recognized the value of studying this older literature for its value in determining the tastes and suppositions of earlier audiences to produce a better understanding of the authors who wrote in such a milieu; this is the point he addresses in the passage quoted (No. 7). Elsewhere, Johnson expressed a preference for the novel, 'written from learning, observation, and general converse, to the romance with its giants, knights, deserts, and imaginary castles, the product of a mind heated with incredibilities'.[21] If art must imitate nature, by the eighteenth century what was not 'real' could not be art. The implausibilities of romance, as well as the mixture of good and bad, thus had come to be another factor militating against their acceptance as worthwhile literature. Johnson did read the *Morte Darthur* and other romances, as did his contemporaries Percy and Warton, and it is perhaps significant that none of these scholars, nor Ritson, nor Ellis, nor Scott, refers specifically to the book's morality.

The *British Bibliographer* of 1810 (No. 11) refers to Malory's loose morality especially in regard to Tristram and to Lancelot's 'notorious' and 'indecorous' relationship with Guinevere, but the writer does not condemn the book out of hand. As has been noted above, one of the 1816 editions of the *Morte Darthur* was expurgated by its nineteenth-century editor; this edition had not sold as well as its rival of the same year, and the announcement that the book in this version was more fit for youth was probably intended to enhance sales.[22] The editor's remark that with his expurgations, the *Morte Darthur* need no longer be 'secreted from the fair sex' implies that theretofore it had been, but the point is dubious. His remark on youth, however, touches another aspect of Malory's nineteenth-century reception. Earlier criticism assumed an adult audience, but in the nineteenth century the *Morte Darthur* was often regarded as a book primarily for boys and limited in its adult appeal (although adults edited the books for boys).

Both Scott and Southey had read Malory as boys, but Scott's ability to extend his pleasure in the book and its essential spirit into adulthood was greater than Southey's. Scott's view was the kind of Romantic medievalism that saw (and reshaped) the Middle Ages as an orderly and in many ways admirable era; Southey's view of the same period was less sanguine. Southey tells us in his introduction (No. 13) that as a schoolboy his favourite book next to the *Faerie Queene* was the *Morte Darthur* and recommends modernization of its orthography and publication as a book for boys. But his introduction also makes it clear that as an adult, he has responsible reservations about romance. Having read several of the French romances that he believed to be Malory's sources, Southey preferred the moral tone of *Meliadus* and *Guiron le courtois* to the story in the prose *Tristan* which 'frequently disgusted' him. Southey acknowledged privately that Arthurian romances were a 'luxurious sort of reading, in which I think I should not afford to indulge were I not paid for it'.[23] Nonetheless, in this paid introduction, he does, if somewhat condescendingly, defend romance and by implication Malory from attacks on plausibility and morality, insisting that the romances of chivalry worked to raise the cruel and barbarous moral standards of the times in which they were written and that what seems implausible to the nineteenth-century reader was not so for the earlier, more credulous age. He concludes by noting that 'for the full enjoyment' of romance, 'a certain aptitude is required ... where that aptitude exists, perhaps no works of imagination produce so much delight'.

That aptitude or the lack of it will be evident in the remarks of a number of nineteenth-century critics: those who have it will vigorously defend the *Morte Darthur*'s morality and its appeal to men as well as boys; those who do not will dwell on the book's inadequacies or find reasons other than delight for reading it. One such reason, cited by Thomas Wright (No. 16) and a number of others, was educational (and thus improving); the *Morte Darthur* was viewed as providing a good comprehensive condensation of a number of Arthurian stories as well as an understanding of the Middle Ages.

The *Christian Examiner*'s review of Wright's edition echoed Wright's comment on Malory as a 'repository of information' but added that his appeal is not merely to a 'childish appetite'. On the contrary, the *Morte Darthur* fulfils the more mature wish that fiction—'even under the unsettled conditions of romance'—reflect the conflict produced by the 'mingled good and evil in men's hearts and fates' (No. 17). *Blackwood's* reviewer (No. 19) of the same edition, on the other hand, announced that the *Morte Darthur*'s absence of moral reflections and its compiling of exciting incident upon incident must render it 'most intelligible to the schoolboy mind ... fresh from foot-ball'. Only a few years before these reviews were written, Rossetti was telling Morris and Burne-Jones that he considered the Bible and the *Morte Darthur* (perhaps deliberately linking them) the two greatest books in the world; Morris himself listed the *Morte Darthur* as one of the best fifty-four books and authors in world literature.[24]

Concern with the moral power of literature in its application to the *Morte Darthur* seemed to become more prominent from about mid-century on, and some of this concern is related to increased emphasis on English studies in the schools. The study of English literature—as opposed to a classical curriculum—was increasingly regarded as a respectable avenue for acquiring an education. At first, perhaps, English studies were seen as providing access to literature to those for whom a classical education was unattainable. One of the first school anthologies of English literature, produced in 1784 by the Reverend Vicesimus Knox, was directed at the schoolboy or the 'mercantile classes, at least of the higher order', and its complete title is instructive:

Elegant extracts; or Useful and entertaining pieces of poetry, selected for the improvement of scholars at classical and other schools in the art of speaking, in reading, thinking, composing, and in the conduct of life.

As D.J. Palmer has pointed out in his valuable study, 'Both utilitarian and literary ideals contributed to develop the importance of English studies as part of a well-rounded general education.'[25] Although the controversy, often bitter, over the place of such studies in the schools and universities would continue through the nineteenth century (the Oxford English School was not established until 1894), new colleges founded in London in the 1820s and 1830s, University and King's, immediately established chairs in English Language and Literature, and teachers appointed there often lectured as well at the London Working Men's College and the Queen's College for Women. Dedicated teachers associated with these institutions endeavoured to shape and regularize English studies as an academic discipline through the study of English literary history; equally important was the 'lofty moral tone of English studies' especially at King's, imparted by F.D. Maurice and others. Through them, Palmer says, 'flows that missionary spirit ... which did even more [than literary history] to promote the study of English literature outside the colleges'.[26]

The aims thus associated with English studies in general have relevance to the discussion of Malory through the remainder of the century, especially when it is noted how much of that discussion was contributed by those engaged in promoting English studies: David Masson, Henry Morley, F.J. Furnivall, and Frederick Ryland were all associated with the London colleges; William Minto and George Lillie Craik taught English literature at Aberdeen and Belfast respectively. And F.D. Maurice's influence reached beyond these circles; his proselytizing is said to have exercised a lasting influence on Edward Strachey.[27]

Reviewing Tennyson's early *Idylls* ('Geraint and Enid', 'Merlin and Vivien', 'Lancelot and Elaine', and 'Guinevere') in 1859, William Gladstone had remarked on the *Morte Darthur* as a 'rich repository' for Tennyson and found the work an appropriate choice: 'It is national: it is Christian. It is also human in the largest and deepest sense; and, therefore, though highly national, it is universal.'[28] David Masson (No. 18) noted the ways in which the Arthurian legend as presented in Malory had served as a 'magazine of ideal subjects' for a number of poets, but thought that it should be read for its own merits, which include the presentation of 'what is eternal and general in human nature and in man's spiritual and social experience'. From time to time, he says, there is the 'quiver of some ethical meaning' arising from an 'intentionally ... half-expressed philosophy'. That is, he seems to say, the work is not didactic, but it is aimed at the ideal.

The character of Lancelot is often used to show that the *Morte Darthur* is actually quite moral or that it is not so at all. So appealing was Malory's portrayal of his character that Lancelot was thought an especially pernicious example for young and passionate minds. (See No. 19, for example.) On the other hand, the idea, mentioned above, that Malory's work and other chivalric romances might provide models for behaviour was sustained through the nineteenth century and into the early twentieth. In America, especially, the identification of 'chivalry' with Southern ideals was particularly strong following the Civil War. Sidney Lanier wrote that 'the days of chivalry are not gone, they are only spiritualized ... the knight of the nineteenth century fights not with trenchant sword but with trenchant soul.'[29] In 1880, Lanier brought out an expurgated version of the *Morte Darthur* in which the character of Lancelot represents an ideal model remarked on in his introduction. An anonymous American publication of 1872 was entitled *The Morte D'Arthur: Its Influence on the Spirit and Manners of the Nineteenth Century* and it was dedicated to the widow of Leonidas Polk, who 'whether as a soldier of the cross when Bishop of Louisiana, or as a soldier of the southern Confederacy when Lieut. Gen. Polk, C.S.A., exemplified in his life and character the spirit of ancient chivalry as handed down to us in the Morte D'Arthur....'[30] To begin with, the author traces our 'modern refinement' back to its 'fountain-head', the *Morte Darthur*, and devotes most of the book to providing examples that show how Southern commanders exhibited the chivalry inspired by Malory, while their Northern counterparts consistently failed to do so.

Between Wright's edition of 1858 and Sommer's in 1889, every edition published was either abridged or expurgated or both. Tennyson was in his *Idylls* presenting Arthur as a blameless king, and many expurgated versions omitted all reference to the begetting of Mordred, implied that Arthur's birth was the natural consequence of Uther's marriage to Igraine, and presented Lancelot's devotion to the queen in an ideal light. Expurgators routinely cited Tennyson's treatment of the story as well as altered moral standards as their justification. (See Knowles, Conybeare, Strachey, and Lanier as examples.)[31]

Edward Strachey was an exception to the general run of expurgators; although he did alter a number of passages to remove physical terminology and to tone down references to Mordred's parentage, he did not completely excise or badly misrepresent the events of the narrative. He dealt earnestly, defensively, and at length with the 'perplexed question' of the morality of the book, the more so, perhaps, because he intended this new edition of 1868 as a book for boys. It is worth noting, too, that in his revised introduction of 1891, Strachey made a greater defence of the book's appeal to the mature intellect and was much more emphatic regarding Malory's positive moral qualities, all but ignoring the moral defects he had mentioned in 1868. Among these positive moral features is 'the silent yet implied judgment which is passed upon lawless love by its tragic end'.

Other critics and reviewers found Tennyson's treatment less appealing than Malory's and, wishing to prove the *Morte Darthur* moral despite its 'immoralities', found in its pages a tragic pattern of unwitting sin come home to roost, as with Oedipus. In this view (that of Herbert Coleridge, Furnivall, Swinburne, Minto, and Ernest Rhys), Arthur's unwitting incest was the cause of his destruction through Mordred, and Lancelot and Guinevere merely provided the necessary agent for the bringing down of doom. Tristram's profligacy and Arthur's open toleration of his adultery compared to Arthur's response to the public disclosure of his own betrayal will be seen as a continuing moral problem, but the suffering of the main characters toward the end is seen as retributive and thus productive of a moral lesson or poetic justice (see Nos 20 and 32 for examples).

Another line of defence provided by Tennyson's treatment of the Arthurian story was the view that Malory's Grail quest, unlike Tennyson's, added an important spiritual significance to his work. It could also be considered moral in its exclusion of both Arthur and Lancelot. This was a view espoused to varying degrees by Furnivall (No. 25), Edward Russell (No. 38), and Frederick Ryland (No. 39) among others, but it was disputed by R.H. Hutton (No. 30c), who argued that when one *reads* Malory, it is not Arthur's sin but his glory that one remembers.

Alfred Nutt further reduced the importance of the Grail quest as a spiritual force motivating the action of the *Morte Darthur* (No. 37B). Nutt declared the enthusiasm of Ernest Rhys and others for the Grail quest as spiritually significant to be unjustified. For one thing, Nutt, like some others, feels distaste for the extremely monastic and ascetic tone of the version that Malory followed; its exaltation of physical chastity and abhorrence of women, he believes, cannot provide an appropriate moral example to the present age. Nutt notes that Malory himself 'occasionally tones down the grossness' of the French *Queste*, but finds it 'hardly too much to say' that Malory's sinful Lancelot offers a 'truer, more human, and therefore more progressive' moral example than the sinless Galahad.

Other critics and reviewers found other ways to regard the *Morte Darthur* as morally improving. One was that Malory's 'outspoken plainness' was less injurious than the insinuative prurience of modern romance (No. 26). While one faction continued to regard 'memorials of an inferior past' as unable to offer 'serious guidance' to the nineteenth-century reader (No. 38), the more Romantic view considered the ethical theory of chivalric romances a distinctly high one—finer, perhaps, than that practised in the present materialistic age (No. 39).

With a number of scholars, the question of morality was never aired; the concerns of literary historians such as Ten Brink, and those of Gaston Paris and H. Oskar Sommer, lay elsewhere. The rise of English studies had an important corollary. As the study of English literature found an accepted place in the curricula of schools and universities, this literature became less the property of the non-specialist or general reader. As the *Morte Darthur* became an object of study rather than a reading experience, its effect on the reader would be of less concern than its construction, its relationship to its sources, and so on. That the scholars just referred to were not English perhaps illustrates the point, and one sees traces of the more detached attitude in Nutt and in Mead. Another example is George Cox (No. 34). It is not simply that his work in mythology and comparative literature had inured him to the irregularities of domestic arrangement that distressed other Victorians; his aim is to show the mythic adaptations and survivals in the Arthurian story, and in that view, certain physical relationships in

Malory are essential to the story. He frankly labels Guinevere's outburst that drives Lancelot to madness a 'sensual fury', and is probably the first writer to focus attention on the genuine moral problem presented by Lancelot's public assertions that he and Guinevere are innocent of any wrongdoing, that they have been falsely accused by liars, and the reader's knowledge that they have in fact committed adultery; Cox notes, though without noticeable repugnance, Lancelot's 'long course of equivocation and lying'.

In two volumes of commentary, H. Oskar Sommer did not discuss the morality or theme of the *Morte Darthur*; in an essay accompanying volume III of this scholarly edition, Andrew Lang (No. 42) said that the book was 'strong on the side of goodness throughout' and noted that Tennyson's 'Touched by the adulterous finger of a time/That hover'd between war and wantonness' was a 'hard judgment' on a work in which evil is neither triumphant nor sympathetic. But he did not belabour the point, and editors of the new, modernized, popular editions that followed Sommer's did not feel obliged to address the question of the book's morality, although the *Nation*'s reviewer of one of these editions noted the appeal of the book to young readers and echoed the earlier-expressed idea that the interest of mature readers would lie in the educative picture of medieval life and manners, and in its piety (No. 46B).

The work of literary historians had helped to place Malory more clearly in a fifteenth-century context, and for Mungo MacCallum (No. 48) Malory's work was not deliberately moral or immoral, but reflected thematically the dissolution of the 'unstable equilib-rium' of medieval chivalry, though he does not seem to regard this theme as consciously produced. Malory himself, MacCallum says, 'means right' and 'has succeeded in the grand lines of the history'. In a quite long introduction (No. 49), William E. Mead, publishing in Boston, found it unnecessary (or perhaps undesirable) to discuss morality except to note that the *Morte Darthur* is 'pervaded with the more enduring qualities of our common humanity'. Saintsbury takes the 'noble morality' of the work for granted; thematically, he says, Malory saw that 'in the combination of the Quest of the Graal with the loves of Lancelot and Guinevere lay the kernel at once and the conclusion of the whole matter' (No. 51b). As an adult reader, Saintsbury finds 'no unpleasant concession to duty' in going through the *Morte Darthur* for perhaps the fiftieth time (No. 51c).

It is tempting to generalize that more perceptive and serious critics and scholars did not find it necessary to defend the *Morte Darthur*'s morality while popularizers, reviewers, and editors presenting new texts to the public did. But such a generalization is too sweeping; it ignores many exceptions and differing objectives, and tends to overemphasize, if that is possible, the role of Victorian notions of propriety in shaping a response to literature and to Malory. While there is a certain degree of smugness in nineteenth-century comments about the differing standards of an earlier age, there is also a recognition that Malory's moral stance cannot be judged by Tennyson's. Among those who dealt with the question from the early record through the later one, some found Malory to be moral, and others did not; the point is that, for both groups, he should be.

IV STRUCTURE AND STYLE

For Caxton, it was enough that Malory's work was in English, that it presented a good many Arthurian stories, and that it provided examples of virtue. Only with the Stansby/Blome edition of 1634 was there sufficient distance for Malory's language to be regarded as the 'best forme and manner of writing and speech that was in use at those times', but a shift of values is already evident in the editor's defence of the work. The book may not be as accurate historically as could be wished, he says, and its style is 'plaine and simple' rather than 'eloquent and ornated', but the *Morte Darthur* can be read with 'pleasure and profit'.

Thomas Warton was the first to comment specifically on the lack of unity in the *Morte Darthur*, although the ways in which romance structure failed to measure up to that of epic had been a topic of criticism for some time, partly as a result of continued interest in the *Faerie Queene*. In 1762, in *Letters on Chivalry and Romance*, Richard Hurd took the view that Spenser should not be judged by classical standards. In arguing this position, Hurd also argued for freeing romance in general from these formal strictures, although his knowledge of medieval romance was scant and second-hand.[32] However well Hurd's comments set the stage for a reconsideration of Spenser, they did not much affect the general perception of the *Morte Darthur* through the next century. Even in the second half of the nineteenth century, the unity of Malory's work was usually defended on the basis that it really was a sort of epic after all.

Early in the century, the *Morte Darthur* was viewed as a compilation lacking in design and harmony of parts. Walter Scott (No. 9) established a view of Malory's structure and style that would reverberate through the nineteenth century, one that would allow enjoyment and delight in Malory while at the same time providing responsible reservations about the work as literature. The solution was to refer to the *Morte Darthur* as a 'bundle of extracts', made 'at hazard, and without much art' but written in excellent prose and 'breathing a high tone of chivalry'. Scott's use of such terms as 'simplicity' and 'sublime' in describing the style show the influence of the Romantic movement, but Romantic theories about organic form and structure did not have any appreciable effect on evaluation of Malory's structure, although Southey (No. 13) deplored the 'inartificial' (he means 'not artful') structure of Arthurian romance by using an organic metaphor: the adventures, he says, lack the 'necessary relation and due proportion to each other' and are therefore to be compared not to trees, but to plants like the prickly pear, 'where one joint grows upon another, all equal in size and alike in shape, and the whole making a formless and misshapen mass'.

Joseph Ritson had called the *Morte Darthur* 'mangle'd' but 'popular', and Ellis, the *British Bibliographer,* Hallam, Craik, and Thomas Wright use only slightly varied terms, describing the book's irregularity, its 'too similar class of incidents' or simply calling it a translation or compilation. But all praise the 'mastery of expression', the spirited language, singling out passages, often Ector's lament, as particularly fine examples. Even Thomas Dibdin, in a straightforward bibliographic description of the complete Caxton (No. 10D), adds a footnote praising the style and including a lengthy extract. Tennyson, unable to read *Palermin* or the *Amadis* preferred by Southey, called the *Morte Darthur* 'much the best' of the romances of chivalry, adding that 'there are very fine things in it; but all strung together without Art'.[33]

Individual segments of the *Morte Darthur* were often singled out as showing unity in themselves. Southey and others noted the 'structure and completeness' of the tale of Gareth and the picturesque and tragic story of Balin and Balan, and almost everyone would find significant design in the *Morte Darthur*'s concluding chapters.

Soon after the mid-century, discussions of structure became more elaborate and more specific. David Masson (No. 18) had said that 'the whole may be taken, in its cohesion, as an Epic Allegory', and developments of this idea would furnish material to earnest defenders of Malory's essential unity. Granted that the *Morte Darthur* lacked the clarity and orthodox construction of modern novels, its allegorical significance, perceptible throughout but especially in Mordred, the 'instrument of infinite ruin', could provide an organizing principle like that of epic (see No. 20 for an example). As seen above, this theme was developed by Coleridge and by Furnivall (who called the work a 'most pleasant jumble') to illustrate the morality of the *Morte Darthur*, but it obviously could be seen as adding structural coherence as well. Edward Strachey (Nos 28 and 45) would insist that the book had a 'properly epic' plan, finding evidence of unity and harmony in the development of the main characters (and of several minor ones) as well as in the tragic end which comes on inevitably despite efforts to avert the catastrophe.

Others, however, continued to find the structure of the *Morte Darthur* unsatisfactory while continuing to praise the style. Expurgators and abridgers like Knowles (No. 21) and Conybeare (No. 27) naturally spoke of the book as 'too long' and referred to 'confusion and want of system' since their presentations would arrange the *Morte Darthur* into a 'somewhat clearer and more consecutive story' than had been achieved by Malory. Ernest Rhys, too, abridged and rearranged Malory's 'rather diffuse and incoherent' narrative, but also called it an epic and praised the style (No. 36). Alfred Nutt's appraisal (No. 37B) is perhaps the most forthright example of divergent views as to the merits of structure and style. Nutt was one of the first scholars in England to write from a close study and knowledge of French, German, and Celtic Grail material, and since he knew how much of this vast corpus never appears in the *Morte Darthur*, his view of Malory's intelligence and skill in compiling a much truncated version is not high. But, he says, Malory's 'language is exactly what it ought to be'.

In discussing the structure of Malory's work, many nineteenth-century critics took a middle ground, not claiming epic unity, but noting qualities that lent consistency and coherence. Perhaps under the influence of Tennyson, reviewers saw in Malory a pattern of movement from the untroubled and sunny light of the earlier parts of the story through gathering clouds of divisiveness, and the failures of so many in the Grail quest, to the final breaking of the storm. Others were content to remark favourably on Malory's organizing power; Harriet Preston (No. 32) and Sidney Lanier (No. 33), for example, note his bringing together of heterogeneous materials into a consistent whole. Swinburne (No. 30b) called the *Morte Darthur* a compilation 'incoherent itself and incongruous in its earlier parts' but 'nobly consistent' and 'profoundly harmonious in its close'. Classicists like Andrew Lang (No. 42) distinguished firmly between the structure of Malorian romance and that of Homeric epic, while maintaining that the *Morte Darthur* 'ends as nobly as the "Iliad"'.

There was, however, some increasing recognition that romance could not be judged by classical standards and that Malory had, by bringing together several related stories, altered the shape of his originals. George Perkins Marsh, the American philologist, had noted as early as 1862 that the *Morte Darthur* is 'harmonized and connected' so far as Malory was able to make a consistent whole out of the various French romances by supplying 'here and there links of his own forging' (No. 23). Ten Brink's comments, too, recognize more than a mere translation. While he takes account of 'repetitions, contradictions, and other irregularities', he finds the *Morte Darthur* 'arranged with a certain degree of skill...a kind of unity'. Here, too, Malory's style is seen as contributing to the success of his efforts (No. 40).

But it was Frederick Ryland (No. 39) who in 1888 expressed the view that the *Morte Darthur* was typically medieval in the subordination of form to matter, and that modern criticism was applying the wrong standards.

> In spite of the work of the romantic school, we are still prone to apply conceptions derived from a study of Greek art to the criticism of art wholly different in spirit, method, and aim. Intelligibility, symmetry, and logical consistency are instinctively sought for, and if they are wanting the picture or the poem is contemptuously dismissed. Some of the best mediaeval work sets such attempts at defiance.

With the publication of Sommer's three-volume text and commentary on the *Morte Darthur*, most discussions of Malory's structure would take into account, as Ryland does, his sources, the study of which will be examined in more detail below. With these source comparisons, though, it was possible for some critics to continue to maintain that Malory had imposed epic structure on his heterogeneous materials. Strachey, in his revised introduction of 1891 (No. 45), John Hales (No. 47B), and MacCallum (No. 48) fall generally into this group.

William E. Mead (No. 49) sums up both sides of the debate over structure and unity. At one extreme the *Morte Darthur* is seen as a 'dry, inartistic compilation, based upon ill-chosen originals'; at the other it is enthusiastically labelled a prose epic. Mead is firm in denying epic structure to the romance, but he does not devalue it as a consequence. It is, he says, 'a collection of charming stories rather loosely tied together'. Like Ryland, he thinks it wrong-headed to look for a classic structure that was never intended. If the *Morte Darthur* is considered an epic, it can only be seen as a botched one; parts of the book, Mead says, may show something of the 'epic breadth of treatment', but the unity and continuity of epic are lacking in the book as a whole, and, he adds, 'we hardly gain in clearness of critical estimate by claiming for Malory what he would probably have been the first to disavow.' Mead also raises the question whether a book constructed to nineteenth-century standards would have been attractive or acceptable to readers of Malory's day. George Saintsbury addresses these last two points, too, when he says that criticism has been posing the wrong questions. Critics have asked, 'Has [Malory] done what *I* wanted him to do?' or 'Has he done it as *I* should have done it?' instead of 'Has he done what *he* meant do do?' and 'Has he done this well?' (No. 51b).

As has been seen, writers who were disparaging of Malory's constructional skills almost invariably praised his style, if often in rather vague terms. Closer analyses of the style began to appear around 1890. Sommer's volume II, for example, had included 'Notes on the Language of "Le Morte Darthur"'. Sommer preferred to refer to Caxton's orthography and syntax rather than label it Malory's, believing that Malory's text must have undergone considerable change in the course of being printed.[34]

Sommer discusses the *Morte Darthur*'s use of personal pronouns, possessives, plural and singular noun forms, and the like, with some brief remarks on peculiarities of syntax. At about the same time,

Leon Kellner brought out an edition of Caxton's *Blanchardyn and Eglantine*; the introduction provides a study of Caxton's syntax based on four works with numerous examples of Malory's usages as well. Kellner considers the two to be more or less separable, and in fact, he compares passages from Caxton's translations with passages from the *Morte Darthur*.[35] Charles Sears Baldwin published *The Inflexions and Syntax of the Morte d'Arthur of Malory* in 1894 and a short study in 1895, 'The Verb in the Morte d'Arthur'.[36] Selections in this volume reflecting more serious and specific examinations of Malory's style are seen in Andrew Lang's analysis of the 'Love and May' passage (No. 42); in Walter P. Ker's comparison of Malory to Herodotus and in his statement that Malory's consciously English prose style is the analogue of Chaucer's poetry (No. 47A); in W.E. Mead's brief grammatical and syntactical analysis (No. 49); and, most elaborately worked out, in the final selection (No. 51c) by George Saintsbury taken from his *History of English Prose Rhythm*.

V SOURCE STUDIES

Caxton mentioned volumes about Arthur in French, in Welsh, and some in English, but says that the *Morte Darthur* was drawn from books in French, as does Malory himself. Bale says that Malory translated from both Latin and French, no doubt because of Geoffrey of Monmouth's Latin work or because some French Arthurian texts claimed to be taken from Latin originals. Oldys adds Welsh manuscripts as sources, probably from a hasty reading of Caxton. Only with Thomas Warton is there specific mention of the French prose *Lancelot*, then attributed to Walter Map. (Map's *Lancelot* was sometimes understood to include what we now refer to as the three later portions of the five-part Vulgate cycle: the *Lancelot* proper, the *Queste*, and the *Mort Artu*, but sometimes it means only the *Lancelot* proper.) Warton adds that the *Morte Darthur* is often 'literally translated from various and very ancient detached histories of the heroes of the round table', which, he says, he has examined, but he describes it as closely resembling a late (1488) printed edition of the latter portions of the Vulgate cycle.

George Burnett (No. 10C) notes vaguely the possibility of 'some additions by the compiler' to the superstructure of French and Welsh materials based on Geoffrey, and the *British Bibliographer* (No. 11) uses 'internal evidence' to deduce that the *Morte Darthur* is a compilation from several different romances, since the *Lancelot* cited by Warton accounts for only one part. The first systematic attempt to study Malory's sources was presented in Robert Southey's introduction to the 1817 edition (No. 13). Southey recognized a basic problem of source study, that works Malory had used might be no longer in existence. An additional concern was accessibility. Many French Arthurian romances had never been printed, and many of the printed editions had become rare collectors' items, like the *Morte Darthur* itself before 1816.

Southey does go through a number of French romances, though with no attempt at close comparison with Malory. In fact, when he ventures a specific statement it is wrong: in describing the 'Lancelot du Lac' (by which he apparently refers to the three Vulgate romances noted above) Southey says that the lament over Lancelot's corpse at the end of the *Morte Darthur* is 'translated from this Romance', when in fact the lament does not appear there and is now accepted as Malory's addition. Among other romances that were Malory's sources, Southey lists what we now call the Vulgate *Merlin*, the prose *Tristan*, the Vulgate *Estoire du Graal* and *Queste*, and the prose *Perceval*, 'from which some parts are blended with the story of the S. Greaal in the *Morte Darthur*'.

Southey is not certain whether the compilation was made by Malory himself or whether he simply translated some existing French compendium, but he does note that the compiler altered incidents and arrangement (as much as could be judged from texts available) and that he may have made additions of his own.

Here, for English scholarship, the question of Malory's sources rested, with little development for some seventy years. There were some interesting but brief remarks relating to other English works, e.g. Ritson, Ellis, Dunlop, and Madden on the relationship of the stanzaic *Morte Arthur* to the French Vulgate version and to Malory's *Morte Darthur*. Furnivall (No. 25) carried the matter a bit further by publishing short corresponding passages showing verbal similarities between the *Morte Darthur* and the stanzaic *Morte* and wondering if perhaps Malory had seen the poem. Madden (No. 15) noticed similarities between Malory's Roman war section and the alliterative *Morte Arthure*; this source of Malory's would be verified in the work of Moritz Trautmann in 1878.[37]

Furnivall (No. 25) noted that Malory had 'abstracted' the French *Queste* at greater length than was his practice with other French romances, and Edward Strachey (No. 28) compared Malory's work with the recently published English prose *Merlin* to show the superiority of Malory's version both in selection and in style. For the most part, writers, editors, and critics confined themselves to rather vague comments naming four or five French prose romances as Malory's main sources.

On the Continent, however, various French and German scholars (Michel, de la Rue, la Villemarqué, Albert Schulz, Simrock, Paulin Paris, Hucher, Birch-Hirschfeld, Foerster) were attempting to sort out the tangled relationships amongst French and German Arthurian romances in both verse and prose, exploring the Celtic origins of this matter, and publishing the essential texts. In its relation to Malory, this work is best represented in the selections from the important contributions of Gaston Paris (No. 35). In working out the relationship between Chrétien's *Lancelot* and the French prose version, Paris noted that Malory's 'compilation' had been 'too little utilized' in various source studies and that the *Morte Darthur* needed a special study, and he included an analysis of the sources of Malory's version of Meliagaunt's abduction of Guinevere in an article of 1883. Paris is here cautious about attributing to Malory's invention those incidents in the *Morte Darthur* not found in known sources, and this caution seemed justified by the discovery and subsequent publication three years later of the Huth *Merlin* or *Suite de Merlin*. This text differed in several ways from the Vulgate *Merlin* and did in fact present episodes—most notably the story of Balan and Balin—which Malory had included but which had not appeared in previously known versions. Paris carries out a brief examination of the first four books (Caxton's divisions) of the *Morte Darthur* as compared to the *Suite de Merlin*, noting, without citing specific examples, that there are in Malory some modifications and additions along with heavy abridgement.

Paris considered the *Suite* inferior in design and in interest to the French *Lancelot* or *Tristan* and regarded Malory's abridgement of it as an improvement. Alfred Nutt, as noted earlier, did not admire

Malory's selective or constructional skills, but because of his familiarity with much of Malory's source material Nutt can say that Malory's narrative style is an improvement on much of Arthurian romance (No. 37B).

Ten Brink (No. 40) had noted the incompleteness of Malory source studies, the possibility of originals no longer accessible, and where sources were known, differences 'difficult to account for', concluding that 'problems still remain to be solved'. Nutt stressed the importance of source study in general, declaring that 'there can be no sound aesthetic criticism of the Arthurian romances until the place of each in, and its relation to the other members of, the whole cycle have been determined.'

In his comments on Malory and the *Suite de Merlin*, Gaston Paris said that he would leave the business of a close comparison of the two texts to some future editor of Malory, and that editor's work appeared in 1891. Volume III of the edition of Caxton and accompanying commentary by the German scholar H. Oskar Sommer was devoted to the first close comparison of the *Morte Darthur* with all its identifiable sources. Here, too, would be realized the 'aesthetic criticism' which Nutt had said must wait for such study.

In the main, Sommer's identification of Malory's sources has stood the test of more recent scholarship. Some adjustments have been necessary as previously unknown manuscripts have come to light, but neither Sommer nor anyone else has discovered sources for Malory's Tale of Sir Gareth or for Lancelot's healing of Sir Urre. Sommer notes Malory's alteration of the sequence of events in Books XVIII and XIX and his addition of several passages, including, finally, the recognition that Ector's much-praised eulogy was Malory's invention.

Sommer's study showed clearly the extraordinary degree to which Malory had reduced the bulk of his sources; Sommer estimated their length as about ten times greater than Malory's condensed version. Always with the provision that the manuscripts being compared with the *Morte Darthur* might not be the very ones Malory used, Sommer's close comparisons also showed Malory's deletions, additions, and other alterations clearly for the first time. This work, too, would not for the most part be challenged, but the conclusions Sommer drew from it would be, and most vigorously. Sommer attributed a great many of Malory's additions and alterations to lost French sources; since it could hardly be disproved, this view could be allowed, with some reservations. But when Sommer maintained that Malory often muddled his sources, ignored important and admirable episodes, added trivia, often fell below the standards of his originals, and oftener still 'servilely' reproduced them, he went too far. Responding to Sommer's work, American and British critics drew far more appreciative conclusions from the source studies.

The *Nation*'s reviewer of Sommer's work (No. 43B), for example, expresses somewhat reserved appreciation for the 'statistical' setting forth of Malory's sources, but seems defensive in the statement that Malory 'is not merely collecting by whim a jumble of good stories. He has a plan.' Both this reviewer and W. E. Mead (No. 49) consider the possibility that the Gareth story is Malory's own; the *Nation*'s reviewer adds that, in any case, its introduction into the *Morte Darthur* shows 'high art'. It is clear that quite a different person reviewed the Rhys/Beardsley edition for the same periodical two years later (No. 46B); that reviewer echoes Sommer and goes further in condemning Malory's undiscriminating selection of materials.

Edward Strachey (No. 45) takes on Sommer direct, pointing out that his estimation of Malory's genius is far higher than Sommer's. Strachey argues that while Malory did often translate and transcribe, he also rewrote and reshaped the vast bulk before him to his own aims and purposes. To illustrate the point, Strachey introduces an apt architectural image that will be reworked by later critics; noting that the 'quarry and the builder are not the same thing', Strachey sees the *Morte Darthur* as a 'great, rambling medieval castle', its walls enclosing 'rude and even ruinous work of earlier times', and not to be mistaken for a Greek Parthenon nor an Italian Renaissance palace.

W. P. Ker (No. 47A) compared Malory with his French sources to show what a difficult thing Malory had accomplished as well as to explore the medieval elements derived from them which Malory retained and revivified. Mead (No. 49) sees the difficulty of Malory's task and his occasional inconsistencies as lying with the structure and lack of motivation of the French romances. He argues that Malory's detractors seem to wish Malory had done either more or less, had used his sources to produce a completely new creation as Tennyson had used Malory, or had simply reproduced his originals as fully as possible. Neither, Mead thinks, would have been as satisfactory as what Malory did do. Saintsbury (No. 51b), like Strachey, directly defends the *Morte Darthur* against Sommer's devaluation of it, maintaining that Malory almost always selected well and for a reason, and that he omitted freely, but with even greater good judgment.

VI TWENTIETH CENTURY

Through the first third of the twentieth century, Malory studies show considerable continuity with the work illustrated in the later selections in this volume. Vida D. Scudder in 1917 wrote the first book-length study of the *Morte Darthur* and its sources; Scudder concluded that Malory had shown 'great original genius in creating the *Morte Darthur* from a number of sources'. J. D. Bruce's *The Evolution of Arthurian Romance* brought together much work of continental scholars on this vast corpus. Ferdinand Lot's term 'entrelacement' in his study of the prose *Lancelot* (1918) and his discussion of its application to the interweaving of separate themes was further developed by Eugène Vinaver to show how Malory restructured his French sources, although Vinaver's early work on Malory (1929) seemed to stress Malory's debt to his French sources more than his originality. E. K. Chambers in a 1922 essay notes both weaknesses and strengths of the *Morte Darthur*; until we are 'clear of the *Tristan*', he says, the work exhibits 'structural incoherence', but like Mead and Saintsbury, Chambers acknowledges the difficulty of Malory's task, and like several nineteenth-century predecessors, finds that in his later books Malory 'rises to the full height of his epic theme'. Chambers also saw that Malory's sense of the importance of the Grail quest was different from that of his source, that the conflict was not 'between the ideals of Camelot and Corbenic, but a purely human one, the familiar conflict between human love and human loyalty' (*Sir Thomas Malory*, 1922).

Through this period, adaptations and expurgated versions continued to be issed, supplemented in 1906 and in numerous reprintings by the complete Everyman's Library version, a reprint of the 1893 Simmons/Rhys edition.

In 1934 came the startling discovery at Winchester College of a manuscript copy of the *Morte Darthur* differing in several ways from Caxton's edition. Caxton's book and chapter divisions, for example, do not appear in the manuscript; there are instead *explicits* marking the ends of what could be considered eight separate tales. In addition, the Roman war section in the manuscript is closer to its alliterative source than the heavily edited version that appeared in Caxton's text. The manuscript was edited by Eugène Vinaver, with immense learning and care, and published in 1947 under the title *The Works of Sir Thomas Malory*. A second edition followed in 1967, and Vinaver also issued a one-volume version of the text and a smaller book of extracts from it.[38]

The discovery of the manuscript and its subsequent publication gave new impetus to Malory studies; Vinaver's 1947 bibliography, for example, listed only 91 books and articles on Malory whereas his 1967 list of critical works (with some omissions) numbered 177, nearly doubling the previous body of work in just twenty years. And a mere fourteen years later, in 1981, Toshiyuki Takamiya brought the 1967 bibliography up to date by the addition of 133 new items. Furthermore, his updated bibliography of 1986 has added more than a hundred items (*Aspects of Malory*, 1981 and 1986). The scope and direction of these critical responses over the last forty years can be but briefly indicated here, but a number of essays and introductions provide useful surveys of recent work.[39]

Vinaver's publication of the Winchester manuscript under the title *Works* and his commentary emphasized the view that Malory had written not one unified work but eight distinct romances. R. H. Wilson called attention to some problems with this approach, and an ensuing controversy over Malory's unity or lack of it dominated Malory scholarship for the next twenty or so years.

Leading proponents of a closely unified work have been R. M. Lumiansky and Charles Moorman; *Malory's Originality* (1964), for example, presented essays defending unity by Lumiansky, Moorman, and several other American scholars. In his second edition of 1967, Vinaver replied to these critics without materially altering his position: 'unity of characterisation and even unity of moral purpose', he said, 'there may well be', but he maintained that the *Morte Darthur* does not exhibit the structural unity of a single work.

As in the nineteenth century, a number of scholars found a middle ground between the two extremes: conscious artistic unity on the one hand and, on the other, eight separate works whose inconsistencies show a lack of connectedness. William Matthews, reviewing *Malory's Originality* (*Speculum*, 1966), said that neither theory 'fits all the facts of the book.' C. S. Lewis pointed out that Malory would not have understood the terms of this modern debate and that modern critics forced upon Malory choices he would not have been making (*Essays on Malory*, ed. J. A. W. Bennett, 1963). Noting that there are forward and backward references in the *Morte Darthur* and more than seven *explicits*, D. S. Brewer argued that the organic unity of a modern novel could not apply to Malory but that the *Morte Darthur* does have 'cohesion' and a cumulative effect dependent upon the ordering of the tales (*Essays on Malory*). Larry Benson has been generally supportive of the unity school; he has analysed the structuring of the 'Tale of Sir Gareth' to show the kind of thematic coherence he sees as underlying the *Morte Darthur* as a whole and has referred to the work as a 'one-volume prose history'. Stephen Knight has pointed out problems associated with both structural patterns—one unit or eight—and concluded that 'there are elements of unity and elements of disunity in the Arthuriad, and it seems impossible to explain either element away' (*The Structure of Sir Thomas Malory's Arthuriad*, 1969).

After the publication of the Winchester manuscript, studies comparing its language to that of the Caxton edition could be carried out; those of Ján Šimko (1957) and Arthur Sandved (1968) are examples. Analyses of Malory's grammar and syntax by Japanese scholars such as Yuji Nakao, Kunio Nakashima, and Shunichi Noguchi have followed, along with a concordance to Vinaver's edition of the Winchester manuscript (Kato, 1974).

P. J. C. Field in the first book-length study of Malory's prose style (*Romance and Chronicle*, 1971) was less concerned with linguistic features than with discussing Malory's style in the context of fifteenth-century literature, especially prose chronicles; Field also dealt with the ways in which Malory's style contributes to meaning, although he did not here consider Malory as a 'conscious artist'. Mark Lambert in *Malory: Style and Vision in Le Morte Darthur* (1975) acknowledges the influence of Field's work and examines Malory's style, often through frequency and context of various word choices, as evidence of Malory's thematic concern, with a particularly helpful section on shame / guilt concepts as an important part of Malory's treatment of Lancelot and Guinevere.

Source study has continued to play a part both in examining the structure that emerged from Malory's reduction of the enormous bulk of the French romances he used and in assessing his originality of treatment. In addition the relationship of the stanzaic *Morte Arthur* to Malory's concluding books has been the subject of more debate. Sommer's remarks on the relationship of Malory, the French *Mort Artu*, and the stanzaic *Morte* were not at all clear and he was challenged by J. D. Bruce. The subsequent exchanges between the two are summed up by Robert H. Wilson (*Modern Philology*, 1939–40), who had decided that while Malory did borrow directly from the stanzaic *Morte* in several passages, he also drew on a version of the *Mort Artu* that showed 'some modification' of the versions that survive. (Malory's ordering of certain major episodes differs from that of either source.) Vinaver, abandoning an earlier view, said that no lost, modified version of the *Mort Artu* need be assumed to account for Malory's additions and alterations (*Works*, 1967).

Recent scholarship has also established Malory's use of a fifteenth-century metrical chronicle by John Hardynge, and an essay by Richard Barber discusses various early accounts of Arthur's death/passing, indicating the possibility of more conscious research and wider reading on Malory's part than has previously been assumed (*Arthurian Literature I*, 1981). Larry Benson noted in 1968 that Malory had been insufficiently studied as an English romancer, and his *Malory's Morte Darthur* (1976) devoted attention to Malory's place in English romance tradition, a context different from the frequent comparisons of Malory with his French sources. Earlier work on the English background had been done by R. H. Wilson and by William Matthews. Other, more recent studies dealing with source material have further explored Malory's adaptation of the French *Queste* and discussed the origins of Malory's Gareth story, with support for the view that it was his own composition.[40]

Despite the Winchester discovery, Caxton's edition of the *Morte Darthur* still had to be considered the basis of Malory criticism, editions, and so on, up to the mid-twentieth century; and a new popular edition by Janet Cowen, published in 1969 and often reprinted, answered the need for an easily accessible text. Further study of the relationship between the manuscript and the printed editions of Caxton and de Worde and recent studies by Lotte Hellinga and Hilton Kelliher presenting evidence linking the manuscript to Caxton's printing workshop have raised questions about the source of the editing for Caxton's text. James Spisak has cited Matthews's suggestion that the editor of the Roman war section may have been the author himself, and if that were true, then Caxton's text would carry more authority than the manuscript. Two editions of Caxton have subsequently appeared, a somewhat modernized edition intended for a general audience (Lumiansky, 1982) and a scholarly edition (Matthews and Spisak, 1983).

Two recent collections of essays on Malory, one edited by Toshiyuki Takamiya and Derek Brewer (*Aspects of Malory*, 1981), the other by James Spisak (*Studies in Malory*, 1985), provide ample evidence of continued interest in questions of style, theme, structure, and Malory's use of his sources; these collections also demonstrate the very great artistry and achievement which modern scholarship attributes to Malory.

This admirably high estimate of Malory's genius, the modern scholar's discernment of a conscious plan in what previous critics regarded as structural imperfections or unenlightening repetitions, should not obscure the fact that in earlier centuries Malory was appreciated, his work was influential, and the *Morte Darthur* was read, probably by a larger proportion of the literate public than actually read through the book today. Some modern critics grant to Malory an early popularity but little 'critical' esteem, a view that seems to indicate that readers in previous times liked and read Malory for the wrong reasons. Fifty or a hundred years hence, no doubt, the preconceptions and motives behind this recent response to Malory (along with the continued popularity of Arthurian themes in modern literature and films) will have been analysed and explored as products of the times and perhaps dismissed as inadequate, too.

Still, modern scholarship has established the concept of Malory that began to be expressed in the nineteenth century—as a conscious artist in control of his materials, as a gifted writer of enduring prose, as an observer of life who recognized the paradoxical splendour and futility of human aspiration. But Professor Brewer's comment made in the introduction to *Aspects of Malory* is pertinent here:

...not much modern criticism has shown Caxton's heartiness of enjoyment, or T. E. Lawrence's capacity to be spiritually sustained by the glory and tragedy that Malory himself, I believe, was deeply moved by. Our modern interest, as revealed in these essays, tends to be historical and, as it were, technical. Perhaps the greatest advance shown by the present collection is in our sense of Malory as far more *intelligent*, more devoted to literature, more purposefully in search of Arthurian material, more ready to revise his work—more like modern literary scholars!—than had previously been realised.

VII BIOGRAPHY

Through most of the period examined here, writers on Malory simply repeated remarks of earlier chroniclers that Malory was Welsh and that he was possibly a priest. Leland had seemed to suggest that the Malorys were a Welsh family and Bale (No. 3B) cited Leland. Holinshed, too, said Malory was Welsh, and the idea that he was a priest was apparently introduced by Oldys (No. 6) in the mid-eighteenth century. Most writers acknowledged that virtually nothing was known of Malory save what he himself says in the *Morte Darthur*, chiefly about the date on which he completed the work.

By the time Edward Strachey published his edition of the *Morte Darthur* in 1868, however, there was an increasing awareness that the author of this great English work must have himself been an English knight. Strachey lists Malory as an old Yorkshire and Leicestershire name (No. 28), and in his new introduction in 1891 (No. 45) carries the point further, finding no reason to believe that Malory was either Welsh or a priest; he must have been of an old English family and a knight 'both in rank and in temper and spirit, and a lover alike of the gentle and the soldierly virtues of knighthood'. Saintsbury took much the same view in 1895. Sommer had found the passage in Bale and had shown that it was based only very generally on Leland. Both John and Ernest Rhys expressed a wish that the Welsh connection might be corroborated, however.

A specific person was not identified until the 1890s and then two candidates were presented. Sir Thomas Malory of Newbold Revel in Warwickshire was strongly supported by G.L. Kittredge, who argued that this was probably the same man as the Malory discovered by T. W. Williams among Lancastrians excluded from a general pardon issued by Edward IV in 1468. However, in 1897, A. T. Martin found the will of another Thomas Malory, this one from Papworth St Agnes in Cambridgeshire and born in 1425, son of Sir William Malory, *miles*. Kittredge's identification of the now familiar Warwickshire knight who served with Richard of Warwick in France in 1415, took the Lancastrian side in the Wars of the Roses, and died at the age of seventy or so in 1470 or 1471, prevailed, and the Papworth Malory was dropped from consideration.

Beginning in the 1920s, new information about Kittredge's candidate came to light. Malory, it seemed, spent the last twenty years of his life in and out of prison, accused of various offences including robbery and mayhem on church property, attempted murder, and rape. These revelations created a quandary for some scholars—how to resolve this brawling rapist with the author of the *Morte Darthur*—and the amended life story produced three approaches. One was that the *Morte Darthur* was not really very moral after all; that, as Caxton had noted, the book included murder, vice, and sin along with more admirable traits; and that Caxton had perhaps tried to hide his own doubts about the author's morality by emphasizing the more positive lessons the reader, if he applied himself carefully to the task, might learn. A second, and more popular, rationale was that the charges were probably trumped up, a result of Malory's being on the wrong side during the Wars of the Roses.

A third response, exemplified in the work of William Matthews, was to reject the flawed Warwickshire candidate and to propose a Yorkshire Thomas Malory in his stead as the author of the *Morte Darthur*.[41] While Matthews's Yorkshireman has not found acceptance among other scholars, his systematic rejection of the case for Malory of Newbold Revel has certainly raised doubts about the Warwickshire knight, and recently Richard Griffith has resurrected Martin's Thomas Malory of Papworth St Agnes with plausible arguments.[42]

Thus, as James Spisak has summed up the case, despite a great deal of work over the past hundred years on the authorship of the *Morte Darthur*, it is difficult to be certain at present of more than Malory's text tells us: that he was a knight, that he was at some time a prisoner, and that he finished his work in the ninth year of Edward IV's reign.[43]

NOTES

1 *Malory: The Critical Heritage* deals exclusively with the reception and reputation of the *Morte Darthur*, although it should be noted that in his 'Malory and *The Wedding of Sir Gawain and Dame Ragnell*', *Archiv*, 219 (1982), 374–81, P.J.C. Field suggests the possibility that Malory composed the Middle English poem.

2 James Merriman, *The Flower of Kings: A Study of the Arthurian Legend in England Between 1485 and 1835* (Lawrence: The University Press of Kansas, 1973), p. 21.

3 In his 'Caxton Prepares his Edition of the *Morte Darthur*', *Journal of Librarianship*, 81 (1976), 272–85, N.F. Blake argued that Caxton's preface and contents pages were printed a little later.

4 Richard R. Griffith, 'The Authorship Question Reconsidered', in *Aspects of Malory*, ed. T. Takamiya and D. Brewer (Cambridge: Brewer, 1981), pp. 171 and 220 n. 7.

5 Cf. Robert P. Adams, 'Bold Bawdry and Open Manslaughter', *Huntington Library Quarterly*, 23 (1959), 33–48; and Ronald Crane, *The Vogue of Medieval Chivalric Romance During the English Renaissance* (Menasha, Wisconsin: George Banta, 1919), pp. 10–13.

6 'The Princely Pleasures at Kenelworth Castle', in *The Complete Works of George Gascoigne*, ed. John W. Cunliffe (1907; reprinted New York: Greenwood, 1969), II, 91ff.

7 Professor Toshiyuki Takamiya has kindly provided information on this rare manuscript, *olim* Phillipps Ms 100, which he intends to publish.

8 See, for example, Mary Lascelles, 'Sir Dagonet in Arthur's Show', in *Shakespeare Jahrbuch*, 96 (1960), 145–54.

9 Marcus Goldman, 'Sir Philip Sidney and the Arcadia' (PhD thesis, University of Illinois, 1931). Reprinted from *Illinois Studies in Language and Literature*, XVII, nos 1–2 (1934), p. 193.

10 Cited, for example, by Roberta F. Brinkley, *Arthurian Legend in the Seventeenth Century* (1932; reprinted New York: Octagon Books, 1967), p. 124.

11 Cf. Brinkley, pp. 128–9.

12 *Selections from the Letters of Robert Southey*, ed. John Wood Warter (London: Longman, 1856), II, 27.

13 *New Letters of Robert Southey*, ed. Kenneth Curry (New York: Columbia University Press, 1965), II, 126–7.

14 'Advertisement', *La Mort D'Arthur* (London: Wilks, 1816), I, iv–v. No close study of these alterations is presently available, but a collation of this 'expurgated' edition and the 1634 text against Caxton is in progress.

15 Barry Gaines, 'The Editions of Malory in the Early Nineteenth

Century', in *Papers of the Bibliographical Society of America*, 68 (1974), 12.

16 Gaines, p. 17.

17 See, for example, Mark Girouard, *The Return to Camelot: Chivalry and the English Gentleman* (New Haven and London: Yale University Press, 1981).

18 See, for example, Arthur Ferguson, *The Indian Summer of English Chivalry* (Durham, North Carolina: Duke University Press, 1960), pp. 42–58.

19 Derek Brewer, Introduction to *Aspects of Malory*, op. cit.; Brewer, Introduction to *Chaucer: The Critical Heritage* (London: Routledge & Kegan Paul, 1978), vol. I.

20 For more detailed views of the treatment of the *Morte Darthur* and other aspects of the Arthurian legend in the seventeenth and eighteenth centuries, see Brinkley, *Arthurian Legend in the Seventeenth Century*; Merriman, *The Flower of Kings*; and Arthur Johnston, *Enchanted Ground: The Study of Medieval Romance in the Eighteenth Century* (University of London: Athlone Press, 1964).

21 Arthur Johnston, p. 71.

22 See Gaines, pp. 10–12.

23 *Selections from the Letters of Robert Southey*, II, 34.

24 *The Collected Works of William Morris*, XXII, xv.

25 D. J. Palmer, *The Rise of English Studies* (London: Oxford University Press, 1965), p. 13.

26 Palmer, pp. 13 and 28.

27 *DNB: Twentieth Century, 1901–1911*, p. 436.

28 W. E. Gladstone, 'Tennyson', *Quarterly Review*, October 1859; reprinted in *Gleanings of Past Years: 1845–76* (London: John Murray, 1879), pp. 153–4.

29 Quoted in Beverly Taylor and Elisabeth Brewer, *The Return of King Arthur* (Cambridge: Brewer, 1983), p. 164.

30 Published at Baltimore by Turnbull Brothers.

31 Various expurgated editions have been discussed in detail in recent papers and articles: Yuri Fuwa, 'The Globe Edition of Malory as a Bowdlerized Text in the Victorian Age', *Studies in English Literature*, English Number (1984), 3–17; David Carlson, 'The Victorians' Malory', paper presented at the Modern Language Association meeting, Chicago, 1985; D. Thomas Hanks, Jr., 'Chivalry Manqué: Malory in Nineteenth-Century Children's Literature', paper presented at the International Medieval Congress, Kalamazoo, 1986; and my 'Malory's Expurgators', forthcoming in *The Arthurian Tradition: Essays in Convergence* (University of Alabama Press).

32 Richard Hurd, *Letters on Chivalry and Romance*, ed. Edith Morley

(London: H. Frowde, 1911), esp. pp. 93–4 and 113–27. See also Arthur Johnston, pp. 60–6 and *passim*.

33 Quoted, for example, by H. J. C. Grierson, 'The Tennysons', *Cambridge History of English Literature*, 13 (1917), 39.

34 H. Oskar Sommer, *Le Morte Darthur by Syr Thomas Malory*, II (London: David Nutt, 1890; reprinted New York: AMS Press, 1973), 29.

35 *Blanchardyn and Eglantine*, ed. Leon Kellner, EETS Extra Series no. 58 (1890; reissued London: Oxford University Press, 1962).

36 Charles Sears Baldwin, 'The Verb in the Morte d'Arthur', *Modern Language Notes*, 10, no. 2 (1895), 46–7.

37 Mauritz Trautmann, 'Der Dichter Huchown und Seine Werke', *Anglia*, I (1878), 143–7.

38 A third edition of the late Professor Vinaver's work is being prepared by P. J. C. Field.

39 These include: (a) Larry Benson, 'Le Morte Darthur', in *Critical Approaches to Six Major English Works*, ed. Lumiansky and Baker (Philadelphia: University of Pennsylvania Press, 1968), pp. 81–131; (b) John Lawlor, Introduction to *Le Morte D'Arthur*, ed. Janet Cowen (Harmondsworth and Baltimore: Penguin Books, 1969), I, vii–xxxi; (c) Derek Brewer, 'The Present Study of Malory', in *Arthurian Romance*, ed. D. D. R. Owen (New York: Barnes & Noble, 1971), pp. 83–97; (d) Page West Life, *Sir Thomas Malory and the Morte Darthur*, an annotated bibliography and survey of scholarship (Charlottesville: University Press of Virginia, 1980); (e) Derek Brewer, Introduction to *Aspects of Malory* (Cambridge: Brewer, 1981), pp. 1–8; (f) James Spisak, Introduction to *Caxton's Malory* (Berkeley: University of California Press, 1983), II, 601–29; and (g) Spisak, 'Introduction: Recent Trends in Malory Studies', in *Studies in Malory* (Kalamazoo, Michigan: Medieval Institute Publications, 1985), pp. 1–12.

40 See, for example, Sandra Ness Ihle, *Malory's Grail Quest: Invention and Adaptation in Medieval Prose Romance* (Madison: University of Wisconsin Press, 1983), and Dhira Mahoney, 'Tradition and Originality in Malory's *Tale of Gareth*: The Comedy of Class', a paper presented at the Southeastern Medieval Association Conference, October 1985.

41 William Matthews, *The Ill-Framed Knight* (Berkeley: University of California Press, 1966).

42 Richard Griffith, 'The Authorship Question Reconsidered', in *Aspects of Malory*, pp. 159–77.

43 James Spisak, Introduction to *Caxton's Malory*, pp. 606–12.

Editions

I COMPLETE EDITIONS OF THE *MORTE DARTHUR*: 1485–1983

1 1485

Le Morte Darthur. (The Noble and Joyous Booke entytled Le Morte Darthur). William Caxton. Westminster, 31 July.

2 1498

The Boke of the Noble Kyng. Kyng Arthur Somtyme Kynge of Englonde and of His Noble Actes and Feates of Armes of Chyvalrye, and His Noble Knyghtes and Table Rounde and is Deuyded in to. XXI. Bookes. Wynkyn de Worde, Westminster.

3 1529

The Boke of the Moost Noble and Worthy Prince Kyng Arthur Somtyme Kyng of Grete Brytayne Now Called Englande whiche Treateth of his Noble Actes and Feates of Armes and of Chyualrye and Of his Noble Knyghtes of the Table Rounde and this Volume is Deuyded in to. XXI. Bokes. Wynkyn de Worde. A reprint, with some variations, of the 1498 edition.

4 1557

The Story of the Most Noble and Worthy Kynge Arthur, The Whiche was the fyrst of the Worthyes Chrysten, and also of his Noble and Valiaunte Knyghtes of the Rounde Table. London: William Copland.

5 c.1578

The Storye of the Most Noble and Worthy Kynge Arthur, the which was the Fyrst of the Worthyes Chrysten, and also of hys Noble and Valyaunt Knyghtes of the Rounde Table. London: Thomas East.

6 1634

The Most Ancient and Famous History of the Renowned Prince Arthur

King of Britaine, Wherein is Declared his Life and Death, with all his Glorious Battailes against the Saxons, Saracens, and Pagans, which (for the Honour of his Country) He Most Worthily Atchieved. As Also, All the Noble Acts, and Heroicke Deeds of his Valiant Knights of the Round Table. 'Newly refined, and published for the delight, and profit of the Reader'. London: Printed by William Stansby for Iacob Bloome.

7 1816

The History of the Renowned Prince Arthur, King of Britain; with his Life and Death, and All his Glorious Battles. Likewise the Noble Acts and Heroic Deeds of his Valiant Knights of the Round Table. 2 volumes. London: J. Walker & Co. [Walker's British Classics.] Based on 1634 edition.

8 1816

La Mort D'Arthur. The most ancient and famous History of the renowned Prince Arthur, and the Knights of the Round Table. 3 volumes. London: R. Wilks. Based on 1634 edition.

9 1817

The byrth, lyf, and actes of Kyng Arthur; of his noble knyghtes of the Rounde Table, theyr merveyllous enquestes and aduentures, thachyeuyng of the Sanc Greal; and in the end Le Morte Darthur, with the dolourous deth and departyng out of thys worlde of them al. With an introduction and notes by Robert Southey. 2 volumes. London: Longman. Based on Caxton.

10 1858

La Mort d'Arthure. The History of King Arthur and of the Knights of the Round Table. Introduction and notes by Thomas Wright. 3 volumes. London: John Russell Smith. [Library of Old Authors.] Second edition, 1866; third, Reeves & Turner, 1889. Based on 1634 edition.

11 1868

Morte Darthur, Sir Thomas Malory's Book of King Arthur and of his Noble Knights of the Round Table. The original edition of Caxton revised for modern use with an introduction, by Sir Edward Strachey, Bart. London: Macmillan & Co. [Globe Edition.] Revised introduction in 1891 reprint.

12 1889–91

Le Morte Darthur by Syr Thomas Malory. The original edition of William Caxton now reprinted and edited with an introduction and glossary by H. Oskar Sommer. 3 volumes. London: David Nutt.

13 c. 1892

I *The Noble and Joyous History of King Arthur.* II *The Book of Marvellous Adventures, & other Books of the Morte D'Arthur.* Ernest Rhys. 2 volumes. London: Walter Scott Ltd. [The Scott Library.] Incorporates partial edition of 1886 (see II, 8). Based on Wright edition of 1858.

14 1893–4

The birth life and acts of King Arthur of his noble knights of the Round Table their marvellous enquests and adventures the achieving of the`San Greal and in the end Le Morte Darthur with the dolourous death and departing out of this world of them all. Edited by F. J. Simmons, introduction by John Rhys, illustrated by Aubrey Beardsley. 2 or sometimes 3 volumes. London: Dent. Based on 1817 edition.

15 1897

Le Morte Darthur. Ed. Israel Gollancz. 4 volumes. London: J. M. Dent and Company. [The Temple Classics.] Based on Sommer (no. 12).

16 1900

Le Morte Darthur, Sir Thomas Malory's Book of King Arthur and of his Noble Knights of the Round Table. Ed. A. W. Pollard. 2 volumes. London: Macmillan & Co. [Library of English Classics.] Based on Sommer (no. 12).

17 1906

Le Morte D'Arthur by Sir Thomas Malory. 2 volumes. London: J. M. Dent. [Everyman's Library.] A reprint of the 1893 Dent edition.

18 1910–11

Le Morte Darthur; the Book of King Arthur and of his Knights of the Round Table. 4 volumes. London: P. L. Warner for the Medici Society. Based on Pollard (no. 16).

19 1913

The Noble and Joyous Book entytled Le Morte Darthur... Chelsea: The Ashendene Press. 1817 edition with 'minor variations.'

20 1933

The Noble and Joyous Boke Entytled Le Morte Darthur. Ed. A. S. Mott. 2 volumes. Oxford: Printed at the Shakespeare Head Press... and published for the Press by Basil Blackwell. A reprint of the 1498 Wynkyn de Worde edition.

21 1936

Le Morte Darthur; the Story of King Arthur and of his Noble Knights of the Round Table. 3 volumes. London: Golden Cockerel Press for the Limited Editions Club, New York. Based on Pollard (no. 16).

22 1947

The Works of Sir Thomas Malory. Ed. Eugène Vinaver. 3 volumes. Oxford: Clarendon Press. Second edition, 1967; third edition forthcoming. Based on the Winchester manuscript.

23 1954

The Works of Sir Thomas Malory. Ed. Eugène Vinaver. London: Oxford University Press. [Oxford Standard Authors.] A one-volume edition of no. 22. Second edition, 1971.

24 1969

Sir Thomas Malory: Le Morte D'Arthur. Ed. Janet Cowen with introduction by John Lawlor. 2 volumes. Harmondsworth and Baltimore: Penguin English Library. Based on Caxton.

25 1976

The Winchester Malory; A Facsimile. Introduction by N. R. Ker.

EETS Supplementary Series no. 4. London and New York: Oxford University Press.

26 1976

Sir Thomas Malory: Le Morte Darthur. Printed by William Caxton 1485. Facsimile from the Pierpont Morgan Library original. Introduction by Paul Needham. London: Scolar Press.

27 1982

Sir Thomas Malory's Chronicles of King Arthur. Revised with an introduction by Sue Bradbury. 3 volumes. London: The Folio Society. Based on Vinaver's one-volume edition (no. 23).

28 1982

Le Morte Darthur. Ed. R. M. Lumiansky. New York: Charles Scribner's Sons. Based on Caxton with emendation from Winchester MS.

29 1983

Caxton's Malory. Ed. James Spisak based on work begun by William Matthews. 2 volumes. Berkeley: University of California Press.

II NINETEENTH-CENTURY ABRIDGEMENTS AND ADAPTATIONS

1 1862

The Story of King Arthur and his Knights of the Round Table. Compiled and arranged by J[ames] T. K[nowles]. London: Griffith & Farran.

2 1868

La Morte D'Arthur: The History of King Arthur. Compiled by Sir Thomas Mallory. Ed. Edward Conybeare. London: Edward Moxon.

3 1871

La Mort D'Arthur: The Old Prose Stories whence the 'Idylls of the King' Have Been Taken. Ed. B. Montgomerie Ranking. London: John Camden Hotten.

4 1871

The Story of Elaine. Illustrated in Facsimile from Drawings by Gustave Doré. The Text Adapted from Sir Thomas Mallory. London: Moxon, Son & Company.

5 1878

Life and Exploits of King Arthur and his Knights of the Round Table, A Legendary Romance. London: Milner & Co.

6 1880

The Boy's King Arthur. Ed. Sidney Lanier. New York: Charles Scribner's Sons; London: Sampson Low.

7 1884

King Arthur and his Knights of the Round Table. Ed. Henry Frith. London: Routledge.

8 1886

Malory's History of King Arthur and the Quest of the Holy Grail. Ed. Ernest Rhys. London: Walter Scott. [Camelot Series].

9 1892

King Arthur and the Knights of the Round Table. A Modernized Version of the Morte Darthur. Ed. Charles Morris. 3 volumes. London: W. W. Gibbings.

10 1896

Selections from Malory's Le Morte D'Arthur. Ed. A. T. Martin. London and New York: Macmillan.

11 1897

Selections from Sir Thomas Malory's Morte Darthur. Ed. William E. Mead. London and Boston: Ginn & Co. [Athenaeum Press Series].

12 1899

The Courteous Knight and Other Tales Borrowed from Spenser and Malory. Ed. E. Edwardson. Edinburgh and London: Thomas Nelson.

13 1900

The Book of King Arthur and his Noble Knights. Stories from Sir Thomas Malory's Morte Darthur. Ed. Mary Macleod, introduction by John W. Hales. London: Wells Gardner, Darton, & Co; New York: Frederick A. Stokes.

1. Caxton's preface

1485

William Caxton (*c.* 1422–91) set up England's first printing press at Westminster in 1476. His preface to the *Morte Darthur*, published in 1485, provides a rationale for publication of the work, offers commentary on its worth, and suggests the proper spirit in which the book is to be read. E. G. Duff, writing in the early twentieth century, said that this preface 'is, perhaps, the best and most interesting piece of writing the printer ever composed, and still remains one of the best criticisms of Malory's romance' (*Cambridge History of English Literature*, II, 358).

The text is that of the Simmons edition, Everyman's Library, I (London: J. M. Dent, 1906), 1–4.

After that I had accomplished and finished divers histories, as well of contemplation as of other historical and worldly acts of great conquerors and princes, and also certain books of ensamples and doctrine, many noble and divers gentlemen of this realm of England came and demanded me, many and ofttimes, wherefore that I have not do made and imprinted the noble history of the Sangreal, and of the most renowned Christian king, first and chief of the three best Christian and worthy, King Arthur, which ought most to be remembered among us English men tofore all other Christian kings. For it is notoriously known through the universal world that there be nine worthy and the best that ever were. That is to wit three paynims, three Jews, and three Christian men. As for the paynims they were tofore the Incarnation of Christ, which were named, the first Hector of Troy, of whom the history is come both in ballad and in prose; the second Alexander the Great; and the third Julius Caesar, Emperor of Rome, of whom the histories be well-known and had. And as for the three Jews which also were tofore the Incarnation of our Lord, of whom the first was Duke Joshua which brought the children of Israel into the land of behest; the second David, King of Jerusalem; and the third Judas

47

Maccabaeus: of these three the Bible rehearseth all their noble histories and acts. And sith the said Incarnation have been three noble Christian men stalled and admitted through the universal world into the number of the nine best and worthy, of whom was first the noble Arthur, whose noble acts I purpose to write in this present book here following. The second was Charlemagne or Charles the Great, of whom the history is had in many places both in French and English; and the third and last was Godfrey of Bouillon, of whose acts and life I made a book unto the excellent prince and king of noble memory, King Edward the Fourth. The said noble gentlemen instantly required me to imprint the history of the said noble king and conqueror, King Arthur, and of his knights, with the history of the Sangreal, and of the death and ending of the said Arthur; affirming that I ought rather to imprint his acts and noble feats, than of Godfrey of Bouillon, or any of the other eight, considering that he was a man born within this realm, and king and emperor of the same; and that there be in French divers and many noble volumes of his acts, and also of his knights. To whom I answered, that divers men hold opinion that there was no such Arthur, and that all such books as be made of him be but feigned and fables, by cause that some chronicles make of him no mention nor remember him no thing, nor of his knights. Whereto they answered and one in special said, that in him that should say or think that there was never such a king called Arthur, might well be credited great folly and blindness; for he said that there were many evidences of the contrary: first ye may see his sepulture in the Monastery of Glastonbury. And also in Polichronicon, in the fifth book the sixth chapter, and in the seventh book the twenty-third chapter, where his body was buried and after found and translated into the said monastery. Ye shall see also in the history of Bochas, in his book *De Casu Principum*, part of his noble acts, and also of his fall. Also Galfridus in his British book recounteth his life; and in divers places of England many remembrances be yet of him and shall remain perpetually, and also of his knights. First in the Abbey of Westminster, at Saint Edward's shrine, remaineth the print of his seal in red wax closed in beryl, in which is written *Patricius Arthurus, Britannie, Gallie, Germanie, Dacie, Imperator.* Item in the castle of Dover ye may see Gawaine's skull and Craddock's mantle: at Winchester the Round Table: at other places Launcelot's sword and many other things. Then all these things considered, there can no man reasonably gainsay but there was a king of this land named Arthur. For in all places, Christian and heathen, he is reputed and taken for one of the nine worthy, and the first of the three Christian men. And also he is more spoken of beyond the sea, more books made of his noble acts than there be in England, as well in Dutch, Italian, Spanish, and Greek, as in French. And yet of record remain in witness of him in Wales, in the town of Camelot, the great stones and marvellous works of iron, lying under the ground, and royal vaults, which divers now living hath seen. Wherefore it is a marvel why he is no more renowned in his own country, save only it accordeth to the Word of God, which saith that no man is accept for a prophet in his own country. Then all these things foresaid alleged, I could not well deny but that there was such a noble king named Arthur, and reputed one of the nine worthy, and first and chief of the Christian men; and many noble volumes be made of him and of his noble knights in French, which I have seen and read beyond the sea, which be not had in our maternal tongue, but in Welsh be many and also in French, and some in English, but no where nigh all. Wherefore, such as have late been drawn out briefly into English I have after the simple conning that God hath sent to me, under the favour and correction of all noble lords and gentlemen, emprised to imprint a book of the noble histories of the said King Arthur, and of certain of his knights, after a copy unto me delivered, which copy Sir Thomas Malory did take out of certain books of French, and reduced it into English. And I, according to my copy, have done set it in imprint, to the intent that noble men may see and learn the noble acts of chivalry, the gentle and virtuous deeds that some knights used in those days, by which they came to honour; and how they that were vicious were punished and oft put to shame and rebuke; humbly beseeching all noble lords and ladies, with all other estates, of what estate or degree they be of, that shall see and read in this said book and work, that they take the good and honest acts in their remembrance, and to follow the same. Wherein they shall find many joyous and pleasant histories, and noble and renowned acts of humanity, gentleness, and chivalries. For herein may be seen noble chivalry, courtesy, humanity, friendliness, hardiness, love, friendship, cowardice, murder, hate, virtue, and sin. Do after the good and leave the evil, and it shall bring you to good fame and renown. And for to pass the time this book shall be pleasant to read in; but for to

49

give faith and believe that all is true that is contained herein, ye be at your liberty; but all is written for our doctrine, and for to beware that we fall not to vice nor sin; but to exercise and follow virtue; by which we may come and attain to good fame and renown in this life, and after this short and transitory life, to come unto everlasting bliss in heaven, the which he grant us that reigneth in heaven, the blessed Trinity. Amen.

Then to proceed forth in this said book, which I direct unto all noble princes, lords and ladies, gentlemen or gentlewomen, that desire to read or hear read of the noble and joyous history of the great conqueror and excellent king, King Arthur, sometime king of this noble realm, then called Britain. I, William Caxton, simple person, present this book following, which I have emprised to imprint; and treateth of the noble acts, feats of arms of chivalry, prowess, hardiness, humanity, love, courtesy and very gentleness, with many wonderful histories and adventures. And for to understand briefly the content of this volume, I have divided it into twenty-one books, and every book chaptered as hereafter shall by God's grace follow. The first book shall treat how Uther Pendragon gat the noble conqueror King Arthur, and containeth twenty-eight chapters. The second book treateth of Balin the noble knight, and containeth nineteen chapters. The third book treateth of the marriage of King Arthur to Queen Guenever, with other matters, and containeth fifteen chapters. The fourth book, how Merlin was assotted, and of war made to King Arthur, and containeth twenty-nine chapters. The fifth book treateth of the conquest of Lucius the emperor, and containeth twelve chapters. The sixth book treateth of Sir Launcelot and Sir Lionel, and marvellous adventures, and containeth eighteen chapters. The seventh book treateth of a noble knight called Sir Gareth, and named by Sir Kay, Beaumains, and containeth thirty-six chapters. The eighth book treateth of the birth of Sir Tristram the noble knight, and of his acts, and containeth forty-one chapters. The ninth book treateth of a knight named by Sir Kay, La Cote Male Taile, and also of Sir Tristram, and containeth forty-four chapters. The tenth book treateth of Sir Tristram and other marvellous adventures, and containeth eighty-eight chapters. The eleventh book treateth of Sir Launcelot and Sir Galahad, and containeth fourteen chapters. The twelfth book treateth of Sir Launcelot and his madness, and containeth fourteen chapters. The thirteenth book treateth how Galahad came first to King Arthur's court, and the quest how the Sangreal was begun, and containeth twenty chapters. The fourteenth book treateth of the quest of the Sangreal, and containeth ten chapters. The fifteenth book treateth of Sir Launcelot, and containeth six chapters. The sixteenth book treateth of Sir Bors and Sir Lionel his brother, and containeth seventeen chapters. The seventeenth book treateth of the Sangreal, and containeth twenty-three chapters. The eighteenth book treateth of Sir Launcelot and the queen, and containeth twenty-five chapters. The nineteenth book treateth of Queen Guenever and Launcelot, and containeth thirteen chapters. The twentieth book treateth of the piteous death of Arthur, and containeth twenty-two chapters. The twenty-first book treateth of his last departing, and how Sir Launcelot came to revenge his death, and containeth thirteen chapters. The sum is twenty-one books, which contain the sum of five hundred and seven chapters, as more plainly shall follow hereafter.

2. Wynkyn de Worde Interpolation

1498

Wynkyn de Worde (Jan van Wynkyn, d. 1534–5), first an apprentice to Caxton, assumed control of the printing business after Caxton's death. He is believed to have taken little interest in the literary aspects of his trade, in contrast to Caxton and continental printers, who were editors and translators as well. The following passage, however, appeared in his edition of Malory in 1498, and thereafter, at book 21, chapter 12. Sir Edward Strachey discovered the interpolation while preparing his edition of Malory (see No. 28), and the text used is from that work (Globe Edition. London: Macmillan, 1868, Note A, p. 488).

Oh ye might and pompous lords, shining in the glory transitory of this unstable life, as in reigning over realms great, and mighty countries, fortified with strong castles and towers, edified with many a rich city. Ye also, ye fierce and mighty chivalers, so valiant in adventurous deeds of arms, behold, behold, see how this mighty conqueror Arthur, whom in his human life all the world doubted—ye also, the noble queen Guenever, that sometime sat in her chair adorned with gold, pearls, and precious stones, now lie full low in obscure foss or pit covered with clods of earth and clay. Behold also this mighty champion Launcelot, peerless of knighthood, see now how he lieth groveling on the cold mould, now being so feeble and faint that sometime was so terrible, how and in what manner ought ye to be so desirous of the mundane honour so dangerous. Therefore me thinketh this present book called La Morte Darthur is right necessary often to be read, for in it shall ye find the gracious, knightly, and virtuous war of most noble knights of the world, whereby they gat praising continual. Also me seemeth by the oft reading thereof ye shall greatly desire to accustom yourself in following of those gracious knightly deeds, that is to say, to dread God, and to love rightwiseness, faithfully and courageously to serve your sovereign prince. And the more that God hath given you the triumphal honour the meeker ye ought to be, ever fearing the unstableness of this deceivable world. And so I pass over, and turn again to my matter.

3. Tudor historians on Malory

A. John Leland

1544

John Leland (c. 1506–52), antiquarian and librarian and collector of manuscripts (many from the dissolved monasteries) under Henry VIII, published his *Assertion of Arthur* in 1544, in response to the attacks on Geoffrey of Monmouth's historical veracity by Polydore Vergil and others. Leland includes 'Thomas Melorius' in a list of authors whose 'testimonies' are to be used, and directly mentions the *Morte Darthur* twice, in the passages recorded below. In both the 'Dictionary of Antiquities' (1543) and the *Itinerary*, Leland notes a region called 'Mailoria' near the Dee in Wales. Bale (see following extract) will use this information to suggest that Malory was a Welshman.

The translation of Leland's Latin treatise used here is that of Richard Robinson, made in 1582, and dedicated to the Society of Prince Arthur, a company of gentleman who called themselves by the names of knights of the Round Table while practising and furthering competitive archery. The translation, along with Leland's Latin text, is included in *Chinon of England*, ed. W.E. Mead for EETS (London: Oxford University Press, 1925); the passages occur on pages 39 and 53–4.

(a)

And because I haue againe entred into the Misteries of sacred Antiquitie and am descended a curious searcher into the bowels thereof, it liketh me to bring forth to light an other matter, namely *Arthures* Seale, a monument most cunningly engrauen, auncient, and reuerent. Concerninge which, *Caxodunus* maketh mention, yet breefly and sclenderly in his preface to the history of *Arthure*: which the common people readeth printed in the English tongue. Being moued with the testimony of *Caxodunus* whatsoeuer it were, I went vnto *Westminster*, to the end that what so as an eare witnesse I had heard, I might at length also as an eye witnesse behold the same.[1]

EDITOR'S NOTE

1 Robinson's side note to this passage reads as follows: 'He meaneth Robert Caxton who translated the history of K. Arthure.' Mead comments on this passage, 'Leland obviously knew Malory's work, whereas Robinson apparently had never read Caxton's preface to the *Morte Darthur* or the romance itself. One may wonder what he thought of Leland's reference to Thomas Mailerius 53/36' (see (b)). (*Chinon*, note following Robinson's translation, n.p.n.)

(b)

Though *Polidore* hold his peace it is not needfull by and by for the whole worlde to be mute: And although *Italy* in times past so esteemed of *Arthure*, and yet still doth, when bookes printed both of his prowesse, & victories (as I haue learned) are read in the *Italian* tongue yea in ye Spanish, and also in the *French* tongue: whereupon also the *English* collection of *Thomas Mailerius* his trauaile, is published abroade. The aduersarie I know will say, that many lyes haue crept into those books. Wherefore this is nothing els, but to *Teach him which is fully taught*. As I contemne fables, so I reuerence & imbrace ye truth of the history: neyther will I suffer this to be taken away from mee at any time, but with losse of life....

B. John Bale

1548, 1557

John Bale (1495–1563), Bishop of Ossory, has been called the first historian of English literature, producing what we would now call biographical dictionaries. Acknowledging his debt to Leland, Bale drew on an unpublished manuscript, *De Scriptoribus Britannicis*, and other of Leland's works augmented by his own considerable travel and research to publish his first catalogue, *Illustrium Maioris Britanniae Scriptorum* at Ipswich in 1548. Although Bale ranks Malory among the 'historians', the following statement from this first edition makes it clear that he had not read the *Morte Darthur* all the way through: 'I have assigned to Malory the most eminent place among historians until such time as I discover in whose reign he flourished.' An expanded edition was published at Basel, 1557–9, under the title *Scriptorum Illustrium Maioris Brytanniae*; the extract below, which takes a more cautious view than the earlier text, is translated from that edition (Basel, 1557–9, pp. 628–9). The source of Bale's remarks on Malory's gifts, government service, and literary enjoyments is not known.

Although 'Briton' (in Bale's opening sentence) was sometimes translated as 'Welsh', and was so considered by later bibliographers citing Bale (and by John Rhys, Introduction to the Simmons/Dent edition, Everyman's Library, I, v), it apparently does not mean Welsh here. As Richard Griffith has pointed out (*Aspects of Malory*, ed. T. Takamiya and D. Brewer, Cambridge, 1981, pp. 161 and 218), only a sentence later 'Cambria' is used specifically to denote Wales, so the more general 'Briton' must be intended in the opening line as, in fact, 'Brytanniae' means British, including England, Scotland, and Wales, in the title of the work.

Thomas Malory was a Briton by race and birth. Because of his magnanimous and heroic temper, due largely to the great variety of virtues and talents he possessed, Malory easily outshone the scholars of his time. Mailoria is, as Leland maintains in his Dictionary of Antiquities, a certain region in Wales in the vicinity of the River Dee. Elsewhere Leland mentions that the area is well known for its agricultural fertility and armament manufactures. Despite his many duties of state, Malory zealously pursued his study of literature. He spent hour after pleasant hour reading historical texts. Some events he would visualize as occurring in their historical context; others he would visualize as occurring in the present—before his very eyes, as it were. Once thoroughly versed in these texts, he collated the many materials written in both Latin and French and painstakingly translated them into our tongue.

The Deeds of King Arthur
Arthur's Round Table

Except for these materials, I have not found anything else he edited nor have I seen any other work authored by him among the booksellers. In my view, his work abounds in old wives' tales which need to be expurgated lest the historical veracity of the work be compromised. In our times, Malory enjoys an illustrious reputation.

4. Renaissance views

A. Roger Ascham

1545, 1570

Ascham (1515–68), classical scholar, reformist, tutor to Elizabeth I, worked on *The Scholemaster*, which contains his famous denunciation of the *Morte Darthur*, from around 1563 until his death. It was first published in 1570; however, the sentiment expressed had been anticipated in a much earlier work on archery, *Toxophilis*, published in 1545.

Both selections are from *The English Works of Roger Ascham*, ed. William Aldis Wright (Cambridge University Press, 1904), pp. xiv–xv and 230–1.

(a) *Toxophilis*

Englysh writers by diuerisitie of tyme haue taken diuerse matters in hande. In our fathers tyme nothing was red, but bookes of fayned cheualrie, wherin a man by redinge, shuld be led to none other ende, but onely to manslaughter and baudrye. Yf any man suppose they were good ynough to passe the time with al, he is deceyued. For surelye vayne woordes doo woorke no smal thinge in vayne, ignoraunt, and younge mindes, specially yf they be gyuen any thynge thervnto of theyr owne nature. These bokes (as I haue heard say) were made the moste parte in Abbayes, and Monasteries, a very lickely and fit fruite of suche an ydle and blynde kinde of lyuynge.

(b) *The Scholemaster*

In our forefathers tyme, whan Papistrie, as a standyng poole, couered and ouerflowed all England, fewe bookes were read in our tong, sauyng certaine bookes of Cheualrie, as they sayd, for pastime and pleasure, which, as some say, were made in Monasteries, by idle Monkes, or wanton Chanons: as one for example, *Morte Arthure*: the whole pleasure of which booke

standeth in two speciall poyntes, in open mans slaughter, and bold
bawdrye: In which booke those be counted the noblest Knightes,
that do kill most men without any quarell, and commit fowlest
aduoulteries by sutlest shiftes: as Sir *Launcelote*, with the wife of
king *Arthure* his master: Syr *Tristram* with the wife of king *Marke* his
vncle: Syr *Lamerocke* with the wife of king *Lote*, that was his own
aunte. This is good stuffe, for wise men to laughe at, or honest men
to take pleasure at. Yet I know, when Gods Bible was banished the
Court, and *Morte Arthure* receiued into the Princes chamber. What
toyes, the dayly readyng of such a booke, may worke in the will of
a yong ientleman, or a yong mayde, that liueth welthelie and
idlelie, wise men can iudge, and honest mē do pitie. And yet ten
Morte Arthures do not the tenth part so much harme, as one of these
bookes, made in *Italie*, and translated in England. They open, not
fond and common wayes to vice, but such subtle, cunnyng, new,
and diuerse shiftes, to cary young willes to vanitie, and yong wittes
to mischief, to teach old bawdes new schole poyntes, as the simple
head of an English man is not hable to inuent, nor neuer was hard
of in England before, yea when Papistrie ouerflowed all.

B. Robert Laneham's letter

1575

This letter was written by Laneham to a fellow mercer in
London and describes the visit of Queen Elizabeth to
Laneham's patron, the Earl of Leicester, at Kenilworth Castle
in July of that year. The entertainment offered for Elizabeth's
amusement was full of Arthurian references; a full account of
the text and staging is to be found in George Gascoigne's 'The
Princely Pleasures at Kenilworth Castle'. See also Warton's
remarks (No. 8 below) and Furnivall (No. 25e).

Laneham displays familiarity with Malory's book as he
describes the entertainments and also introduces Captain
Cox, a Coventry mason, whose extensive library includes the
Morte Darthur. F. J. Furnivall, who edited the letter for the
Ballad Society in 1890, surmised that the list of books
provided was 'as much one of Laneham's own books as

Captain Cox's' (Hertford: Ballad Society, 1890; reprinted New York: AMS Press, 1968, pp. 28–30 and 41).

(a)

But aware, keep bak, make room noow, heer they cum! And fyrst, captin Cox, and od man I promiz yoo: by profession a Mason, and that right skilfull, very cunning in fens, and hardy az Gawin; for hiz tonsword hangs at his tablz éend: great ouersight hath he in matters of storie: For, az for king Arthurz book, Huon of Burdeaus, The foour suns of Aymon, Beuys of Hampton, The squyre of lo degrée, The knight of courtesy, and the Lady Faguell, Frederik of Gene, Syr Eglamoour, Sir Tryamoour, Sir Lamwell, Syr Isenbras, Syr Gawyn, . . . with many moe then I rehearz héere: I beléeue hee haue them all at hiz fingers endz.

[The list continues through books of moral and natural philosophy, poetry, astronomy, ballads and songs, 'almanacs of antiquity', etc.]

(b)

[The minstrel] after a littl warbling on hiz harp for a prelude, came foorth with a sollem song, warraunted for story oout of King Arthurz acts, the first booke and 26. chapter, whearof I gate a copy, and that iz this.

> So it befell vpon a Penticost day,
> When King Arthur at Camelot kept coourt rial,
> With hiz cumly Quéen, dame Gaynoour the gay,
> And many bolld Barrons sitting in hall,
> Ladies apparaild in purpl and pall,
> When herauds in hukes herried full by,
> 'Largess! Largess! cheualiers treshardy!'

[The ballad that follows treats of King Rience's sending to Arthur demanding his beard; see Caxton, Bk I, chap. 26.]

C. Nathaniel Baxter

1577

Baxter (c. 1550–1635) was a poet, preacher, author of Puritan tracts, and Greek tutor to Sir Philip Sidney. His translation of

Calvin's sermons on the prophet Jonas appeared in 1578; thus his comment on a recent issue of the *Morte Darthur* must affect the conjectural dating of East's edition of Malory, usually placed at around 1585, as Baxter could scarcely be referring to Copland's edition of 1557. See Josephine Bennett, *The Evolution of 'The Faerie Queene'* (University of Chicago Press, 1942), p. 76 n. 46.

Baxter's concerns in this introduction are the baits of the world, death, and hell, and he clearly considers romances to be among the leaders, although he blames printers for pandering to men's humours. The extract is from the Dedicatory Epistle, dated 1577, but printed in a later edition (London: Edward White, 1580).

We see some men bestowe their time in writyng, some in printyng, and moe men in readyng of vile & blasphemous, or at least of prophane and friuolous bookes, suche as are that infamous legend of K. Arthur (whiche with shame enough I heare to bee newly imprinted) with the horrible actes of those whoremasters, Launcelot du Lake, Tristram de Liones, Gareth of Orkney, Merlin, the lady of the Lake, with the vile and stinking story of the Sangreall, of K. Peleus, etc. Some again studie the liues of Huon of Burdeaux, and king Oberon, the king of the Fairies, of Valentine & Orson, & the lady Cleremond, with the Iuggler Paccolet and king Trumpert, and the Giant Ferragus and the liues of the fower sonnes of Aymon, with the worthie actes of Oliuer & Rouland, Guichard and Richard: some are expert in Beuis of Hampton that notable man, with the death of Boniface, Arundel & Trunchifice: some in the court of Venus, some in the Iestes of Skoggen the kinges dizzard: some in the subtelties of Howleglas, & Garagantua: some again (and to many) in the pestilent policies of that Mahounde Matchiauile: in the puddle of pleasure, and Forist of histories, and such like which doe manifestly shewe that Gods word is either shamefully neglected, or despitefully condemned. For if any good booke be written, it lieth in the printers hands, smally regarded, seldome enquired after: so that the printer is scarce paied for the paper that goeth to the booke. And this maketh many printers which seketh after gaines, to take in hand rather those thinges that are profitable to the purse (though they bee ridiculous) and so satisfie mens humors, then to print without profite those bookes that be Godly....

D. Sir Philip Sidney

1581

Sidney (1554–86), it is thought, drew on the *Morte Darthur* for episodes in his *Arcadia*, and here, in the *Defence of Poesie*, he first comments (a) on the power of literature to move men—even through a less than perfect romance such as *Amadis*; the second passage (b) deals with the same theme while refuting the notion that literature and learning weaken a man's capacity for action. It is here that Sidney uses the *Morte Darthur* as an example. It should be noted that after Caxton, the fifteenth- and sixteenth-century editions of Malory were not called the *Morte Darthur*, but did use the words 'King Arthur' in such titles as 'The Book of the Noble King Arthur ...'

The selections are from *The Complete Works of Sir Philip Sidney*, ed. Albert Feuillerat (Cambridge University Press, 1923), III, 20 and 31–2.

(a)

Truly I have knowne men, that even with reading *Amadis de gaule*, which God knoweth, wanteth much of a perfect *Poesie*, have found their hearts moved to the exercise of courtesie, liberalitie, and especially courage.

(b)

... it is a manifest that all government of action is to be gotten by knowledge, and knowledge best, by gathering manie knowledges, which is reading; ... [concerning the notion that literature and learning weaken the capacity for action] as for *Poetrie* it selfe, it is the freest from this objection, for *Poetrie* is the Companion of Camps. I dare undertake, *Orlando Furioso*, or honest king *Arthure*, will never displease a souldier: but the quidditie of *Ens & Prima materia*, will hardly agree with a Corcelet.

5. Two seventeenth-century comments

A. Stansby's edition

1634

William Stansby (d. 1639), a printer, acquired the rights to the *Morte Darthur* in 1626 and published a new edition, for Jacob Blome, in 1634. The preface gives a brief summary of events of British history drawn mainly from Geoffrey, 'set down to confute the errours of such as are of an opinion that there was never any such man as king Arthur'. After additional urging that Arthur be accepted and honoured, the author/editor, possibly Blome, introduces Malory's book, as seen in the first passage (a) below; phrases in this section seem to echo Bale (see No. 3B above). He also explains his expurgations.

This edition altered Caxton's divisions of the text, so after repeating Caxton's prologue down to the contents of the twenty-one books, this preface substituted the second passage (b) to explain the new arrangements. Both passages are taken from Thomas Wright's edition of Malory, based on Stansby, *La Mort d'Arthure* (London: John Russell Smith, 1858), I, xxiv–xxv and xxxii–xxxiii.

(a)

This following history was first written in the French and Italian tongues, so much did the poets and chronologers of forraine nations admire our Arthur. It was many yeares after the first writing of it, translated into English, by the painfull industry of one Sir Thomas Maleore, knight, in the ninth year of the raigne of king Edward the Fourth, about one hundred and fifty two yeares past; wherein the reader may see the best forme and manner of writing and speech that was in use at those times. In many places fables and fictions are inserted, which may be a blemish to the reputation of what is true in this history, and it is unfitting for us to raze or blot out all the errours of our ancestours, for by our taking consideration of them, wee may be the better induced to beleeve and reverence the truth. It is 1114 years since king Arthurs raigne, which was long before the dayes of Edward the Fourth, whereby it may be mused what speech they used above 1100 yeares agoe, when as it was so plaine and simple in king Edwards time.

And therefore, reader, I advertise thee to deale with this book as thou wouldest doe with thy house or thy garment, if the one doe want but a little repaire thou wilt not (madly) pull downe the whole frame, if the other hath a small spot or a staine thou wilt not cast it away or burne it, gold hath its drosse, wine hath its lees, man (in all ages) hath his errours and imperfections. And though the times are now more accute and sharp-witted, using a more eloquent and ornated stile and phrase in speech and writing then they did, who lived so many yeares past, yet it may be that in the age to come, our successours may hold and esteeme of us as ridiculously as many of our over-nice critickes doe of their and our progenitours, as we are refined in words I wish we were reformed in deeds, and as we can talke better, it were well if wee would not doe worse. Wee perceive their darknesse through our light, let not our light blind us that we may not see our owne ignorance. In many places this volume is corrected (not in language but in phrase), for here and there king Arthur or some of his knights were declared in their communications to sweare prophane, and use superstitious speeches, all, or the most part, of which is either amended or quite left out, by the paines and industry of the compositor and corrector at the presse, so that as it is now it may passe for a famous piece of antiquity, revived almost from the gulph of oblivion, and renued for the pleasure and profit of present and future times.

(b)

In which all those that dispose them to eschew idlenesse, which is the mother of all vices, may read historicall matters. Some are willing to reade devout meditations of the humanitie and passion of our Saviour Jesus Christ; some the lives and painefull martyrdomes of holy saints; some delight in moralisacion and poeticall stories; and some in knightly and victorious deeds of noble princes and conquerours, as of this present volume, which treateth of the noble acts and feates of armes, of chivalry, prowesse, hardinesse, humanitie, love, courtesie, and gentilnesse, with divers and many wonderfull histories and adventures. And for to understand briefly the contents of this present volume, comprehending the valiant acts of this noble conquerour, with his lamentable death caused by sir Mordred his sonne and the subjects of his realme, I have devided it into three parts, and every part into sundry chapters, as hereafter, by Gods grace, shall follow.

B. William Nicolson

1696

Nicolson (1655–1727), later Bishop of Carlisle, Bishop of Derry, and, at his death, Archbishop of Cashel and Emly, produced the *English Historical Library* in three parts between 1696 and 1699. The description of this work, with the addition of Scottish and Irish material, reads as follows in the edition of 1776: 'giving a short view and character of most of our historians, either in print or manuscript', indicating that Nicolson did in fact consider Malory an historian. Judging from his otherwise odd remark near the end of this passage, it is likely that Nicolson knew the *Morte Darthur* only through Stansby's edition, the only one divided into three books rather than twenty-one. The extract is from the later edition (London: T. Evans, 1776), I, 31.

King Arthur, and his knights of the round-table, made so considerable a figure in the British history, that many learned men have been at a great deal of trouble to clear up that Prince's title, and to secure that part of Geoffrey's story, whatever fate might attend the rest. The first stickler ... was one Grey [who is said to have been Bishop of Norwich and died 1217].... About 200 years after him, Thomas Malory, a Welsh gentleman, wrote King Arthur's story in English; a book that is, in our days, often sold by the ballad-singers, with the like authentic records of Guy of Warwick and Bevis of Southampton. This was first published, as Geoffrey of Monmouth's, under the title of a Translation, by William Caxton; who finished the mighty work at Westminster, on the last day of July, 1485.... John Bale makes W. Caxton write King Arthur's history in no less than one and twenty several books;

which if they could have been found, might have saved Richard Robinson the trouble of translating Leland's *Assertio*, etc. into English. But, in truth, honest William was only T. Malory's printer, as has been already observed.

6. *Biographia Britannica*

1747–1766

This work, often cited through the early nineteenth century, is subtitled 'The Lives of the Most Eminent Persons who have flourished in Great Britain and Ireland from the earliest Ages, down to the present Times'; it is 'digested in the manner' of Bale's history. A number of its articles, including the one on Caxton in which this selection appears, are attributed to William Oldys (1696–1761), antiquary, bibliographer, editor, and biographer, whose most important work was perhaps his life of Ralegh (1736) and who worked with Samuel Johnson on the cataloguing of the Harleian library.

Oldys introduces the notion, repeated through successive decades, that Malory was a priest; he also attributes the popularity of the *Morte Darthur* to its loose standards of morality. The entry appears in volume II (London: W. Innys, 1748; reprinted Hildesheim: G. Olms, 1969), 1243.

But what was accounted his [Caxton's] capital work this year [1485], is a large thick volume, intituled, *The Byrth, Lyf, and Actes of King* Arthur; *of his noble* Knyghtes *of the* Round Table, *their marvayllous Enquestes and Adventures; th Achyeviyng of the* Sang real; *and in the end*, Le Morte D'Arthur; *with the dolorous Deth and Departyng out of thys World of them Al. Whiche book was reduced to the Englisshe by Syr* Thomas Malory, Knight, *and by me* (William Caxton) *divyded into twenty one bookes; chaptyred and emprynted, and fynysshed in th' Abbey Westmestre, the last day of July, the yere of our Lord* 1485. That Sir Thomas Malory seems to have drawn this volumious romance out of several manuscripts, written in the French and Welsh tongues, of the said King Arthur and his Knights; and to be conversant in the adventures of such redoubted champions, Caxton thought would inspire a noble spirit of valour in our gentry, which made him recommend it to them, as was before observed.[1] If this Sir Thomas Malory was a Welshman, as Leland, and others after him assert, he was probably a Welsh Priest; as appears not only by the legendary vein which runs through all the stories he has thus extracted and wove together, but by his conclusion of the work itself, in these words: 'Praye for me, whyle I am on lyve, that God sende me good delyveraunce; and when I am deed, I praye you all, praye for my soule; for this booke was ended the 9th yeer of the reygne of Kyng Edward the Fourth, by Syr Thomas Maleore, Knyght, as Jesu helpe him for his grete myght, as he is the *servaunte* of Jesu, bothe day and nyght.' As the author has not made his heroes any great commanders of their passions in their amours, nor rigorously confined them to honour and decorum, in point of fidelity and continence, his book became a great favourite with some persons of the highest distinction for a long time. It had two or three impressions afterwards, and seems to have been kept in print, for the entertainment of the lighter and more insold readers, down to the reign of King Charles I,[2] though Mr. Ascham had long before passed such a censure upon it as might have put it out of continuance....

NOTES

1 Caxton's Book of the Ordre of Chivalry, in the Rehearsal.
2 One edit. called The Storye of the most noble and worthy Kynge Arthur, &c. folio, emprinted by Thomas East. Another is, The most ancient and famous Hist. of the Renowned Arthur, &c. 4to 1634, &c.

7. Samuel Johnson

1765

Samuel Johnson (1709–84) was said by Bishop Percy to have been 'immoderately fond of reading Romances of Chivalry', and, added Percy, 'he retained this fondness through Life' (Boswell's *Life of Johnson*, cf. Everyman's Library edition, London, 1906, I, 20). Johnson also defended the reading of romances by students of history and literature. However, he refers directly to the *Morte Darthur* rarely in his works.

The first passage below, from the preface to Johnson's *Shakespeare*, explains why Shakespeare was obliged to include fabulous or fantastic events in his plots. The second is a note to the line in Henry IV, Part 2, where Shallow refers to taking the part of Sir Dagonet in 'Arthur's Show'. Extracts are from the Yale edition of the Works of Samuel Johnson, VII, *Johnson on Shakespeare* (New Haven: Yale University Press, 1968), pp. 81–2 and 506–7.

(a)
The English nation, in the time of Shakespeare, was yet struggling to emerge from barbarity. The philology of Italy had been transplanted hither in the reign of Henry the Eighth; and the learned languages had been successfully cultivated by Lilly, Linacer, and More; by Pole, Cheke, and Gardiner; and afterwards by Smith, Clerk, Haddon, and Ascham. Greek was now taught to boys in the principal schools; and those who united elegance with learning, read, with great diligence, the Italian and Spanish poets. But literature was yet confined to professed scholars, or to men and women of high rank. The publick was gross and dark; and to be able to read and write, was an accomplishment still valued for its rarity.

Nations, like individuals, have their infancy. A people newly awakened to literary curiosity, being yet unacquainted with the true state of things, knows not how to judge of that which is proposed as its resemblance. Whatever is remote from common appearances is always welcome to vulgar, as to childish credulity;

and of a country unenlightened by learning, the whole people is the vulgar. The study of those who then aspired to plebeian learning was laid out upon adventures, giants, dragons, and enchantments. *The Death of Arthur* was the favourite volume.

The mind, which has feasted on the luxurious wonders of fiction, has no taste of the insipidity of truth. A play which imitated only the common occurrences of the world, would, upon the admirers of *Palmerin* and *Guy of Warwick*, have made little impression; he that wrote for such an audience was under the necessity of looking round for strange events and fabulous transactions, and that incredibility, by which maturer knowledge is offended, was the chief recommendation of writings, to unskilful curiosity.

(b)
III.ii.271 SHALLOW. when I lay at Clement's Inn, I was then Sir Dagonet in Arthur's show

[The only intelligence I have gleaned of this worthy wight, Sir Dagonet, is from Beaumont and Fletcher in their *Knight of the Burning Pestle.* THEOBALD]

The story of Sir Dagonet is to be found in *La Mort d'Arthure*, an old romance much celebrated in our authour's time, or a little before it.

[Quotes part of Ascham's comment.]

In this romance Sir Dagonet is King Arthur's fool. Shakespeare would not have shown his Justice capable of representing any higher character.

8. Thomas Warton

1762, 1777

Warton (1728–90) was the first to present Malory as an influence on later writers. In *Observations on the Fairy Queen*,

Warton discusses Spenser's debt to the *Morte Darthur*, citing many parallel passages which show his familiarity with Malory, and then goes on to provide evidence of Malory's popularity and influence in Elizabethan times and after. His citations of Malory are to the 1634 edition, in three books and numerous chapters. Extracts combined as (a) below are from the second edition (London: R. and J. Dodsley, 1762), I, 17–44.

In his *History of English Poetry*, Warton refers again to Malory's popularity in his comments on Shakespeare's Shallow/Dagonet passage (see previous extract), suggests that Malory's work influenced that of Stephen Hawes in *The Pastime of Pleasure* (1509), and comments not very favourably on the structure of the *Morte Darthur* in an addendum on French romance. Here Warton reviews Caxton's twenty-one books. All three passages are from volume II (London: J. Dodsley et al., 1778); (b.i) pp. 404–5; (b.ii) p. 235 note; and (b.iii) 'Emendations and Additions to Volume I', addition to I, 15, line 4, 'Robert Borron', no page number.

(a) *Observations*

Although Spenser formed his *Faerie Queene* upon the fanciful plan of Ariosto, yet it must be confessed, that the adventures of his knights are a more exact and immediate copy of those which we meet with in old romances, or books of chivalry, than of those which form the Orlando Furioso....

Among others, there is one romance which Spenser seems more particularly to have made use of. It is entitled, MORTE ARTHUR, *The Lyf of Kyng Arthur, of the noble Knyghtes of the round table, and in thende the dolorous deth of them all*. This was translated into English from the French, by one Sir Thomas Maleory, Knight, and printed by W. Caxton, 1484 [sic]. From this fabulous history our author has borrowed many of his names, viz. Sir Tristram, Placidas, Pelleas, Pellenore, Percivall, and others. As to Sir Tristram, he has copied from this book the circumstances of his birth and education with much exactness.

[Cites corresponding passages from Spenser and Malory referring to Tristram's birth, his mastery of hunting and hawking, etc.]

From this romance our author also took the hint of his BLATANT BEAST; which is there called the QUESTING BEAST.

[Quotes Malory's description of the Questing Beast.]

Spenser has made him a much more monstrous animal than he is here represented to be, and in general has varied from this description. But there is one circumstance in Spenser's representation, in which there is a minute resemblance, viz.—speaking of his mouth,

> And therein were a thousand tongues empight,
> Of sundry kindes, and sundry qualities,
> Some were of dogs that barked night and day.
>
> (6.12.27)

By what has been hitherto said, perhaps the reader may not be persuaded, that Spenser, in his BLATANT BEAST, had the QUESTING BEAST of our romance in his eye. But the poet has himself taken care to inform us of this: for we learn, from the romance, that certain knights of the round table were destined to persue the QUESTING BEAST perpetually without success: which Spenser, speaking of this BLATANT BEAST, hints at in these lines.

> Albe that long time after Calidore,
> The good Sir Pelleas him took in hand,
> And after him Sir Lamoracke of yore,
> And all his brethren born in Britaine land,
> Yet none of these could ever bring him into hand.
>
> (6.12.39)

Sir Lamoracke and Sir Pelleas are two very valourous champions of Arthur's round table.

This romance supplied our author with the story of the mantle made of the beards of knights, and locks of ladies. The last circumstance is added by Spenser.

> For may no knight or ladie passe along
> That way (and yet they needs must passe that way)
> By reason of the streight and rocks among,
> But they that ladies lockes do shave away,
> And that knights berd for toll, which they for passage pay.
>
> (6.1.13)

Afterwards,

> His name is Crudor, who through high disdaine,
> And proud despyght of his selfe-pleasing mynd,
> Refused hath to yeald her love againe,
> Until a mantel she for him do find,
> With berds of knights, and lockes of ladies lynd.

(6.3.15)

Thus in MORTE ARTHUR. 'Came a messenger—saying, that king Ryence had discomfited, and overcome eleaven [sic] knights, and everiche of them did him homage; and that was this; they gave him their beards cleane flayne of as much as there was: wherefore the messenger came for king Arthur's berd: for king Ryence had purfeled a mantell with king's beards....' After this passage we have an antient ballad, the subject of which is this insolent demand of king Ryence [see No. 4B above]....

And though further proofs of Spenser's copying this romance are perhaps superfluous, I shall add, that Spenser has quoted an authority for an antient custom from MORTE ARTHUR in his *State of Ireland*. 'The knights in antient times used to wear their mistresses or lover's sleeve upon their arms, as appeareth by that which is written of Sir Launcelot, that he wore the sleeve of the Faire Maid of Asteloth in a tournay: whereat queen Genever was much displeased.' This is the passage. 'When queen Genever wist that *Sir Launcelot* beare the red sleeve of the Faire Maide of Astolat, she was nigh out of her minde for anger.'

There is great reason to conclude, not only from what has already been mentioned concerning Spenser's imitations from this romantic history of king Arthur and his knights, but from some circumstances which I shall now produce, that it was a favorite and reigning romance about the age of queen Elizabeth; or at least one very well known and much read at that time. Spenser in the *Shepherd's Kalendar* had the following passage.

> And whither rennes this bevie of ladies bright
>> Raunged in a row?
> They been all LADIES OF THE LAKE behight,
>> That unto her go.

Upon the words LADIES OF THE LAKE, E.K. the old commentator on the pastorals has left us the following remark. 'LADIES OF THE LAKE be nymphes: for it was an old opinion among the antient heathens, that of every spring and fountaine was a goddesse the soveraine; which opinion stucke in the minds of men not many years since by meanes of certain fine fablers, or loose lyers; such as were the authors of KING ARTHUR the great—Who tell many an unlawfull leesing of the LADIES OF THE LAKE.' These fine fablers or loose lyers, are the authors of the romance above-mentioned, viz. MORTE ARTHUR, where many miracles are performed and much enchantment is conducted, by the means and interposition of the LADY OF THE LAKE. Now it should be observed, that the LADY OF THE LAKE was introduced to make part of queen Elizabeth's entertainment at Kenelworth; as evidence of which, I shall produce a passage from an antient book entitled, A LETTER, *wherin part of the entertainment untoo the queens majesty at Killinworth-castl in Warwicksheer in this soomers progress*, 1575, *is signified*. The passage is this. 'Her highness all along this tilt-yard rode unto the inner gate, next the baze coourt of the castle: whear the LADY OF THE LAKE (famous in KING ARTHUR'S BOOK) with too nymphes wayting upon her, arrayed all in silkes, attended her highnes comming, from the midst of the pool, whear upon a moveable island bright-blazing with torches she floting to land, met her majesty with a well-penned meter, and matter, after this sorte; first of the aunciente of the castl; who had been owners of the same e'en till this day, most allways in the hands of the earles of Leycester; how she had kept this lake syns king Arthur's dayes, and now understanding of her highnes hither coming, thought it both offis and duety; to discover, in humble wise, her, and her estate, offring up the same, hir lake, and power thearin; with promis of repair to the court. It pleased her highness to thank this lady, &c.'...

She [the Lady of the Lake] is afterwards introduced complaining to the queen, that sir Bruse had insulted her for doing an injury to Merlin, an incident related in MORTE ARTHUR [see also Mead, No. 49] and that he would have put her to death had not Neptune delivered her, by concealing her in that lake; from which confinement the queen is afterwards supposed to deliver her, &c.

Without expatiating upon the nature of such a royal entertainment as this, I shall observe from it, that as the LADY OF THE LAKE was a very popular character in the reign of queen Elizabeth, so consequently the romance, which supplied this fiction, was at the same time no less popular. We may add, that it is not improbable that Spenser might allude in the above-cited verses [April eclogue] to some of the circumstances in this part of the queen's entertainment; for queen Elizabeth, the Fayre Elisa, is the lady whom the LADIES OF THE LAKE are represented as repairing to, in that eclogue. Nor is it improbable that this lady was often exhibited upon other occasions: nor is it improper to remark in this place, that Ben. Jonson has introduced her, together with king Arthur and Merlin, in an entertainment before the court of James I. called, PRINCE HENRIES BARRIERS.

The above antient letter acquaints us, that the queen was entertained with a song from this romance, which is a corroborative proof of its popularity at that time.

[Quotes passages quoted above, No. 4B.]

We find Spenser in another place alluding to the fable of the lady of the lake so much spoken of in this romance.

———— A little while
Before that Merlin dyde, he did intend
A brasen wall in compas to compyle
About Cairmardin, and did it commend
Unto these sprights to bringe to perfect end;
During which time, the LADIE OF THE LAKE,
Whom long he lov'd, for him in haste did send,
Who therefore forst his workmen to forsake,
Them bound till his returne, their labour not to slake.

(3.3.10)

In the mean time, thro' that false ladies traine
He was surpris'd and buried under beare,
Ne ever to his worke return'd againe.

These verses are obscure, unless we consider the following relation in MORTE ARTHUR. 'The LADY OF THE LAKE and Merlin departed'

[Quotes Malory's account of Merlin's enchantment by Nimue.]

Our author has taken notice of a superstitious tradition, which is related at large in this romance.

————Good Lucius
That first received christianitie,

The sacred pledge of Christs evangelie:
Yet true it is, that long before that day
Hither came Joseph of Arimathie,[1]
Who brought with him the HOLY GRAYLE, they say,
And preacht the truth; but since it greatly did decay.

(2.10.53)

The HOLY GRALE, that is, *the real blood* of our blessed Saviour.
What Spenser here writes GRAYLE, is often written SANGREAL, or *St.
grale,* in MORTE ARTHUR; and it is there said to have been brought into
England by Joseph of Arimathea. Many of king Arthur's knights
are in the same book represented as adventuring in quest, or in
search of the SANGREAL, OR SANGUIS REALIS. This expedition was
one of the first subjects of the old romance.

This romance seems to have extended its reputation beyond the
reign of queen Elizabeth. Jonson, besides his allusion to it
concerning the LADY OF THE LAKE, mentioned above, hints at it
more than once:

> Had I compil'd from Amadis de Gaule,
> Th' Esplandians, ARTHURS, Palermins, &c.[2]

And afterwards, in the same poem,

> —— The whole summe
> Of errant knighthood; with the dames and dwarfes,
> The charmed boates, and the enchanted wharfes,
> The TRISTRAMS, LANC'LOTTS, &c.

And Camden[3] refers to this history of king Arthur, as to a book
familiarly known to the readers of his age. Speaking of the Name
TRISTRAM, he observes, 'I know not whether the first of his name
was christned by king Arthur's fabler.' Again, of LAUNCELOT he
speaks, 'Some think it to be no auncient name, but forged by the
writer of king Arthur's history, for one of his douty knights.' And
of GAWEN, 'A name devised by the author of king Arthur's table.'

To this we may add, that Milton manifestly hints at it in the
following lines,

> ——Damsels met in forrests wide
> By knights of Logris, or of Lyones,
> Lancelot, Pelleas, or Pellenore.

These are Sir Lancelot (or Sir Meliot) of Logris; Sir Tristram of

73

Lyones, and king Pellenore, who are often mentioned in MORTE ARTHUR, and represented as meeting beautiful damsels in desolate forrests....

To which we may subjoin,

> ———— What resounds
> In fable, or romance, of Uther's son,
> Begirt with British, and Armoric knights.

Before I leave this romance, I must observe, that Ariosto has been indebted to it; I do not mean, to the old translation, which Spenser made use of. He has drawn his enchanter Merlin from it, and in these verses refers to a particular story concerning him, quoted above. Bradamante is supposed to visit the tomb of Merlin.... Thus translated by Harrington,

> Heere is the tombe that Merlin erst did make
> By force of secret skill, and hidden art,
> In which sometimes the lady of the lake
> (That with her beauty had bewitcht her hart)
> Did force him enter fondly for her sake;
> And he was by a woman over-reached
> That unto others prophesied, and preached.

(xii. 12)

> His carkas dead within this stone is bound

This description of Merlin's tomb, says Harrington in a marginal note, is out of the BOOK OF KING ARTHUR. Ariosto has transferred the tomb from Wales into France....

He also mentions some of the names of the knights of our romance. When Renaldo arrives in Great Britain, the poet takes occasion to celebrate that island for its singular achievements in chivalry, and for having produced many magnanimous champions; these are,

> ———— Tristano,
> Lancillotto, Galasso, Artu, e Galuano.

Afterwards, in b. 32. Tristram makes a great figure.

From this romance is also borrowed Ariosto's tale of the enchanted cup....

As it is manifest, from a comparison of passages, that Ariosto was intimately conversant in this romance; so I think we may fairly suppose that he drew from it the idea of his Orlando running mad with jealousy. In Morte Arthur, Sir Lancelot, smitten with a jealous fit, is driven to madness, in which state he continues for the space of two years, performing a thousand ridiculous pranks, no less extravagant than those of Orlando; and, like him, at last he recovers his senses. A popular and ridiculous romance was a sufficient hint for what we think a fine effort of poetry.

I had forgot to remark before, that our author has borrowed the name of Materasta's castle from that of Lancelot in Morte Arthur.

> ———The goodly frame
> And stately port of Castle Joyeous.

(3.1.31)

Lancelot's Castle is styled, by Caxton, Joyous Gard, or castle.

This romance, or at least the stories formed from it, sometimes furnished matter for theatrical exhibitions, as we learn from Shakespeare. '*Shallow.* I remember at Mile-end Green, when I lay at Clements-inn, I was Sir Dagonet in Arthur's Show.'... Sir Dagonet is an important character in Morte Arthur.... In our author's age, we find him introduced among the entertainments exhibited at the splendid reception of lord Leicester [see above on Kenilworth, and No. 4B].... Sydney, as appears from a curious conversation between B. Jonson and Drummond of Hawthornden, recorded by the latter, intended to turn all the stories of the *Arcadia* into the admired legend of Arthur and his Knights. In his *Defence of Poesie* he plainly hints at Caxton's romance [see No. 4D above]. . . .

(b) *History of Poetry*

(i)

... The performance of this part of Sir Dagonet was another of Shallow's feats at Clement's-inn, on which he delights to expatiate: a circumstance, in the mean time, quite foreign to the purpose of what he is saying, but introduced, on that account, to heighten the ridicule of his character.... Not to mention the satire implied in making Shallow act Sir Dagonet, who was King Arthur's Fool. Arthur's Show, here supposed to have been presented at Clement's-inn, was probably an interlude, or masque, which actually existed, and was very popular, in Shakespeare's age: and seems to have been compiled from Mallory's Morte Arthur, or the history of king Arthur, then recently published, and the favorite and most fashionable romance. . . .

(ii)

[From Warton's discussion of Stephen Hawes's knowledge of Malory]

Of Arthur and his knights he [Hawes] says, that their exploits are recorded 'in royall bokes and jestes hystoryall.' Sir Thomas Maillorie had now just published his MORTE ARTHUR, a narrative digested from various French romances on Arthur's story. Caxton's printed copy of this favourite volume must have been known to our poet Hawes, which appeared in 1485. . . .

With regard to Maillorie's book, much, if not most, of it, I believe, is taken from the great French romance of LANCELOT, translated from Latin into French at the command of one of our Henrys. . . .

(iii)

. . . Caxton's MORTE ARTHUR, finished in the year 1469, professes to treat of various separate histories. But the matter of the whole is so much of the same sort, and the heroes and adventures of one story are so mutually and perpetually blended with those of another, that no real unity or distinction is preserved. It consists of twenty-one books. The first seven books treat of king Arthur. The eighth, ninth, and tenth, of sir Trystram. The eleventh and twelfth of sir Lancelot.[4] The thirteenth of the SAINGRAL, which is also called sir Lancelot's Book. The fourteenth of sir Percival. The fifteenth, again, of sir Lancelot. The sixteenth of sir Gawaine. The seventeenth of sir Galahad. (But all the four last mentioned books are also called the *historye of the holy Sancgreall*.) The eighteenth and nineteenth of miscellaneous adventures. The two last of king Arthur and all the knights. . . . MORTE ARTHUR is often literally translated from various and very ancient detached histories of the heroes of the round table, which I have examined; and on the whole, it nearly resembles Walter Map's romance abovementioned [*Histoire de Roy Artur*, 1488], printed at Rouen and Paris, both in matter and disposition.

SELECTED NOTES

1 Concerning the preaching of Joseph of Arimathea there was an old song or legend, 'The olde man had an harpe, and there he sung how Joseph of Arimathea came into this land.' MORTE ARTHUR, B. iii, c. 5. See also c. 38.

2 An execration upon Vulcane, in the Underwood. [Warton does not mention that Jonson is making fun of the *Morte Darthur* and other romances.]

3 *Remains*, printed 1604. Artic. NAMES.

4 But at the end, this twelfth book is called *the second booke of* SYR TRYSTRAM. And it is added, 'But here is no rehersall of the thyrd booke [of SIR TRISTRAM].'

9. Sir Walter Scott

1804–24

Walter Scott (1771–1832) was making notes on the *Morte Darthur* as early as 1792 and, during the first decade of the nineteenth century, planned at intervals to bring out a new edition (see Introduction, pp. 6–7). Washington Irving, who visited Abbotsford in 1817, records that an evening's entertainment consisted of Scott's reading aloud from the *Morte Darthur*. Like Saintsbury's (see No. 51), Scott's remarks become increasingly more appreciative.

The extracts below are drawn from several sources:—from Scott's letters, ed. H. J. C. Grierson, 12 vols (London: Constable, 1932–7; reprinted AMS Press, 1971); from the introduction to Scott's edition of *Sir Tristrem*, 1804 (3rd edition, Edinburgh: Archibald Constable, 1811, pp. lxxix–lxxx); from *Marmion* (Edinburgh: Constable, 1808, Notes to Canto First, p. iii); and from an 'Essay on Romance', first published in the *Encyclopaedia Britannica* (1824), then in Scott's *Prose Works*, VI (Edinburgh, 1834, reprinted Freeport, N.Y.: Books for Libraries, 1972, pp. 183 and 212).

(a) Letter of 27 January 1804, to Richard Polwhale (Grierson, I, 211)
… The Morte Arthur which you mention, is a book of still less authority than the Paris folio. It is not a history of the Cornish hero in particular; but a bundle of extracts made by Sir T. Mallory, from the French romances of the Table Round, as Sir Lancelot du Lac,

and the other folios printed on that subject at Paris in the beginning of the 16th century. It is therefore of no authority *whatever*, being merely the shadow of a shade, an awkward abridgement of prose romances, themselves founded on the more ancient metrical *lais* and *gests*. . . .

(b) *Sir Tristrem*
The *History of Tristrem* was not, so far as I know, translated into English as a separate work; but his adventures make a part of the collection, called the *Morte Arthur*, containing great part of the history of the Round Table, extracted at hazard, and without much art or combination, from the various French prose folios on that favourite topic. This work was compiled by Sir Thomas Malory, or Maleore, in the ninth year of the reign of Edward IV., and printed by Caxton. It has since undergone several editions, and is in the hands of most antiquaries and collectors. Those, unaccustomed to the study of romance, should beware of trusting to this work, which misrepresents the adventures, and traduces the character, of Sir Gawain, and other renowned Knights of the Round Table.

[The third edition, 1811, adds the following sentence:]

It is, however, a work of great interest, and curiously written in excellent old English, and breathing a high tone of chivalry.

(c) *Marmion*
Note 1: The romance of the Morte Arthur contains a sort of abridgement of the most celebrated adventures of the Round Table; and, being written in comparatively modern language, gives the general reader an excellent idea of what romances of chivalry actually were. It has also the merit of being written in pure old English; and many of the wild adventures which it contains are told with a simplicity bordering upon the sublime. Several of these are referred to in the text; and I would have illustrated them by more full extracts, but as this curious work is about to be republished, I confine myself to the tale of the Chapel Perilous, and of the quest of Sir Launcelot after the Sangreal.

[Quotes lengthy passages from the *Morte Darthur*, interspersed with paraphrase and summary.]

(d) Letters about the proposed new edition of the *Morte Darthur*

(i) 11 October 1807, to William Miller, publisher (Grierson, XII, 296 n. 1)

[Along with copy for his edition of Dryden's works, Scott has put into Ballantyne's hands] ... copy for a book which I intend to reprint and which you may publish if you please. It is the famous black Letter Romance called the *Morte Arthur* which contains much good old English and some very spirited adventures. I intend to make a page or two of preface perhaps a sheet or two of preface and put my initials to it. I have referred to this curious work so frequently in Marmion that I am sure if that poem sell a small edition of the romance (say 500 or 700 at most) will go off and perhaps lead the way to reprint others in the same stile. If you do not like to be concernd in this *keep my secret*.... With regard to terms (if inclind to take printing &c off my hands) I fancy you will think 30 gu a volume copy money not extravagant. I think it will be two volumes. In fact it will cost me very little trouble and I am only availing myself of my popularity when I make any charge at all. But I want to pick up a few books at the Roxburgh sale and I must make one black letter pay for others if I can.

(ii) 18 November 1807, to Richard Heber (Grierson, XII, 296–297)

Now though a little alien from the genius loci I must implore your advice upon the subject of republishing the old romance of the Morte Arthur. I have determined upon this (I mean anonymously & without notes) in order to preserve a curious specimen of old English Romance. I don't want to make it an antiquarys book & shall therefore print from Stansby's edition in 1636 I think, because the language is perfectly intelligible. But before printing I should like to have your opinion or rather your instruction concerning the earlier editions and what extent of collation will be necessary. All that I can find in Scotland are copies in the 17th Century. Caxton's copy I believe is not now known to exist but I am most desirous to know what is the earliest I presume the refaciamento in Edward VIths. time. I should not be unwilling to replace the oaths profanity & so forth which that Editor piques himself on having exploded from Sir Thomas Mallore's copy. Of course the Bookseller makes a very limited edition in a small old fashioned 4to—Should this succeed at all or even save itself I think of going through our old

Bibliotheque Bleue—Do write me on this subject with unwashd hands as Falstaff says—Palmerin you have seen of course it is I think far inferior to Amadis & infinitely so to the Morte Arthur in which I take great pleasure.

(iii) 15 December 1807, to Robert Southey (Grierson, I, 401)
I am very glad the Morte Arthur is in your hands; it has been long a favourite of mine, and I intended to have made it a handsome book, in the shape of a small antique-looking quarto, with wooden vignettes of costume. I wish you would not degrade him into a squat 12mo; but admit the temptation you will probably feel to put it into the same shape with Palmerin and Amadis.

(iv) 10 September 1809, to Southey (Grierson, II, 2)
Don't tease yourself or Pater noster about the Morte Arthur but take your own time. My idea was entirely different from yours, to reprint namely the whole from the only original Caxton which is extant with all the superstition and harlotrie which the castrator in the reign of Edward VI chose to omit. A Classic of Henry VII[ths] time is so valuable that I still think once you have been afloat for a year or two I will give a very limited edition of Sir Thomas Mallory in his native dress. But this is a distant vision.

(e) 'Essay on Romance'

(i)
Churchmen, however, were by no means the only authors of these legends. . . . As education became improved, and knowledge began to be more generally diffused, individuals among the laity, and those of no mean rank, began to feel the necessity, as it may be called, of putting into a permanent form the 'thick-coming fancies' which gleam along the imagination of men of genius. Sir Thomas Malory, who compiled the *Morte d'Arthur* from French originals, was a person of honour and worship; and Lord Berners, the excellent translator of Froissart, and author of a Romance called *The Chevalier de la Cygne*, is an illustrious example that a nobleman of high estimation did not think his time misemployed on this species of composition.

(ii)
If the Metrical Romances of England can boast of few original compositions, they can show yet fewer examples of the Prose

Romance. Sir Thomas Malory, indeed, compiled, from various French authorities, his celebrated *Morte d'Arthur*, indisputably the best Prose Romance the language can boast.

10. Early nineteenth-century scholars and bibliographers

A. Joseph Ritson

1802

Joseph Ritson (1752–1803), a precise and careful editor and scholar, published several collections of early ballads and romances. In addition, he wrote a *Life of Arthur*, published posthumously in 1825, which examined the evidence for an historical Arthur. His brief comments on Malory appeared in the 'Dissertation on Romance and Minstrelsy', prefixed to *Ancient Englëish Metrical Romanceës* (London: William Bulmer & Company, 1802), pp. cv–cvi and cxlii–cxliv.

(a)
The fragment of a metrical romance, intitle'd *Le Mort Arthure*, preserve'd in the Harleian MSS. Num. 2252, and of which Humphrey Wanley has say'd that the writeër 'useth many Saxon or obsolete words;' and doctor Percy, fancyfully and absurdly, that 'it *seems* to be quoted in *Syr Bevis*,' is, in fact, nothing more than part of the *Morte Arthur* of Caxton turn'd into easey alternate verse, a very unusual circumstance, no doubt, in the time of Henry the seventh, to which Wanley properly allots it. The antiquateed words use'd by this versifyer are manifestly affected. Caxtons book is the onely one known by the name of *La mort D'Arthur*, which he took as he found it.

(b)
... Caxton, our first printer, had so little taste for poetry, that he never printed one single metrical romance, nor, in fact, any poetical

composition whatever, beside Gowers *Confessio amantis*, The Canterbury tales, and a few other pieces of Chaucer, Lydgate, &c. He translateëd, indeed, Virgil and Ovid, out of French, into Engleish, prose; and we are indebted to him, by the like mean, for several venerable black-letter romanceës in folio, or quarto, such as *Mort Darthur*, compile'd, it seems, by sir Thomas Malory; *Charlemagne, Reynard the fox*, and others; the first of which, though most abominablely mangle'd, became exceedingly popular, and was frequently reprinted; allthough no copy of the original edition is now known to exist.

B. George Ellis

1805

Ellis (1753–1815) published *Specimens of the Early English Poets* in 1790 and in 1805 brought out *Specimens of Early English Metrical Romances* where he included portions of 'Arthour and Merlin' and of the stanzaic *Morte Arthur*. Like Ritson, he regards Malory as primarily a compiler, but he admires the style of the *Morte Darthur* and substitutes its language for a paraphrase of the 'rather insipid' concluding portion of the stanzaic *Morte*.

The excerpt is from *Specimens of Romances*, new edition, ed. and rev. by J.O. Halliwell (London: H.G. Bohn, 1848; reprinted New York: AMS Press, 1968), p. 143.

Ellis is here discussing the stanzaic *Morte Arthur*.

The late Mr. Ritson was of opinion that it was versified from the prose work of the same name, written by Malory, and printed by Caxton; in proof of which, he contended that the style is marked by an evident affectation of antiquity, But in truth it differs most essentially from Malory's work, which was a mere compilation; whilst it follows, with tolerable exactness, the French romance of Lancelot; and its phraseology, which much resembles that of Chester, and other authors of the fifteenth century, betrays no marks of affectation.

C. George Burnett

1807

Burnett (1776?–1811) had a varied if brief career which
included an early association with Coleridge and Southey in
their pantisocracy scheme. His last publication was a selection
from Milton's Prose Works.

The selection below is from *Specimens of English Prose Writers*
(London: Longman, 1807, I, 247–59), which was intended as a
companion work to Ellis's *Specimens of Early English Metrical
Romances*.

The title of this book at full length is—'The Birth, Life and Acts of
King Arthur; of his noble Knights of the Round Table; their
marvellous Enquests and Adventures; the achieving of the
Sangreal; and in the end, *La Mort d'Arthur*; with the dolorous death
and departing out of this world of them all: which book was
reduced to the English by sir Thomas Malory, knight; and by me,
William Caxton, divided into twenty-one books; chaptered and
emprinted and finished in the abbey of Westminster, the last day of
July, the year of our Lord 1485,' being about a month before the
battle of Bosworth, in which Richard III. was slain.

If we are to credit Leland, and others after him, sir Thomas
Malory was a Welchman; and from the legendary cast of some of
the stories, he was probably a priest. The history of king Arthur,
who died in 542, occupies the seventh book of Geoffrey of
Monmouth; which undoubtedly furnished the ground work of the
romance in question. The superstructure was completed by
materials derived from MSS. written in the French and Welch,
concerning the said king Arthur and his knights; perhaps with
some additions by the compiler.

[Quotes Caxton's preface.]

The blowing of the horn, in the beginning of the following
passage, furnishes a fine instance of the sublime, founded on
particular costume.

[Quotes 'Balin and Balan' from Balin's warnings down to the deaths of the brothers.]

The speech of sir Bohort, towards the end, over the dead body of sir Lancelot, has been often quoted as the perfect character of a knight errant.

[Quotes Ector's eulogy.]

D. Thomas Frognell Dibdin

1810

Dibdin (1776–1847), a bibliographer, was librarian to Lord Spencer and helped to extend the famous collection of rare books and editions at Althorp. He was the author of several anecdotal, gossipy works on book collecting and collectors. In his bibliographical descriptions, Dibdin relied heavily on secondary sources, especially in his enlarged edition of Ames and Herbert's *Typographical Antiquities*, and his description of Caxton's edition brings together much of what was currently known about Malory and the *Morte Darthur*.

The extracts below exclude most of Dibdin's quotations and summaries from previously cited commentaries; they are taken from 'William Caxton', *Ames' Typographical Antiquities*, ed. Thomas F. Dibdin, I (London, 1810; reprinted Hildesheim: Georg Olms, 1969), pp. 241–55.

A BOOK OF THE NOBLE HYSTORYES OF KYNGE. ARTHUR and of certeyn of his knyghtes. Whiche book was reduced in to englysshe by syr Thomas Malory knyght *and by me deuyded into xxi bookes chapytred and enprynted, and fynysshed in thabbey Westmestre the last day of Juyl the yere of our lord* M. CCCC. LXXXV. Folio. (Type No. 4.)

This title is gathered from the prologue and colophon; there being no title 'at full length,' as Mr. Burnett supposed, prefixed to the edition. Of all the productions of Caxton's press, the present is probably the most curious, amusing, and scarce; and is well called by Oldys, the printer's 'capital work this year.' Lewis[1] does not appear to have ever seen a copy of it; and I suspect that Oldys has taken his account from the imperfect description of Ames, who has extracted, with many errors, what he considered to be, Caxton's proheme or preface, and mentions 'a wooden cut to each book'—whereas there is not a single cut throughout the volume.[2] Herbert had never seen a copy; but as Ames noticed it, he doubted not of its existence, and accordingly transcribed his account literally....

By the politeness of the Earl of Jersey, I am enabled to lay before the reader a particular, and I trust interesting, account of this singularly rare book; it having been originally obtained from the Harleian library, by Bryan Fairfax, and purchased of this latter, with his entire collection, for the Osterley Library, by the late Mr. Child, grandfather of the present Countess of Jersey.

Caxton, in his prologues to Godfrey of Boulogne and the Order of Chivalry, had spoken so enthusiastically of Prince Arthur and the Knights of the Round Table, that he most probably seized with avidity the present opportunity of *printing* a work written in commendation of this illustrious corps.[3]

[Quotes extensively from Caxton's prologue.]

In the Harleian Catalogue, vol. iii. no. S72, this copy is very justly described to be 'choicely preserved; bound in red morocco, and richly adorned with gold.' The margin is ample, the press work exact, and, upon the whole, the book is one of the finest specimens extant of Caxton's typography. It has capital initials, like those of the first, second, and fourth form in the plate prefixed to the Disquisition on early Printing and Engraving: the pages are about 550 in number. Lord Oxford's autograph is on the recto of the first leaf of the body of the work; and a pencil mark of £5. 5. is on the corner of a fly leaf—the price at which Bryan Fairfax probably obtained it from Osborne the bookseller, who purchased the Harleian collection: a sum, at least, forty times below its present value!

Of the translator and the work itself, we will say a few words by way of conclusion to this article.

[Quotes Oldys, No. 6 above.]

It underwent several impressions afterwards, and seems to have been popular even as late as the reign of Charles I.

[Quotes Ascham, No. 4A above.]

SELECTED NOTES

1 *Life of Caxton*, p. 96.
2 I incline to think that some one sent Ames an account of East's edition of the romance of King Arthur, which edition agrees, in the prologue adopted by Ames, and contains 'a wooden cut to each book.'
3 In order that the possessors of subsequent editions of the HISTORIES OF ARTHUR may compare their copies with the present one—and to shew the niceties and peculiarities of our language in the course of two centuries—as well as to afford, to the uninitiated, a specimen of the curious things which happened in the ancient days of chivalry, I subjoin a few extracts from this *third book*; giving fragments of the first four, and the entire fifth, chapters, with a few immaterial variations from East's edition. Those who do not discover therein a certain simplicity or naïveté of style, may be accused of possessing a fastidiousness of feeling, of which no scholar of taste will envy them the possession.

11. *The British Bibliographer*

1810

The British Bibliographer was a journal (1810–14) devoted to antiquarian concerns, primarily the description of old or rare books. The selection below is from volume I (London, 1810; reprinted New York: AMS Press, 1966, pp. 44–61); the article is signed only with the initial 'W', and the editor, Sir Samuel Egerton Brydges, in the introduction to this volume 'regrets that he is prohibited from mentioning the name of the learned and ingenious communicator, to whom the Volume is under such essential obligations'.

This description and abstract of the 1634 edition of the *Morte Darthur* is the first substantial commentary on the work, offering structural, moral, and stylistic comments along with an outline of the book's contents.

...The pleasures derived from the recital of romances, although confined to the great for several centuries, were, by the introduction of printing, afforded a wider range; and the great mass of readers were benefited by a more familar acquaintance with those fascinating scenes of extravagance and fiction. Some of the earliest productions of Caxton and de Worde were prose versions of the old metrical tales; and by a reference to Herbert, we see, that even after the Reformation had deluged the press with the wranglings of theological polemics, no inconsiderable employment of the printer arose from the multiplication of romances, many of which are now only known by tradition. The wondrous acts narrated in the romance, its splendid scenery, and the frequent successes of human prowess over the strength of diabolical agency, offered, to an illiterate population, unacquainted with the more polished models of classic elegance, a never-failing source of amusement and study. Notwithstanding the introduction of more varied reading, toward the middle of the sixteenth century, the volumes of chivalry retained their hold on popular favour until a very late period of the succeeding century, when the improvement of taste, and more familar acquaintance with classic lore eventually expelled the magician and the tournament from the hall of the mansion, to the shelves of the collector. One of the earliest and most justly favoured of these now neglected works, was that under review: it carried with it, in addition to its interesting narrative, a certain degree of authenticity in the opinion of our forefathers, who listened to, and perused, the work containing the deeds of Arthur and his knights, with twofold interest; first, as it amused the hour of indolence, and secondly, as bearing with it the authority of a chronicle.

[Discusses the belief in Arthur's return, the denunciations of the romance by Ascham and others, and Milton's interest in Arthurian romance.]

The prose romance of the Mort Arthur, of which this work

before us is a transcript, was, according to Warton, 'much or most of it taken from the old French romance of Lancelot, translated from Latin into French, at the command of one of our Henries.'

From internal evidence, I should imagine it to have been a *compilation* from several different romances, rather than a translation of one individually. The acts of Lancelot form but a portion of the body of the book, in which are related the histories of various other knights, and also the achievements of the Saint Greall.

[Quotes from Caxton's prologue to support the idea of a compilation from several sources.]

Of the translation and compiler of the Morte Arthur, little, I believe, is known; Hollingshead, who, although not always inimical to legendary tales, does not appear to have had much of the fashionable taste for romances of chivalry, mentions, among the learned men that lived in the reign of Henry the VIIth, 'Thomas Maillorie, a Welshman borne, wrote I wote not what of King Arthure, and of the Rounde Table.' H. Chr. vol. ii. 1462. ed. 1577.

The translation was finished the ninth year of the reign of King Edward the IVth. The first edition was printed by Caxton, and bears the following title, 'A book of the noble hystoryes of Kynge Arthur, and of certyn of his knightes. Whiche booke was reduced into Englysshe by Syr Thomas Malory, knyght, and by me devyded into xxi bookes chapytred and emprynted, and fynyshed in thabbey Westmestre, the last day of Juyl, the year of our Lord M. CCCC. LXXXV. fol. The second edition, according to Herbert, was printed by W. de Worde, 1498; in folio; the third also in folio, by Thos. East, without date, after which, I am not aware of its being reprinted until 1634, the edition herein mentioned.

This edition commences with a preface or advertisement to the reader, for the better illustration and understanding of this famous history. This is a short chronicle of rulers in England, from the departure of the Romans from the island, until the death of Arthur, in confutation of the error, that no such person as that prince existed.

[Quotes also from the editor's remarks about amending certain passages (see No. 5A above) but adds this note:]

The variations are trivial, and little affect the construction of the sentence: by Mr. Dibdin's kindness, I have been enabled to compare several passages of Caxton's edition with the present one.

[Summarizes from the remainder of Blome's preface and continues:]

I shall select a few specimens of the language and incidents, which will be less numerous, from the probability that this now scarce work, will, ere long, be given to the public in a reprint.

[Summarizes at some length the events leading to Arthur's assuming the crown.]

Chapters xii. xiii. xiv. and xv. are occupied with a tedious battle between his united foes and the intrepid Arthur, all the incidents of which are minutely related; at which we cannot be surprised, when we learn that after the battle, 'Merlin (who acted as commander in chief) took his leave of King Arthur for to goe see his master Bleise which dwelt in Northumberland.'—'And so Bleise wrote the battayle word by worde as Merlin tolde him, how it began, and by whom, and in like wise how it was ended, and who had the worst. All the battayles that were done in King Arthur's dayes, Merlin caused Bleyse his master, to write them. Also he caused hym to wryte all the battayles that every worthy knyght did of King Arthur's court.'

Merlin, although he amused himself with Arthur's ignorance of the powers of sorcery (for he frequently appeared in different disguises for the purpose of playing tricks upon the simple monarch) uniformly stood his friend. He preserved his life repeatedly; and put the famous Excalibur into his possession; that celebrated falchion 'which was so bright in his enemies eyes that it gave light like thirtie torches.' Victorious as Arthur had generally been, yet was not his personal prowess or his political consequence sufficient to prevent the insult offered him at ch. xxviii.

[Summarizes the episodes involving King Ryence's cloak of beards.]

At length Arthur, in compliance with the wish of his barons, takes a wife; and disregarding Merlin's prophetic advice, yields to his passions, and selects Guenever, daughter of Leodegraunce, king of the Land of Cameliard, to share his throne. This lady possessing every grace save that of chastity, (for her amours with the famous Sir Lancelot have been celebrated in romances and fabliaux innumerable,) brought as her portion the much-famed Round-table. Merlin, notwithstanding his advice to Arthur, and spite of his necromantic skill, appears to have been unable to resist the tender passion, as we are told, ch. 60. that he 'fel in a dotage on the damosel that King Pellinore brought to the court with him, and she was one of the damosels of the lake which hight Nimue.' Sorcerers are sometimes equally unlucky in pleasing the fair sex with less learned suitors: the lady obtained a knowledge of his art from his attachment, but refused him all remuneration in her favours, 'and faine would haue been deliuered of him, for she was afraid of him, because he was a divels sonne.' We occasionally meet with 'gyants' who possess the same qualities which are common to all giants in our old romances—viz. ferocity and cruelty. In one instance, however, a gyant rauisher is introduced, and falls beneath the edge of Arthur's sword, whose rapes are attended with effects not usually consequent on that crime. The series of adventures, relating to Arthur and his knights, are related without any regularity; and however we may give credit to Merlin's Master Bleise for the fidelity of his narration, we certainly cannot praise him for the *lucidus ordo* of his arrangement. He travels from Sir Gareth to Sir Gauaine, leaving the feats of each respectively neglected to introduce the deeds of Sir Gringamor and Sir Tristram, who in their turn quit the stage for a time to inferior actors. His morality is as loose as his style: although Sir Tristram and Sir Lancelot are allowed to persist almost uninterruptedly in their adulterous intercourse with Isonde and Guenever, Sir Gareth is less fortunate in the less blameable pursuit of the dame Lyones; since the nocturnal visits of the latter to the knight are disturbed by the intrusion of a supernatural visitant, who, although beheaded and hewn in pieces by the disappointed Sir Gareth, fails not to wound in return that gallant knight. Amongst other qualifications which he possessed, and which claimed the notice of the ladies, was an extremely good appetite—'Then Sir Gareth list well to eate, & knightly he eate his meat & egerly, there was many a faire lady by him, & some of them said they neuer saw a goodlier man nor so well of eating.' The second part is chiefly occupied with the adventures of Sir Tristram, which much resemble those in the romance of that name, edited by Mr. W. Scott. In the third part, Sir Lancelot is the most prominent character, although the achievements of the Sancgreal, and the death of Arthur, add materially to its stock of variety. Continual combats fill the pages: as a specimen of one of them, I will extract that between Sir Lancelot and Sir Tristram.—Part ii. ch. 92. . . .

The greatest of all achievements, in a court like Arthur's, where heroism had scarcely aught left to feed upon, was that of the Sancgreall. An account of the Sancgreall, and its disappearance, is to be found in Mr. W. Scott's edition of Sir Tristram, to which I refer the reader. This adventure was not to be achieved by persons tainted with sin—Sir Lancelot had failed in the completion, as had his brother, Sir Ector de Maris: the former lay twenty four days and nights in a stupor resembling death, as a punishment for his unhallowed attempt. This honour was reserved for Sir Galahad, who, accompanied by Sir Percival and Sir Bors, and King Pelles and Eliazer his son, and some other knights, met at the spot on which the Sancgreall rested. King Pelles and his son, however, not being in the quest of the Sancgreall, were warned by a voice from heaven to depart.

[Quotes one of Malory's Grail passages where the figure of a child 'smote himselfe into the bread' (Caxton, Bk XVII, chap. 20) with the note, 'The simplicity and rudeness of this method of describing the transubstantiation of the catholic church must strike every reader.']

The succeeding part of this chapter is wild in the extreme. The singular devotion of Sir Lancelot, coupled with his criminal passion for Queen Guenever, are quaintly narrated in ch. 105 [Caxton, Bk XVIII, chap. 1].

'Now after the quest of the Sancgreall was fulfilled, and that all the knights that were left aliue were come againe to the round table, as the booke of the Sancgreall maketh mention. Then was there great joy in the court. And especially King Arthur and Queen Gueneuer made great joy of the remnant that were come home. And passing glad was the king and the queene of Sir Launcelot and of Sir Bors, for they had beene passing long away in the quest of the Sancgreall. Then Sir Launcelot began to resort unto Queene Gueneuer againe, and forgat the promise and the profession that he made in the quest; had not Sir Launcelot beene in his priuy thoughts, and in his minde set inwardly to the queene, as hee was in seeming outward unto God, there had no knight passed him in the quest of the Sancgreall, but euer his thoughts were priuely upon the queene.'—— 'And so it bee fell, that Sir Launcelot had many resortes of ladyes and damosels, that daily resorted unto him, which besought him to be their champion. And in all such manners of right, Sir Launcelot appealed him daily to doe for the pleasure of our Lord Jesu Christ.'

Notorious as this connexion was, and indecorous as it ought to have been in the eye of the church, our author makes the Pope interest himself in favour of the lovers, at a period when Sir Lancelot had taken away the queen, and was in open rebellion against his patient sovereign.

'Sir Launcelot which was called the most noble knight of the world, wherfore the Pope called unto him a noble clarke, that at that time was there present, which was the bishop of Rochester. And the Pope gaue him bulls under lead unto King Arthur of England, charging him, upon pain of interditing of all England, that he take his queene dame Gueneuer to him again, and accord with Sir Launcelot.'

Arthur, in compliance with the Pope's commands, again received the faithless Guenever to his bosom. The period when Arthur's life was to be shortened now approached, of which he was warned in dreams, and by spectres.

[Quotes Arthur's Wheel of Fortune dream and his dream of Gawaine's warning.]

Arthur, notwithstanding these friendly advices, falls a sacrifice to the traitor Sir Modred. Lancelot did not long survive the master whom he had so grossly injured; but as he had been more fortunate than Arthur in possessing the affections of Guenever, so was he more fortunate in having time to repent of his misdeeds, and dying a natural death. His brother, Sir Ector de Maris, 'that had sought seuen yeare all England, Scotland & Wales, seeking for Launcelot,' arrived in time to see the body of the deceased hero.

[Quotes Ector's lament for Lancelot.]

Few panegyrics, (allowing for the manners of the age) in ancient or modern story, appear to me more comprehensive, or less affected: the simplicity of the diction is only equalled by the energy of the thoughts; and, if I am not misled by my partiality for a favourite work, I shall not hazard too much in saying, that this short funeral oration over the lifeless Lancelot is one of the most interesting specimens of the pathetic in the English or any other language.

[Concludes by quoting from Scott's note to *Marmion*; see No. 9 above.]

12. Walker's British Classics

1816

In 1816, two new editions of the *Morte Darthur* were published, the first since 1634. Both were based on the Stansby/Blome edition. The two-volume edition put out by J. Walker for Walker's British Classics had a preface which is unsigned but which has been attributed to Alexander Chalmers (1759–1834). On both editions, as well as Southey's (No. 13), see Barry Gaines, 'The Editions of Malory in the Early Nineteenth Century', *Papers of the Bibliographic Society of America*, 68 (1974), 1–17. Chalmes's preface is derivative (the last line, for example, is borrowed from Scott without acknowledgment), but appreciative. For the reference to Dibdin's work, see No. 10D above.

Although our information respecting the domestic habits of our ancestors is but scanty, it seems agreed upon, that, in the infancy, or rather the absence of literature and literary taste, romances were very generally read, and served to fill up the hours that are now devoted either to study, or to more refined amusements. Such, indeed, was the demand for these extravagant fictions, that our earliest printers employed their skill on them, and gave them a much wider circulation than when confined to manuscripts, and in the hands of the wealthy only. The book now before the reader was first printed by Caxton, in 1485, and is reckoned one of the finest specimens of his typography. The only copy, however, now known, is one in the library of the Earl of Jersey; which was originally obtained from the Harleian Library, by Brian Fairfax, whose books were purchased by the late Mr. Child, grandfather of the present Countess of Jersey. It is from this copy that Mr. Dibdin was enabled to rectify the many errors of his predecessors, and give an accurate description of the volume in his 'Typographical Antiquities.'

The second edition was printed by Wynkyn de Worde in 1498, and may be accounted yet more rare than the preceding, as there is but one copy extant, (in Lord Spencer's library,) and that very imperfect. It was purchased by his lordship at the memorable Roxburgh sale, for £31 10s. A third edition was printed by Thomas East, but without date; after which no edition can be traced until that of 1634, of which the volume now before the reader is an exact reprint.

The long interval between the first three editions and this of 1634, may be accounted for from the state of public affairs, both ecclesiastical and civil—but principally the former. That great event, the REFORMATION, engaged the attention of the public for nearly the whole of the sixteenth century; and the transactions of the seventeenth, as far as the Restoration of Charles II. were very unfavourable to works of imagination and amusement.

[Summarizes Malory's biography as presented by Oldys, No. 6 above.]

It is remarkable, that Caxton was at first very unwilling to print this work, because he doubted whether such a person as Arthur ever existed; and it is amusing to read the arguments by which he was persuaded of the existence of that noted monarch. The modern reader, however, need not be told, that the Arthur of *history*, and the Arthur of *romance*, are very different personages. Still its merit, as a fiction, is very great. It gives the general reader an excellent idea of what romances of chivalry actually were: it is also written in pure English; and many of the wild adventures which it contains, are told with a simplicity bordering upon the sublime.

13. Robert Southey

1817

Robert Southey (1774–1843) had planned a new edition of Malory as early as 1807, but the project was long delayed (see Introduction, pp. 6–7, and Scott, No. 9). Letters of this period indicate ambitious plans for a history of Arthur drawn from Welsh sources as well as a chapter-by-chapter source study using the French romances. The introduction and notes that appeared with the edition of 1817 did not fulfil these aims, but they do offer the first systematic attempt to identify many of Malory's sources.

Although Southey admits to a great fondness for the *Morte Darthur* in his youth, his adult estimate of the narrative method of romance and of some of its incidents is not high. Some of Southey's statements about Malory and the *Morte Darthur* are inaccurate, but no more so than other commentaries of the period. Some examples are the statement in section XI that Ector's lament is from the French *Lancelot* (it is Malory's addition) and the assumption that Malory drew on late compilations like that of Rusticien (see also Madden, No. 15). The statement in section XVIII that the text is a scrupulous rendering of Caxton is not quite true either (see Strachey's 1868 preface, extracted in No. 28 below and de Worde, No. 2 above). Southey's preface is divided into twenty-one sections, perhaps in imitation of Caxton (the divisions seem a bit arbitrary); some sections are merely summarized below. (London: Longman, et al., 1817), I, i–xxxii.

I. Rich as the English is in every other branch of literature, it is peculiarly deficient in prose romances of chivalry, a species of composition in which the Portugueze and the French have excelled all other nations. The cause of this deficiency may perhaps be found in our history. At a time when the feelings and fashion of the age tended to produce and encourage such works, and when the master-pieces in this kind were composed, our language had not found its way among the higher classes, and our prose-style in consequence was wholly unformed. We had metrical romances in abundance, because these were in the proper sense of the word popular; they were designed for recital, and all who had ears to hear were fit audience. But for long compositions in prose readers were required, and in those ages reading was a rare accomplishment even in the highest ranks: this is one reason, among others, why poetry has in all countries preceded prose; and in this country French was at that time the language of those for whom books were written. Just as the English tongue acquired a decided prevalence, and had been stampt for immortality by Chaucer, the civil wars began, and the men, without whose patronage literature could make no progress, were engaged in a fierce struggle, not merely for power, but for life. When the long contest between the houses of York and Lancaster was terminated, and the government assumed a settled form under the Tudors, the glory of chivalry was on the wane. The character of war had been changed by the general use of gunpowder; this produced, though somewhat more slowly, a change in its costume; and the intellectual activity of the age was at the same time excited and almost engrossed by the momentous struggle for religious liberty.

II. For the same reasons that during the golden age of chivalry no original compositions of this description were produced among us, no translations were made from the numerous works which had appeared in French. To this circumstance the Morte Arthur is owing: it is a compilation from some of the most esteemed romances of the Round Table. Had the volumes from which it is compiled existed in English, Sir Thomas Malory would not have thought of extracting parts from them, and blending them into one work. This was done at the best possible time: a generation earlier, the language would have retained too much of its Teutonic form; a generation later, and the task of translation would have devolved into the hands of men who performed it as a trade, and equally debased the work which they interpreted, and the language in which they wrote.

III–VII. [Origins of romance; Charlemagne versus Arthur as subject of romance; the Arthur of history.]

VIII. All which can be gleaned from Welsh authorities, respecting the real actions of Arthur, may be found in Mr. Turner's elaborate and most valuable history of the Anglo-Saxons: it is sufficient to prove that he made a brave stand against the Saxons, though not always a successful one, and that he was sometimes engaged in destructive wars with the petty princes of his own country. To trace the fictions to which he has given birth, would be a work of extraordinary labour and difficulty,—greater, perhaps, than any individual could accomplish. Many of the oldest works have never been published, and some, perhaps, are no longer in existence. The printed romances are of extreme rarity, and their bulk is such that they cannot be perused without a serious expence of time, more than commensurate with the importance of the object. Such, however, as I have been able to obtain, I have gone through, and among them are the most important of those from which the Morte Arthur has been compiled.

IX. Merlin is the first of these in order.

[Southey discusses the Vulgate *Merlin*, calling it 'one of the poorest books of the Round Table' and summarizing its plot.]

X. [Prophecies of Merlin.]

XI. A much larger portion of the Morte Arthur is taken from Lancelot du Lac than from Merlin.

[Description of the printed texts.]

This is the bulkiest of all the Round Table Romances, but it is also one of the best; and the hero might be considered as the ideal of a perfect Knight for honour, generosity, and constancy, as well as courage, if it could be forgotten that he lives in adultery with the wife of the King whom he serves, and who regards him as one of the best and most faithful of his court. The lamentation over Sir Lancelot's dead body, toward the close of the Morte Arthur, which has often been quoted for its beauty, is translated from this Romance.

XII. Sir Thomas Malory has also drawn liberally from the following romance.

[Southey cites printed texts of the prose *Tristan* and Scott's *Sir Tristrem* and the British origin of this romance.]

XIII. The Romance of Meliadus de Leonnoys, the father of Tristram, is, in my judgement, very superior to that of the son.

[Plot summary.]

XIV. Gyron le Courtoys is the work of the same author, whose style indeed is distinctly marked, especially in dialogue, and who in his tone of morals is infinitely superior to all the other Romancers of this school.

[Titles of printed texts, plot summary.]

XV. *Lhystoire du sainct greaal* and *Le second volume du sainct greall* [Vulgate *Estoire* and *Queste*]... great part of which is incorporated in the Morte Arthur.

[Southey here confines his comments mainly to a discussion of the opening attribution of the *Estoire* to the pen of Christ himself.]

Whether this blasphemous fiction be the unpardonable license of a romancer's fancy, or the pious fraud of some zealous believer in transubstantiation, I presume not to determine.... Legends not less impudent have obtained belief in the Romish church....

XVI. This personage [Perceval] is the hero of a Romance... from which some parts are blended with the story of the S. Greaal in the Morte Arthur.

[Southey identifies and discusses briefly what we now call the prose *Perceval*.]

XVII. There are other Romances which I have not met with, from whence materials for the Morte Arthur have been drawn; but these are the principal sources, Lancelot, Tristan, and the Sainct Greaal, having furnished nearly two thirds of the whole. Whether this compilation was made originally by Sir Thomas Malory, or translated by him from a French compendium, has not been ascertained; nor is it of importance, as there is no claim to originality on his part. The compiler seems to have altered the incidents as freely as the arrangement, and may perhaps have made some additions of his own; Mr. Douce has suggested that he used manuscripts to the texts of which we may probably always be strangers, and this therefore must remain doubtful.[1] It is probable also that some of his materials have never been printed. 'O blessed Lord,' says Caxton, 'when I remember the great and many volumes of St. Graal, Ghalehot, and Lancelot du Lac, Gawain, Perceval, Lionel and Tristram, and many other, of whom were over long to rehearse, and also to me unknown.'...

It seems too, from the exclamation of Caxton, that Gawain and Lionel had each their history; but I believe none are known to be in existence, or at least that none have been published. The story of Beaumayns has, from its structure and completeness, the appearance of having been a metrical Romance. I do not know from whence the story of Balin and Balan has been derived; it has finer circumstances in it than any other part of the Morte Arthur.

The history of the Round Table Romances may be investigated with better opportunities in France than in England; but it must be sought for also among the remains of the Welsh and Breton fictions, and something may perhaps be discovered in the Walloon tongue....

XVIII. The Morte Arthur was favourite book among our ancestors. It continued to be printed till the middle of the 17th century, with much alteration of orthography, but very little change of language; and were it again modernized in the same manner, and published as a book for boys, it could hardly fail of regaining its popularity. When I was a schoolboy I possessed a wretchedly imperfect copy, and there was no book, except the Faery Queen, which I perused so often, or with such deep contentment.

The present edition is a reprint with scrupulous exactness from the first edition by Caxton, in Earl Spencer's library, that nobleman having, with his wonted liberality, permitted a transcript to be made from this most rare and valuable volume for this purpose.

XIX. [Southey dismisses Addison's mocking of romance: he 'appears not to have read the books which he...characterises.']

The morals of the chivalrous romance were however always taken at the highest standard of the age,... but the ferocious spirit of the times frequently appears.

[Examples of ferocity, from *Merlin* and *Meliadus*.]

The history of Europe during the middle ages, is full of cruelties like these: it must be considered as a great merit in the romance writers, that they have not introduced them more frequently; that they have sometimes reprehended them, and that in their ideal heroes they held up for imitation fairer models of heroic virtue than were to be found in real life.[2]...

XX. The authors of these books never supposed that they were outraging probability; none of the marvels which they feigned were regarded as impossible; they were all founded upon the received opinions of the age; the belief in magic, the science of gems, and the wonderful properties of wells, fountains, and lakes, whose effects were described in books, the authenticity of which had never been questioned. Travellers and naturalists told of more monsters than the romance writers ever devised....

It is in describing their tournaments, and the exploits of their knights on horseback, that the Romance writers have committed the greatest exaggeration: their heroes seldom encounter without breaking a lance, and giving or receiving a fall....

The prowess of the knights of Romance in other respects is not much exaggerated. Lancelot and Tristram in armour are what the Chicken and Gulley were without it; men of the greatest skill, strength, and courage, in a mode of fighting wherein those qualifications rendered success certain.

XXI. Nothing can be more inartificial in structure than the Romances of the Round Table. Adventure produces adventure in infinite series; not like a tree, whose boughs and branches bearing a necessary relation and due proportion to each other, combine into one beautiful form, but resembling such plants as the prickly pear, where one joint grows upon another, all equal in size and alike in shape, and the whole making a formless and misshapen mass. Even this clumsy mode of transition is often disregarded, and the author passes from adventure to adventure without the slightest connection, introducing you without prologue or prelude of any kind to a new scene, and bringing forward a new set of personages. In this respect Amadis is greatly superior to every other work of the same description. Lobeira was the first Romance writer who formed a clear and connected plan, and bore it steadily in mind throughout the whole progress of his narrative. The skill with which his fable is constructed is not less admirable than the beauty of the incidents, and the distinctness with which the characters are conceived and delineated. Amadis infinitely surpasses every earlier romance in all these points, and has not been equalled in either of them by any of later date.

These folios were the only books of recreation when they were composed and printed; and in those ages large volumes were not regarded with that fear which is now felt by the busy, and affected by the superficial and the vain....

As the manners have become obsolete, the fashion for such works has passed away; and now for the full enjoyment of them a certain aptitude is required, as it is for poetry and music: where that aptitude exists, perhaps no works of imagination produce so much delight. It is something like that pleasure which the poet and the painter partake from forest scenery, or in following the course of a mountain stream.

SELECTED NOTES

1 *Was the Morte Arthur compiled in French or in English?*—A passage in the beginning of the sixth book implies that the compilation was in French, and Sir Thomas Malory only the translator.—'Sir Launcelot increased marvellously in worship and in honour, therefore he is the first knight *that the French book maketh mention of after King Arthur came from Rome.*'

The title also appears to warrant a like inference. I believe all the poems with a French title which are printed with Chaucer's works are translations from that language.

2 [In an explanatory note to the text at the point where Lancelot is being told that his failure in the Quest is due to his sin with Guinevere, Southey cites Ascham's condemnation of the morals of the *Morte Darthur*, but adds:] Notwithstanding the severity, and in some degree the truth of this censure, I believe that books of chivalry, instead of increasing the corruption of the age, tended very greatly to raise the standard of morals.

14. Three literary historians

Malory receives but brief mention in most literary histories of the nineteenth century.

A. John Colin Dunlop

1816

Dunlop (d. 1842) published his *History of Fiction* in 1814; the work was enlarged in 1816 and its title changed to *History of Prose Fiction*. Under this title it went through many editions. Dunlop gave lengthy synopses of many French Arthurian romances and noted Malory's debt to them at appropriate intervals; an example is (a) below. Another brief mention of Malory appears in a section on the 'origin and progress of the English novel' in which he has announced that lengthy analyses of relatively well-known works would be tedious.

The extracts are from a new edition, revised (though not in these portions) by Henry Wilson in 1888 (London: George Bell, 1986), I, 185, and II, 547.

(a)

In some of the editions, [the Vulgate] Lancelot is divided into three parts, comprising the adventures of Agravain, the Quest of the Graal, and the Morte d'Artus, which is the origin of the celebrated metrical romance Morte Arthur. The English prose work of that name, also called the·History or Boke of Arthur, was compiled from the romances of Lancelot, Merlin, and Tristan, by Sir Thomas Malory, in the beginning of the reign of Edward IV., and was printed by Caxton in 1485. Mr. Ritson imagines that the English metrical romance of Morte Arthur was versified from the prose one of the same title, but as it differs essentially from Malory's prose work, and agrees exactly with the last part of the French romance of Lancelot, it is more probable that it has been versified from this composition.

(b)

...I shall confine myself to a very short and general survey of the works of English fiction.

We have already seen that, during the reigns of our Henrys and Edwards, the English nation was chiefly entertained with the fables of chivalry. The French romances concerning Arthur and his knights continued to be the most popular productions during the rule of the Plantagenet monarchs. In the time of Edward IV. the fictions of chivalry were represented in an English garb in the Morte Arthur, which is a compilation from the most celebrated French romances of the Round Table; while, at the same period, the romantic inventions concerning the history of Troy and classical heroes were translated and printed by the indefatigable Caxton. Artus de la Bretagne and Huon of Bourdeaux were *done* into English by Lord Berners in the reign of Henry VIII., and continued along with the Morte Arthur, to be the chief delight of our ancestors during the sway of the family of Tudor....

B. Henry Hallam

1839

Henry Hallam (1777–1859), besides his monumental historical works (*A View of the State of Europe during the Middle Ages* and *Constitutional History of England from Henry VII to the Death of George II*), brought out his *Introduction to the Literature of Europe in the 15th, 16th, and 17th Centuries* from 1837 to 1839. His brief remark on Malory appears in volume II (London: John Murray, 1839), p. 442.

Mallory's famous romance, La Morte d'Arthur, is of much earlier date [than 1592], and was first printed by Caxton. It is, however, a translation from several French romances, though written in very spirited language.

C. George Lillie Craik
1844, 1861

Craik (1798–1866), Professor of English Literature and History at Queen's College, Belfast, from 1849 until his death, published *A Compendious History of English Literature* in 1861; it was a revised and enlarged edition of his *Sketches of Literature and Learning in England*, published in 1844. Such literary manuals, in part the product of the rise of English studies in the schools, provided standard information and illustrative extracts.

The extract below is from a later impression, volume I (New York: Charles Scribner, 1866), pp. 399–400.

Although both Pecock and Fortescue lived to see the great invention of printing, and the latter at any rate survived the introduction of the new art into his native country, no production of either appears to have been given to the world through the press in the lifetime of the writer. Perhaps this was also the case with another prose-writer of this date, who is remembered, however, less by his name than by the work of which he is the author, and which still continues to be read, the famous history of King Arthur, commonly known under the name of the Morte Arthur. This work was first printed by Caxton in the year 1485. He tells us in his prologue, or preface, that the copy was given him by Sir Thomas

Malory, Knight, who took it, out of certain books in French, and reduced it into English. Malory himself states at the end, that he finished his task in the ninth year of King Edward IV., which would be in 1469 or 1470. The Morte Arthur was several times reprinted in the course of the following century and a half, the latest of the old editions having appeared in a quarto volume in 1634. From this, two reprints were brought out by different London booksellers in the same year, 1816; one in three duodecimos, the other in two. But the standard modern edition is that which appeared in two volumes quarto in the following year, 1817, exactly reprinted from Caxton's original edition, with the title of The Byrth, Lyfe, and Actes of Kyng Arthur; of his noble Knyghtes of the Rounde Table, &c., with an Introduction and Notes, by Robert Southey. Malory, whoever he may have been (Leland says he was Welsh), and supposing him to have been in the main only a translator, must be admitted to show considerable mastery of expression; his English is always animated and flowing, and, in its earnestness and tenderness, occasionally rises to no common beauty and eloquence. The concluding chapters in particular have been much admired. We extract a few sentences:—

[Quotes the death of Lancelot, Wynkyn de Worde's interpolation (see No. 2), and Ector's eulogy.]

15. Frederic Madden

1839, 1847

Sir Frederic Madden (1801–73) refers to Malory in passing in *Sir Gawayne* (1839) and in his edition of Layamon's *Brut* (1847). Madden's editorial achievements were impressive, but some of his comments on Malory were in error. Such was his authority, however, that some of them were uncritically repeated for decades. Madden believed, for example, that Rusticien's late thirteenth-century compilation based probably on a prose *Tristan* and another compilation, the *Palamedes*, was the source of Malory's translation. (See also No. 13 above.) Like Ritson (see No. 10A), Madden believed the stanzaic *Morte* to be a late versification of the closing books of Malory. Although Ritson and Madden have the influence backwards, they did recognize genuine verbal similarities in the two works. In addition, Madden was the first to comment on the verbal similarities between Malory's account of the Roman Wars and the alliterative *Morte Arthure*, still in MS when he wrote in 1839. The similarities were not referred to again for fifty years. However, in his note on Arthur's passing in the *Brut*, Madden ignores Malory's ambiguous passage on the possibility of Arthur's return.

Extracts (a), (b), and (c) below are from *Sir Gawayne*, Bannatyne Club (London: Richard and John Taylor, 1839), pp. xxviii–xxix, xxii, and xxv. The last, (d), is from *Layamon's Brut*, 3 vols (London: Society of Antiquaries, 1847), III, 411.

(a) *Sir Gawayne*

... To the same author who completed the [prose] Tristan we are indebted for a huge compilation intitled [*sic*] *Gyron le Courtois*, in which the exploits of Gyron, Meliadus, Branor le Brun, the Chevalier sans Peur, and a fresh race of worthies are commemorated, to whom even the Lancelots and Tristans are represented as inferior. Of course Sir Gawayne occupies here a very inferior grade, and is so changed from the all-conquering hero of the *Merlin*, as scarcely to be recognised. From this compilation, as well as from the prior works of Robert de Borron and Map, was formed the abridgment made by Rusticien de Pise in the reign of Edward the First; and in the course of the succeeding two centuries other compilers arose, who selected what portions they pleased, and formed them into distinct bodies of romance. These more recent compilations must be regarded as the immediate originals of the romances printed under the titles of *Gyron le Courtois* and *Meliadus de Léonnois*. The former of these first issued from the press of Verard, and represents with tolerable accuracy a portion of Rusticien's work. In this Sir Gawayne is only mentioned on two occasions, and in both passages as a vanquished knight. In the

Meliadus he is oftener introduced, but without a much greater degree of praise. His character for courtesy is indeed acknowledged, and an awkward fiction is alleged to account for his inferior powers.... From the work of Rusticien de Pise it is probable that Sir Thomas Malory compiled the English prose *Morte d'Arthur* in the year 1469, in which, as Scott and Southey have remarked, the character of Gawayne is traduced, and his history misrepresented. There are a few adventures of Gawayne in this work which I have not found elsewhere, but they were doubtless furnished by the French manuscript originals, which I have had no opportunity of consulting.[1]...

(b) *Sir Gawayne*
The substance of this romance [the Vulgate *Mort Artu*, attributed to Walter Map], but much abridged, is to be found in Malory's *Morte d'Arthur,* books 18, 20, and 21, and the latter text was versified in the reign of Henry the Seventh by an anonymous English author, who follows it in some instances verbally.[2]...

(c) *Sir Gawayne*
The alliterative Scotish [*sic*] romance of *Morte Arthure*, in the library of Lincoln Cathedral, marked A.1. 17, is very much amplified in its account of the destruction of the Round Table, and does not agree with any other authority I have consulted.[3]...

(d) Layamon's *Brut*
...It is singular, that neither here [in the Vulgate *Mort Artu*] any more than in Geoffrey's history, is a syllable added of Arthur's expected return. In Sir Thomas Malory's compilation, made in 1469, from the french romances of Rusticien de Pise and others (which are themselves compilations from the earlier texts), the story of Arthurs being carried away in 'a lytyl barge wyth many fayr ladies in hit,' occurs, lib. xxi, c. 5, with some variations, and in the next chapter he says, 'Thus of Arthur I fynde neuer more wryton in bookes that ben auctorysed, nor more of the veray certente of his deth herde I neuer redde; but thus was he ledde aweye in a shyppe, wherin were thre quenes....'

SELECTED NOTES

1 There are no copies in the British Museum or Bodleian Library of the compilations of Helie de Borron and Rusticien....

'2 This metrical version is preserved in MS. Harl. 2252, and was printed in 1819 for the Roxburghe Club. Ellis [see No. 10B above] is in error in stating that it was translated immediately from the French text...(copied by Dunlop, *Hist. of Fiction* [see No. 14A above])....Had he taken the trouble of comparing them together, he would not have hazarded such an assertion.

3 It is a singular circumstance that it often coincides verbally with Malory's prose version, and the episode of *Gawayne and Priamus* is found in both, and nowhere else.

16. Thomas Wright

1858

Thomas Wright (1810–77) was actively associated with a number of the literary and historical societies of his day, was a prolific writer on medieval and archeological topics, and edited several medieval manuscripts as well. His enthusiasm and industry were not always matched by scholarly depth and exactitude, and his introduction to this 1858 edition adds little that is new to Malory criticism at mid-century. However, his carefully edited text, based on Stansby, but with notes on Caxton variants, met an apparent need for an accessible version and, except for the changes made by the seventeenth-century editor, this edition was the last unexpurgated one until Sommer's scholarly edition of Caxton's text came out in 1889. Wright's introduction also provides the first full if somewhat waspish discussion of all previous editions.

At the point at which this excerpt begins, Wright has traced Arthurian romance from Geoffrey, Wace, and Layamon through de Boron, Walter Map, *Tristan*, and several metrical romances. (London: John Russell Smith, 1858, pp. v–xvii.)

... As the feudal manners began to degenerate, and the practice of chaunting the romances was abandoned, the metrical versions, the language of which became sooner obsolete, began also to lose their popularity, and gave way to almost a rage for the romances in prose, which, especially among the great chiefs on the continent, were looked upon with a feeling of reverential respect, as the grand and almost sole repositories of the spirit and principles of feudalism; and such was the state of feeling when the invention of the art of printing came to facilitate the multiplication of copies of books. The French printers of the latter half of the fifteenth century, and of the earlier part of the century following, produced a considerable number of editions, generally in folio, of the long French prose romances relating to the St. Graal, to king Arthur and his knights, and especially to the adventures of sir Tristram, whose story appears to have become permanently the most popular of them all.

Although this cycle of romances had, as we have seen, first made its appearance in England, it seems never to have been so popular here as in France; and it held by no means a prominent place in our literature at the time when so many editions were issuing from the presses of the French printers. A few English metrical romances belonging to this class are found in manuscripts of the fifteenth century, but they are generally unique copies, and I doubt whether they were in any degree of vogue. Even Caxton, who had evidently a taste for French literature, did not think of printing a book on this subject, until he was pressed to do it, as he informs us, by 'many noble and dyvers gentylmen of thys royame;' and then he seems to have been at a loss to find any book which would suit his purpose, until he was helped out of this difficulty by sir Thomas Malory, who had compiled a book 'oute of certeyn bookes of Frensshe, and reduced it into Englysshe.' All we seem to know of sir Thomas Malory is, that he tells us himself, at the conclusion of his book, that he was a knight, and that he completed his compilation in the ninth year of the reign of Edward IV., that is, in the course of the year 1469, or early in 1470, or more than fifteen years before Caxton printed it. The statement of some of the old bibliographers, that he was a Welshman, is probably a mere supposition founded on the character of his book.

We have no exact information as to the method pursued by Malory in his compilation, or as to the materials he used, although it is clear that a large portion of his book is taken from the great prose romances of Merlin, Lancelot, Tristram, the Queste du St. Graal, and the Mort Artus. He has adopted throughout the unfavourable view of the character of sir Gawaine which appears to have been established in France by the popularity of Tristram, although it was quite contrary to the general tone of the English romances. He has considerably modified some parts of the story in the course of abridgment, and omitted many of the most important and characteristic incidents—in Tristram and Lancelot especially— while he sometimes gives incidents which are not found related in the same way elsewhere, and which seem to show that he made use of some materials which are no longer known to exist. Malory takes care to remind us continually that his authorities were in the French language, by his frequent references to the 'French book,' which references, it may be remarked, are in the greater number of cases omitted in the text from which the present edition is taken.

Caxton tells us that he finished the printing of La Mort Darthur, as he entitles the book, in the abbey of Westminster, on the last day of July, 1485. This book has now become so rare that only one complete copy is known, which was formerly in the Harleian library, and is now in that of the earl of Jersey at Osterley park, Middlesex. An imperfect copy, now in earl Spencer's library, was purchased, as we learn from Lowndes, for the large sum of £320. These, I believe, are the only copies of Caxton's edition known to exist.

Two editions of this work were printed by Caxton's successor in the art of printing, Wynkyn de Worde, one in 1498, the other in 1529. Only one copy of each is at present known to be in existence. Wynkyn de Worde entitled his editions, 'The Booke of Kynge Arthur.'

William Copland, another well-known early English printer, reprinted this work in 1557, under the title of 'The Story of Kynge Arthur, and also of his Knyghtes of the Rounde Table.'

This title was also adopted by Thomas East, who printed two editions, one in folio, the other 4to., and both equally without date.

It is probable, from the similarity of the title, that East printed from Copland's edition.

We can trace no other reprint of this work until the year 1634, when the last of the black-letter editions was published in three parts, in 4to., with three separate titles. It is proved, by a considerable omission in this edition, that it was printed from a copy of the folio edition by East, in which a leaf in the third part was wanting.

Malory's history of king Arthur appears not to have been printed again until 1816. In that year two different popular editions appeared, undertaken apparently quite independently and unknowingly of each other. Both were printed in the same size, 24mo., the one in three volumes, the other in two. The edition in three volumes is understood to have been edited by Joseph Haslewood, and is spoken of as an especially 'correct reprint' of the edition of 1634. This, however, is so little the case, that in reading it over we are led to conclude that the correcting of the text in this edition was left to the printers themselves. Here and there alterations were made to fit the narrative for the taste or understanding of the ordinary modern reader; yet, though alterations of this kind are often made without much judgment, gross and evident misprints of the edition of 1634 are left uncorrected, and others are added which as evidently arose from the misreading of the old black-letter by the modern compositor....

The edition in two volumes, which appears thus to have come out before Haslewood's, belonged to a series of popular editions known as 'Walker's British Classics.' The text is quite as little recommendable as that of Haslewood, and the editor, or printer, has taken as great liberties with it in various ways, especially in altering phrases when he did not understand them....

Finally, in the year following that of these two editions, in 1817, appeared the well-known 4to. edition of the original text of Caxton, which has gained a reputation, as the publishers, no doubt, intended it should, from having the name of Robert Southey attached to it. The text is a mere reprint of Caxton, without any attempt at editing, and was probably left entirely to the care of the printers. It is, therefore, a book useless to the general reader, and is only useful at all because, for reference, it supplies the place of the original, which is inaccessible. The introduction and notes by Southey display the extensive and indiscriminate reading for which the poet was celebrated, but he has done little towards explaining or illustrating his text.

These are all the known editions of the story of king Arthur, as it was given originally to the English reader in the text of sir Thomas Malory and in the types of William Caxton. It is remarkable that the two popular editions published in 1816 have both become rare, and the want of a good edition of this romance has been felt generally. A knowledge of it is, indeed, necessary to enable us to understand the later Middle Ages in one of their important points of view; while it possesses an intrinsic interest, as giving us, in a comprehensive form, a good general sketch of a cycle of romances which through many ages exercised an influence upon literature and art. To meet this want, the present edition has been undertaken. It has been judged advisable to adopt for the text the latest of the old editions, that of 1634; for it is evident that the choice lay between the last and the first, between this we have selected and that of Caxton; as the moment we decided on abandoning Caxton, there was no reason why we should not take that of the reprints which was most readable. This choice was made with the less scruple, as no particular philological value is attached to the language of Caxton's edition, which would certainly be repulsive to the modern reader, while all its value as a literary monument is retained in the reprint. On the other hand, the orthography and phraseology of the edition of 1634, with the sprinkling of obsolete words, not sufficiently numerous to be embarrassing, preserves a certain clothing of mediaeval character which we think is one of the charms of the book. The edition of 1634 contains the whole text of Malory's work, and presents in general a verbal copy of it. Not unfrequently, however, the words are a little transposed, while some words are here and there added, and others are exchanged, as obsolete, for words that were better understood, with the notion evidently of making the language more correct or more readable. Many of these alterations are probably the mere work of the compositors; but some appear to have been made by design by some better informed person employed to read over the sheets of that or of some of the preceding editions.

In the present edition I have carefully collated the text of 1634 with that of Caxton, and given in the notes any variations in the latter which seem to be of importance or to present any particular interest. I have only ventured to alter the later text in cases where there were evident misprints or omissions. The old printers, especially those of the seventeenth century, when left to themselves, were, as it is well known, extremely careless, and the books of that period, if not corrected by the authors, are generally full of printers' errors. These I have carefully corrected from the text of Caxton, and in general, where the blunders are self-evident, I have not thought it necessary to point them out. If I have erred at all in this respect, it has been by over caution, and as I advanced in the book I found it necessary to correct the text more than in the earlier part. . . .

I have thought it advisable in a work like this, where the obsolete words and phrases are after all not very numerous, to explain them in the notes. Every reader has not at hand a dictionary of obsolete English; nor, if he had, is it convenient, in reading a book of this description, to be interrupted at every page or two in order to trace out a word in a dictionary. When the same obsolete word recurs after some interval, I have, for the same reason, not hesitated to repeat the explanation. I have avoided loading the text with illustrative and what may perhaps be termed historical notes, confining myself to what seemed almost necessary to render the perusal of the text easy and agreeable to a modern reader. It would not be difficult to increase notes and illustrations of this description to an almost indefinite extent.

With these explanations, it is hoped that the present edition of Malory's *Mort d'Arthure* will be a work acceptable to the public. It contains, as has been stated before, a good comprehensive condensation of the romantic cycle of king Arthur and his knights, as it first appeared in the great prose compilations of the latter part of the twelfth and beginning of the thirteenth century, and as it remained popular in those same compilations in the fifteenth. Although a similar class of incidents are perhaps too uniformly repeated, yet these romances are full of life and activity, and are often picturesque; while some knowledge of them is absolutely necessary for those who would understand those Middle Ages which have of late years been so much talked of and have excited so much interest. They differ from the Chansons de Geste and the generality of the other mediaeval romances in this, that while the former are plain and practical pictures of life in the feudal ages, these embody a sort of mythic code, if I may use such a phrase, of the more elevated principles and spirit of chivalry which the high-minded knight was supposed to labour to imitate. The tone of the morality of this code is certainly not very high; but—it was the morality of feudalism.

17. Unsigned review of Wright's edition, *Christian Examiner*

67 (November 1859), 391–408.

The *Christian Examiner* was established under Unitarian auspices (later becoming transcendentalist) as an American religious and literary periodical; it is considered of special importance for distinctive work through the second half of the nineteenth century in literary criticism and book reviews. The anonymous reviewer also discusses Bulfinch's *Age of Chivalry* (1859), Bulwer-Lytton's *King Arthur* (1851), and the early *Idylls of the King* (1859). This article and other reviews of Wright, Bulwer, and Tennyson (see, for example, Nos 19 and 20 below) show a developing interest in Arthurian topics in the periodical press.

The article begins by discussing Sharon Turner's picture of the historic Arthur and Geoffrey's 'lying chronicle', and then proceeds as follows:

But the real Arthur is the Arthur of romance. More real he than the actual historic king.... And it is in ballads, *Volkslieder*, and fables, songs of minstrelsy and the annals of story-tellers, that the life and fame of the real Arthur are set forth. They are the royal archives from whose records his chivalric glory and goodness draw the popular interest and liking, throughout a boundless realm of pleasant imaginings and day-dreams. Here, among the mind's marvels and the heart's delights, he holds a sovereignty beside which the remote and dim state of that petty British chief makes no show. The prophecy of his epitaph is fulfilled,—'Rex quondam, rexque futurus,'—'Once king, and king to be;' for here he continually rules in the full splendor of his court and bravery of his Round Table, a real presence to all children of Saxon and British stock, and to as many of their elders as are fortunate or wise enough to retain still something of the child in their hearts, and to carry along with them a little of that happy credulity which, in the nursery, heard with favor,

> When as King Arthur ruled the land,
> He was a goodly king,

and which, cultured to a more delicate fancy, enables them to read with delight these new Idyls, where his goodliness and gracious times are so fairly set forth. Here he is always 'Flos Regnum,'—the Flower of Kings,—in comparison with whose splendid bloom many historic potentates are but 'kings of shreds and patches.'

With this real Arthur the books at the head of this article have to do. Jeffry of Monmouth may be supposed to have gathered up in A.D. 1147 [*sic*], after his tedious way, and with feeble romancing of his own, a good deal of the floating story which for six centuries had been collecting around the name of the historic Arthur, and with fond exaggeration perpetuating the fame of his patriotism. This foolish chronicle of his seems, however, to have done much good in this, that it set the fancy of singers and story-tellers to work. For shortly after his time many romances appear, written, for the most part, in the Anglo-Norman dialect, telling the tale of the 'Queste du St. Graal,' 'Lancelot du Lac,' and the 'Morte d'Arthure,' with the life and deeds of Merlin the enchanter, and of many knights and dames like Tristan and Galahad, Isoude and Guinevere. These romances, and a mass of legendary verse and prose on the same theme of Arthur and his chivalry, furnish to one Sir Thomas Malory, in 1470, material for the compilation of a book 'oute of certeyne bookes of Frensshe and reduced into Englysshe,' which William Caxton, in 1485, printed in the Abbey of Westminster, with the title 'La Mort Darthur.' Of this book many reprints have been made, the most famous of which is the elegant quarto edited by Southey. Beside these, certain translations of it into modern and readable English have appeared. Of these, the edition of 1634 furnishes Mr. Thomas Wright the basis of his handsome book, published last year in that 'Library of Old Authors'. . . .

This 'La Morte d'Arthure' is the treasury of informati‹ concerning the king, his brave knights and lovely ladies, feas‹ tourneys, wars, enchantments, and all the brilliant haps and s‹ mishaps of his life, court, and renowned Round Table. It is fro‹ this source that book-makers, story-writers, fabliasts, balladis‹ and poets have drawn their stories of Sir Tristram and his devoti‹ to La Beale Isoude, and how Sir Lancelot and the queen joined th‹ guilty loves,—of the young and pure knight, Sir Galahad, who w‹ blessed with the sacrament from the holy chalice of the very blo‹ shed by the Lord upon the cross, and how the Lady of Shalott di‹ for love of Lancelot, and crafty Viviane shut up Merlin f‹ herself,—with many other fables of strange adventure and magi‹ fortune, fit to lead and please the fancy.

Yet it does not merely feed the childish appetite for marvels, b‹ answers the more mature wish, which exacts of fiction that ‹ should, even under the unsettled conditions of romance, ke‹ something of the interest of that conflict which goes on by t‹ mingled good and evil in men's hearts and fates. It is not Fancy r‹ wild, but, with all her lawless magician-work and fairy extrav‹ gance, bound still to deal with and present, 'after what flourish h‹ nature will,' some memorial of that strife of human affectior‹ powers, and destinies, in which are born equally the prose a‹ commonplace with the poetry and heroism of life. 'Herein,' sa‹ Caxton, in the Prologue to his edition, 'may be seen nob‹ chyvalrye, curtosye, humanyte, frendlynesse, hardynesse, lov‹ frendshyp, cowardyse, murdre, hate, vertue, synne.' So mu‹ semblance of the unfanciful truth of things and enforcement fro‹ actual humanity these fanciful stories of elfdom have, to give r‹ pleasure and profit, and to bear out the pious conclusion of t‹ Preface.

[Quotes Caxton's conclusion.]

18. David Masson

1859

David Masson (1822–1907), who held chairs in English Literature at University College, London, and then at Edinburgh, is perhaps best known for his *Life of Milton*, the first volume of which appeared the same year as his *British Novelists and their Styles*, the work from which this extract is taken. The latter book was based on lectures given in Edinburgh in the spring of 1858; it is a good example of the combination of historical perspective and impressionistic enthusiasm that often characterized English studies at the mid-century and after. The extract is from *British Novelists* (London: Macmillan, 1859), pp. 49–54.

Malory's *Mort d'Arthur*, or *History of King Arthur and of the Knights of the Round Table*, is one of those books the full effect and significance of which in the history of our literature it would require much research and much disquisition to exhaust. On the origin of the book alone there might be a historical essay of much interest. How the original groundwork came forth to the world in 1147, in the legends of Arthur and Merlin, which formed part of the Welsh Geoffrey of Monmouth's Latin 'History of the Britons,' the materials of which he professed to have derived from Breton tradition and from Breton writings of which there is no trace; how Geoffrey's book at once seized the imagination of the age, and his legends were appropriated, amplified, and developed by contemporary metrical chroniclers, and especially by the Anglo-Normans, Gaimar and Wace, and the Saxon Layamon; how, within the next century, new tissues of chivalrous and religious romance were woven out of the material thus accumulated, or attached to it and woven into it, by Anglo-Norman poets, themselves not wholly the inventors of what they wrote, but deriving the incidents and the names which they worked up from legend already afloat,—Robert de Borron adding the Roman du St. Graal and the developed History of Merlin, and Walter Mapes adding the Adventures of Sir

Lancelot, the Queste du St. Graal, and the Mort d'Arthure specially so called, and two later writers, Lucas de Gast and Helie de Borron, supplying later fragments in the Romances of Sir Tristram and other knights; how the total mass so aggregated was shaped, adjusted, and again morselled out in parts by subsequent minstrels and writers in France and in England, gradually loosening itself from the restraint of verse, and flowing into oral prose; and how, at length, an unknown Sir Thomas Malory, living in the reign of Edward IV., did his service to posterity by recompiling the whole in connected English, according to his own taste, and perhaps for his own amusement, in some castle in the country, or old city-dwelling, where he had the French scrolls and folios about him, and so provided Caxton with his copy:—here is a story of a book which might employ ingenuity as well as the story of the Homeric poems, and in connexion with which there might be discussed some of the same problems. It is as if the book were the production of no one mind, nor even of a score of successive minds, nor even of any one place or time, but were a rolling body of British-Norman legend, a representative bequest into the British air and the air overhanging the English Channel, from the collective brain and imagination that had tenanted that region through a definite range of vanished centuries.

[Quotes from Caxton's preface, where Caxton tells how he was approached by 'dyvers gentylmen' and asked why he had not published a history of Arthur, and Caxton's excuse (some people think there never was an Arthur).]

The antiquarian arguments used by the gentlemen in reply seem to have but half convinced Caxton of the possibility that Arthur had ever had a real existence; but, on other grounds, he was willing to print the book. 'For to passe the tyme,' he says, 'this book shal be plesaunte to rede in, but for to gyve fayth and byleve that al is trewe that is contayned herein, ye be at your lyberte; but al is wryton for our doctryne, and for to beware that we falle not to vyce ne synne, but texercyse and folowe vertu, by whyche we may come and atteyne to good fame and renomme in thys lyf, and after thys shorte and transytorye lyf to come unto everlastyng blysse in heven.' The book fully answers to this description. All in it is ideal, elemental, perfectly and purely imaginative; and yet all rests on a basis of what is eternal and general in human nature and in man's spiritual and social experience, so that, to use Caxton's very happy enumeration, 'herein may be seen noble chyvalrye, curtosye, humanyte, frendlynesse, hardynesse, love, frendshyp, cowardyse, murdre, hate, vertue, synne.' We are led over a vague land of plain and hill, lake and forest, which we know to be Britain, and which contains towns and fair castles; over this dreamland we pursue valiant knights riding in quest of adventures, justing with each other whenever they meet, rescuing enchanted maidens, and combating with strange shapes and horrors; all occurs in a manner and according to laws totally out of relation to the real world; but every now and then there is the gleam of some beautiful spot which remains in the mind as a vision for ever, the flash of some incident conceived in the deepest spirit of poetry, the sudden quiver of some ethical meaning—many parts, moreover, obviously challenging interpretation as involving intentionally a half-expressed philosophy, while the whole may be taken, in its cohesion, as an Epic Allegory. It is the kind of book into which a poet may go for hints and fancies already made to his hands, in dealing with which by way of elaboration and expansion he may follow his own free will without sense of constraint, evolving meanings where they seem concealed, or fitting his own meanings to visual imaginations which start out of their apparent arbitrariness into pre-established connexion with them. Accordingly, the body of Arthurian legend here locked up has served as a magazine of ideal subjects and suggestions to some of the greatest poets of our nation, from Spenser and Milton to our own Tennyson. No wonder that to so many in these days Malory's *King Arthur* has become once again a favourite pocket volume. To recline in a summer's day, for example, under the shelter of a rock on the coast of the Isle of Arran, and there with the solitary grandeurs of the Isle behind one, and with the sea rippling to one's feet and stretching in haze towards the opposite mainland, to pore over Malory's pages till, in the mood of poetic listlessness, the mainland over the haze seems again the very region where Arthur ruled and the knights journeyed and justed, and the romantic island itself an exempt spot on the contemporary margin whither the noise of them was wafted—this is reading such as is possible now but once or twice in a lifetime, and such as was known perhaps more when books were scarce. . . .

19. Unsigned review of Wright's edition, *Blackwood's Magazine*

88 (September 1860), 311–37

The *Wellesley Index* identifies the reviewer as W. Lucas Collins (1817–87), who had been a regular contributor to *Blackwood's* since 1843, providing criticism, essays, stories, and reviews. He was in addition the editor of 'Ancient Classics for English Readers' and the author of books and articles on classical subjects, public schools, and French literature. This article also reviews Hersart de la Villemarque's *Les Romans de la Table Ronde*, to which Collins is indebted for a discussion of the Celtic origins of much of Arthurian romance. Though contemporary with No. 20 below and, like it, published in a conservative journal, Collins's review offers a distinct contrast in appreciation of Malory's work and best audience.

'Rossetti's mediaeval tinting' in the first paragraph is a reference to the Arthurian frescoes painted by the Pre-Raphaelites at the Oxford University Union in 1857, and Miss Yonge in the next sentence was the author of *The Heir of Redclyffe* (1853), whose hero reads the *Morte Darthur* and comments on its virtues.

Collins's plot summaries of parts of Malory and his comments on Celtic backgrounds and related topics are omitted here.

'*Arturum expectare*' is no longer a taunting proverb. Arthur is come again! Bardic prophecy and popular tradition, after all, spoke truly. Once more the name of the hero-king rings through the length and breadth of England. Years ago, the Laureate caught his first glimpse of him, in poetic trance, when he sang of Excalibur and the Lady of Shalott, before he brought the full vision before us—'The Dragon of the great Pendragonship'—in his 'Idylls.' Sir Lytton Bulwer was the first to herald this new *avatar* with a grand and stately march-music, which has yet to find its due appreciation.

Clothed in the old prose version, Mr Russell Smith has presented him in three volumes of undeniable type and paper. A host of minor lyrists swell the triumph. The British king is more ubiquitous in his resuscitation than even in the days of his mortality. He looks down upon the undergraduates of Oxford from the gallery of their new reading-room, grim and gorgeous, in the richest hues of Messrs Riviere and Rossetti's mediaeval tinting. Young ladies are introduced to his court in Miss Yonge's pleasant fictions, and ask the most puzzling questions of their well-read governesses touching Sir Galahad and the San Greal. Children even find him reigning in their story-books, *vice* King Cole and King Alfred superseded. Enterprising lady-tourists demand of their astonished Breton guides to be led forthwith to the 'Fontaine de Barenton.' We seem to have gone back suddenly some eight or nine centuries, and are once more become enamoured of the grand chain of romance which held captive all readers—or rather hearers—in the days of Edward III.

Yet, probably, to the great body of his admirers, the outline of this favourite hero is very dim and indistinct. They see little more of him than Guenever saw at their last parting—

> The moony vapour rolling round the King,
> Who seemed the phantom of a giant in it.

Mr Tennyson's 'Idylls,' and the graceful presentations of Sir Lancelot and Sir Galahad, and their companions of the Round Table, which now crowd upon us everywhere in prose and poetry, produce, we very much suspect, upon the minds of the reading public in general, much the same tantalising and half-disappointing effect, as those snatches of tempting scenery which flash upon our eyes at intervals between the cuttings of the railway and the smoke of the engine—informing us of a pleasant and interesting country close at hand, but with which we have no present means of making further acquaintance. For the early English and French romances which contain the story at large are not very easily accessible; the MSS. themselves not to be thought of except by professed antiquarians; the printed editions few and scarce, and their quaint wording and orthography, so charming in the eyes of their true lovers, presenting rather a forbidding front to mere passing acquaintances. Even the most accessible and most readable of all—'the noble and joyous hystorye of the grete conquerour and excellent kyng, Kyng Arthur'—first printed by Caxton, and several times reprinted since with more or less accuracy, had become in all its editions comparatively scarce; and it may fairly be doubted whether the late reprint, with all the advantage of an attractive typography, is likely to become a popular book. Southey spoke indeed quite truly when he said it had a marvellous attraction for boys. It was so in his youthful days; it was so, we can ourselves testify, a generation later, in at least one large public school, when a solitary copy in two disreputable little paper-bound volumes, claiming to belong to 'Walker's British Classics' (even that wretched edition must have been scarce), was passed from hand to hand, and literally read to pieces, at all hours, lawful and unlawful. And the spell works to this day; boys seize upon the volumes still, wherever they fall in their way, and sit absorbed in them as did their forefathers. They will tell you more of Sir Bagdemagus and King Pellinore in a week, than they can of Diomed and Hector at the end of a school half-year. The taste is a genuine one on their part, wholly independent of Mr Tennyson and his fellow-poets, explain it how we will. The truth is, that the style of these romances recommends itself at once to the schoolboy mind, healthfully active and energetic; with very little love-making, few of the finer flights of fancy, and no moral reflections, there are plenty of terrific encounters and hard blows. The interest, such as it is, never flags; incident crowds on incident, adventure succeeds adventure; the successful champion disposes of one antagonist just in time to be ready for another—the discomfited knight is either despatched forthwith to make room for some new aspirant, or is healed of his wound with marvellous rapidity by some convenient hermit, and fights as well, or better, than ever. The plot and machinery are of the simplest kind, most intelligible to the schoolboy mind, and appealing strongly to his sympathies, fresh from foot-ball. Everybody runs full tilt at everybody he meets, is the general stage direction. Whether the antagonist be friend or foe by right, is quite a secondary consideration; these kind of questions are generally asked afterwards, being considered rather a waste of precious time beforehand. 'It doth them good to feel each other's might.' There you have the key-note of Round Table philosophy; and young England thoroughly appreciates it. True, there is a wonderful sameness in the heroes and their achievements; Sir Tristram's performances are precisely like Sir Lancelot's. In the encounters with which almost every page is filled, there is not even the graphic variety of Homer's wounds; commonly, the knight who is worsted goes 'over his horse's croupe;' occasionally, by way of change, we find that his opponent has 'gate him by the necke, and pulled him cleane out of his saddle.' But to the admiring readers in question this never seems to occur as an objection; sufficient for them that the action of the piece never stands still for an instant; Sir Ban or Sir Bors, or whoever may be the hero of the hour, has no sooner overthrown the knight with the black shield, than he 'fewtres his spear afresh, and hurles him' straightway at him of the red shield. The 'disport' is fast and furious. And when half-a-dozen champions are unhorsed in the space of a single page, it would be unreasonable to expect that each should fall in different fashion.

This kind of repetition, however, vigorous as it is, must be confessed to pall occasionally upon less voracious appetites. One gets tired of reading for ever of '*fortemque Gyan, fortemque Cloanthum*;' and we can readily imagine the disappointment of those gentle and enthusiastic readers, who, with the grand chant of the Laureate or the classic rhyme of Bulwer still in their ears, turn to the volumes of the *Mort d'Arthure* as their fount of inspiration. The gentle Enid they will not find there. Such passages as the love of the fair maid of Astolat are rare indeed; and even Arthur and Lancelot, like living mortal heroes, lose something of their herohood on more familiar acquaintance. They will hardly be consoled by a succession of chapters recording 'how Sir Lamoracke justed with Sir Palomides, and hurt him grievously;' and 'how Sir Tristram smote down Sir Sagramore le Desirous and Sir Dodinas le Savage.' Yet these tales of chivalry, though they threaten to be wearisome to the general reader when encountered at full length, have a very deep interest both in a literary and an antiquarian point of view; the more so, because now for the first time there appears a general consent as to the real sources of their origin, while they have sprung afresh into the full sunshine of popular favour, after centuries of comparative obscurity, by one of the most remarkable resurrections in the history of fiction. We will endeavour here to lay before our readers some sketch of that great cycle of romance which for ages was the literature *par excellence* of Christendom, and which has once more become the treasure-house from which poet and painter draw subjects for their pictures, and in which essayists—wearied of the old heathen classics—seek for illustrations and allusions....

The form, however, in which these romances are far more accessible to general readers than Welsh MSS. or Norman *fabliaux*, is that which stands at the head of this article as 'Mort d'Arthure,' or 'The Booke of King Arthur,' as Wynkyn de Worde more correctly entitles it—a compilation made in the year 1469 by a Sir Thomas Mallory 'out of certayne bookes of Frensshe,' as he tells us, and first printed by Caxton in 1485 at the request of 'noble and dyvers gentylmen.' Who this Sir Thomas Mallory was is not known; the Welsh antiquaries of course claim him as a countryman. His work is but a piece of patchwork, not always very cleverly put together; but its terse idiomatic language has been said to be the purest English extant, next to the Bible. It appears to have been founded chiefly on the great prose romances of Merlin and the St Graal, written by Robert de Borron aforesaid—the 'Mort Artus,' 'Lancelot du Lac,' and the 'Queste de St Graal,' all commonly ascribed to Walter Mapes—and the two romances of 'Sir Tristram,' by Lucas de Gast and Helie de Borron. These three last sources are said by Southey to have supplied two-thirds of the whole compilation; they supply, in fact, more; unless portions of what forms the third volume in the present edition are taken, as seems most probable, from a separate romance known to have existed, of which Sir Galahad was the hero. There would appear also, from the arrangement of the earlier portions of the book, to have been a distinct romance of Balin le Savage, and another of Sir Gareth of Orkney, which Mallory has either worked in bodily, or upon which he drew largely for materials. The result is a not very harmonious whole, somewhat confusing to the reader who has no previous acquaintance with these heroes of chivalry. He will find constant allusions to circumstances not recorded in the work itself, and anticipations of characters and incidents which are not introduced until long after. But Sir Thomas, it must be remembered, was addressing himself to those who might fairly be supposed to be already more or less familiar with the subject which he was reproducing. To imagine a knight or gentleman of the days of Edward IV. to be unacquainted with the history (true or fabulous) of Arthur, and Merlin, and Lancelot, would have been as strange as to suppose an educated Englishman of the present day to know nothing of Wellington or Napoleon. We think, however, that Mr Wright, who edits the present volumes, would have consulted the reader's comfort more, and given him a better chance, as Caxton wished, 'to understande bryefly the contente,' if he had preserved the old printer's original division into twenty-one books (the headings of which supply a very useful clue), instead of following the edition of 1634 in its more arbitrary arrangement into three parts. To attempt to give any continuous outline of what is in fact seven or eight separate stories, would be tedious, if it were not almost impossible; but a slight sketch of the principal heroes, as they appear here and in the Welsh legends, may not be uninteresting. And to begin with the Hero-King himself.

[Plot summary.]

But we have somewhat anticipated the course of the main narrative, if narrative that can be called which is at best but a conglomerate of disjointed legends.

[Plot summary.]

But Arthur's barons 'will let him have no rest' until he takes a wife. In evil hour he sets his affections on Guenever, Gwynhyfar, or Guanhumara, as Geoffrey calls her, daughter of King Leodegraunce of Camelyard. He had very little rest afterwards. This lady did her best throughout her wedded life to justify the character given her in the old Welsh distich, said to be still current—

> Gwenhyfar merch Gogyrfan gawr,
> Drwg yn fechan, gwaeth yn fawr.[1]

Merlin, with a prophetic insight into the fact that she was 'not wholesome' for the king to take to wife, would have had him choose better; but is fain to let him have his own way, with the admission that 'whereas a man's heart is set, he will be loth to return.' The sole dowry, besides her fatal beauty, which Guenever brings with her, is the world-renowned Round Table. It had belonged to Uther Pendragon, and had been given by him to Leodegraunce. Merlin had made it, as we learn from the romance which bears his name, 'in the likeness of the world:' if we are to take the romance of Tristan as any authority, it turned round like the world itself....

From the date of Arthur's marriage, the compilation before us is little more than an unconnected series of adventures, ascribed to the king and his knights, until it breaks into what are, in fact, separate romances, containing the achievements of Sir Tristram, Sir Galahad, Sir Percival, and Sir Lancelot. Again does Arthur's evil sister, Queen Morgan la Faye, aim at his life, by the gift of a poisoned mantle, and again he is preserved by his tutelary genius, the Lady of the Lake. Enraged at such treachery, he banishes from his court her son, Sir Ewaine, in the belief that he is privy to her treason, and his cousin, Sir Gawaine, elects to share his exile. They ride forth together in quest of adventures; and falling in with one Sir Marhaus (or Morolt) of Ireland, they make his acquaintance after the usual fashion of the Arthurian chivalry.

[Plot summary.]

The compiler dashes off at once into a new romance, the main features of which exist in Geoffrey of Monmouth's work, on the subject of Arthur's triumphant expedition against the Emperor of Rome.

[Plot summary.]

Sir Gawaine, in this campaign, does knightly execution upon the 'Sarrasins' with his good sword Galatine. Amongst the enemies' ranks he meets with some strange dignitaries, such as the 'Duke of Duchmen' and the 'Marques of Moises' Land;' but the most remarkable of all is one Sir Priamus, who is 'lineally descended of Alexander and Hector by right line,' and claims also 'Duke Josue and Machabeus' amongst his kindred, and is 'right inheritor of Alexandry and Affrike, and all the out isles.' This pagan knight Sir Gawaine overcomes after a terrific combat; Sir Priamus then stanches his adversary's wound with a vial 'full of the four waters that came out of Paradise,' and requests to be made a Christian. These victories are not won without the loss of some of the good knights of the Round Table, for whose fall, we are told, King Arthur 'wept, and dried his eyes with a handkercher'—a touch of the genuine realistic which we commend to the notice of our modern novelists.

[Plot summaries.]

[The Graal], then, becomes the object of ambition to all good knights of Arthur's court; and the 'Quest of the Saint Graal,' accordingly, is taken up by the most renowned amongst them; and it is a portion of these adventures, adapted from the romances which bore the name, which fills nearly the whole of the third volume of Mallory's compilation. But the sketch which we have given of the history of the Graal has been altered and amplified by the Anglo-Norman writers, until it has become a puzzling mass of contradictions. The 'maimed king' is sometimes called Pellam or Pellas of Lystenoise, and is said to have been wounded by the lance for attempting to draw a sword which 'no man might begripe but one;' or again the wound is said to have been inflicted by a knight named Balin, who seizes the lance in self-defence, and so smites what passes into a proverb as 'the dolorous stroke;' sometimes Joseph himself is spoken of as having been 'smitten through the thigh;' sometimes the maimed king, who is to be healed by the Sangreal, would appear to be one King Evelake, who lies in a bed—'three hundred winters old.' These incongruities may serve as additional evidence of the looseness with which Mallory blended his materials. In the hands of the ecclesiastics who, like Walter Mapes and the brothers De Borron, became romancers—employed or at least patronised by Henry II.—the legend of the Saint Graal grew in mystery and splendour. They even went so far as to assert that the Latin original was written by 'le vrai Crucifix'—Christ himself. The cup is formed from a diamond that fell from the crown of Satan in his contest with St Michael; it is located in a temple of its own upon 'Mount Salvage,' a dome of sapphire, round which rise thirty-six towers surmounted by crosses of crystal; knights 'Templistes,' all armed, keep watch about it day and night, but it is visible only to the pure in flesh and spirit. In this compilation of Mallory's it appears as a 'vessell of gold,' borne by a maiden, emitting 'all manner of sweetnesse and savour,' healing the wounds of those who approach it; but it may not be seen 'but by a perfect man'. Sir Percival has 'a glimmering' of it, because he is a maiden knight . Or it stands upon a 'table of silver,' 'many angels about it,' in King Pelles's castle of Corbin or Corbonek,—called elsewhere the 'castle adventurous,' or *Chateau de Merveilles*; lions guard the entrance, and the chamber which contains the holy vessel is 'as bright as though all the torches in the world had been there.' All the mystical fancies of a half-idolatrous Christianity are here combined with the picturesque painting of mediaeval chivalry. In fact, as will be seen, these romances of the Graal are of a totally different colouring from the genuine tales of Arthur; the personages introduced into the action are the same, but the parts allotted to them are rather those of armed pilgrims than knights adventurous.

But the Holy Vessel and the Bleeding Lance, though they fall into their places so easily and naturally amongst the *regalia* of a fanciful Christianity are indisputably of pagan origin....

Foremost amongst the knights-companions who engage in the holy Quest is Sir Lancelot of the Lake. Son of King Ban of Benwicke (probably Benoit in Brittany), he is carried away in his infancy by the fairy Viviane, and brought up in her enchanted island. In him we have the romanciers' ideal of chivalry; so noble and so fascinating is his character in many points, that we can scarcely wonder if we see it exercising even at this day a dangerous influence in the pages of modern literature. But for one thing, Lancelot had been indeed the knight '*sans peur et sans reproche;*' and unhappily his one fault—coupled, too, as it is in his case, with a certain truth and loyalty, though to an unworthy cause—is of that nature which wins pardon easiest from the young and passionate. We need no more than to allude to his amour with Queen Guenever, the blot on his escutcheon which the poets of the 'Courts of Love' were not ashamed to blazon into a virtue. In the eyes of the Norman gestours, from whom Mallory draws in the earlier portion of these volumes, he 'has not his peer of any earthly sinful man.' 'At no time was he overcome, but it were by treason or enchantment.' Brave, gentle, and true, he wins honour and love from knights and ladies. To him alone the haughtiest champions of Arthur's court are content to yield the prize of the tournament without a murmur; defeat from such a hand confers almost as much honour as victory over others. Even Arthur, whom he has so deeply wronged, feels the spell upon him; he bursts into tears, when Lancelot assists him to remount—'thinking on the great courtesie that was in Sir Lancelot more than in any other man.' So successful was the portrait which they had drawn of all that was noble and admirable—writing as they did for a licentious age and a corrupt court—that it was only left for the later mythists of the Graal to point out how one deadly sin disqualifies the flower of chivalry from approaching the church's mysteries. 'Had he not been in his privy thoughts and in his mind set inwardly to the queen, as he was in outward seeming unto God, there had no knight passed him in the Quest of the Saint Graal.' 'It had been most convenient for him of all earthly knights, but sin is so foul in him that he may not achieve such noble deeds.' Once, indeed, he wins his way to a sight of the Holy Vessel; before it a priest elevates the Host, with the miraculous weight of which he seems to stagger; Lancelot puts forth a sacrilegious hand, like Uzzah, to help him; and is struck down in a swoon which lasts for twenty-four days—in punishment, as he learns afterwards, for as many years of sin. Weary and dispirited, he returns to Camelot, to find half the companions of the Round Table slain. Knights 'of evil faith and poor of belief,' their presumptuous quest has been fatal to them.

Three there are, however, to whom success is foretold—Sir Percival, Sir Bors de Ganis, and Sir Galahad. The first and the last are pure and maiden knights; Sir Bors has never sinned but once. Sir Galahad is the beautiful creation of the later fictions. He belongs to the romance of the Graal, and would be quite out of place in the earlier Arthurian story. He is the son of Sir Lancelot and King Pelles's daughter; his birth is illegitimate, but it has been brought about by enchantment. He is introduced suddenly by an old man amongst the assembled knights, and placed in the 'siege perilous.' The knights all marvel that he 'durst sit there, that was so tender of age;' but his name is found written there in letters of gold, and he is acknowledged as the rightful occupant that 'shall win the Saint Graal.' It is hopeless to trace any connected allegory in the long train of adventures which follow, in which the mystical sometimes descends to absurdity, and sometimes rises to the sublime: we have probably here, as in the other portions of Mallory's book, a rude attempt to combine portions of separate romances into a connected story.

[Plot summary.]

Sir Bors...returns, with an account of the achievement of the Quest, to Arthur's court at Camelot.

Thither, somewhat unwillingly, we return too. The tangled web of adventure begins afresh (in fact, it is a new romance), and Lancelot is again the hero. In vain for him have been his own resolve to lead henceforth a pure life, and Galahad's parting charge to him by Sir Bors's mouth, 'to remember this unsteadfast world;' he 'began to resort unto Queen Guenever again, and forgat the promise and the profession that he had made in the Quest.' Their guilty love runs on its course, only interrupted by the pathetic tale of Elaine la Blaunche, the maid of Astolat, of whose scarlet sleeve, worn by Lancelot at the tournament, the queen is jealous, and who floats down dead, in her barge, 'covered with black samite,' amongst all the gay company 'at Westminster.' Twice the queen is detected, and condemned to the stake; and twice Lancelot delivers her; the last time, at the expense of the lives of Sir Gareth and many of his companions of the Round Table. Concealment from this time is hopeless; yet such is his renown and popularity that his nephew Sir Bors, with many other of the knights-companions, who 'will take the woe with the wealth,' espouse his cause, and he carries off Guenever to his castle of Joyous Garde, until the king's wrath cool. On some strange principle, wholly repugnant to our modern feelings, the Pope charges Arthur to receive his queen back again 'on pain of interditing all England;' and she is restored to him in a sort of triumphal procession—'in white cloth of gold tissue'—a sentimental display which is represented by the trouveurs as affecting the bold knights who were there present even to tears. But 'King Arthur sate still, and spake not one word.'...

Arthur leaves the stage of his mortal glory in right royal fashion. The passage which records his disappearance, and which has given the name of *Mort d'Arthure* to the whole of this body of legend, may claim to stand almost unrivalled, for the grand simplicity of its conception and language, amongst the masterpieces of English prose. It is too well known to justify extraction here. How the brothers Sir Lucan and Sir Bedivere, sole survivors of that deadly fight, left the king to carry him 'to some toune;' how, in the effort, Sir Lucan, wounded as he is to the death, swoons and falls—'and his noble heart brast;' how Arthur knowing that 'his time hieth fast,' bids Sir Bedivere take Excalibur, his good sword, and cast it into the water, and bring him word of what he shall see there; how Sir Bedivere, as he looks upon the 'pummell and haft all of precious stones,' thinks it 'sinne and shame to throw away that noble sword,' and twice hides it, and returns answer to the dying king's inquiry, that he had done his bidding, but had seen nothing but 'water wap, and waves waune;' and how at the last, after stern chiding for his faithlessness, he 'threw the sword into the water as far as he might, and there came an arme and a hand above the water and met it and caught it, and so shook it thrice and brandished; and then the hand vanished away with the sword in the water'—is not all this written in the chronicles of a thousand memories?

So Sir Bedivere carries his lord down to the water-side, where there waits a barge with many fair ladies—amongst them the royal sorceress, Morgan la Fay—no longer, as it would seem, her brother's enemy—the Queen of North Wales, the queen of the waste-lands, and Nimue, 'chief lady of the lake;' and they bear him away to Glastonbury, where an aged hermit, 'that had some time been Archbishop of Canterbury,' buries him at midnight....

But the Arthur of legend and song fills no grave at Glastonbury or in Cornwall. The last words which the romancers put in his mouth contradict their own story of the midnight burial—'I will to the isle of Avallon, to heal me of my deadly wound.' 'Men say that he will come again and win the holy cross.' The popular belief in this second advent is perhaps the strongest evidence of his historical existence. Like all the darlings of a people—like Frederick Barbarossa, like Sebastian of Portugal, like 'the three Tells' of Switzerland, like the last Duke of Burgundy, like the first Napoleon—men could not believe in his death. The noble heart can never die....

Of the ends of Guenever and Lancelot we do not care to say much. Both pass, according to the due course of religious and poetical justice of the time, from the worst vanities of the world into the purest odour of sanctity. Guenever takes the veil at Amesbury, and in time becomes abbess there. Of the beautiful parting scene between her and Arthur, where we almost lose the sense of her guilt in the reality of her repentance, it is but just to Mr Tennyson to say that it is wholly a fair creation of his own. Very different is the spirit in which these romances part from her; 'while she lived she was a true lover, and therefore she had a good end.' Lancelot, who has meanwhile also taken the religious habit, sees her buried with Arthur at Glastonbury, and after six weeks of 'grovelling and praying' on the tomb, he too is found dead. But there is no sound of penitence in the grand proud words pronounced over him by his comrade Sir Bors; after a life of falsehood to his king and his friend, red with the blood of unarmed companions slain in an unhallowed quarrel, faithful only to an adulterous love, he goes to his grave with that well-known eulogy, whose magnificent language has blinded many an admiring reader to its perilous application.

But such is the morality of these romances throughout; an evil imported into them by their Anglo-Norman adapters, for the tales of the *Mabinogion* are free from it. It is not that we find here the seductive licence of the Italian novelist; it might be hard to point even to a licentious passage; but intrigue and unchastity are treated as the boldest matters of fact, and the writers appear utterly unconscious of even a moral rule in such cases. The two love-tales are adulteries, for the relations of Tristram and Iseult are but a repetition of those of Lancelot and Guenever; the *preux chevaliers* are disloyal, both as friends and as subjects, in that which is rightly held to be the very soul of modern honour. Even Arthur himself, in whom M.de la Villemarqué sees the model of Christian chivalry, is here neither saint nor hero: to say nothing of his massacre of the innocents already alluded to, or his unintentional incest, he is habitually faithless in his own conjugal relations. We can feel little interest in his own wrongs, when he congratulates Tristram and Iseult on being safe from King Mark in Joyous Gard, and says that 'they are right well beset together.' Such, indeed, is the line in which the reader's sympathies are always directed; King Mark's aims at avenging himself by taking Tristram's life, are always denounced as 'treason;' when King Lot's wife is slain in adultery, Arthur and Lancelot hold it 'a felonous treason;' and when King Mark, for the most excellent reasons, banishes Tristram from his court for ten years, he is denounced by the hero—in the apparent conviction that he is expressing a popular sentiment—as *'very ungrateful.'* But enough of such instances; is it too much to exclaim with old Leland—honest, even if he was credulous—'O scelera, O mores, O corrupta tempora!'

The religion—in all but the latter portion, the Quest of the Graal—is a mere *parergon*, though we have abundance of its phraseology. In all essentials it is at least as much pagan as Christian. There are strong proofs how long the old heathen belief survived,—a blind unreasoning fear of the mysterious powers of nature, a very worship of the groves and rocks. Morgan la Faye, who can turn herself and followers into stones at pleasure, is a far more awful personage than the Archbishop of Canterbury, who appears in strange conjunction almost on the same page. Nature and art are alike inexplicable, except on supernatural principles.

The works of the latter are miracles, as in the instance of Excalibur. The powers of the former are magnified into prodigies. We have an example in that strange creation, the 'Questing Beast,' or the 'Beast glatisant,' the undoubted original of the 'Blatant Beast' of Spenser; which, introduced as it is abruptly into the narrative, is evidently supposed to be already well known. It has 'a noise as of questing hounds in its belly'—'a marvellous beast and a great signification,' of which 'Merlin prophesied much;' some of the most renowned knights of Arthur's companionship follow it successively, apparently without success. The 'great signification' we confess ourselves unable to explain; but the legend, like so many of the rest, is Cymric. It is undoubtedly the *Twrch Trwyth*, the wild-boar king, of the tale called 'Kilhwch and Olwen,' the wildest and perhaps the most curious of the Mabinogion. ...

It will be seen that our estimate of these romances is scarcely the popular one. The remarkable interest which attaches to them seems to us independent of, and far beyond, their intrinsic merit. As to the life and morals which they paint, the most satisfactory reflection is, that it was never real. There was no golden age of chivalry, whatever Sir Bulwer Lytton may try to persuade us—

When what is now called poetry was life.

Few of these heroes wore in their hearts the noble motto, which one of them—Gyron le Courtois—bore upon his sword, '*Loyaulté passe tout, et faulseté honnet tout.*' This would-be heroic and chivalric age was very mean and poor in some of its phases. Even its good, such as it was, was all for the knight and noble; the 'churl' is only introduced for their disport and mockery. 'Then were they afraid when they saw a knight.' What a picture of the social relations!

After all, this antiquarian hero-worship is unreal: ... They were not the giants that they seem, looming through the mist of ages. If we lay our bones beside their bones, they hardly suffer by the comparison; nerve and sinew have not degenerated. The ancient armour which had borne the brunt of actual tourney, was found somewhat scant of girth for the limbs that jousted in sport at Eglinton. The gentlemen of modern England, who, instead of sitting at home at ease, ride across the stiffest country they can find, or climb Monte Rosa and the Wetterhorn for pure amusement, are at least king Arthur's equals in this,—they 'will not go to meat till they have seen some great adventure.' And if it come to what the romancers call 'derring-do,' we can fight as well as they did; though the sober columns of the modern 'correspondent' have not the grand faculty of lying that was accorded to the trouveur of old, our poor prosaic annals can tell their story too. The lads that stood back to back at the Alma—the men who rode at Balaclava—the raw recruits, 'churls' though they were, who fired their own death-volley as they went down in their ranks on board the Birkenhead—were truer heroes than any knight of the Round Table.

NOTE

1 'Gwenhyfar, daughter of Gogyrfan the tall—wicked when little, worse when big.'

20. Unsigned review of Wright's edition, *Dublin University Magazine*

55 (April 1860), 497–512

The *Dublin University Magazine* was founded from and long associated with Trinity College; its guiding principles were Tory, Anglican, and Irish. The reviewer find 'epic' qualities of sin and retribution (Morgawse and Mordred) in Malory's sources and, of course, in Malory (cf. No. 24 below), and through his plot summaries from the *Morte Darthur* runs a thread of moral and spiritual allegorizing. Although the reviewer considers Malory a compiler, it is Malory's version, not the 'Anglo-Norman originals', that he examines, admires for its style, explicates, and quotes extensively.

The reviewer begins by contrasting the eighteenth century's rejection of romance with the nineteenth's revival of interest and discusses Arthurian influences on Tennyson, Arnold, Kingsley, and others. The *Morte Darthur*, he says, is but one of 'the crowd of mediaeval works re-issued lately', and the Napoleonic wars account in part for the shift in attitude.

... And paladinism has never been more nobly manifested than within the last years of English life. We return to the ancient legends, for the deeds which they relate seem no longer impossible and lying fables. Colonel Inglis at Lucknow, Mr. Stafford in the infected transports and terrible hospitals of Scutari, are representatives of the knight errantry, fostered by the extremes of modern life and perhaps first roused into practical revival by the personality of Napoleon. The heroic fires, latent in the sons of God, may be kindled by a spark from a volcano as by a ray of the sun. Let us be thankful that our age is warmed by their glow—that men are once more soldiers of the Cross—that religion is a motive power. The warrior saint Havelock fights his good fight against the Eastern miscreants. Florence Nightingale inaugurates a new order of charitable women. Westminster Abbey is once more the church of the poor. On a day of humiliation the *Times* fills its columns with sermons, while the voice of the English nation rises in supplication as intense as that offered by the crusading host before the walls of Jerusalem. Everywhere is the same reviving faith manifested. The World's Fair of 1851 is redeemed from vanity by prayer and praise—the temporary bond between old and new worlds is consecrated by the angelic message, *Gloria in excelsis Deo*. The heroic element has been kindled, and we open our hearts to the tales of the Norman past, and find in them sympathy with the feeling which animates our modern literature. Mr. Carlyle gives us a Heldenbuch, and sings as Romans in wild, warlike cadence, such as Taillefer might have used when he tossed his lance in air, before the hosts at Hastings.... But it is time to examine the book which prompts these thoughts, with an interest, we will hope, quickened by the foregoing remarks on the causes of its reappearance among us.

We have probably received the popular history of King Arthur and his round table from Walter Calenius, archdeacon of Oxford, who, in the twelfth century, made, as is once more the fashion, a tour in Brittany. He brought from thence to England a collection of legends and Armorican traditions which he committed to the care of the British chronicler, Geoffrey of Monmouth, who, with more or less sincerity, incorporated them as a true history of the British race. We need not examine too harshly into his conscientiousness, owing him as we do the fables that were afterwards so well employed by Shakespeare and Spenser. The discredit which attached to his account of our national hero for long destroyed faith in the existence of an Arthur; but historians seem disposed to admit his place in history as Prince of the Silures; and the defeat of the Saxon Cerdic at Mount Badon, in the sixth century, has been ascribed to his arms. Heroism and even genius must have conducted the defence of Britain during her long struggle against the Northern races, and we need not be surprised to find that the process of deification goes on in barbarous as in civilized communities; but a further mystification seems to have been occasioned by the confusion of the historical hero with a personage of Welsh mythology—the symbolic Arthur whose harp yet shines on the Cymri in the constellalation Lyra, and traditions of whom are so largely scattered through the Scotch lowlands, as well as in the west of England. However the doubtful place held in history by the Prince of Silures need not be discussed in reference to the Arthur of Anglo-Norman romance. The cycle of round-table fiction but adopts his name, and the dim tradition of his story, as a skeleton to be clothed in the flesh and blood of knightly life, wearing the raiment of the Plantagenet court, and adorned by the ideal graces of chivalry. The budding of fiction in England was, it is true, coloured by the British legends made popular by Geoffrey, but its growth was Norman; and if the celebrated litterateur, Walter Mapes, and his fellow romancers, took for their ground-plan the fables of Armorica, the superstructure of their works was according to the newest rules of chivalry.

From the earliest novels of Europe our 'History of King Arthur' is compiled. The chief part in its incidents is assigned to Walter Mapes, who was attached to Henry the Second's court. The 'Tale of Lancelot,' the 'Quest du Sangréel,' and the 'Mort Artus,' are ascribed to him, while his contemporary, Robert de Borron, is supposed to have written the 'Roman du Sangréel,' and the 'History of Merlin.' 'The Adventures of Sir Tristram'—a popular development of this cycle of fiction—were added by Helie de Borron, and Lucas de Gast, who, probably, wrote as late as the reign of the third Henry. . . .

We do not deny that the sword-points of the crusaders

contributed to the universal circulation of these romances in eastern as in western Europe, but we claim for the tales themselves an interest even beyond that which must gather round the first efforts of an art that tells us, however rudely, the thoughts and aspirations of our national youth. Though they were quickly overgrown with grotesque fancies from the countries of magic and diablerie, Arabia and Africa, the purpose and meaning in them insured their vitality in the memory of all who ventured through their verbiage to their inner sense. If we remove the few clumsy contrivances of spells, giants, and enchantments, from these stories, they remain to us a very perfect monument of chivalry, as it was, in the tale of 'Lancelot and Guinevere,' but of its highest ideal, in the portraiture of Sir Galahad.

It is difficult to account for much in these volumes, too evidently unharmonious with this higher standard to have been the pure creations of those who could so well portray the perfection of knighthood, unless we accept the probability that under fictitious names real personages were drawn. The choice of the British champion as the centre figure most likely but veiled the flattery addressed to the reigning king. . . .

A direction was thus given to the imagination of the gestours at Henry's court, whose romances rapidly circulated wherever a Norman knight and his attendant jongleur were found, providing a new pleasure for the barbarian, and forming for the better civilized the maxims of chivalry into a code of honour more binding than any law enforced by the government of the day. By these fictions were popularized to the crusading millions—to the lawless baron in his impregnable castle as to the fierce leader of free companies—the precepts framed at the assises de Jerusalem and promulgated by the royal Galahad, St. Louis. As exemplars of their practice King Arthur and his knights gained a celebrity which even obscured the fame of Charlemagne and his paladins. The loves of Lancelot and Guinevere became more popular in Southern Europe than the purity of Galahad; and it is strange to find that Dante chooses a British love-tale as the subtlest poison for Francesca da Rimini's ear, and significant of the power of these earliest romances on the hearts and actions of all Christendom.

In short, it is difficult to over-estimate the influence traceable to them on the youth of Europe; and to those who value the fresh conceptions, the simple pathos, the unconscious power of a world's first utterances, as compared with the rounded beauty of its complete eloquence, we commend heartily even this dry compilation from the cycle of round-table fiction now published by Mr. Russell Smith.

To Sir Thomas Malory, a knight and amateur antiquary of the fifteenth century, we owe the popular shape to which the old romances have been cut down. In the preface to his 'Hystorye of Kynge Arthure' Caxton gives us an account of its parentage and birth under the patronage of the new art of printing...and in 1485 these old-world fabled truths or truthful fables were ushered into the new age that was to be illumined by a brighter, if not a steadier, light than the past had known. We can imagine how those who survived of the noble families decimated by the Civil Wars of the Roses desired to see perpetuated by the magic of type the customs of their ancestors. The French press teemed with copies of the old romances during the first years of its existence, and Caxton evidently found ready for his purpose the English condensation which he used in his edition of the voluminous tales connected with the round table.

Throughout Europe there was an Indian summer for the forms, if not the spirit of chivalry, before the Rabelaisian winter that even Columbus, in whom knight-errantry was fulfilled, could not enlighten; before the scepticism of Montaigne who turned, he tells us, from the foolish tales of Amadis to the interests of egotism; before the spring which followed of enterprise and discovery, when Spaniard and Briton jousted à l'outrance in the lists of Eldorado, and the world was new clothed from the seeming death of the past.

Several editions of Malory's compilation were published during the sixteenth century, but the last of the black-letter 'Hystoryes' appeared in 1634. We may imagine it to have been a sort of protest against the fashionable exaltation of Cervantes' great work which just then loosed the ridicule of the world on Quixotism, and gained for the sensualism of Sancho an applause its narrator had scarcely intended. There were fast growing tendencies in English society, singularly opposite to the traditionary knightly manners. To the reader of 1634–1690, the loyalty, yet freedom of Arthur's champions must have appeared as remote from the revolutionary spirit of Puritanism as from the adulation of the Stuart courtiers. Yet we are wrong, for surely in the time of the Restoration, the gaudy cavaliers who figured on the Mall were farther removed from the heroes of the round table than the lowest born of the Ironsides. The satire of Hudibras was more destructive to the spirit of chivalry than the wildest fanaticism; and Cromwell might surely have better claimed a place in Arthur's fellowship of noble knights than Zimri, or Ahitophel, or the handsome Absalom of Charles's court.

In truth, chivalrous faith, and courteous justice, and loyal devotion ceased to be public virtues in the land, until the great Revolution scared men from a torpor that Pope's lyre had but increased—that the drowsy drone of State Church preachings had well-nigh made mortal to the honour of England. But at last the Laputa philosophies and the Yahoo princedoms were swept away in the surge of self-asserting human suffering. There was no more leisure to twist the sand-ropes of unbelief. The value of men was ascertained when war replaced tactics, and governors had become necessary in the failure of corruption. Heroes were raised from the dust of time in which dynasties were buried. Necessarily, poets and romancers had once more an office as trouvères of the noble incidents scattered thickly in the history of the new nations. Side by side with gazettes of battles appeared Walter Scott's revival of chivalric legends; and the year after Waterloo two editions of the long-forgotten 'Mort D'Arthur' were called for by a public no longer sceptical of heroes. Within twelve months Southey's folio followed, which for a time satisfied the general desire for news of the men whose effigies bear witness in our land of the living foundation on which our modern Church rests.

And yet, though we have said thus much in honour of round-table romance, we warn our readers that in Malory's condensation of it there is much to discourage a beginner in antique literature. He has drawn at will from 'the Frenssche bookes,' and there is not the clearness of dates and parts in his plot that is expected by those who read modern novels of orthodox construction. Malory's plan is still further confused by the editor of 1634, from whose work Mr. Wright has taken his present copy. The omission of Caxton's division of the work into books taxes largely our critical intelligence to separate the minor events from the main narrative, and draw the necessary lines between the Iseults and Eleynes who are the heroines of the several Romans that contributed to Malory's book. We would endeavour to make order in the chaos of incidents did our limits admit of their analysis, but we must confine ourselves to a sketch of the chief purpose that connects them, and pass over episodes which interrupt the action of the principal personages.

The first volume opens abruptly with the birth of Arthur, and nothing is told us of his father Uther Pendragon's reign as related by Geoffrey, though the vicissitudes of his life, and the strange portents which marked its events, might well have served as a prologue to his son's marvellous history. There is little said of Arthur's mother, Igrayne, the fresh-made widow of a Duke of Cornwall, except that she is wise and virtuous, though deceived by Uther. She was for a time left ignorant of her son's parentage, while he, the Christian Hercules, was committed to the care of a faithful and discreet knight, by Merlin's advice. The great enchanter himself is suddenly and slightly introduced to us merely in the character of Uther's counsellor, and the protector of Arthur's youth.

The characteristics of this representative of worldly wisdom are made notable in their symbolism when we are told that in the legends of the day he is described as the son of the fiend, born black, but possessed of intelligence that soon gives him power over all who are at first disgusted by his origin. He is shown to us as the fruit of union between human weakness and the subtilty of the devil. Wiser than all men, yet 'assotted' when his hour comes, he knows the evil from the good with perfect knowledge. He provides with infinite sagacity for his ward Arthur's marriage, and for the government of his realm. He institutes the Round table fellowship, or image of the world's completed council of the best. He foresees and prepares for every exigency with supernatural prevision; yet, in all he attempts with present success, the fiend's son finally fails. The best plans organized by his craft, wretchedly break down with ruin to all concerned, and he himself is at last entrapped in his own enchantment, and bound in his own net until the End.

But, meantime, the education of the child Arthur is committed to him; and while the boy is trained to the life of a subordinate squire in his foster-father's home, he is kept ignorant of his pretentions to the sceptre of Uther. In due time Merlin contrives that he shall attain his right position; he imposes a test on the many competitors for the vacant throne, which his ward can alone fulfil. Arthur draws forth the magic sword of empire that none other can wield, with unconscious power, and Merlin proclaims him the king of England. But there were many to dispute his title; his half-sisters,

Morgause, Morgan la fay, and Eleyne, with their husbands, the Kings of Orkney, Garlot and Gore, leave his court at Careleon in anger and disdain, and many a battle rolled across the plains of England before the young prince assured his sovereignty.

He had Merlin on his side, however, and good counsel secured the victories won by his prowess; by the enchanter's advice the Kings Ban and Bors of outre mer were summoned to his aid, a final battle was fought (in which were done marvellous deeds by the three confederate princes), and Excalibur proved itself worthy of its name, which an old legend tells us means

> Kerve steel and yren and al thing.

No sooner were his rebel relations dispersed than Ryence, of North Wales, sent fierce defiance and a demand for Arthur's beard, 'to purfile his mantle withal;' but Arthur made short work of him, and delivered from his attack Leo de Graunce, the King of Camelyard. The far-famed Guinevere was his daughter, at the shrine of whose perfect beauty the young conqueror could not but worship, nor did she disdain Arthur, the 'star of tournament,' now fresh in the grace of victory. But their marriage was not yet to be; and even now, in the first flush of his successes, the small cloud appeared that should shadow Arthur's life and darken his end. Not all Merlin's craft could save him, though his prescience foretold the retribution that should visit sin.

In manner of a messenger from Lot of Orkney her husband, came to Arthur's court, Morgause, his half-sister. Arthur was ignorant of his parentage, and he proffered love to her—for she was 'passing fair.' She accepted it; and Modred—at once the king's son and nephew—was born; Modred, the instrument of the infinite ruin that lay piled in such thunderous shadows beyond the sunshine of the young king's prime. The first indication of his future Arthur receives through a dream, in which his troubled end was prefigured. Merlin interprets its meaning to him; and, with a cynicism of prophecy, strange in the simple language of the romance, informs him of his fate and foretells his own.

The king's mother, Igrayne, confirms Merlin's account of her son's relationship with Morgause—but too late; Arthur's weak and cruel effort to avert the meed of his sin by a massacre of innocents is of no avail, and Mordred escapes to be his father's curse.

In all the episodes that follow—when Arthur's glory rises to its highest pitch, by his invasion of Italy—through the brilliant splendour of his wedding feast—in all his high festivals of Pentecost and Whitsuntide, when from far and near the chivalry of the world came to honour him—the handwriting on the wall is seen throwing on all the spectral glare of retribution. By its light the vague chaos of character and incident that gathered round Arthur's court assumes the form of an epic poem, preaching of the great vengeance due to great crime, and making of his history a moral lesson that must strike every heart. . . .

The punishment that dogs Arthur is great in outline as Chriemhilde's revenge in the Nibelungen Lied—too vast to have had its birth in the imagination of one man; it is probably a shadow thrown by some national tradition of a great disaster. But the king's character as drawn in these volumes does not fill up the ideal of the Welch hero; and, as we before remarked, the lineaments of Henry and Richard appear somewhat incongruously under the white plumes of the fabled Arthur. We are disappointed to find, instead of the Christian Hercules and the coming saviour of his race, the features of a wily statesman, who thrives by craft rather than by faith—the pupil of Merlin and the unworthy son of the Church, who is incapable to receive her higher graces—the weak husband of an intriguing wife—the unhappy father of a rebellious son. It is impossible not to see in these characteristics a portrait of Henry II., the parent of Geoffrey—the husband of Eleanor—the adversary of Thomas à Becket. Without this explanation of the inconsistencies of Arthur's life, we could not understand why authors capable of imagining a Galahad should have left so many stains on the robe of their chief hero. It would probably have been impolitic to have exalted too highly the standard of a reigning monarch's life; and the fate of Luc de la Barre, who, for his satires on Henry Beauclerc's court, had his eyes put out, of course kept Walter Mapes and his fellows within due limits of praise or censure. Their wish to please Queen Eleanor and her successors most likely produced the gaillard sketches of Guinevere and Isault of Ireland— heroines better suited to preside in the popular courts of Love than the less prominent maidens of Astolat or of Carbonecke, who yet witness well how tenderly and nobly the old romancers could draw a fair and perfect woman. However with all their carefulness to avoid offence, the historians of the Round table followed tradition, and obeyed the dictates of moral truth in describing the ruin that followed the ill-doing of their heroes and heroines. The terrible groundswell of just judgment sounds grimly even through the love-makings and triumphs of Arthur's and Guinevere's youth. We may note well in the writings of these first novelists that there are crimes enough on their canvas; but the worse vice of painting them as virtues had not then infected writers of fiction. Chivalry had but recently laid its axe at the root of outrage, and the Christian code was new in the north; yet in spite of courtly deference, in the face of too general licence, we find in these romances of Arthur that no crime goes unpunished. For all his courtesy, his high-bred courage and deeds of arms, Tristram of Lyoness dies miserably, stabbed in the back by his most despised enemy; Lamoracke de Galis is murdered by the sons of his unlawful love; Gawain, in his implacable pride, is denied the benefits of faith; Lancelot even—but we must not forestal the main incidents of the romance.

We have not space to give a detailed account of the episodes which, though coherently interwoven with the whole design, and tuned to the same harmony of moral purpose, do not concern the chief persons of the story. Of Balin and Balan, Arthur's wars in France, the adventures of Gareth under the nickname of Beaumains, the loves of Tristram and la beale Isoud, we will not speak, but turn at once from the wedding of Guenevere, and the institution of the Round-table fellowship which followed, to the point where Arthur's fate first visibly darkens in the wrath of God.

Having raised him to the highest pinnacle of worldly glory, Merlin is gone from his court; he has been taken captive by fay Viviane, the lady of the lake. We do not accept Mr. Tennyson's portrait of her; we rather love to think that she, perhaps, symbolizes the natural religion which at once strengthens revelation to the believing, yet ensnares those to their perdition who are 'assotted' on her, and adore the creation rather than the Creator. While Vivien imprisons Merlin by his own spell, that shall have power until the great day when craft shall render an account of its deeds, she nourishes in her retreat Lancelot, surnamed du Lac, the noble image of the perfect man. He goes forth to the world arrayed in every virtue but those peculiar to the Christian; he wins the highest place in Arthur's council; he becomes the star that governs Guinevere's stormy passions; honour, courtesy, truth, and justice illumine his actions; he has beauty and grace such as no other knight possessed; his dexterity and strength are only equalled by his generosity and mercy; he even practises the virtue of self-denial; he seeks with all the energy of his character for the unknown God; he wins the love of many, yet is constant to his one love of many years through all. Sir Lancelot has splendid virtues, yet lacks he one thing—the humility which would sacrifice the world's praise for the love of Christ—the purity of thought which, when there is need, can tear a man's best and dearest from his heart when they offend the Spirit that should dwell there.

Yet he is for long the best prop and chief ornament of Arthur's court, and the robes of the good knight do not show the stains which so mar his wedding garment when he is bidden to the feast of the Sangréel. For him, as for nearly all the Round-table fellowship, the mystic benefits of the True Blood are a stumbling-block. As its herald, Lancelot's son, Sir Galahad, appears for the first time at the Court of Camelot, and in the fulness of Arthur's splendour, the mystery is announced which shall at once bring spiritual good and physical evil to the realm. In the era of the first crusades there was throughout Christendom a strong expectation of the immediate advent of our Lord, and Galahad, the sinless knight, seems to us an impersonation of the expected Saviour, who, by his coming, should, as the son of Lancelot does, disperse the world's fair fellowship, while he alone is worthy to occupy the highest place at the Round table—the 'siege perilous' of mortal life. The account of his arrival at Arthur's court strengthens our belief. He is unknown and humble in his coming; he is introduced by an ancient prophet who, at the same time, foretels the Gospel of the Sangréel; he is clothed in red, the colour of love, yet by his first act he draws the sword that shall divide the kingdom.

Seated next to Arthur, on a pinnacle of earthly glory, the holy youth looks on at the high festival around him,—the crowd of noblest knights assembled at Pentecost from all lands to earn Ios in the court of Britain—to learn the discipline of chivalry, which seemed the perfection of human law. Guinevere's beauty threw glorious light on the best champions of the world as they jousted in the daisied meadow, by 'many towered Camelot.' She added her meed of praise to the universal acknowledgment of Galahad's strength and beauty; but the pure knight was proof against the world's attractions as against the world's pride.

That very night, in the banquet hall, was revealed to Arthur's court the mystery which Galahad came to solve....

But Arthur knew not yet what should follow. His nephew, Gawain, when power of speech returned to him, presumptuously proclaimed a vow, that he would for a year and a day seek to pierce the hidden mystery which had passed among them, yet without being revealed. The most part of the knights present, when they heard him, avowed the same resolve, and thus the Quest or search of the Sangréel was begun.

In vain Arthur grieved, and Guinevere wept and entreated; the leaven had stirred in the hearts of the knights, and whether for death or life the feverish thirst for salvation was on them. The sense of infinite but unknown good had roused them from their tourney games and May-day achievements, and a gleam from the inner world shone in on them, which they sought with wild, ignorant courage, to pursue to its source. Can this legend of the True Blood mean other than the gospel of justification by faith in its efficacy. The Quest that fills so many pages of Arthur's history surely signifies the thirst that seizes on the souls of those who, even as mere hearers, have experienced the benefits of Christian revelation.

Parables lie hid in every page of this romance; in more than one passage we are reminded of the most perfect of all allegories—the Pilgrim's Progress—and this part of our subject we recommend especially to those who dislike the occasional coarseness of the first volumes, and are fatigued by their monotony. We can but hurry through its incidents, merely glancing at the fate of Gawaine and his fellow-intruders into the mysteries of faith. They are warned in vain that penitence and purity must train their sight ere the Sangréel could be seen by them. They fare forth in hot haste, but disgust visits them when they find themselves in 'the meadow of herbs unsavoury,' the bitter but wholesome food to the soul, of self-denial, prayer, and fasting. Their zeal is quenched by difficulty of various kinds, and one by one they shamefully return to their old lives at Arthur's court, to revel and sin, which can be no longer excused by ignorance; for since the true faith of justification by the Sangréel had been revealed, the whole world was changed, and its former good had darkened in the new supernatural light of revelation.

Four of the seeking knights alone engage our sympathies, and but three finally attain the spiritual city of Sarras, the new Jerusalem of this mystic tale—the good knights Galahad and Percivale, and Sir Bors de Ganis.

In this group of Christian heroes, the ante-type, we may remark, of Christian, Faithful, and Hopeful, Galahad stands supreme. We can, gathering together his traits from the romance, picture him to ourselves as not unlike a pre-Raffaelite painting of St. Michael—a conqueror, yet passionless in the hour of victory, piercing the dragon Evil, yet unsullied by its dark breath. There is no shadow on him of coming death. He wears his immortality with the calm of perfect faith. There is no dint of conflict on his white shield; and if he has fought with Satan, no soil mars his radiant and unstirred robes. His portrait is a symbol to us, not of what is or has been, but of the ideal which is ever unrealized on earth. We imagine for such a figure a background of celestial blue, studded with golden stars. The landscape in which he stands is not a scene of this rent and dying earth, nor can our world produce the lilies and roses that enshrine the picture, yet our hearts beat with the sense of their hidden meaning, while the long line of light beyond the blue distant hills shines on us as a gleam from the 'spiritual place.'

By Galahad's side Sir Percevale stands in the same glow of faith and love, yet on a lower level. There is more of the human and less of the angelic in his attitude. His eyes are full of visionary light, and his compressed lips tell of conflict with the world, the flesh, and the devil. He has been in Patmos, and has seen the mysteries of God in the 'wilde mountaine.' He attains the communion of the Sangréel, yet so as by penance, before he can enter into the ship of faith 'from the Orient.' The Christian Church is here evidently symbolized, which bearing him safely through the waves and whirlpools of this troublesome life, reaches finally the holy place of Sarras, where his sister, who has followed the shorter road of martyrdom, awaits to celebrate with him the communion of saints. One more champion is associated in the victory which overcometh the world, and though Sir Bors de Ganis lacks the strength of Galahad, and the constancy of Percevale, we welcome him in this mediaeval group of Christians as an encouragement to those who have sinned yet are forgiven. We can imagine how his story stirred the zeal of those who sought in the military orders at once the office of soldier and missionary. He was, though denied the rapturous death of Sarras, counted worthy to return to Arthur's court on the sacred errand of the Gospel, and to tell how Galahad had achieved the Quest of Salvation—how, while fulfilling the highest tasks of earthly existence, the perfect knight had scattered the illusions of its possible perfection, unless through the Sangréel, the Divine influence on heart, and thought, and strength were obtained.

We said that four were earnest in their Quest, yet one, and he the most famous of all earthly knights, failed in the high enterprise. There is an impressive lesson in the fact that Lancelot, noblest of the world's champions, sans peur et sans reproche, the representative of Adam's race, earnest as he is in religion, and eager for justification, never attains the Divine communion which only can give spiritual life. We follow him in shrift and penance—in the ship of faith,—even in the moment of religious exaltation, when the benefits of the True Blood are visibly set before him. We share his dejection when they elude his grasp, and marvel at the sentence which gives him over to farther sin and life-long remorse; yet it is so, and from the time of his failure in the Quest du Sangréel, there is for him no more peace in the world; he returns to the dark place of his former sin. . . .

The end glares on us with such visible fire from the moment of Lancelot's return to the court of Arthur and Guinevere, that we have scarce a thought for the tale of Eleyne la Blanche, yet it makes a belt of pale pure light across the way, that might well have kêpt Sir Lancelot within its radiance, as he hurried to the Tophet of ruin beyond. . . .

Our readers, if they have read Mr. Tennyson's idyll of 'Elaine,' will note the art with which he has retained the simple beauty of Malory's style in his re-cast of [Eleyne's] lament.

But Heaven was now shut to Lancelot, and much must happen ere he can pray again. Through tourney and joust the shadow darkens on Arthur's court. Day by day Guinevere's moody love and angry jealousies bound the falling knight in closer bands, until even his worldly honour was sullied in her cause, for it befel that, as she 'rode on maying, in great joy and delight, her knights clothed in green in the freshest manner,' that a treacherous enemy carried her away prisoner, and Lancelot must drag his fair fame through the mire to release her, and even wage his life in her false quarrel.

At last the great anger that shall winnow all that is grain in Lancelot's character from the chaff, breaks over the court. The Queen's treachery to her husband, and Lancelot's part in it, is made manifest. Taking stern vengeance on the spies who have discovered the knight's ill-doing, Arthur retires from the Castle of Caerleil, where Guinevere then was. She is doomed to be burned, but few knights will attend to witness her execution, and men's minds already fall off from Arthur. Many side with Lancelot, and join him in the rescue of the Queen;—and she must have been a sight to move pity—her proud and perfect beauty, shorn of its rays, and sinking in such lurid clouds;—but, like a sudden storm-rift, her lover tore apart the imminent shade of death, and carried her off to his castle of Joyous Gard. Not without dishonour, even in victory, the blood of his unarmed friends, Gareth and Gaheris, struck down defenceless in the fray, reddens Lancelot's hands, and their brother Gawaine turns on his old friend to whom, up to this cruel fate, he had been loyal.

In vain Lancelot restores Guinevere to Arthur, and prays for pardon: he is hunted as a wild beast to his fortresses in France. In vain he offers what reparation he can to his outraged master, and proves all the courtesy and patience of his strong heart, forbearing the king and humbling himself to Gawaine. The bitterness of death in life is before him, and he must drink to the dregs the chalice of suffering.

War sways to and fro between the king and Lancelot. The scene is shifted from England to France; and marches and sieges, defiances and knightly deeds, follow each other as we may imagine the Plantagenet wars to have ebbed and flowed in the plains of Anjou and Guienne. But while he pursues his enemy, Arthur himself is in the toils. His sin at last finds him out; and Modred, his illegitimate son and nephew, to whom, in his absence, he had committed the regency of England, levies war against him. He even insolently proposes marriage to Guinevere, and lays siege to the Tower of London, to which she has fled for safety....

Of Modred's host, who had shouted so 'grimly' in the morning, he only remained. 'Then was King Arthur ware where Sir Modred leaned on his sword, among a great heape of dead men; and King Arthur gate his speare in both his hands and ran towards Sir Modred, crying, "Traitor! now is thy death-day come." And when Sir Modred felt that he had his death-wound, he thrust himself with all the might he had up to the end of King Arthur's speare, and righte so he struck his father, Arthur, with his sword on the side of the head, that it pierced the helmet and the brainpan———.'

A dolorous blow in truth—a terrible back stroke of Divine

lightning, laying low the splendid edifice of mortal glory. What availed Merlin's craft or the charmed Excalibur, the heroism of knightly valour, or the wise ordinances of human government? Sin had gnawed at the root of Arthur's glory, and in a day it was laid low.

We come now upon the scene which Mr. Tennyson has chosen for his epic fragment of the 'Mort D'Arthur.' That our readers may compare his noble verse with the antique prose, we give the whole passage. It lacks some touches peculiar to Mr. Tennyson's idyllic fancy, for he has painted the back ground with mystic light and shade, that might have been studied in Dante's selva oscura. Arthur's figure looms colossally from the mirror of Mr. Tennyson's imagination, but as a dim and superhuman form that loses its true outline in the dazzling Arctic landscape. Perhaps he is the more fitted to speak the ambiguous prophecy with which the modern poem ends. Our readers are familiar with its beauties; we bespeak their approval of the simple power in Malory's tale....

The legend of Arthur's re-appearance as harbinger of a future golden age is but hinted in the chapter which follows that which we have quoted; but the vague hope of a To come centred on him among the Brétons—the yearning for some millenium which is found in Pagan as in Christian hearts. In the Armorican colony of the Cymri, the people, up to a late date, used to cry aloud at certain of their feasts, 'Non le Roi Arthur n'est pas mort.' 'Unknown is the grave of Arthur' say the Welch bards of this Celtic Prometheus, for the thoughts of the sons of Adam turn to the hope of a resurrection from death, through the discords of all ages. The writers of the Crusade era dwell less on this barbaric form of truth, the dim faith in some 'good time coming,' however, than on the Christian perfections of repentance and purity. They leave the question of Arthur's reappearance on earth, to set before us the sorrow and penance of Lancelot and the broken-hearted Guenevere.

The proud, passionful Queen, struck to the ground by remorse, bows her head low in Amesbury Convent, while Lancelot, too late to succour his lord, arrives in England and finds consummated the ruin he had entailed on those he loved best. Leaving his following of kings and knights he rides in search of her who had been the false light of his life. We will follow the language of the old tale to describe their last meeting....

There is now no more place for him in the world. Well for him and Guinevere if they can gain one in heaven, re-baptised in bitter tears and chanting misereres heartfelt as David's.

For six years Lancelot and seven of his knights remained in great penance as postulants, 'and then he tooke the habite of priesthood, and twelve moneths he sung the masse. And thus upon a night a vision came to him and charged him, in remission of all his sinnes, to hast him towards Amesbury, "and by that time thou come there thou shalt find Queene Guinevere dead."'

He started or it was day, taking his fellows with him; but 'they were weak and weary to goe,' and ere they reached her bedside Guinevere was dead. For two days before her prayer had been, that she might never again see Lancelot, and it was granted to her weakness to be spared further trial of her repentance. 'Then Sir Lancelot saw her visage and hee wept not greatly, but sighed; and so hee did all the observance of the service himself, both the dirige at night and the masse on the morrow.'

To the dregs he drank the cup of suffering. He led the funeral to Glastonbury, where she was buried by Arthur; 'and when she was put into the earth Sir Lancelot swooned and lay long upon the ground, while the hermit came and awaked him, and said, "Yee are to blame, for yee displease God with such manner of sorrow making." "Truly," said Sir Lancelot, "I trust I do not displease God, for hee well knoweth mine entent, for my sorrow was not, nor is, for any rejoicing of sinne; but my sorrow may never have an end."'

The whole tale of treachery and ingratitude, of sin and its results at last was bare to him. Six weeks he lay 'grovelling' and praying continually upon the tomb of Arthur and Guinevere; but at last came to the weary penitent rest. He died in the night alone, and when the hermit bishop, who has been shown in a vision Lancelot's reception into heaven, goes with his fellows to the dead man's cell he finds him lying 'as he had smiled.' His sorrow was over. His 'soul is with the saints we trust,' for we cannot look on Lancelot as a mere embodiment of chivalric ideas. If during the first volumes he was but part of Arthur's pageant, in his grief and death a human interest gathers round him, and this hero of the old gestours seems to us warm with the same life that we live. Are there not Lancelots in society as well as Lancelots in India or the Crimea? So strong, yet so weak, offering noblest qualities at an evil shrine, and consummating self-sacrifice which is but self-immolation.

Some of our readers will know, too, that the end of Lancelot's life is not without daily example. His bitter sorrow and surrender to the keenest suffering are yet the price paid by noble natures who have sinned, and such will comprehend the skill of the trouvère who left Lancelot's last years in the shadow of lifelong grief, and who troubled not the penitent with the garish light of worldly good. 'Blessed are they that mourn'.

[Digression on the defects of Muscular Christianity and some modern novels.]

But the leaven of revealed ethics worked in the tales of romance as in the graver literature that spread throughout Christendom. The fables of the gestours, with all their licence, and through all their verbiage, on the whole point us forward to the distant light that yet attracts the Christian poet or historian. In the failure of chivalry to attain all it aimed at and still aims at, we must not forget the lawlessness and brutality of the society it first was instituted to civilize—the lawlessness and brutality of the human heart, which still render it sometimes powerless in the best examples of civilization. If many blots were on the knight errantry of the middle ages, we must remember that the very splendour of its enterprise increased their apparent darkness, and reading these tales which Malory has edited we can but feel surprised at the purity of their aim, and the place given in them to religion, when we consider the conditions of their origin.

They greet a world fresh from change and newly-born now as in the youth of Europe, vibrating with battle, ready for crusades, and credulous of heroes. They are popular now as then—sung by poets, and woven into modern fictions, because they teach us the eternal lessons of this world's incapacity to fulfil our higher aspirations—of our failure in our best-planned schemes, if they are not hallowed by faith in the power and necessity of sanctification through the blood of the Atoner. They satisfy the hero-worship which now, as then, ennobles manhood, by showing us the warfare between the spiritual and the fleshly life, and they give us examples of the Christian paradox, that the noblest victory is gained by humility—the highest happiness by self-denial. Now, as then, when the race of life seems crowded with competitors, and the world is ready to crown the victor, of whatever rank, the truth is preached to us in these old myths that by obedience men are made more than kings, and that faith is the substance—the very present possession—of things hoped for.

21. James T. Knowles

1862

James T. Knowles (1831–1908), architect and editor, brought out in 1862 a 'popular abridgement' of Malory's *Morte Darthur*, with a few additions from Geoffrey and elsewhere. *The Story of King Arthur and his Knights of the Round Table* was in an eighth edition by 1895. The book is not only abridged but heavily expurgated, and Knowles's introduction points out the defects in the original that make these alterations obligatory. (London: Griffith & Farrow, 1862, pp. i–iii.)

The story of King Arthur will never die while there are English men to study and English boys to devour its tales of adventure and daring and magic and conquest.

King Arthur was to our forefathers what and more than what 'Robinson Crusoe' and 'The Arabian Nights' are to the present generation. They feasted on its legends for centuries, and never grew tired of the grand chivalry of the 'blameless king,' and the wanderings, feats, and dangers of his chosen band of knights. Caxton only ministered to the public appetite when he took it for one of the first printed books, and if in our own time it has disappeared from the popular literature and the boys' bookshelves, the cause is, probably, that, since the days of cheap books, it has never been modernised or adapted for general circulation.

Concealed in antiquated spelling and quaint style, it has become a treat for scholars rather than for the general reader, who would find it too long, too monotonous, and too obscure. Still less is it fitted for boys, who would probably become the principal readers of the Arthur legends in a popular form.

To supply the gap still existing, therefore, and provide a popular abridgment of the Story of King Arthur and his Knights is the object of the following pages—an endeavour to carry out the suggestion of the poet Southey, who says, 'were it modernised and published as a book for boys it could hardly fail of regaining its popularity.'...

The author of the following compilation has done little but abridge and simplify Sir Thomas Mallory's Collection of the Legends as printed by Caxton—adding from Geoffry of Monmouth and other sources where it was desirable, and arranging the many tales into a somewhat clearer and more consecutive story than appears heretofore to have been formed from them. He has modernised the style only so much as seemed indispensable; the ancient manner suiting the ancient matter better than a purely modern dress could do.

He has endeavoured, nevertheless, at however great a distance, to follow the rule laid down in the 'Idylls of the King;' and has suppressed and modified where changed manners and morals have made it absolutely necessary to do so for the preservation of a lofty original ideal.

If he shall succeed in paving the way for such a popular revival of the Story as is its due, and which would place it in boys' libraries anywhere beside 'Robinson Crusoe' and 'The Arabian Nights,' he will have obtained his reward. For he is sure of the gratitude of all whom he may be fortunate enough to present for the first time to King Arthur and his Knights.

22. D. W. Nash

1861

David William Nash (1809–76) in his book *Taliesin* (1858) questioned the early dating of surviving Welsh Arthurian material, maintaining that the twelfth- and thirteenth-century manuscripts argue a late tradition; he also debunked elaborate attempts to find remnants of Druidic lore in the Welsh poetry. The remarks below were solicited and quoted by F. J. Furnivall for the introduction to an edition of Lovelich's *Seynt Graal, or The Sank Ryal: The History of the Holy Graal* (2 vols, Roxburghe Club, London: J. B. Nichols, 1861, 1863), I, pp. vi–vii). While Nash is ostensibly discussing the entry of the Holy Grail material through French romances, he is not familiar with these sources and in fact bases his remarks about the thematic significance of the Grail and the structure of the whole romance upon Malory's version.

The reference to M. Schulz is to Albert Schulz, whose *Essay on the Influence of Welsh Tradition upon the Literature of Germany, France, and Scandinavia* (translation published 1841) won the prize of the Abergavenny Cymreigyddion Society at the Eisteddfod of 1840.

I quite agree with the opinion put forward by M. Schulz, that the legend of the Graal was originally distinct from the histories of Percival and the other Arthur knights, and that it was first woven into them by North French poets. One can pretty well see, on reading the old romance of Arthur printed by Caxton in 1485, where the monkish 'trouvere' took up the old chevaleresque story, and commenced interweaving the Graal-legend,[1] improving, in a pious sense, the popular romance, but altogether marring the unity of the original design by the introduction of modes of thought and action altogether inconsistent with those belonging to the genuine characters of the earlier story.

NOTE

1 What I mean about the interweaving of the Sangreal romance with the Arthurian is this:—In the first part of the 'Prince Arthur' the knights are all jovial, damsel-loving, hard-fighting heroes, who trouble themselves very little about the mysteries of Christianity. Merlin plays a conspicuous part amongst them. The Sangreal is incidentally mentioned—in C. 36. Merlin prophecies that the adventures belonging to it are to commence after his death. In C.C. 38–44 we find it stated that certain adventures are afterwards rehearsed in the 'Book of the Sangreal.'

In the third part commences the history of a new generation, Galahad the son of Sir Lancelot, and Sir Bors his nephew; and now the knights are chaste and religious, and have much to do with monks and hermits, who interpret their dreams or visions. The adventures in quest of the Sangreal accomplished, we get back to the old style of adventure. Sir Lancelot goes back to his adultery with Queen Guenever, with a slight show of compunction, and matters go on as before. King Arthur himself has nothing to do with the quest; and if all relating to the Sangreal were cut out of the story, the history of the Knights of the Round Table would remain sufficiently complete. In connecting the two stories— Arthur and the Graal,—it was necessary to introduce a pure spiritual knight, chaste and pious, and this is done by the union of the best knight, Lancelot, and a maiden of the race of Joseph of Arimathaea, whose issue is Galahad, predestined to accomplish the adventure of the Sangreal.

This seems to be M. Schultz's view . . . but I do not agree with him that 'the point of union is Percival, the Peredur of the Welsh.' I am not sufficiently acquainted with the subject to know what was the original of Sir Thomas Malory's legend, but of course he must have found it as he gives it. . . .

23. George Perkins Marsh

1862

George Perkins Marsh (1801–82), an American lawyer, diplomat, scholar, and philologist, was an early volunteer for the work of the *New English Dictionary*, serving as American secretary from 1862; he published *The Origin and History of the English Language* in 1860. In his brief mention of Malory, Marsh speaks of him as more than a mere compiler and discusses his 'Teutonic' vocabulary.

The extract is from the second edition (New York, Charles Scribner, 1863), pp. 486–8.

Perhaps there is no better method of enabling the reader to form an idea of the condition in which Caxton found the English of his time, and the state to which he contributed to bring it, than by introducing extracts from the Morte d'Arthur and from Caxton himself. The Morte d'Arthur is not, indeed, a work of English invention, nor, on the other hand, is it just to style it simply a translation. No continuous French original for it is known; but it is a compilation from various French romances, harmonized and connected so far as Malorye was able to make a consistent whole out of them, by supplying here and there links of his own forging.

In the introduction to the reprint of 1817, Southey says: 'The Morte d'Arthur is a compilation from some of the most esteemed romances of the Round Table. Had the volumes from which it is compiled existed in English, Sir Thomas Malory would not have thought of extracting parts from them, and blending them into one work. This was done at the best possible time: a generation earlier, the language would have retained too much of its Teutonic form; a generation later, and the task of translation would have devolved into the hands of men who performed it as a trade, and equally debased the work which they interpreted and the language in which they wrote.' This is very superficial criticism.

'A generation earlier' would have carried us back to the time of Pecock; 'a generation later' would have brought us down to that of Lord Berners, the translator of Froissart. If Pecock be taken as the standard of his age, I admit the language must be regarded as still retaining much more of its Teutonic *form* than it showed in the hands of Sir Thomas Malorye. But while Pecock was grammatically behind his age, he was rhetorically far in advance of it; and I am by no means certain that he could not have given us a better translation of the patchwork put together by Malorye than Malorye has done. On the other hand, I cannot admit that Lord Berners 'debased' either 'the work he interpreted' or 'the language in which he wrote,' in his sometimes slovenly, but always marvellously spirited, translation of the great chronicler Froissart.

The narrative of the death of Arthur, which I take from the fifth chapter of the twenty-first book of the Morte d'Arthur, according to Southey's reprint of Caxton's edition of 1485, is a favourable specimen of Malorye's style. The proportion of French words, which does not exceed four per cent., is smaller than Malorye's general average; but it would be difficult to find any author of later date than the middle of the fourteenth century whose vocabulary is so 'Teutonic' as his....

24. Herbert Coleridge

1864

Herbert Coleridge (1830–61), great-nephew of Samuel Taylor Coleridge, was primarily a philologist and until his early death he was the general editor for the project to issue a New English Dictionary. His essay on Arthur was published posthumously by F.J. Furnivall twice, first in the introductory material to Lovelich's *Seynt Graal* (Roxburghe Club, 1861, 1863) and again as part of the preface to his edition of the stanzaic *Morte Arthur* (London: Macmillan, 1864), pp. xxviii–lvi; these extracts from the 1864 publication show Coleridge's sense of the dramatic unity of the Arthurian story as seen in Malory's version.

Coleridge's essay begins with a lengthy summary of the life and career of Arthur taken from Geoffrey with minor additions from Wace, Layamon, and the alliterative *Morte Arthur*.

Such is the legend of Arthur when stripped of all those adventures and marvels which have conferred on it as deep and undying a fascination as the venerable myths of Roman history have upon the earliest annals of imperial Rome; such is the tale which our ancestors not a century ago gravely received and repeated as historical truth. Many readers, however, will find this version quite as new to them as—indeed, perhaps more so, than—many of the more marvellous editions of the story.

We will now pass on to the account given us by Sir T. Malory in his great compilation made in the reign of Edward IV., and printed by Caxton in 1485; and this for the future, with several minor works—such as 'The Romance of Arthur and Merlin,' a second metrical Morte Arthur, a romance of Lancelot; 'The Romance of the San Graal,' and others—I shall refer to as the Legend, reserving the term 'history' to denote the version given by Geoffrey and his followers. It will of course be understood that I attach no more historical weight to the latter than to the former; and that the terms 'history' and 'legend' are simply employed as convenient modes of reference. In analogy with the divisions I have employed for the history, we shall find that Malory's work also falls into three principal sections, which we may denote by the three well-known names of Merlin, Lancelot and the Sangreal, and Guinever.

The legend is prefaced, as it were, by a relation of the miraculous birth and adventures of Merlin, which we pass over here; then comes the story of Uther and Igerna as before, with this addition, that Merlin stipulates as the price of his services that the education of the future prince be left in his hands.

[Summary.]

This division of the legend ends with the disappearance of Merlin. The enchanter is fooled by a woman: he becomes 'assotted' on one of the Ladies of the Lake, Nynene, who does not reciprocate the admiration of her semi-diabolical lover, and contrives at length to rid herself of his importunate addresses by boxing him up in a hollow stone, through a charm, which in an evil hour, though with a full foreknowledge of his coming doom, he had taught his treacherous mistress. There are several versions of this story; but in none is the lady represented as actuated by such abominable motives as Tennyson has ascribed to her in his last and greatest work.

There remains, however, still one matter which it is important to notice, because it supplies the thread of connexion for the maintenance of the dramatic unity of the legend. I allude to the seduction by Arthur, in ignorance, of his own sister Margause, the wife of King Lot, who, with her four sons, Gawain, Gareth, Agravain, and Gaherys, was paying a visit at her brother's court. From this adulterous, not to say incestuous, amour was Modred born; and Merlin, as may be supposed, did not fail to improve the occasion for his sovereign's benefit, by a prophecy of the evils that should arise in consequence of this sin. I am not aware that this incident is mentioned by any other writer than Malory,[1] but it is evidently of considerable importance to the legend if looked upon as an epic or dramatic whole, just as the original sin of Tantalus pervaded every generation of his house till the curse finally worked itself out in the madness and deliverance of Orestes; just as also in the great Scandinavian Epos, the curse first pronounced on the golden hoard of Andvari destroyed each possessor in succession till the destined atonement was made in the death of Atli and his sons.

In this first section Arthur appears chiefly in the character of an ordinary knight errant seeking adventures, and relieving distressed damsels, and not unfrequently getting sorely mauled by older hands than himself, not to mention the machinations of more than one hostile enchantress. Occasionally, too, he acts as commander-in-chief of an army, as in the battle against the eleven confederate kings in the forest of Bedegrayne, where, however, he appears to have owed more to his miraculous sword than to his skill as a tactician. This latter part of a general's duties he had the sense to leave in the hands of Merlin, who managed admirably;—indeed, in these romances the round men slip into the round holes, and the square men into the square holes, with marvellous precision. In the next section, however, Arthur is a married man and king, and thereby retires somewhat into the background, while the narrative is occupied with the deeds of other important personages, who are now for the first time brought forward. The principal figures are those of Lancelot, Tristram, Lamorak, Galahad, and Percival. Each of these heroes has a private history of his own, which is united to that of Arthur by some secret link of connexion, such as Lancelot's love for Guinever, his unconscious amour with Elayne (not her of Astolat), and the consequent birth of Galahad, who is devoted to the quest and achievement of the Sangreal, and proves to be the true occupant of the Siege Perilous. These matters occupy in the legend a considerable length of time, and find place between the epoch of the conquest of Rome and the revolt of Modred, which in the history immediately succeeded each other. In this part of the legend, which we cannot here, from want of space, do more than allude to in general terms, the curse of Ate which hung over Arthur and his family is slowly gathering strength, as each of the greater knights, whose separate destinies seem to be inextricably inwoven with that of their sovereign, add by their indiscretion and lawless amours to the weight of that inexpiable sin for which a terrible atonement was, in the fulness of time, to be exacted and paid. Other symptoms of the beginning of the end may be observed in the weakening of the bond of fellowship among the knights of the Round Table. Lamorak, the elder brother of Percival, is treacher-ously slain by Gawayne and two of his brethren, for the seduction of their mother, Queen Margause, who thus, by a double adultery, contributes to her royal brother's ruin. Her own crimes she expiates by her death at the hands of her son Gawayne [Gaheris], who surprises her with her paramour *flagrante delicto*, and cuts her head off without further delay, allowing the defenceless Lamorak to escape for a time, in order to ensure a revenge as base and treacherous in the manner of its execution as the motives alleged for it were mean and unknightly.

We might adduce other instances, but our rapidly diminishing space warns us imperatively to resume the thread of the main narrative.

[Summary.]

This legend of the Sangreal extends, as we have said, over a period of three centuries or nine generations, commencing with Joseph of Arimathea himself, and his convert Evalach, King of Sarras, who, though smitten almost blind for a too daring inspection of the Sangreal, was nevertheless allowed to live by God's own promise until he should see the achiever of the adventure, in whose presence he should regain his sight and die—a promise duly fulfilled by the agency of Galahad. It is therefore attached to the Arthurian cycle only by its conclusion, and must not occupy us further at present, to the prejudice of our main subject. In the closing scenes of Arthur's life and reign the mythus once more runs parallel with the history: that is, in the French and English versions. There are, however, others of Keltic origin, curious enough in themselves, but diverging so considerably from the former, that we cannot here do more than pay them the tribute of a passing allusion.

The reunion of the knights after the achievement of the Sangreal was but a melancholy one. Sad gaps were seen in the Round Table, and many seats once occupied by those who bore names of high renown were empty—Tristram, Galahad, Percival, Lamorak, all were gone; bad and angry feelings had established themselves between several of the knights individually, and a tendency to clownishness, and towards separation of the entire body into sections united by family ties, was only too perceptible. Sinister rumours of another kind began to be heard, for Lancelot's pious resolves soon faded away before the smiles of Guinever; their interviews became more frequent, and conducted with less precaution, and although he himself saw only too clearly how things must in every tournament sooner or later end, and endeavoured to bring his infatuated mistress to a sense of her danger, he only succeeded in awakening a fresh fit of jealousy, in consequence of which he was peremptorily ordered to leave the Court. Retribution follows with no lame foot on this occasion, and Guinever is soon made to rue her folly bitterly.

[Summary.]

One day, when she and her suite were out Maying in the woods, an old but unsuccessful admirer, Sir Melegrance, with his men, captures the whole bevy of knights and ladies, after an ineffectual resistance, and carries them off in triumph to his castle. Lancelot, hearing of it, soon manages to effect an entrance, and not only that, but also contrives to pass the night in the arms of his mistress. Being, however, unfortunately wounded in the hand in a desperate attempt to break the iron stanchions which guarded the window of her chamber, he left a bloody mark on the bed; and when Sir Melegrance comes in the morning to visit the wounded knights of Guinever's suite, whom she had insisted on tending herself, he very coolly draws the curtains, discovers the blood, and at once charges the queen with a clear and manifest adultery. As before, in Mador's case, Lancelot appears at the nick of time in the lists, and Guinever's life is once more safe; but these repeated misfortunes affect her reputation only too plainly; and Arthur himself, at the conclusion of the affair, seemed to think that the bottom of the mystery had not been fathomed satisfactorily.

At length the fatal hour arrives. Under pretence of loyal duty, Agravaine and Modred, in spite of the earnest remonstrances of their nobler brethren, Gawayne, Gaherys, and Gareth, formally acquaint Arthur of what had been long obvious to all eyes but his. With his sanction, a trap is laid for the lovers, which succeeds, as Tennyson tells us; but only Modred, out of a party of twelve, survives to tell the tale. Arthur's fury at this information of the truth of the scandal is unbounded; his queen, he declares, shall have the law; nor do the supplications of Gawayne and his two brothers avail to turn him from his wrath. Once more Guinever sees her doom approach, and once more she is rescued by main force by him for whose love she had thrown away both honour and happiness. Unfortunately, in the *mêlée* which took place, Lancelot, blinded with rage, and intent only on saving his beloved mistress, kills, without recognising them, Gaherys and Gareth, who were present by the king's peremptory command; but who, determining to lend no sort of countenance to the proceeding, appeared unarmed, and by some chance were mixed up in the combat. This terrible oversight costs all parties dear. Up to this time Gawayne has been the foremost in defending Lancelot, and deprecating the idea of war between him and the king; but now the resentment which the king had formerly tried to arouse in him against Lancelot, by reminding him of the death of Agravaine, blazes forth on hearing the bitter news of what seemed like a wilful and cruel murder. The result is a war between Lancelot and Arthur, or rather a siege by Arthur of Lancelot's castle of Joyous Gard, conducted with the utmost forbearance on the part of the former, and which might have been brought to an amicable termination had not Gawain's inextinguishable anger, and the pledged honour of the king, rendered all attempts at negotiation fruitless. At length Lancelot does come forth, and Sir Gawain is compelled to relinquish the combat he had provoked with a dangerous wound, from which he has hardly time to recover before news of worse evils force Arthur to return and punish a far less noble foe. Guinever had, in the meantime, by force of a letter or bull from the Pope, been restored to Arthur, under a stipulation that her life should be safe and the past forgotten. In the absence of her husband, however, Modred attempts to assume the place of Sir Lancelot, and on her indignantly resisting such a substitution, he revolts and lays siege to London, where she had entrenched herself. Then follow the incidents I have before detailed, diversified by a few poetical ornaments, such as the appearance of Gawain's ghost to Arthur on the eve of the battle of Camlan, warning him not to fight the next day; the accommodation, in consequence, proposed by Arthur, and destroyed by a mere chance accident; and lastly, the death or translation of Arthur himself to the Isle of Avalon, and the restoration of Excalibur to its mysterious owner by the hands of Sir Bedivere, just as Tennyson has given it in his noble 'Morte Arthur.' The legend closes with Guinever's retirement to a convent, and Lancelot's vain attempt to induce her to return to the world and himself; failing which, he himself, at her instance, becomes a hermit;

and, after a few years of repentant sorrow, gradually pines away, and is found dead on the tomb of the queen [Lancelot dies in his cell], whose decease had been communicated to him a short time previously. Bedivere, the sole survivor of the battle of Camlan, also takes to a religious life; and with his death and the accession of Constantine, the legend is brought to a close.

Our sketch of this world-famous legend has been but an imperfect one, and many portions of the tale have of necessity been altogether passed over; still enough has been detailed to enable us, by a comparison of the two versions, which we have termed the historical and legendary, to elicit some results which may not be wholly devoid of interest. It will have been observed that the two stories coincide in three points—the miraculous birth of Arthur, the Roman expedition, and the final battle; but between these several points of contact they diverge widely. In the former, Arthur stands out alone, and his knights occupy but subordinate positions, and exercise little influence on his fortunes; in the latter, Lancelot is the true centre of the action, which is otherwise carried on almost entirely by the knights of the Court, and not by the king. Moreover, by means of Arthur's early sin, and his ill-omened alliance with Guinever, the legend acquires a kind of dramatic unity; it exhibits in Aeschylean phrase the working out of an Ate, a retribution long delayed, but surely developing itself at last; while in the historical version no trace of such design appears. Now, when we remember that this so-called 'history' is as purely legend as the other, and that we are not here, as in the case of Charlemagne, comparing one really historical account with another, which represents that central arc incrusted with a vast accretion of legendary matter, the inference would seem to be that, in very early times, and without taking the Keltic transformations of the story into consideration, the accounts of the mythus had become current in two distinct though partly parallel forms. For be it observed that no amount of mere excision will make Malory's work agree with Geoffrey's; Malory is not Geoffrey *plus* a mass of romantic detail; the 'motives' of the two accounts are different in kind, and cannot be reconciled. This is further supported by the difference observable in the characters of the knights, such as Gawain, Kay, and Modred, who are all systematically vilified in the legend, but appear in a very different light in the works of Geoffrey and Layamon. Even the queen herself is represented by these writers as more sinned against than sinning. And I believe that, out of the remains of Keltic literature, another edition of the mythus might be given, even more distinct from those we have been considering than they are from each other, a fact which lends additional probability to the hypothesis I have brought forward. Another discrepancy of some importance, is the importation into the Arthurian legend of the adventure of the Sangreal, which would not certainly have been excluded from a mediaeval history by means of its marvellousness; and, therefore, by its absence seems to favour the supposition of the independence of the two versions. This, too, is not a mere episode in Malory's work, as might be supposed at first sight, and as the books devoted to Tristram and to Balyn really are—it has a root in the legend, which would be manifestly incomplete by its elimination. I pass over minor points of variation, such as the parentage ascribed to Guinever; the locality and circumstances of the last battle, the extent of the Roman expedition, the ceremonies attending Arthur's death, and the glaring discrepancy as to the fate of Bediver, all of which, however, have a weight, rendered more perceptible when taken in conjunction with the other matters already alluded to. But to discuss the origin of these divergences, or even to enumerate the lesser variations in the legendary account, would require a separate essay and much additional detail. On some future occasion we may revert[2] to the subject, which is one of high interest as mythology to the scientific inquirer, and of hardly less as poetry to the genuine lovers of old Romance.

FURNIVALL'S NOTES (SELECTED)

1 It is by his French original.—F.
2 The writer's early death prevented his accomplishing this and other more important literary undertakings that he had planned.

25. F.J. Furnivall
1864–8

Frederick James Furnivall (1825–1910) was the energetic
editor of several Arthurian texts among a number of other
medieval and Elizabethan editions. Founder of several literary
societies including the Early English Text Society, he planned
an edition of Caxton's Malory for the EETS in the early
1860s, but the project was eventually abandoned. His
references to Malory in the introductions to other Arthurian
editions reflect typical attitudes of the period, dismissive of
Malory's constructional skills but admiring of tone and style.
As may be seen in the second selection below, Furnivall was
the first to point out in detail the verbal similarities between
Malory's concluding chapters and the stanzaic *Morte Arthur*
and to suggest that Malory borrowed from the poem.

(a) *Queste del Saint Graal* (London: Roxburghe Club, 1864),
pp. iii–vii
... Syr Thomas Maleore, in his most pleasant jumble and summary
of the Arthur Legends, has, with a true instinct, abstracted the
Quest at much greater length than the other portions of the story,
rightly recognising its greater beauty and deeper spiritual meaning.
Well does he—or Caxton rather, perhaps—finish it with these
words, 'Thus endeth thistory of the Sancgreal that was breuely
drawen oute of Frensshe in to Englysshe, the which is a story
cronycled for one of the truest and the holyest that is in this world,
the whiche is the xvii book' (chapter 29 to chapter 104 (both
inclusive) of Part III. in the later editions).

I find this preference of his, and other men's, wholly justified; for
in the Quest is no question of exalting the Kelt above the Saxon,
the Briton above the Roman, or of narrating the effort of an impure
king to establish as a model for the world a Society in which his
own incest has sown the seeds of corruption: not for these things
does the Quest-writer strive: he sets before men the Lifeblood of
God, and the light of His presence as the highest prizes for earthly

endeavour, and shows his hearers that not by arms of human strength or worldly make can these glorious gifts be won, but by entire chastity and purity of spirit, soul, and flesh. ... This Graal-legend and its incorporation into the Arthur story seem to me distinctly to have this end, to bring a spiritual Presence into halls and camps of armed men, to lift up before them the ideal of the scholar and the monk, and so to purify and ennoble the soldiers' coarse and careless lives. ... we may be thankful for the inbringing of this more than mortal holiness into so much of human weakness and sin.

And we may feel thus without holding that the *Flos Regum Arthurus* of the chronicler was a much less noble person than the chronicler's more legendary follower. ... Moreover, Arthur, though under the doom for his early sin, is still allowed in the Legend to fight gallantly and with all earthly glory for a time against his fate; and is at last saved, 'yet, though as by fire,' and carried to his happy Apple-valley, there to heal him of his grievous wound. If he does not appear as the undoubted centre of interest in the legend,—as he does not to me,—this is because, as a pure and Christian knight, he is far below Galahad; as a doer of doughty deeds, as a man of human nobleness and human infirmity, he is, or is put, below Lancelot. Not for him was it to be the chosen of God, because no heat of earthly lust had ever inflamed his flesh; not for him did Bohors mourn, the man whom Christ had fed; not for him was the warrior's death-song sung: 'A, syr Launcelot, thou were head of all crysten knyytes. ... '

Again, as to Arthur's relation to Guinevere, I cannot feel that the modern representation is the truest one. To any one knowing his Maleore,—knowing that Arthur's own sin was the cause of the breaking up of the Round Table, and Guinevere's the means only through which that cause worked itself out,—having felt Arthur's almost purposed refusal to see what was going on under his own eyes between his queen and Lancelot, so as to save a quarrel with his best knight till it was forced on him; having watched with what a sense of relief, as it were, Arthur waited for his wife to be burnt on her second accusal,—then, for one so primed to come on Mr. Tennyson's representation of the king, in perfect words, with tenderest pathos, rehearsing to his prostrate queen his own nobleness and her disgrace; the revulsion of feeling was too great; one was forced to say to the Flower of Kings, 'if you really did this, you were the Pecksniff of the period.' I quite admit that any one, and especially Mr. Tennyson, (who is to me personally more than all the other English poets put together, save alone Chaucer,) has a right to take Arthur's nobleness from the early Legend, and Guinevere's sin from the later one, and combine them together as he will, (and whatever he has done or may do with them the English world will be grateful;) but I desire to point out that the early legend, which says nothing of Arthur's sin, says nothing of Guinevere's sin with Lancelot either; and that some, if not all, of the later legends which point out Guinevere's sin, point out, too, Arthur's earlier incest, which, in accordance with Merlin's prophecy, must and does ruin his Round Table; the destruction being wrought out through the less unnatural though more wilful sin of his wife, and his own old passions working in Lancelot's breast. . . .

(b) Stanzaic *Morte Arthur* (London and Cambridge: Macmillan, 1864), p. xvi
. . . That the writer took it more or less from the French romances written in England by Robert de Borron, Walter Mapes, and others of Henry the Second's and Richard the First's time, I do not doubt.[1] . . .

NOTE

1 Did he and Syr Thomas Maleore translate from one original (which was not the version of the French *Mort* or *Lancelot* (as far as I can see) mentioned above) or had Syr Thomas seen the present poem? Compare

> Thenne said sir Lyonel
> that was ware and wyse,
> 'My lord syr Launcelot I will gyue this counceylle,
> lete vs kepe oure stronge walled Townes
> untyl they have hongre and cold, and blowe on their nayles;
> and thenne lete vs fresshely sette vpon hem,
> and shrede hem doune as shepe in a felde, that Alyaunts
>   may take ensemple for euer how they lande vpon
>   oure landes.'

with the following lines of the present poem—

> Lyonelle spekys in that tyde,
> That was of warre wyse and bolde,
> 'Lordyngis, yit I rede we byde,
> And oure worthy walles holde;
> Let them pryke wyth alle ther pryde,
> Tylle they haue caught bothe hungre and colde,
> Than shalle we oute vppon them Ryde
> And shredde them downe as shepe in folde.'

There are many other coincidences of expression in the poem and Maleore.

(c) *Arthur: A Short Sketch of his Life and History*, EETS (London: Trübner, 1864), p. vi (a fragmentary English poem of the fourteenth century, based on Geoffrey).

The story he tells is an abstract, with omissions, of the earlier version of Geoffry of Monmouth, before the love of Guinevere for Lancelot was introduced by the French-writing English romancers of the Lionheart's time (so far as I know), into the Arthur Tales. The fact of Mordred's being Arthur's son, begotten by him on his sister, King Lot's wife, is also omitted; so that the story is just that of a British king founding the Round Table, conquering Scotland, Ireland, Gothland, and divers parts of France, killing a giant from Spain, beating Lucius the Emperor of Rome, and returning home to lose his own life, after the battle in which the traitor whom he had trusted, and who has seized his queen and his land, was slain.

> 'He that will more look,
> Read on the French book'

says our verse-writer: and to that the modern reader must still be referred, or to the translations of parts of it, which we hope to print or reprint, and that most pleasantly jumbled abstract of its parts by Sir Thomas Maleor, Knight, which has long been the delight of many a reader,—though despised by the stern old Ascham, whose Scholemaster was to turn it out of the land.—There the glory of the Holy Grail will be revealed to him; there the Knight of God made known; there the only true lovers in the world will tell their loves and kiss their kisses before him; and the Fates which of old enforced the penalty of sin will show that their arm is not shortened, and that though the brave and guilty king fights well and gathers all the glory of the world around him, yet still the sword is over his head, and, for the evil that he has done, his life and vain imaginings must pass away in dust and confusion.

(d) *Bishop Percy's Folio Manuscript,* I (London: Trübner, 1868), p. 414.

Sir Thomas Maleore's 'Morte Darthur,' (Caxton, 1485, Southey 1817; modernised 1634, ed. twice 1816, ed. Wright 1858, 1866), an abstract of the books of 'Merlin,' 'Balyn and Balan,' 'Lancelot,' 'Tristram,' 'Quest of the Holy Graal,' 'Percival,' 'Gawayne,' 'Morte Arthur'; an epitome, more or less complete, of the French romances, containing what is for the English student *the* history of Arthur.

(e) Robert Laneham's letter (see No. 4B), from Furnivall's introductory notes, pp. xv−xvi, identifying 'King Arthurz book'.

This is Sir Thomas Maleore's or Malory's well-known *Morte Darthur,* or abstract of the several prose French Romances of *Merlin,* ... *Les Prophecies de Merlin, Lancelot del Lac, Tristan, Queste del Saint-Graal, Morte d'Arthur,* etc. Sir T. Maleore finished his work in the 9th year of king Edward the Fourth .... and Caxton printed the first edition of it in 1485. Wynkyn de Worde reprinted Caxton's edition, with a few variations ... in 1498, and again in 1529. Then Wyllyam Copland reprinted it again in 1557, at his predecessor Robert's old shop, at the sign of the Rose Garlande in Fleet Street; and these are all the editions that we know before Laneham's date. ...

Maleore's and Tennyson's conceptions of Arthur differ widely. Our Victorian poet makes him a sinless king,—a type of Christ,—whose work is marred by the guilt of his wife and his friends. Maleore, on the other hand, makes Arthur what a Norman knight, a Keltic chieftain, would certainly have been, a gratifier of his own lust: he sins, not only with Lionors,—he begat Borres on her (ed. 1816, p. 34, bk. i. ch. 15),—but with his own half-sister Margawse, King Lot's wife, and the son of his incest works his father's death. The prophecy of Merlin on Arthur's committing his crime is fulfilled; and for his own sin the Flower of Kings withers and dies. The Fate is on him from his youth; and over all his glory hangs ever the dark cloud of unatoned-for sin.

26. Samuel Cheetham

1868

'The Arthurian Legends in Tennyson', *Contemporary Review*,
7 (April, 1868), 497–514.

Samuel Cheetham (1827–1908), later archdeacon of Rochester, was at the time of writing this article, professor of
pastoral theology at King's College, London. He was a
contributor on varied subjects to the *Quarterly Review* and to
the *Contemporary Review*; his other publications were chiefly
sermons and church history.

The title of the article suggests its intent, which is partly to
show Tennyson's art and skill in transforming the old stories.
The early part of the essay is concerned with tracing the
legend from the historical Arthur, through Geoffrey and
Wace, to Anglo-Norman, French, and German romancers.
Cheetham finds that the *Morte Darthur*'s lack of prurience and
sensuousness renders it, though indelicate at times, far less
injurious to morals than many contemporary novels. The
extract combines passages from pp. 501–3 and 513.

When Caxton set up his press in Westminster Abbey, he was (as he
tells us) pressed by 'many noble and dyvers gentylmen of this
royaume' to print an English history of King Arthur. He printed,
accordingly, a work by Sir Thomas Malory, who had compiled a
book 'oute of certeyn bookes of Frensshe, and reduced it into
Englysshe.' Of this Sir Thomas, the compiler of one of the most
famous books in the English tongue, we know no more than he
tells us himself, that he was a knight, and that he finished his work
in the ninth year of Edward IV. (1469–70). Caxton completed the
printing of it in the abbey of Westminster on the last day of July,
1485. This is the famous 'Mort d'Arthure' which was once the
favourite reading of English knights.

If forms a strange tangled thread of many colours. Round the
leading story of King Arthur are twined the principal incidents of

the various romances just mentioned, until the original foundation is almost lost. The constant features of Arthurian legend are there. King Arthur and his peerless queen, Guenevere, are always the centre of the bright throng. It is from Arthur's court that the brave knights go forth on their high emprises; it is to Arthur's court that the vanquished knights render themselves, and do homage in accordance with their plighted troth. As in all the versions of the great king's story, the treachery of Modred, himself the offspring of Arthur's sin, is the cause of the ruin of that goodly fellowship of the Table Round. In the great fight between the army of the king and the usurper, the flower of British chivalry is cut down, Modred is slain, and Arthur, wounded to death, resigns to the mystic hand that gave it the wondrous sword Excalibur. But round this simple story of King Arthur are clustered the adventures of various knights. Now we follow Sir Tristram or Sir Gawain,—now Sir Percival or Sir Galahad. They cross and recross each other's path, but there is no attempt to make all these adventures tend to one artistic *dénouement*. Each knight fights for his own hand, and we must be content to follow his devious course without caring for the time about his fellows. Of the romances which Sir Thomas Malory twined into his 'History of King Arthur,' it will be sufficient for my purpose to mention those of the 'Holy Grail,' of 'Merlin,' and of 'Sir Lancelot.'. . .

Such is the old English history of King Arthur. It reveals to us in these days, more completely than any other English book, a phase of thought which has passed away or assumed other forms. The delight in prowess, in daring, and dexterity, and feats of bodily strength, has clearly not vanished from the race. We feel at least as keen an admiration for the brave deeds which have won the Victoria Cross as our ancestors did for deeds done in mail; and I hope that in England the strong still feel the same desire to aid the weak, the same loathing for meanness and unfairness and breach of faith, which are expressed so vividly in the pages of the chivalrous romance. But along with this nobleness and manliness we find traces of the strange feeling with regard to love and wedlock which appears in the mediaeval courts of love. Sir Lancelot loves Queen Guenevere, *par amours*, yet he is the dear friend and devoted follower of the king, and towards Guenevere herself he seems to feel the same obligation to fidelity which in a healthy state of society is felt towards a wife. He is horror-stricken when he finds that he has been betrayed into unfaithfulness to her. The coarseness of the romance is but a kind of *naïveté* and absence of reserve which is common to most writings of the age. It is never prurient, while many modern novels are prurient and sensuous in a high degree without being, in terms at least, coarse or indelicate. For myself, I believe that the outspoken plainness of the old romances is far less injurious than the delicate insinuation of the modern. The religion of chivalry bears, as is natural, very strongly the stamp of the mediaeval church. There is, in the 'Mort d'Arthure,' scarcely a trace of the gentle mysticism, the yearning of the soul after direct communion with God, which we trace (for instance) in the 'Theologia Germanica.' Everything is definite and concrete. The knight in distress of mind is sure to find some hermitage or chapel where a good priest shrives and assoils him, and administers to him the sacrament, according to the due order of Holy Church: and the same concrete conception of things divine appears in the most spiritual of legends—that of the Holy Grail itself. And this mingled story of love and war, of sin and devotion, is told in sweet, clear, unaffected English,—not the affected *Saxon* English to which some aspire now-a-days, but the natural language of a well-bred Englishman of Edward IV.'s days, who wishes only to express his meaning in a direct and simple way. It bears much the same relation to the cultivated prose of our own time that the style of Herodotus does to that of Demosthenes. And this story of King Arthur and his 'goodly fellowship' delighted many generations of Englishmen. Chivalry proper had, indeed, almost passed away when it appeared; but the delight in the high thoughts and valorous deeds of chivalry remained still. Poets caught at the noble and unworldly spirit which shines through all the imperfections of the old romances. The old stories of chivalrous eld inspired Spenser with the conception of the 'Faëry Queen,' though his immediate sources were probably rather Italian than English. They were the delight of Milton when his young feet wandered 'among those lofty tales and romances which recount, in solemn cantos, the deeds of knighthood.' To pass over others who have taken up themes from the Arthurian cycle, they inspired Lord Lytton's Ariostean 'King Arthur,' and many lays and idyls of the Poet-Laureate. . . .

In the 'Morte d'Arthur' alone Mr. Tennyson has adopted the incidents, the tone, and something even of the diction of Malory's romance; but in the 'Idyls' it is far otherwise. No one who has taken the trouble to compare the old prose with the modern verse can fail to admire the skill with which the somewhat crude originals have been transformed by the brilliant word-painting of the poet. The contrast between the older and the newer form of the stories is something like that between a mediaeval illumination and a finished picture by Mr. Millais or Mr. Holman Hunt. The miniatures in an old MS. have often great beauty and expressiveness, but the bloodless figures are devoid of life, and the surroundings are purely conventional; the touch of the modern painter gives life and movement to the stiff forms. So it is in Mr. Tennyson's pictures of the Arthurian heroes. No doubt Sir Lancelot is a 'modern gentleman,' and the fair Guenevere a modern lady, thrown back into the olden time; but so are the Lancelot and Guenevere of the old romance characters of the Plantagenet era thrown back so far as to derive from distance a new charm; and we are grateful to the poet for having painted for us the old heroes with the thoughts and feelings which animate this 'wondrous mother-age.'

27. Edward Conybeare

1868

J.W. Edward Conybeare (1843–1931), in addition to an abridged and expurgated edition of the *Morte Darthur*, wrote guide books to Cambridgeshire and, later in his life, works on Alfred and on Roman Britain. Here, as an expurgator, he takes a stronger position than that of Knowles (see No. 21) on the defects of Malory's work that his edition will remedy, but he, too, guides the reader back to the unexpurgated version.

His remarks appear in *La Morte D'Arthur: The History of King Arthur Compiled by Sir Thomas Mallory*, abridged and revised by Edward Conybeare (London: Edward Moxon, 1868), pp. iii–v.

In bringing out this edition of the History of King Arthur, the object of the Editor has been to put into a more popular form one of the least appreciated works in the English language. It would be hard to name any other book which, while containing so many of the elements which render books popular—a story the interest of which never flags, characters grandly conceived and sustained throughout with wonderful skill, and a style which though now antiquated is singularly clear and forcible—has gained so little popularity. In earlier days indeed it met with the favour which it deserved, at least six editions having been published between 1470, the date of Sir Thomas Mallory's compilation, and 1634. Very shortly after this last date all such literature was suppressed as 'vain and fabulous' by the Puritans; nor were the old romances, though frequently coarse, sufficiently licentious to be popular in the years that succeeded the Restoration. Thus Mallory's work seems to have become entirely forgotten, no further reprint appearing till 1816, when two editions, equally remarkable for the gross inaccuracy of their text, were brought out simultaneously, followed in the next year by Southey's black letter edition. All these, however, speedily went out of print, and are now very scarce. Finally, in 1858 appeared by far the best edition that has yet been published, an accurate reprint of that of 1634, with notes by Mr. Wright, F.S.A. But even this has scarcely made its way beyond a few, and has by no means realised the popularity which such a book as King Arthur deserves. Indeed the work in its original form could never be a general favourite at the present day. Its great length, the confusion and want of system in the divisions, and the occasional coarseness are insuperable obstacles to popularity; and in spite of the attention which the Idylls of the King have attracted towards the Arturian romances, Mallory's book has never become generally known, and though it may be read and esteemed at its true rate by some few, remains essentially unpopular.

The object of the present Editor has been to obviate, if possible, this unpopularity. To this end he has taken liberties with the text which he fears will appear to many quite unjustifiable, and for which his only excuse is his belief that nothing less would attain his object. The coarse passages have been cut out, the book generally much abbreviated, and divided anew into Books and Chapters, not according to the plan of any previous edition, but with regard to the several stories which compose the work. In doing this, though nothing has been added, much has been unavoidably left out which the Editor would gladly have inserted, and for the omission of which he would apologise most earnestly to those who, like himself, are lovers of this noble romance in its original form. If his work leads any who do not already know King Arthur to read and appreciate the book in its integrity, his object will have been gained.

28. Edward Strachey

1868

Sir Edward Strachey (1812–1901) edited a popular Globe edition of the *Morte Darthur* for Macmillan in 1868. He collated the two Caxtons with Southey's 1817 edition to establish a text, but then expurgated it; unlike Conybeare and Knowles, however, he did not omit whole episodes. His defence of Malory's 'morality' is spirited, and his admiration of style, characterization, and epic structure is strongly stated as is his insistence that the *Morte Darthur* continues and deepens its appeal past boyhood. Strachey's is the earliest comprehensive appreciation of Malory's work, and his tone will become even more positive in the revised introduction (see No. 45) that followed Sommer's scholarly edition and assessment of Malory (No. 41).

Extracts are from the introduction (London: Macmillan, 1868), pp. vii–xviii.

1. THE ORIGIN AND MATTER OF THE BOOK.

We owe this our English Epic of Morte Arthur to Sir Thomas Malory, and to William Caxton the first English printer. Caxton's Preface shows (what indeed would have been certain from his appeal to the 'Knights of England' at the end of 'The Order of Chivalry') that however strongly he, 'William Caxton, simple person,' may have been urged to undertake the work by 'divers gentlemen of this realm of England,' he was not less moved by his own love and reverence for 'the noble acts of chivalry,' and his deep sense of his duty and responsibility in printing what he believed would be for the instruction and profit of his readers, 'of whatever estate or degree.' But to Sir Thomas Malory he gives all the honour of having provided him with the copy which he printed. I retain the more usual spelling of Sir Thomas Malory's name, though it is also written Malorye and Maleore. The last indeed is the form in the words with which he himself concludes his work; but as Caxton printed, and therefore knew, this no less than the other forms, and as even so late as the time of Marvell and Pym men of education did not keep to one way of writing their own names, we cannot infer that one is more correct than the others, though probably we may that Malory most nearly represents the pronunciation to us. Malory was an old Yorkshire name in Leland's time, and is mentioned in the next century in Burton's 'Description of Leicestershire'; but we have nothing but the name to connect Sir Thomas Malory with these families. Leland indeed, according to the 'Biographia Britannica,' says he was a Welchman.[1] From his own words we learn that he was a knight, and from his adding that he was 'a servant of Jesu both day and night,' as well as from the general tone of the book, it has been inferred that he was a priest. And he tells us that he ended his book in the ninth year of Edward the Fourth, or about fifteen years before Caxton finished printing it. It has been usual to assume that, because Caxton says that Sir Thomas Malory took his work 'out of certain books of French and reduced it into English,' he was a mere compiler and translator. But the book itself shows that he was its author—its 'maker,' as he would have called it. Notwithstanding his occasionally inartificial manner of connecting the materials drawn from the old romances— 'in Welch many, and also in French, and some in English'—there is an epic unity and harmony, and a beginning, middle, and end, which, if they have come by chance and not of design, have come by that chance which only befalls an Homeric or a Shakspeare-like man. If we compare the first part of Malory's work with the old prose romance[2] which supplied the materials for it, we see at once how he has converted that prose into poetry, giving life and beauty to the coarse clods of earth, and transmuting by his art the legends which he yet faithfully preserves. For the long and repulsive narrative of Merlin's origin he substitutes a slight allusion to it; without disguising what he probably believed to be at least an half historical

record of Arthur's birth, he gives a grace and dignity to the story
by the charms of his mother's character, the finer touches of which
are wanting in the original: and so through the whole of this part of
the story. The plan of the book is properly epic. While the glory of
Arthur as the head of the kingdoms no less than of the chivalry of
Christendom is only in its early dawn, Merlin warns him that the
seeds of death will spring up in all this fair promise through the sin
of himself and of his queen. Still the fame and the honour of the
king and his knights of the Round Table open continually into new
and brighter forms, which seem above the reach of any adverse fate,
till the coming of the Sancgreal, into the quest of which all the
knights enter with that self-reliance which had become them so
well in the field of worldly chivalry, but which would be of no avail
now. They are now to be tried by other tests than those by which
they had been proved as 'earthly knights and lovers,' tests which
even Launcelot, Ector de Maris, Gawaine, and the other chiefest of
the fellowship could not stand. The quest is achieved by the holy
knights alone: two depart from this life to a higher, while Sir Bors,
not quite spotless, yet forgiven and sanctified, the link between the
earthly and the spiritual worlds, returns to aid in restoring the glory
of the feasts and tournaments at Camelot and Westminster. But the
curse is at work: the severance between good and evil which had
been declared through the Sancgreal cannot be closed again; and the
tragic end comes on, in spite of the efforts—touching from their
very weakness—of Arthur and Launcelot to avert the woe, the one
by vainly trying to resist temptation, the other by refusing to
believe evil of his dearest friend. The black clouds open for a
moment as the sun goes down; and we see Arthur in the barge
which bears him to the Holy Isle; Guenever, the nun of Almesbury,
living in fasting, prayers, and alms-deeds; and Launcelot with his
fellowship, once knights but now hermit-priests, 'doing bodily all
manner of service.'

Nor are the marks of harmony and unity less plain in the several
characters than in the events of the story. Arthur is a true knight,
sharing the characteristics of his nobler knights, yet he differs from
them all in showing also that he is, and feels himself to be, a king; as
when—with an imperiousness which reminds us of Froissart's
story of Edward III refusing to listen to Sir Walter Manny's
remonstrances on behalf of the burgesses of Calais—he tells Sir
Launcelot that he 'takes no force whom he grieves,' or insists on his

entering the lists against a tired knight whom he is not willing to see victorious over the whole field; or as when he sadly regrets that he cannot do battle for his wife, though he believes her innocent, but must be a rightful judge according to the laws. There are many others of the Round Table who are 'very perfect gentle knights,' yet we feel that Launcelot stands distinct among them all in the pre-eminence of his knightliness, notwithstanding his one great sin. Thus, to take one of many instances, who but Launcelot would have borne the taunts and the violence of Gawaine with his humble patience and ever-renewed efforts for a reconciliation, when he was leaving the realm, and when he was besieged in Joyous Gard. Modern critics of great name agree in censuring Sir Thomas Malory for departing from the old authorities who represented Gawaine as the very counterpart of Launcelot in knightly character: but I rather see a proof of Malory's art in giving us a new Gawaine with a strongly individual character of his own. Gawaine's regard for his mother's honour, his passion for Ettard, and his affection for his brothers, are savage impulses driving him to unknightly and unworthy deeds, yet he is far from being represented as a mere villain. If Malory depicts him thirsting to revenge upon Launcelot the unintentional killing of Gaheris and Gareth, he depicts also his long previous affection for Launcelot and his opposition to the hostility of his other brother, Mordred, against him; his devotion to his uncle Arthur; his hearty repentance towards Launcelot at the last; and his entreaty that he would 'see his tomb, and pray some prayer more or less for his soul.' Nor must we forget that it was by the prayer of those ladies for whom Gawaine had 'done battle in a rightwise quarrel,' that his ghost was permitted to give Arthur a last warning. Distinct again from the character of this fierce knight is that of the Saracen Palamides, whose unquestionable courage and skill in deeds of chivalry also want—though in another way than Gawaine's—the gentleness, the meekness, and the delicate sense of honour of the Christian knight. Sir Dinadan again, who can give and take hard knocks if need be, though he has no great bodily strength, and who is always bantering the good knights who know and esteem him with his humorous protests against love and arms, is a distinctly drawn character. So is Merlin; so are many others whose names I might recite. The dignity of queen Guenever towards her husband and her court is not less marked than her guilty passion for Launcelot, and the unreasoning jealously it excites in her. The wife-like simplicity of Igraine, the self-surrender beyond all limit, though from different impulses, of the two Elaines, the pertness of the damsel Linet, and the piety and self-sacrifice of Sir Percivale's sister, will occur to the reader among the distinctive characteristics of the different ladies and damsels who live and move, each in her own proper form, in the story. Sir Thomas Malory, as we know, found many of these men and women already existing in the old romances as he represents them to us; but we may believe that those earlier books were to him something of what the pages of Plutarch and Holinshed were to Shakspeare.

In the Introduction to Southey's edition of Morte Arthur the student will find an account of the principal early prose romances in which sources of Sir Thomas Malory's book have been found, and the English translation of one of these has been mentioned above; while the volumes of Ellis, Sir Walter Scott's 'Sir Tristrem,' and the publications of the Early English Text and the Camden Societies, and of Mr. Furnivall, supply specimens of the metrical romances of the like kind. But as they are only attractive to the antiquarian student, who requires the originals and not abstracts, I shall say no more of them here.

Nor shall I attempt to illustrate Malory's book by the ancient historical or legendary accounts of the British King Arthur. The most recent critics are disposed to prefer Gibbon's belief to Milton's scepticism as to the actual existence of Arthur: but of the history and the geography of the book before us we can only say that they are something.

> Apart from place, withholding time,
> But flattering the golden prime

of the great hero of English romance. We cannot bring within any limits of history the events which here succeed each other.

[Strachey summarizes events of Arthur's career, remarks on Malory's geography ('The geography of Arthur's Roman war is very coherent; but that of the rest of the book it is often impossible to harmonise'), and discusses various place names including Camelot, which he places at Cadbury Castle.]

Lastly, the perplexed question of the morality of the book

demands our notice. If it does not deserve the unqualified denunciation of the learned Ascham, it cannot be denied that Morte Arthur exhibits a picture of a society far lower than our own in morals, and depicts it with far less repugnance to its evil elements, on the part either of the author or his personages, than any good man would now feel. Still—with the exception of stories like those of the birth of Arthur and Galahad, which show not only another state of manners from our own; but also a really different standard of morals from any which we should now hold up—the writer does for the most part endeavour, though often in but an imperfect and confused manner, to distinguish between vice and virtue, and honestly to reprobate the former; and thus shows that his object is to recognise and support the nobler elements of the social state in which he lived, and to carry them towards new triumphs over the evil. And even where, as in the story of Tristram, there is palliation rather than reprobation of what Sir Walter Scott justly calls 'the extreme ingratitude and profligacy of the hero,' still the fact that such palliation, by representing King Mark as the most worthless of men, was thought necessary in the later, though not in the earlier, romance on the same subject, shows an upward progress in morals; while a real effort to distinguish virtue from vice is to be seen in the story of Launcelot, with his sincere though weak struggles against temptation, and his final penitence under the punishment of the woes which his guilt has brought on all dear to him as well as to himself. Or if we look at the picture which Chaucer's works give us of the co-existence in one mind—and that perhaps the noblest of its age—of the most virtuous Christian refinement and the most brutish animal coarseness, and then see how in the pages of Malory, inferior as we must hold him to be to Chaucer, the brutish vice has dwindled to half its former size, and is far more clearly seen to be vice, while the virtue, if not more elevated in itself, is more avowedly triumphant over the evil, we find the same upward progress. And I cannot doubt that it was helped on by this book, and that notwithstanding Ascham's condemnation of Morte Arthur, Caxton was right in believing that he was serving God and his countrymen by printing it; and that he justly estimated its probable effect when he says, 'Herein may be seen noble chivalry, courtesy, humanity, friendliness, hardiness, love, friendship, cowardice, murder, hate, virtue, sin. Do after the good, and leave the evil, and it shall bring you to good fame and

renommée.... All is written for our doctrine, and for to beware
that we fall not to vice nor sin, but to exercise and follow virtue,
by which we may come and attain to good fame and renomme in
this life, and after this short and transitory life to come unto
everlasting bliss in heaven; the which He grant us that reigneth in
heaven, the blessed Trinity. Amen.'

2. THE TEXT, AND ITS SEVERAL EDITIONS.

The first edition of Le Morte Darthur was printed by Caxton at
Westminster in 1485, as he tells us in the colophon. Two copies
only are known: they are folio, black-letter, with wide margin, and
among the finest specimens of Caxton's printing. One is in the
library of the Earl of Jersey at Osterley; and the other in that of Earl
Spencer at Althorp. The Osterley copy... is perfect, except that it
has no title-page, though, as the Proheme or Preface begins at the
top of the recto of signature ij (not 'a ij' as Dibdin says), I infer that a
title did exist on the leaf j, thus shown to be wanting. The Althorp
copy... had eleven leaves deficient; but these were supplied by Mr.
Whittaker in fac-simile from the Osterley copy with remarkable
skill,[3] though on collation with the original I have found some
oversights.

The two next editions of Morte Arthur were printed by Wynkyn
de Worde, the chief workman and successor of Caxton, in 1498 and
1529. Only one copy of each is known. That of 1498 is in the
Althorp Library: it wants the Title and part of the Table of
Contents, but contains the Preface, which is a reprint of that of
Caxton, though it here follows instead of preceding the Table of
Contents. This edition, which has numerous woodcuts, is not an
exact reprint of Caxton's; there are differences of spelling and
occasionally of a word; and the passage in the last chapter but one,
beginning 'Oh ye mighty and pompous lords,' and ending with
'turn again to my matter,' which is not in Caxton's edition, appears
here, as in all later editions.[4] The edition of 1529 is in the British
Museum, and wants the Title, Preface, and part of the Table of
Contents.

In 1557 the book was reprinted by William Copland, with the
title of 'The story of the most noble and worthy kynge Arthur, the
whiche was one of the worthyes chrysten, and also of his noble and
valiaute knyghtes of the rounde Table. Newly imprynted and

corrected mccccclvij. Imprynted at London by Wyllyam Copland.' And on the title-page, above the last line, is a woodcut of St. George and the Dragon, of which that on the title-page of Southey's edition is a bad copy. A copy of this edition is in the British Museum, with a note that this is the only one with a title which the annotator has seen.

There is a folio edition by Thomas East, without date, in the British Museum; and there is said to be a quarto edition, also without date.

The next, and last black-letter, edition is that of 1634, which has been reprinted by Mr. Wright, and which contains the woodcut of the Round Table with Arthur in the middle and his knights around, a copy of which is familiar to many of us in one of the small editions of 1816. From the fact of an omission in this edition which exactly corresponds with a complete leaf in East's folio, Mr. Wright concludes that the one was printed from the other. Each succeeding edition departs more than the previous one from the original of Caxton; but if we compare this of 1634 with Caxton's, we find the variations almost infinite. Besides remodelling the preface, dividing the book into three parts, and modernising the spelling and many of the words, there are a number of more or less considerable variations and additions, of which Mr. Wright has given some of the more important in his notes, but which I estimate at above twenty thousand in the whole; and which have plainly arisen in the minor instances from the printer reading a sentence and then printing it from recollection, without farther reference to his 'copy,' but in the others from a desire to improve the original simplicity by what the editor calls 'a more eloquent and ornated style and phrase'.

No new edition seems to have been published till 1816, when two independent editions appeared, one in two, and the other in three 24mo. volumes. Both are modernised for popular use, and are probably the volumes through which most of us made our first acquaintance with King Arthur and his knights; but neither has any merit as to its editing.

In 1817 Messrs. Longmans & Co. published an edition in two volumes quarto, with an introduction and notes by Southey, who says, 'The present edition is a reprint with scrupulous exactness from the first edition by Caxton, in Earl Spencer's library.' As it appears from a note that he had nothing to do with the superintendence of the press, which was undertaken by Mr. Upcott, he was probably unaware that eleven leaves were, as I have mentioned above, then wanting in the copy from which this reprint was made. These had not then been restored in fac-simile; for Earl Spencer's copy contains a note, signed by Messrs. Longmans and dated 1816, which gives a list of the pages then wanting; and, in fact, the substitutes for them which actually appear in Southey's edition differ widely from the restored, or the original, text. Thus in chapter xii of the last book, besides the interpolation of the long passage 'O ye myghty and pompous lordes,' &c., which is not in Caxton, there are in the first eleven lines thirty-five variations of spelling and punctuation, besides the introduction of the words 'but continually mourned un—' and 'needfully as nature required,' which are not in Caxton, and the change of Caxton's 'on the tombe of kyng Arthur & quene Guenever' into 'on kynge Arthur's & quene Gwenever's tombe.' And thus throughout the pages in question—seventeen in number—the spelling constantly, and words and even sentences occasionally, differ from the real text of Caxton.[5]

When at page 113 of volume i. the editor introduces the words 'certayne cause' to complete the sense, he is careful to call attention, in a foot-note, to the fact that these words are not in the original, but taken from 'the second edition,' by which I presume he means that of 1498. But when he subsequently supplies seventeen pages which were also not in his original, he gives no hint of the fact; and his reticence has been so successful that for fifty years the interpolations have passed as genuine among learned critics, who have quoted from them passages wholly spurious as Caxton's genuine text. It was only last year that, in collating Earl Spencer's copy with the edition of Southey, I discovered that these passages—to which my attention was directed by Messrs. Longmans' note above mentioned—did not correspond with Caxton's text, as represented by Whittaker's restorations: and on afterwards collating them with the Osterley text itself I found the like result.... That the interpolated passages are not taken from the Osterley Caxton itself, even in the roughest and most careless manner, is quite evident.

Lastly, in 1858 Mr. Wright published an edition reprinted from that of 1634, with an introduction and notes of considerable interest.

The Early English Text Society promise us a reprint of the original Caxton which shall be free from the faults of that of Southey, which meanwhile is, except in the interpolated passages, a very faithful representation of that original for the purposes of the antiquarian and philologist; and whatever like interest there may be in the edition of 1634 is available in the reprint of Mr. Wright. But neither is readable with pleasure by any but the student, and the two modernised editions are out of print. What is wanted, therefore, is an edition for ordinary readers, and especially for boys, from whom the chief demand for this book will always come; and such an edition the present professes to be. It is a reprint of the original Caxton with the spelling modernised, and those few words which are unintelligibly obsolete replaced by others which, though not necessarily unknown to Caxton, are still in use, yet with all old forms retained which do not interfere with this requirement of being readable. For, when, as indeed is oftenest the case, the context makes even an obsolete phrase probably, if not precisely, known, I have left it in the text, and given its meaning in the Glossary, in which I have chiefly followed Roquefort, Halliwell, and Wright. In the Glossary I have also added a few geographical notes for those readers who may care for them. And for the like reason—of making the book readable—such phrases or passages as are not in accordance with modern manners have been also omitted or replaced by others which either actually occur or might have occurred in Caxton's text elsewhere. I say manners, not morals, because I do not profess to have remedied the moral defects of the book which I have already spoken of. Mr. Tennyson has shown us how we may deal best with this matter for modern uses, in so far as Sir Thomas Malory has himself failed to treat it rightly; and I do not believe that when we have excluded what is offensive to modern manners there will be found anything practically injurious to the morals of English boys, for whom I have chiefly undertaken this work, while there is much of moral worth which I know not where they can learn so well as from the ideals of magnanimity, courage, courtesy, reverence for women, gentleness, self-sacrifice, chastity, and other manly virtues, exhibited in these pages.

The omissions, not many, were essential to the publication of the book at all for popular reading; but if any one blames the other departures from the exact form of the original, I would ask him to judge from the specimens of the old type and spelling which I have given at the end of each book, and of the volume, whether a literal and verbal reproduction of the whole would not be simply unreadable except by students of old English. And if some departure from the original was necessary, it was reasonable to carry it so far as, though no farther than, my purpose required. And, subject to these conditions, the present volume is in fact a more accurate reproduction of Caxton's text than any other except that of Southey. I have, indeed, made use of Southey's text for this edition, having satisfied myself by collation with the Althorp and Osterley Caxtons that it is an accurate reprint excepting as to the passages above mentioned; and these have been taken by me, in like manner, from the only existing original.

There is no title-page, as I have already mentioned, to the Osterley or the Althorp Caxton, that which is given by several bibliographers being only an extract, not very critically selected, from Caxton's preface. But it is evident from Caxton's colophon that the real title or name of the book was LE MORTE DARTHUR, and he explains that it was so 'entitled' notwithstanding it treated of Arthur's birth, life, and acts as well as death, and also of the adventures of his knights of the Round Table. And the concluding words of Malory, 'Here is the end of the death of Arthur,' taken with their context, point to the same title. It was indeed before Malory's time, and has been ever since, the traditional title of this story. We have Mort Artus and Morte Arthure in the earlier times; Ascham, in Henry VIII's reign, calls this book La Morte d'Arthure; Tyrwhitt, Mort d'Arthur; and Walter Scott and Southey, Morte Arthur, which last probably many of us are familiar with as the old name which we heard from our own fathers.

SELECTED NOTES

1 Biographia Britannica, art. 'Caxton;' but no reference is given by which to verify the quotation. [See No. 6 above.]
2 Merlin, or the Early History of King Arthur, edited by Henry B. Wheatley, for the Early English Text Society, 1865–8. This is a translation, contemporary with Malory's work, from the French which he doubtless used.
3 Dibdin's Supplement to the Bibliotheca Spenceriana, vol. ii., p. 213; or Aedes Althorpianae, vol. vi., p. 213. I would here express my thanks to

Earl Spencer for sending to the British Museum for my use his Caxton, and his unique copy of Wynkyn de Worde's first edition of Morte Arthur, as also for favouring me with details of information respecting the former; and to the Earl of Jersey for permitting me to examine his Caxton at Osterley.

4 As the passage is worth preserving I have given it at the end of the volume, Note A, p. 488. [See No. 2.]

5 An account of these interpolations was given by me in the Athenaeum of Sept. 7 and Dec. 10, 1867, and Feb. 10, 1868.

29. William Blake Odgers

1871

Odgers (1849–1924) later had a distinguished career as an authority on the law ('Odgers on Common Law', 'Odgers on Libel and Slander', etc.) but in 1871, as a young man, he read a paper for the Bath Literary and Philosophical Association; the paper, published the following year under the title *King Arthur and the Arthurian Romances*, provides a good survey of generally current laymen's views on Arthurian history and romance. In comparing Malory and Tennyson, Odgers is complimentary to both, but seems to prefer Malory. (London: Longmans, 1872), pp. 56–61

... Thus was printed that famous 'Book of King Arthur and of his noble Knights of the Round Table' which inspired the chivalry of Sir Philip Sidney, and which has been the food of our poets for many generations. To it we owe the recent edition of the Arthurian Romances by the Poet Laureate. It is interesting to see how alike are Tennyson's version and Malory's, and yet how different. Often Tennyson borrows Malory's actual phrase. Thus, Malory says, speaking of Sir Lavaine, Elaine's brother, 'and his fellow did right well and worshipfully.' Tennyson's line is—

Then Sir Lavaine did well and worshipfully.

The last sentence in Elaine's letter is in Malory, 'Pray for my soul, Sir Launcelot, as thou art peerless.' In Tennyson—

> 'Pray for my soul, thou too, Sir Lancelot,
> As thou art knight peerless.'

And Arthur says to Launcelot—'It will be to your worship that ye oversee that she be interred worshipfully,' which is in the Idyll—

> 'It will be to your worship, as my knight,
> And mine, as head of all our Table Round,
> To see that she be buried worshipfully.'

Thus, in parts, they are very much alike; but on the whole they are very different. If you will pardon me while I read rather a longer extract, you will see this at once. This is Malory's account of the passing of Arthur:—

[Quotes from arrival of barge down to 'that it was pity to hear.']

This is the corresponding passage in the Morte d'Arthur:

[Quotes Tennyson, 41 lines.]

I have given the first part in full, in the second I have pared away all the flesh and blood which Tennyson has placed on the skeleton which Malory had furnished him. The speeches of Arthur and Bedivere, in Tennyson, are more beautiful and artistic; in Malory, more natural and simple. It is scarcely probable that a dying king who is fast being rowed away from the shore, would stay to discourse on the efficacy of prayer, and the development of God's order in the world. And in the narrative portion, Malory is more straightforward, that is, more truly epic; Tennyson has enriched the bare statement of facts, with beautiful pictures and exquisite metaphors. Still the comparison of the ladies' lamentation to a cry in a land where no man hath come scarcely illustrates or explains his meaning, though it impresses on us a sense of weirdness. And that last most beautiful comparison of Arthur as he was then to Arthur in the pride of his manhood and glory is, strictly speaking, dramatic and not epic; for it supposes an ideal spectator capable of contrasting the two.

The difference between Malory and Tennyson is pretty much the difference between Homer and Virgil. Malory has all Homer's freshness and simplicity; Tennyson has Virgil's finish and exquisite grace. I think I do no wrong to the Father of Epic Poetry if I call Malory the English Homer; for the 'Iliad' and the 'Morte d'Arthur' have many points in common. But you must remember in reading Malory's book that it is a picture not of the time when the historic Arthur lived, but of the days of the Plantagenets. It interprets to us the vices and the virtues, the coarseness and the refinement, the sad superstition and the glorious religious earnestness of the Middle Ages.... Sir Lancelot, the first of all the knights of the table round; 'the truest lover, of a sinful man, that ever loved woman; the kindest man that ever strake with sword; the goodliest person ever came among press of knights; the meekest man and the gentlest that ever ate in hall among ladies; the sternest knight to his mortal foe that ever put spear in the rest.' And towering above all his knights stands out the majestic figure of King Arthur. He is 'a very perfect, gentle knight,' but, moreover, he is something higher than a knight; he is a king as well; a king with a will of his own which must be obeyed; with a 'power in his eye that bowed the will' of all his subjects. In the Idylls, Arthur is a somewhat shadowy aggregate of all kingly virtues; he is Tennyson's 'own ideal knight'; and we can sympathise with Guinevere when she cries—

> 'I could not breathe in that fine air
> That pure severity of perfect light.'

But in Malory he is not a 'blameless king;' he is flesh and blood like the rest of us; not an ideal of the sinless man. In his youth he had sinned, and bitterly does he reap the consequences of that sin. There is a poetic justice in the sad catastrophe which overtakes him in the end, for in this book Modred is his own illegitimate son.

Such, then, is the work which I have called the English Iliad that history by Sir Thomas Malory, which Wm. Caxton 'after the simple conning that God had sent to him under the favour and correction of all noble lords and gentlemen, enprised to imprint....'

30. A. C. Swinburne and R. H. Hutton

1872, 1886, 1888

Algernon Charles Swinburne (1837–1909), like other critics
and reviewers, included remarks on Malory in his criticism of
Tennyson's *Idylls of the King*. Tennyson's conception of a
'blameless king', he believes, vitiates the force of Malory's
version, a version that Swinburne, like Morris, Rossetti, and
Burne-Jones, drew upon for artistic inspiration.

The first selection is from *Under the Microscope* (London: D.
White, 1872), pp. 35–42. Swinburne's remarks on the *Idylls*
constitute a longish digression here considerably abridged.
The second is from an essay, 'Tennyson and Musset',
published in *Miscellanies* in 1886 (London: Chatto & Windus,
1911), pp. 248–51. The third selection is the response of the
critic Richard Holt Hutton (1826–97) to Swinburne's
criticism of Tennyson's Arthur. His essay first appeared in
Macmillan's Magazine in 1872; the extract here is from
Hutton's *Literary Essays* (London: Macmillan, 1888),
pp. 400–7.

The lines in Greek in (a) are the concluding lines of Aeschylus'
The Libation Bearers: 'Oh when will it work its accomplishment, when will the fury of calamity, lulled to rest, find an
end and cease?' —H. W. Smyth, *Loeb Classical Library* (1926).

(a) *Under the Microscope*
... the enemies of Tennyson ... are the men who find in his
collection of Arthurian idyls,—the Morte d'Albert as it might
perhaps be more properly called, after the princely type to which
(as he tells us with just pride) the poet has been fortunate enough
to make his central figure so successfully conform,—an epic poem
of profound and exalted morality. Upon this moral question I shall
take leave to intercalate a few words. ... It seems to me that the
moral tone of the Arthurian story has been on the whole lowered
and degraded by Mr. Tennyson's mode of treatment. Wishing to

make his central figure the noble and perfect symbol of an ideal man, he has removed not merely the excuse but the explanation of the fatal and tragic loves of Launcelot and Guenevere. The hinge of the whole legend of the Round Table, from its first glory to its final fall, is the incestuous birth of Mordred from the connexion of Arthur with his half-sister, unknowing and unknown; as surely as the hinge of the *Oresteia* from first to last is the sacrifice at Aulis. From the immolation of Iphigenia springs the wrath of Clytaemnestra, with all its train of evils ensuing; from the sin of Arthur's youth proceeds the ruin of his reign and realm through the falsehood of his wife, a wife unloving and unloved. Remove in either case the plea which leaves the heroine less sinned against indeed than sinning, but yet not too base for tragic compassion and interest, and there remains merely the presentation of a vulgar adulteress. ... Mr. Tennyson has lowered the note and deformed the outline of the Arthurian story, by reducing Arthur to the level of a wittol, Guenevere to the level of a woman of intrigue, and Launcelot to the level of a 'co-respondent'. Treated as he has treated it, the story is rather a case for the divorce-court than for poetry. ...

... In the old story, the king, with the doom denounced in the beginning by Merlin hanging over all his toils and triumphs as a tragic shadow, stands apart in no undignified patience to await the end in its own good time of all his work and glory, with no eye for the pain and passion of the woman who sits beside him as queen rather than as wife. Such a figure is not unfit for the centre of a tragic action; it is neither ignoble nor inconceivable; but the besotted blindness of Mr. Tennyson's 'blameless king' to the treason of a woman who has had the first and last of his love and the whole devotion of his blameless life is nothing more or less than pitiful and ridiculous. ... such a man as this king is indeed hardly 'man at all'; either fool or coward he must surely be. Thus it is that by the very excision of what may have seemed in his eyes a moral blemish Mr. Tennyson has blemished the whole story; by the very exaltation of his hero as something more than man he has left him in the end something less. The keystone of the whole building is removed, and in place of a tragic house of song where even sin had all the dignity and beauty that sin can retain, and without which it can afford no fit material for tragedy, we find an incongruous edifice of tradition and invention where even virtue is made to seem either imbecile or vile. The story as it stood of old had in it something almost of Hellenic dignity and significance; in it as in the great Greek legends we could trace from a seemingly small root of evil the birth and growth of a calamitous fate, not sent by mere malevolence of heaven, yet in its awful weight and mystery of darkness apparently out of all due retributive proportion to the careless sin or folly of presumptuous weakness which first incurred its infliction; so that by mere hasty resistance and return of violence for violence a noble man may unwittingly bring on himself and all his house the curse denounced on parricide, by mere casual indulgence of light love and passing wantonness a hero king may unknowingly bring on himself and all his kingdom the doom imposed on incest. This presence and imminence of Ate inevitable as invisible throughout the tragic course of action can alone confer on such a story the proper significance and the necessary dignity; without it the action would want meaning and the passion would want nobility; with it, we may hear in the high funereal homily which concludes as with dirge-music the great old book of Sir Thomas Mallory some echo not utterly unworthy of that supreme lament of wondering and wailing spirits—

ποῖ δῆτα κρανεῖ, ποῖ καταλήξει
μετακοιμισθὲν μένος ἄτης;

The fatal consequence or corollary of this original flaw in his scheme is that the modern poet has been obliged to degrade all the other figures of the legend in order to bring them into due harmony with the degraded figures of Arthur and Guenevere. The courteous and loyal Gawain of the old romancers, already deformed and maligned in the version of Mallory himself, is here a vulgar traitor; the benignant Lady of the Lake, foster-mother of Launcelot, redeemer and comforter of Pelleas, becomes the very vilest figure in all that cycle of more or less symbolic agents and patients which Mr. Tennyson has set revolving round the figure of his central wittol. . . .

(b) 'Tennyson and Musset'
. . . Lord Tennyson has missed few opportunities of denouncing [gossip] with emphatic if not virulent iteration. But the lesson of abstinence from promiscuous tattle can hardly be considered by itself as 'the law and the gospel.' And whatever else there is of

sound doctrine in Lord Tennyson's *Idylls* was preached more simply and not less earnestly in the grand old compilation of Sir Thomas Mallory. But, says the Laureate, it is not Mallory's King Arthur, nor yet Geoffrey's King Arthur, that I have desired to reproduce: on the contrary, it is 'scarce other than' Prince Albert. And in that case, of course, there is no more room for discussion. All I can say is that most assuredly I never heard 'these Idylls' attacked on any moral ground but this: that the tone of divine or human doctrine preached and of womanly or manly character exalted in them, directly or indirectly, was poor, mean, paltry, petty, almost base; so utterly insufficent as to be little short of ignoble: that it is anything but a sign of moral elevation to be so constantly preoccupied by speculations on possible contact with 'smut' and contamination from 'swine'. . . . [In the earlier version of Tennyson's 'Morte d'Arthur'] the great dying king had been made to say, in words which 'give a very echo to the seat' where conscience is enthroned,

> I have lived my life, and that which I have done
> May He within himself make pure!

If this be taken as the last natural expression of a gallant, honest, kindly, faulty creature like the hero of old Mallory, it strikes home at once to a man's heart. If it be taken as the last deliberate snuffle of 'the blameless king,' it strikes us in a different fashion. We feel that even at Almesbury, when denouncing the fallen Guinevere in such magnificent language that the reader is content and indeed thankful to take the manliness and propriety of such an address for granted, this blameless being had not attained to the very perfection of pretence—a flight beyond his preceding pretence of perfection.

The real and radical flaw in the splendid structure of the *Idylls* is not to be found either in the antiquity of the fabulous groundwork or in the modern touches which certainly were not needed, and if needed would not have been adequate, to redeem any worthy recast of so noble an original from the charge of nothingness. The fallacy which obtrudes itself throughout, the false note which incessantly jars on the mind's ear, results from the incongruity of materials which are radically incapable of combination or coherence. Between the various Arthurs of different national legends there is little more in common than the name. It is essentially impossible to construct a human figure by the process of selection

from the incompatible types of irreconcilable ideals. . . . the result is
to impress upon us a complete and irreversible conviction of its
absolute hopelessness. Had a poet determined to realize the Hora-
tian ideal of artistic monstrosity, he could hardly have set about it
more ingeniously than by copying one feature from the Mabinogion and the next from the Morte d'Arthur. So far from giving us
'Geoffrey's' type or 'Mallory's' type, he can hardly be said to have
given us a recognizable likeness of Prince Albert; who, if neither a
wholly gigantic nor altogether a divine personage, was at least, one
would imagine, a human figure. But the spectre of his laureate's
own ideal knight, neither Welsh nor French, but a compound of
'Guallia and Gaul, soul-curer and body curer,' sir priest and sir
knight, Mallory and Geoffrey, old style and middle style and new
style, makes the reader bethink himself what might or might not be
the result if some poet of similar aim and aspiration were to handle
the tale of Troy, for instance, as Lord Tennyson has handled the
Arthurian romance. The half godlike Achilles of Homer is one in
name and nothing else with the all brutish Achilles of Shakespeare;
the romantic Arthur of the various volumes condensed by Mallory
into his English compilation—incoherent itself and incongruous in
its earlier parts, but so nobly consistent, so profoundly harmonious
in its close—has hardly more in common with the half impalpable
hero of British myth or tradition. . . .

(c) R.H. Hutton
In taking his subject from the great mediaeval myth of English
chivalry, it was of course open to Tennyson to adopt any treatment
of it which would really incorporate the higher and grander aspects
of the theme, and also find an ideal unity for a number of legends in
which of unity there was none. It is obvious that in dealing with the
chivalric story with which strange and grand fragments of
mediaeval Christian mysticism are closely interwoven, it was
impossible to avoid the blending of the distinct themes of ideal
courage and honour, ideal love and purity, and the rapt visions of
an ideal faith. This could not have been avoided. But undoubtedly
these various elements might have blended in various ways; and it
would have been possible, no doubt, to make the central figure of
the poem one in which the highest ideal aims were crossed by the
tragic consequences of a youthful sin, so that everywhere his own
sin rose up against him till it brought to ruin the fair dream of his

life. This is the view of the story of Arthur which Mr. Swinburne and his school maintain to be the only natural and legitimate one. And there is no doubt that the treachery which finally undermines and ruins Arthur's work is the treachery of Modred, nor that, according to the story of the old legend, Modred is Arthur's own son, the offspring of Arthur's guilty passion for one whom he did not then know to be his half-sister Bellicent. According to the old story, Merlin prophesied to him the evil destiny in store for him as the penalty of this sin, and also forbade him to take part in the search for the Holy Grail, as being rendered unworthy of it by that sin. Nor can it be denied that there are various other traces in the early part of these legends of the moral taint which Arthur's nature had thus incurred. For instance, the sword brought by the lady of the isle of Avelyon cannot be drawn by Arthur, because it can only be drawn by a knight in whom there is no hidden shame.

For the rest, the picture of Arthur as given in the old legends is exceedingly wavering and uncertain. For the most part it is the picture of a gracious and noble figure of mysterious origin and mysterious destiny, — 'Rex quondam, Rexque futurus,' according to the legendary inscription on his tomb, — whose nobility inspires a passion of love and fidelity in his knights, and the profoundest agony of remorse in his unfaithful queen; but also at times crafty, and at times weak, trying in the beginning of his reign, like Herod, to exterminate the infants amongst whom Merlin's lore pronounces that the cause of his own ruin and death is to be found; and yielding at the end of his reign, against his own better mind, to the bloody and vindictive counsels of his nephew Gawain in the war with Lancelot. I will venture to say that if only those legends collected by Sir Thomas Malory were to be taken as authorities (and though I do not profess a knowledge of the various other collections, it is quite clear that many of them are far more favourable to the ideal view of Arthur than Sir Thomas Malory's), and if everything they say of Arthur were put together, no coherent character at all could be constructed out of them. It would have been impossible to draw any poetical portrait of the king without the freest principle of selection. Had Tennyson taken the view which Mr. Swinburne affirms, — with a pert dogmatism quite unworthy of the exquisite English in which he writes, and the frequent flashes of genius in the substance of what he writes, — to be the only possible one; had the story of Arthur been turned into that of a kind of mediaeval Oedipus, and the awful destiny which avenged his voluntary sin but involuntary incest, that of death by the hand of his own son, been made the subject of it,—there would have been no room at all for the spiritual halo which the mysterious stories of Arthur's birth and of his return from the island of his rest shed round the subject. No Greek tragedian would have dreamt of investing Oedipus with such a halo as that. This view of the story is a tragic one in the true old sense of a story purifying the heart by pity and by fear. The subject of so dread and dark a destiny may be enabled to answer Sphinx-riddles as a step to his own doom, but he cannot be one whose coming is preceded by heavenly portents, and whose passing takes place amidst the wailing of unearthly mourners, the bitter grief and remorse of faithless companions, and the mystic presage of a glorious return. It seems to me perfectly evident that Tennyson, as every true poet—Mr. Swinburne himself, for example—had to choose between the various inconsistent elements in the Arthurian legends, which of them he would keep and which he would eliminate, that it would have been simply impossible to keep the element of shame and retribution along with the element of mystic spiritual glory, and that the last is far the most characteristic and the most in keeping with the Christian mysticism of the San Grail legends, of the two. Let any one read either Sir Thomas Malory's book, or the brief, graceful, and classical compilation of the Legends of King Arthur by J.T.K., and then judge for himself whether the sin of King Arthur or his unearthly glory be the more deeply ingrained element of the two, and I suspect he will end by accepting as the overruling idea, and also as by far the better adapted for coherent treatment, the verdict of the old chroniclers, of Joseph of Exeter, for example: 'The old world knows not his peer, nor will the future show us his equal; he alone towers over all other kings, better than the past ones, and greater than those that are to be'; and again another old compiler: 'In short, God has not made, since Adam was, the man more perfect than King Arthur.' It is perfectly evident that this tradition of unrivalled spiritual glory was a development of elements of the story quite inconsistent with that of his great sin and shame.

Mr. Swinburne asserts, however, that Guinevere's sin is closely implicated with Arthur's: 'From the sin of Arthur's youth proceeds the ruin of his reign and realm through the falsehood of his wife—a wife unloving and unloved.' I believe this is not only without basis in the story as told by Sir Thomas Malory, but wholly inconsistent with it. So far is Guinevere from being 'unloved,' that when Merlin asks Arthur, 'Is there any faire lady that yee love better than another?' he answers, 'Yea, I love Guinevere the King's daughter, Leodegrance of the land of Camelyard, which Leodegrance holdeth in his power the Table Round that yee told hee had of my father Uther. And this demosell is the most gentilest and fairest lady that I know living, or yet that I ever could find.' 'Sir,' said Merlin, 'as of her beautie and fairenesse, she is one of the fairest that live; *but an yee loved her not so well as yee doe, I would finde yee a demosell of beautie and of goodnesse that should like yee and please yee, and your heart were not set. But there as a man's heart is set, he will be loth to return.*' 'That is truth,' said Arthur;—and here not only is Arthur's passion for his queen represented as beyond resistance, but Merlin treats the want of love of Guinevere as the root of the calamities that were to come, and intimates that by a happier choice these calamities might have been avoided. And the simple truth is, that this is the whole drift of the legends, from the date of Arthur's marriage to the close. After Arthur's mysterious death, Guinevere freely takes upon herself and Lancelot the whole guilt of the ruin of Arthur's kingdom. 'Through this knight and mee all these warres were wrought, and the death of the most noble knights of the world; for through our love that we have loved together is my most noble lord slaine. ... For as well as I have loved thee, Sir Lancelot, now mine heart will not once serve mee to see thee; for through thee and mee is the floure of kings and knights destroyed.' And her last prayer is not to see Sir Lancelot again with her bodily eyes, lest her earthly and disloyal love should return upon her, but that he should bury her beside her true lord and master, King Arthur. No one can read Sir Thomas Malory's book without being struck by the complete disappearance, as it proceeds, of all trace of remorse or shame in King Arthur, and by the weight of guilt thrown upon the passionate love of Lancelot and Guinevere. Obviously, if Tennyson was to keep to the legends which cast so mysterious a halo of spiritual glory around King Arthur, he had no choice but to ignore those which connected, Oedipus-fashion, his youthful sin with the final catastrophe.

But it has been said that Arthur's exclusion from the search for the San Grail is only intelligible on the ground of his youthful guilt. Here again, I think, Tennyson's poetic instinct proves triumphant.

For in the story of it as told by Sir Thomas Malory, there is not only no trace of this, but a distinct justification of the Poet Laureate's view that Arthur looked on this search for the San Grail as almost a disloyalty to the higher though humbler task that he had set himself and his knights—of restoring order on earth; while, on the other hand, knights, who, like Sir Lancelot, are stained with far deeper and more voluntary guilt than any with which the King, even on Mr. Swinburne's view, is chargeable, are allowed to join in the search. I do not know anything happier or more true in its instinct, in English poetry, than the tone Tennyson has attributed to Arthur's reluctant assent to the search for the San Grail. It is amply justified by the old legends, and it just enables the poet to express through Arthur that spiritual distrust of signs and wonders which, while it serves to link his faith closely with modern thought, is in no way inconsistent with the chivalric character of the whole story. In Sir Thomas Malory's version, after the descent of the Holy Ghost, the vision of the holy vessel, and that Pentecostal scene in which all the knights, amid profound silence, had beheld each other invested with a higher beauty than their own, Arthur yields thanks to God 'of his grace that hee had sent them, and for the vision hee had showed them at the high feast of Pentecost,' yet not only suggests no quest, but imagines none; nor is it the holiest of the knights, nor one of those who are to succeed wholly or partially in achieving it, who proposes it. It is Sir Gawain;—though Tennyson, who has accepted for other reasons a lower conception of Sir Gawain than the old chroniclers, puts the first oath into the mouth of the mystic-minded Percivale. Arthur at once expresses his displeasure in language at least fairly interpretable as implying disapprobation of the surrender of a prior earthly duty for a visionary spiritual aim. '"Alas!" said King Arthur unto Sir Gawain, "yee have nigh slaine mee with the vow and promise yee have made; for through you yee have bereft mee of the fairest fellowship and the truest of knighthood that ever were seene together in any realme of the world. For when they shall depart from hence, I am sure that all shall never meete more in this world, for there shall many die in the quest, and so it forethinketh (repenteth) mee a little, for I have loved them as well as my life; wherefore it shall grieve me right sore the separation of this fellowship, for I have had an old custome to have them in my fellowship."' And again, more passionately: '"Ah, Sir Gawain, Sir

197

Gawain, yee have betraied mee, for never shall my heart be amended by you, but yee will never be sorry for mee as I am for you"; and therewith the teeres began to runne downe by his visage. And therewith the King said: "Ah, knight, Sir Lancelot, I require thee that thou wilt counsaile mee, for I would this quest were undone, and it might bee."' This is not the language of one too guilty to join in the quest himself, but of one who sincerely disapproves it, as the exchange of a clear prior duty undertaken by his knights, for one of doubtful obligation, though of spiritual ambition.

On the whole, I cannot help thinking that Mr. Swinburne's hostile criticism of 'The Idylls of the King' for their omission of the taint in the king's life and character, is virtually a complaint that the poet has not excluded the whole halo of spiritual glory from the Arthurian traditions, and substituted an old Greek tragedy for a mystic mediaeval vision. . . .

31. William Minto

1874

William Minto (1845–93), Professor of Logic and English at Aberdeen from 1880 until his death, and before that critic, author, and editor, published in 1872 *A Manual of English Prose Literature*. Such manuals were in part a response to the rise of English studies in the schools. Two years later, Minto brought out *Characteristics of English Poets from Chaucer to Shirley*, from which this excerpt is taken. Minto was an independent and sometimes penetrating critic; his remarks on Malory and Tennyson take a commonsense approach and suggest that it is foolish to judge one's work on the basis of the other's. He is responding here to Swinburne's attack and Hutton's defence (No. 30).

Extracts are from a later edition, *Characteristics of English Poets*, Authorized American Edition (Boston: Ginn & Company, 1889), pp. 81–5.

Sir Thomas Malory's 'Morte d'Arthur' is a condensation of an extensive literature—the prose romances on the subject of Arthur and the Knights of the Round Table. Its humble prose is all that we have to show as a national epic. It is compiled and abridged from French prose romances written during the thirteenth, fourteenth, and fifteenth centuries, and contains the most famous exploits fabled of our national heroes. Its chief pretence to unity is that it begins with the birth of Arthur and ends with his death. It is, furthur, consistent in recognising throughout the invincible superiority of Lancelot of the Lake. Otherwise, its variety is somewhat bewildering, in spite of the obliging printer's division into twenty-one books. It is a book to choose when restricted to one book, and only one, as the companion of solitude; there might then be some hope of gaining a clear mastery over its intricacies, a vivid conception of each several adventure of Gawain and his brothers, of Pelinore, Lancelot, Pelleas, Tristram, Palamides, Lamorak, Percival, Galahad, and their interminable friends, foes, and fair ladies.

Lord Tennyson's 'Idylls of the King' have drawn especial attention to Malory in this generation. The old knight is very pleasant reading. He describes warlike encounters with great spirit and graphic homely language; and his simple old English is very telling in the record of such pathetic incidents as the unhappy love of the maid of Astolat. His work being more or less of an abridgment, he is obliged to sacrifice much of the picturesque detail of his originals, and the story sometimes becomes a catalogue of encounters, with but little variation of the familiar incidents of knights hurled over their horses' tail, swords flashed out, shields lifted high, and helmets struck with stunning blow. Yet the 'Morte d'Arthur' is, as it was designed to be, a most entertaining book.

Lord Tennyson has taken considerable liberties in his adaptation of the legends or fictions collected by Malory. This he was fully entitled to do: there is nothing sacred in them, and an artist may do with them as he pleases, bearing always the responsibility of treating the subject in such a way as to justify himself. So far from being offended at any modification of the story of the 'Morte d'Arthur,' we should owe no gratitude to a modern poet who should simply versify Malory's prose, whether in substance or in detail. We can have no quarrel with a modern poet for using the 'Morte d'Arthur' as so much raw material to be worked at discretion. It is vain to look for any profound and consistent unity in such a compilation of the unconcerted labours of different authors—authors working not only without concert, but even with conflicting aims. And therefore I think that Mr Hutton, in his eloquent defence of the 'Idylls of the King' from the strictures of Mr Swinburne, commits a mistake when he tries to make out that Lord Tennyson's conception of the story is more consonant with the original designs than Mr Swinburne's. Lord Tennyson is fully entitled to bend the story to his own purposes; and Mr Hutton is much more happy in his interpretation and justification of the Idylls upon their independent merits.

What the laureate has really done, has been to take up one motive to the creation of Arthur, and to regenerate his whole life in rigorous conformity thereto. This generating or regenerating motive is considerably different from any of the several motives that produced the heterogeneous character of the 'Morte d'Arthur,' but it may be said to be the modern and idyllic equivalent of one of them. So far, the character and achievements of Arthur may be described with Mr Hutton as a 'mystic mediaeval vision.' There is a certain 'halo of spiritual glory' round Arthur's head. He ministered to other sentiments than religious enthusiasm: he was a mirror of perfect knighthood, an object of national pride, and the adventures of himself and his knights furnished a luxurious feast to the passion for the marvellous. But religious enthusiasm was undoubtedly one motive, and a great motive, for his creation. He was the champion of Christianity against the heathen, and his return was looked for to aid in the recovery of the Holy Cross. And it is this side of Arthur's character that Lord Tennyson has set himself to treat in his own way. His Arthur is still a perfect knight, a national hero, and a centre of marvellous adventure; but he is, above everything, a defender of the faith according to Lord Tennyson's ideal, and according to the moral sense of the present generation—a hero of divine origin, of immaculate purity, of unwavering and unintermitting singleness of purpose. Now, in these particulars, the modern poet departs from the Arthur of the old story. There was something supernatural in the origin of the old Arthur, but he was not literally heaven-sent: he was a child of shamefulness—not begotten in lawful wedlock. His father, Uther Pendragon, was transformed by the art of the magician, Merlin, into the likeness of Ygerne's husband, and Arthur was the issue of this illicit love and supernatural delusion of a faithful wife. Again, the Arthur of the old story was not stainless in the sense of loving one woman and cleaving to her. When he was a young squire, and before his origin was known either to himself or to the public, he lay with Morgause (or Bellicent), the wife of Lot, his half-sister; and in that unwittingly incestuous connection begat Mordred, who became afterwards his fatal enemy. After the battle with the eleven kings at Bredigan, he gratified, by the help of Merlin (who would not seem to have been scrupulous about playing the pander), a passing fancy for Lionors. And even after his marriage with Guinevere, not to mention his unwitting adultery with the false Guinevere, he was not the high, cold, self-contained Arthur of the Idylls. On one occasion, at least, he showed the wantonness of gallant curiosity, when he persisted, against Lancelot's dissuasion, in riding up to the fair Isoud, and staring at her until he was smitten off his horse by Sir Palamides for his discourtesy. Finally, as regards his singleness of purpose in driving out the heathen, therein also the modern Arthur is a refinement upon the Arthur of the old story, who made great war for the common selfish purpose of 'getting all England into his hand;' and did not scruple to try to secure his power by committing to the mercy of the waves all children born on May-day, because Merlin told him 'that he that should destroy him should be born on May-day.'

Arthur is not the only personage in the old story whose character Lord Tennyson has chosen to modify. ... The sons of Bellicent, again, are seriously transfigured in the Idylls. In the old story, Arthur's death, through the treason and by the hand of Mordred, his own son by unconscious incest, appears as the inexorable vengeance of an iron law that accepts no plea of ignorance. The king is punished by the fruit of his own involuntary crime. Lord Tennyson wipes off this blot of incest from the life of his spotless hero, and attributes the treason of Mordred, whom he represents as the lawful son of Lot, to simple depravity of nature. And to deepen the colours of this natural taint, he extends it to Gawain, the son of Bellicent and Lot, incriminating the whole of them as a crafty deceitful race, with traitor hearts hid under a courteous exterior.

These modifications of the old story and the old characters must be left to justify themselves, very much as if the modern version were a wholly new creation. It is best on all grounds to regard it as such: we should spoil the 'Morte d'Arthur' were we to read it by the light of Lord Tennyson's conceptions; and we should be unfair to Lord Tennyson were we to condemn him for departing from the somewhat uncertain outlines of the 'Morte d'Arthur.' We must take the 'Idylls of the King' on their own merits. If the poet had been writing a tragedy on a theme that appears on the surface, at least, so admirably suited for tragedy, one cannot see that he would have gained anything by rejecting the incestuous birth of Mordred and its fatal consequences. But the 'Idylls of the King' are idylls; it is obvious that their greater simplicity is in accordance with the idyllic nature of the poetry. We are not distracted by bewildering mixtures of good and evil in the 'Idylls of the King': the king is blameless; Mordred is wholly vile, with no justification as an instrument of Nemesis, or a revenger of the inhuman attempts upon his own infant life; Lancelot and Guinevere are noble natures stained by one great sin. As the simple clearly outlined figures pass before us, we are not agitated by changing admiration and abhorrence; their first impression is ever deepened as they come and go by repeated strokes on the same spot of our moral vision. When the catastrophe comes, and death passes over them, we look back upon their lives without the conflict of emotion that appertains to tragedy. They affect us as visionary types, not as men and women of mixed passions.

32. Harriet W. Preston

1876

'The Arthuriad', *Atlantic Monthly*, 38 (August 1876), 132–41.

Harriet Preston (1836–1911), an American author and translator of French and Latin works, made a speciality of Provençal literature. Besides scholarly editions and translations, she wrote several novels and contributed to periodicals, often to the *Atlantic Monthly*. The review below appeared in that magazine as the lead article for August 1876; the occasion was the recent publication in Boston (1875) of a newly organized collection of Tennyson's *Idylls*. 'Balin and Balan' was not published until 1885, and 'Geraint and Enid' was not yet being printed as two separate books; this is why Miss Preston refers to ten books.

The article begins with a summary of Tennyson's story line as presented in the 1875 version, and it continues by tracing the legend through early British lore and Geoffrey.

... Not until 1485 did Sir Thomas Malory sum up the growth of legend concerning the king and his knights in his Morte d'Arthur, the latest and finest of the great chivalric romances, whose artless and beautiful phraseology Tennyson himself has not always cared to alter.

The following is the story of Arthur's birth as it is told by Geoffrey, afterwards with more fullness of detail by the French romancers, and finally, with that added grace of characterization which was far beyond Geoffrey's range, by Malory.

[Plot summary.]

It will be seen that Malory has not distributed the balance of censure, so to speak, for the wizard's unhappy end precisely as Tennyson does. But the passage is quoted entire because it illustrates better and more briefly than almost any other the miraculous development which Tennyson sometimes gives his material. The breathless interest and appalling beauty of the story of Merlin and Vivien as we have it in the Idyls, the sublime fitness of the scenery, the subtle analysis of instinct and motive, and, above all, the irresistible force and solemnity of the lesson conveyed,—they are all here in embryo, in this dreamy fragment of a garrulous old tale. But the power which can evolve the one out of the other seems to us like the power which causes the seed to grow.... This is indeed the *maker's* proper function among men, but here we see it almost in its highest exercise. Sir Thomas Malory himself must have possessed no small share of this vivifying and organizing power, or he never could have wrought, as he assuredly has, the heterogeneous materials which he collected from so many sources into a *naïve*, consistent, and affecting whole. But usually, except in one remarkable instance to be noticed hereafter, Tennyson's mode of treatment is as great an advance in art and in refinement on Malory's, as Malory's is on the crudeness and puerility of Wace or the lusty coarseness of Thomas the Rhymer of Ercildoune.

The story of Geraint and Enid is more purely episodical than any other Idyl, and is derived from an entirely independent source. The story of Gareth and Lynette, as we have it in Tennyson, belongs wholly to the earlier and happier period of Arthur's reign. Its events bear a general resemblance to those which are recounted, in this instance very much more at length, in Malory; and the marked peculiarities of Lynette, her rudeness and petulance and entire lack of the softer graces which belonged, as a rule, to the lady of chivalry, are fully indicated in the old story. In fact, Lynette, or Linet, is called in Malory the 'damsel savage,' although considerable stress is laid on her skill in the arts of healing, which she practiced on many a wounded knight besides Gareth in the Castle Perillous of her beautiful sister Lyonors. There is a very life-like scene in Malory where the mother of Gareth, Queen Belicent, alarmed at his protracted absence on his first adventure, appears at Arthur's court and reproaches the king for the lad's non-appearance, with the true, unreasoning fierceness of feminine anxiety; there is also a particularly pretty scene at court where Gareth and Lyonors finally meet and both confess to Arthur their love for one another.

[Quotes from Bk VII, chap. 34.]

Malory's Gareth continues to figure with distinction throughout Arthur's reign, and is closely involved in its catastrophe. He was slain by Launcelot's own hand 'unwittingly,' amid the bloodshed which followed the discovery by Modred of the great knight's treason, thus causing Gawain, who, up to this time, quite consistently with his character in Malory, had been inclined to screen the distinguished lovers from Arthur's wrath, to swear an oath of mortal vengeance against Launcelot, in performing which he was himself slain. Tennyson's Gawain is identical with the Gawain of Malory, and hardly more elaborated: a brave, unprincipled man, adorned with all chivalric accomplishments, but of a vindictive temper, as unlike as possible to the proud and patient magnanimity of Arthur, Launcelot, and his own young brother, Gareth. 'For,' says Malory, 'after Sir Gareth had espied Sir Gawain's conditions, he withdrew himself from his brother Sir

Gawain's fellowship, for he was vengeable, and where he hated he would be avenged with murder, and that hated Sir Gareth.'

Gawain though a frequent is seldom a principal actor in the great scene of Arthur's life, and the sad story of Pelleas and Ettarre, in which he figures most conspicuously, is but the briefest of episodes in Malory, illustrating, hardly less remarkably than the story of Merlin and Vivien, Tennyson's magnificent power of amplification. It is proper, however, to observe that the Gawain of all elder romance is a very different person from Malory's, much more admirable and commonplace. His chivalric rank is second only to that of Launcelot and Tristram. He is the hero of many an honorable adventure, and is confidently identified with the golden-tongued Gwalzmai of the Welsh triads, as Tristram is identified with Tristan the Tumultuous, the son of Tallwyz.

Let us now consider briefly Tennyson's treatment of the world-renowned story of Tristram and Isolt. The high antiquity of this tale, its peculiar picturesqueness, and the prominent place which it occupies in the Arthurian cycle of romances, including Malory's, of which it constitutes at least a quarter part, would have led us to expect that the laureate would give it more space than he has done in the dreary fragment of The Last Tournament. . . . And we cannot rid ourselves of the fancy that he once meant to have told it in full in a separate and earlier idyl. The epic, even in its latest form, falls short of the canonical number by two books. We infer from the introduction to the fine fragment which first appeared a generation ago under the title of Morte d'Arthur, and has since been expanded into the Passing of Arthur, that this, in the poet's original scheme, was to have been the eleventh book of the epic. It seems impossible but that the earlier missing canto was to have rehearsed all of the romantic story, except its grim catastrophe, of those lovers who are so constantly compared with Launcelot and Guinevere in all old romance, nay, even poetically styled the only two in the world beside them. Why was this classic tale rejected? Was it because the poet deemed it too hackneyed, or because of its utter impracticability for that strenuous moral purpose which came so palpably to modify his treatment of the Arthurian story, and which must have deepened so fast between the purely aesthetic days of the Morte d'Arthur and those of the supreme idyl of Guinevere? Sir Walter Scott, in the fascinating preface to his edition of Thomas the Rhymer's Tristram, speaks of the 'extreme ingratitude and profligacy of the hero.' In Malory, and apparently in the later French prose romance which he closely followed, these ugly qualities are veiled by every lesser chivalric grace, by consummate skill in music and the arts of the chase, and by an almost fantastic magnanimity in combat. But the character is essentially the same. Tristram is the most notorious and the most elegant of libertines; and the full knowledge and open toleration of his intrigues on the part of Arthur himself, as compared with his noble incredulity and righteous wrath when he was himself wronged, constitute the most glaring inconsistency in Malory's romance, and the greatest blemish on the character of his king. In Malory, indeed, the *dénouement* of the story, which is the same as that recorded in The Last Tournament, is retributive, and so may be considered, in a general way, moral. . . .

We have now glanced at the originals of nearly all the great Arthurian heroes whom Tennyson has restored, except the two who move us most deeply—Launcelot the Peerless, and Galahad the Spotless. To these immortal figures we must allow a purely French origin. In Malory, and in the French prose romances of Launcelot du Lac and the Saint Grael, they are father and son. In the refined version of Tennyson it would hardly have been possible to admit this relation, yet it adds a peculiar interest and pathos to some of the scenes in that quest of the Holy Grail in which from motives so dissimilar they both engaged. For example, Malory tells us how once, during that fateful year of the quest, they met on board the ship which was conveying to their last rest the remains of Percivale's holy sister. It was just before Sir Launcelot had the veiled vision which taught him that his own quest was vain, in an interval of his so-called madness, when he was enjoying a great but transitory peace of mind. . . .

Galahad's death occurred shortly after, and Launcelot was never again at ease in his sin. The mighty struggles of this great and tender soul with the guilt that was crushing it are plainly foreshadowed in Malory, but of course they do not receive anything like the searching examination with which he is made in Tennyson to face his own 'remorseful pain' at the close of the thrilling episode of Elaine of Astolat; although otherwise, in this episode, Tennyson follows Malory with unusual closeness. The cruel reaction of Launcelot's divided loyalties, the deep 'dishonor in which his heart's honor was really rooted,' are set in stronger light than ever in Tennyson's last edition in two interpolated passages of such unusual beauty and significance that we make room for them, our last quotations from the Idyls here. The first occurs on the threshold of the story, before Launcelot had sought and brought Guinevere to be Arthur's wife,—which, by the way, in Malory, he does not do,—when Arthur had finally broken the might of the last insurgent army. . . .

So the king goes away into the mist and darkness of that 'last, dim, weird battle in the west,'—a marvelous picture in its wintry tints of white and monotonous gray, indelibly drawn on the memory of the present generation. And this, with Tennyson, is the end. But here at last we venture to think that the poet's art has overreached itself, and that his *finale*, fine and imaginative though it be, is less impressive than that of the simple old master. It seems impossible to read the Idyls in their connection, and to go directly from Guinevere to the Passing of Arthur, from the verity, solemnity, and intense humanity of the former, and the extraordinary moral elevation which it induces, to the mists and portents and fairy uncertainties of the latter, without experiencing a painful shock and chill. The two poems, both so beautiful, belong to different spheres. There is a life-time, a spiritual revolution, between the two. Malory's story and that of his 'French book' by no means end with the battle. Is it possible that the absent twelfth book of Tennyson's epic was to have related these subsequent incidents?

At all events Malory's ending is realistic and credible, sad but satisfying.

[Quotes from scene of Lancelot and Guinevere's last meeting.]

In all this there is a grave and simple fitness to the inalienable majesty of the guilty pair. They never met again; but six years later, after long prayer and penance, there came to Launcelot one night a vision, warning him to seek once more the convent at Almesbury, where he would find Guinevere dead, and to see that she was buried beside her lord, King Arthur.

'Then Sir Launcelot rose up or day, and told the hermit. "It were well done," said the hermit, "that ye made you ready, and that ye disobey not the vision." Then Sir Launcelot took seven followers with him, and on foot they went from Glastonbury to Almesbury, the which is little more than thirty miles. And thither they came within two days, for they were weak and feeble to go. And when Sir Launcelot was come to Almesbury, within the nunnery, Queen Guinevere died but half an hour before. And the ladies told Sir Launcelot that Queen Guinevere told them all, or she passed, that Sir Launcelot had been priest near a twelvemonth. "And hither he cometh, as fast as he may, to fetch my corpse; and beside my lord King Arthur he shall bury me." Wherefore the queen said, in hearing of them all, "I beseech Almighty God that I may never have power to see Sir Launcelot with my worldly eyes." "And thus," said all the ladies, "was ever her prayer these two days till she was dead." Then Sir Launcelot saw her visage, but he wept not greatly but sighed.'

The Idyls themselves contain no touch finer than this last. . . .

33. Sidney Lanier

1880

Sidney Lanier (1842–81), the American poet, also edited a series of books for boys: one drawn from Froissart, one from the *Mabinogion*, one from Percy, and *The Boy's King Arthur*, based on Malory, though extensively abridged and expurgated. Lanier's introduction of 1880 is addressed to boys, not to adults, much less to scholars, but a well-educated audience is anticipated as Lanier quotes Geoffrey in translation, Layamon in the original with interliner translation, and the Vulgate *Queste* in French. His comments on 'this beautiful old book' show Malory to be more than a compiler.

This version of the *Morte Darthur*, especially in the later editions with illustrations by N.C. Wyeth, for perhaps half a century dominated the popular children's versions in America. The comments of Malory are from the introduction (New York: Charles Scribner's Sons, 1880), pp. xvi-xxi.

If we now leave out of sight the numerous writers, besides Wace and Layamon and Map, who sent forth all manner of romances in prose and verse growing out of Geoffrey's original stock; and, passing at one step along nearly three hundred years, if we come to an English author who is still re-telling the Arthurian stories, and find an English audience still desiring to hear them retold: we cannot fail to be struck with the hold which Geoffrey's tales had taken upon men's minds.

This author is our own simple, valorous, wise, tender Sir Thomas Malory, who wrote the History of King Arthur and his knights of the Round Table found in the following pages. I regret that I can give no personal account of one who must have been an interesting man: so far as I can discover, we know absolutely nothing of him save what is contained in the... words, which form the last clause of the last sentence of his work.... The ninth year of the reign of Edward IV would be somewhere in 1469 or 1470: thus, while the Wars of the Roses were thundering about England, while Edward and Warwick the king-maker were apparently shaking the world with their desperate struggle, our Sir Thomas Maleore, knight, was sitting down quietly day by day, and poring over the five great French romances—the Merlin, the Tristram, the Launcelot, the Quest of the Saint Grail, and the Death of Arthur—which appear to have furnished the main materials of his book....

And so, after running over England and France, in the twelfth century, like a Scott's novel in the nineteenth; after growing, branching into new tales, absorbing new heroes, embodying new ideas, employing new writers, and delighting whole countries, through Wace, Map, Layamon, Gaimar, de Borron, and many other authors, until the latter part of the fifteenth century: all the separate stories originating in Geoffrey's history are brought together and moulded into one work, with a sort of beginning, a plot, and a crisis, by Sir Thomas Malory, who may thus, with but little strain, be said to have written the first English novel. And his modifications and general treatment of his material—of which no details can be given here—suffice, I think, to give him a claim to this book, not as a mere compilation, but as a work in which so much of himself is mingled that it is largely, and in some of its best features, his own. This is indeed almost a peculiar circumstance characterizing the successive improvements of the Arthurian story as it comes on down the ages....

And now,—when four hundred years after Caxton printed this book for 'many noble and divers gentlemen of this realm of England,' you find a later editor rearranging the old grown-people's story for many noble and divers boys both of England and America,—perhaps the foregoing account may justify you in a certain sense of proud responsibility as you recall the question with which I began this long inquiry.

No book ever needed less pointing-out of its intrinsic faults and beauties than this frank work of a soul so transparent that one is made to think of the Wakulla Spring in Florida where one can see a penny on the bottom at a hundred feet depth. I will but ask you to observe specially the majestic manhood of Sir Launcelot during those dolorous last days when King Arthur, under the frenzied advice of Sir Gawaine, brings two great armies in succession to besiege Joyous Gard. Day after day Gawaine, and sometimes Arthur, call out the vilest taunts and dares and accusations over the walls; but ever Sir Launcelot, though urged even by his own indignant followers within, replies with a grave and lordly reasonableness which shames his enemies beyond measure; twice he fights a great single-handed battle with Sir Gawaine, and, although Gawaine is miraculously helped, wounds him sorely, yet spares his life; he charges his knights to be still loyal to King Arthur, and to do the king no hurt, upon pain of death; and one day in a general engagement when King Arthur is unhorsed Sir Launcelot himself flies to the rescue, places the king on horseback again, and sees him safe, with perfect tenderness and loyalty. Larger behavior is not shown us anywhere in English literature. And from this point on, the pictures of the passing of Arthur, of Launcelot grovelling on the tomb of the king, of Launcelot's own strange departure, and of Sir Ector lamenting Sir Launcelot and describing that great knight in his lamentation,—are wrought with a simple art that is as perfect as artlessness....

34. George W. Cox

1883

George William Cox (1827–1902) produced a number of historical books on Greece, Persia, and England, as well as *Popular Romances of the Middle Ages* (1871), which went through several English and American editions. He was more original, however, in his equally popular work in comparative mythology. As a follower of Max Müller (1823–1900), he was a strong proponent of the solar or nature myth theory as the origin of much folklore and legend. *The Mythology of the Aryan Nations* (1870) had related this theory to the Arthurian legend, and *An Introduction to the Science of Comparative Mythology and Folklore* (1881) elaborated it with specific references to Malory's version.

While Cox, like most comparative mythologists, is not much concerned with Malory as an author, his remarks are included here for two reasons: they illustrate the early application of comparative mythology to Arthurian studies (although Welsh scholars had long been discussing Arthur's mythological origins), and they reveal a willingness to deal frankly with the sexual relationships between Malory's characters, in fact to insist upon them, with a candour not typical of the times.

The extracts below are from *Introduction to Comparative Mythology*, second edition (London: Kegan Paul, Trench, & Co., 1883), (a) pp. 313–23, (b) pp. 330–7, and Appendix IV, pp. 367–8 n. 1.

(a)
... The likeness [among stories from various cultures] may be the result of direct borrowing or importation, or it may be caused by independent growth as of plants from seeds which once came from a single tree; but whatever be the cause, the likeness is still there, and according to these points of likeness, these stories may be

211

grouped and classified. These remarks apply with special force to the romance, or rather the body of romances, in which King Arthur is a more or less prominent figure. There can be no question that in the chronicle of Malory we have a number of stories, the connexion between some of which is very slender, and which have been pieced together with no great dexterity and skill. The whole story, as he gives it, resolves itself into cycles, the heroes of which had each his own separate legend or tradition, which probably at first made no reference to Arthur. Of the whole narrative it may be said that its general outlines and its special features may be traced not only in other mediaeval romances, but in the traditions of almost every Aryan tribe.... The incidents which mark the Arthur story are confessedly extraordinary, or miraculous, or impossible; and it is the recurrence of these features either in different portions of the story, or in other legends, which both shows how each romance has been brought into space and determines its affinity with other versions of the same tale....

[Comparisons of Uther/Amphitryon, Arthur/Sigmund.]

According to the later ideal, Arthur is the king or knight of spotless purity. With this notion the earlier traditions stand out in striking contrast. The incidents relating to the daughter of Earl Sanam and the wife of the king of Orkney are cardinal points in the story. As in the Theban tradition, the ruin of the hero or of his kingdom must be brought about by his own son or descendants; and Mordred and the wife of the king of Orkney stand to Arthur in the relation of Polyneikes and Iokastê to Oedipus. The queen of Orkney is Arthur's sister, the daughter of Igerne, although he knows it not, as Oedipus knows not that in wedding Iokastê he is wedding his mother. But in the Arthur story it must be remembered that he dallies with the queen of Orkney, though she comes to his court with her four sons, as he dallies with the daughter of Earl Sanam, for the mere attraction of her beauty. In neither case has he any misgivings of conscience. If his relations with the mother of Mordred cause him sadness, this sadness is not awakened until he has dreams which forbode the ruin to be one day wrought. But if Arthur really belong to the same heroic company with Herakles and Sigurd, with Phoebus, or Indra, or Agni, this sensuous characteristic is precisely what we should look for. All these must be lovers of the maidens.... Nor may we pass over the incident which closes the first portion of the Arthur myth, and which tells us that Arthur, on hearing that his destroyer should be born on Mayday, orders that all the children born on that day shall be brought to him. With these Mordred is placed in a ship, which is wrecked, and, as we may suppose, Mordred is the only one saved....

The reluctance which Uther's nobles show to receive Arthur as their lord, on the ground that he is but a base-born boy, brings before us another familiar feature in this whole class of legends. Without exception the Fatal Children, as Grimm calls them, have to spend their early years in banishment or disguise or humiliation; and when they come to claim their rightful inheritance, they are despised or jeered at by men of meaner birth, who can never be their match in strength and wit. The wise Odysseus is mocked for his beggarly garb as he stands on the day of doom in his own hall; and this passing shame before the great victory is reflected in countless popular stories which tell us of a degradation culminating in the Gaelic lay of the Great Fool. This story is repeated in the episode of Sir Tor, who is brought in by a cowherd....

The recurrence of precisely the same ideas in the story of the poor knight Balin, throws light on the method in which a crowd of originally independent stories have been sorted and pieced together in order to produce the Arthur story of Jeffrey of Monmouth, and still more of Malory. In truth, the myth told of Arthur is now told all over again of Balin, and Arthur becomes altogether subordinate to the new protagonist. Here, as before, the first incident is that of the drawing of a sword; but in this case the weapon is attached not to an anvil or a stone, but to the side of a maiden who cannot be freed from it save by a true knight guileless of treason. No knights of the court of King Ryons have been able to rid her of the burden; and Arthur himself is now not more successful. Hence, when Balin, the poor-clad knight, who has just been let out of prison, begs that he may be suffered to try, the maiden tells him that it is in vain for him to do so, when his betters have failed before him. To his hand, however, the weapon yields as easily as those which were drawn forth at the touch of Arthur or of Galahad.

With the death of Balin and his brother Balan the story returns to the myth of Arthur and his wedding with Guenevere, whose character approaches more nearly to that of the Helen of the Greek lyric and tragic poets, than to the Helen of our Iliad and Odyssey. As Helen is with Aeschylus the ruin of ships, men, and cities, so is Arthur here warned by Merlin that Guenevere is not wholesome for him; and at a later time the knights who are besought to come forward as champions in her behalf demur to the request, on the ground that she is a destroyer of good knights. Their reluctance is fully justified. The real Guenevere of the Arthur story is sensual in her love and merciless in her vengeance; nor is Lancelot the austerely devoted knight which sometimes he declares himself to be. By equivocation or direct falsehood Lancelot contrives to avoid or rebut the charge brought against him by Sir Meliagrance; but when, in the encounter that follows, that knight goes down beneath the stroke of Sir Lancelot and yields him to his mercy, the latter is sorely vexed, because he wished to destroy the evidence of his guilt; and when he looks to Guenevere, she makes a sign which expressed the will of the Roman ladies in the amphitheatre, that the vanquished gladiator should die. It may, of course, be said that the incident which furnished grounds for the accusation of Meliagrance has been interpolated into the myth; but the process is perilous which rejects from a legend every portion that clashes with our conceptions of the character of certain heroes. Assuredly it cannot be maintained that the acts which roused the suspicions of Meliagrance are consistent with any notion of merely Platonic affection; nor is it safe to impute the coarseness which characterises Lancelot and Guenevere, Tristram and Isolte, wholly to the coarseness of the mediaeval storytellers. There is everything to support, and little or nothing to invalidate the conclusion, that the harsher and more repulsive portraits are the older; and if in the original myth Lancelot had been a man such as later poets have painted him, the quest of the Sangreal could not have been accomplished, for it is only by personating Guenevere that Elaine becomes the mother of Galahad.

But Guenevere, like Helen, has her treasures as well as the rich dower of beauty; and her special gift to Arthur is the Round Table....

With his election as king begin the toils and the wanderings of Arthur. No sooner is one enemy overcome than another assails him from some other quarter. 'Alas!' he complains when he hears that the king of Denmark is ravaging his northern lands, 'never have I had one month's rest since I became king of the land.' It is but the doom which lies on the mythical heroes of all countries. . . .

. . . In short, there is but one being of whom this tale is eternally true, and that being is the sun, who can never rest until he joins in the evening the beautiful maiden from whom he was parted in the morning. The force of the evidence becomes irresistible, as we ascend from the wanderers of folklore stories to the great company of epical heroes, and beyond these to the divine persons whose real nature was closely known to those who spoke of them—to Dionysos, the wine god; to Phoebus, who cannot rest in Delos, but who, having wandered far away to the west, ever comes back to his bright birth-place; to Wuotan or Odin, who is Wegtam, the pilgrim of the road, and to Indra the wonderful, who, like all the rest, is a wanderer.

Nothing can grow without a root; and the most grotesque fictions are not altogether unreasonable and absurd. Thus, when in these Arthur legends we come across men whose strength increases from nine to twelve o'clock, so that towards noon they become almost irresistible, while from the moment of noon their power begins slowly but steadily to decline, it becomes impossible to resist the conclusion that here, again, we are reading of heroes who have had transferred to them the properties which belong only to the one-eyed wanderer who daily performs his journey through the heavens. This power of growth until noon is possessed by Sir Gawaine, while his adversary, Marhaus, who here represents the opponent of the sun-god, waxes bigger and bigger at sundown, as the shades deepen. It is shared also by the Red Knight of the Red Lawns. This magical power in Gawaine (of which, with one of the many direct contradictions exhibited by the legends pieced together to form the Arthur story, we are told that Arthur alone was aware), is especially manifested in the last desperate struggle with Lancelot, which ends in the death of Gawaine.

If any doubt yet remained that these otherwise inexplicable characteristics of the Knights of the Round Table or their antagonists are remnants of nature-myth, these would be removed by the transparent scene in which the three fatal sisters are brought before us by the stream side in the forest of Alroy. The images of the Past, the Present, and the Future with its budding hope, cannot be mistaken in the three maidens, of whom the eldest wears a circlet of gold on hair white with the snows of more than threescore winters, while the second has seen thirty years, and the third, whose head is crowned with flowers, is but in her fifteenth summer. These maidens sit where the road parts, watching for errant knights, whom they may teach strange adventures. It is enough to say that Uwaine and Marhaus choose the more sober and discreet of the sisters; the youngest falls to the share of Gawaine, and by her early desertion of him illustrates the truth that the young and his hopes, like the fool and his money, are soon parted.

[Discusses the 'cycles' of Lancelot, Gareth, Tristram.]

(b)

We have seen that in the stories of Balin and Gareth Arthur himself becomes a subordinate personage, and that too in the very points in which in his own myth he is the peculiar hero. In each case a sword is to be drawn forth from a stone or an anvil; and in each case it moves lightly as a feather at the touch of the one knight who is destined to draw it out. It follows that if this peerless hero is elsewhere secondary or defeated, we have passed out from the cycle of traditions immediately relating to him; and thus we find Arthur unhorsed by Tristram in the legend which relates the career of the latter.[1] In a still more striking scene, the power of healing, which Arthur vainly strives to exercise on Sir Urre of Hungary, is made to depend on the touch of Lancelot, for here we are in that portion of the tale in which Lancelot is the bravest and best knight in all the world.

[Discusses various motifs: horns, ships, life-giving and fertility vessels.]

But although almost all the closing scenes of the romance are lit up with the splendour of Christian feeling, there are features in it which we can no more regard as Christian, or even as human, than we can look on the narrative of certain events related in the Odyssey as in conformity with Achaian character. The high ascetic tone imparted to the close of Lancelot's relations with Guenevere may be and is probably due entirely to the force of Christian opinion; and this fact must clearly distinguish the earlier and later forms of the myth. Rather it must be said that the whole romance, as we have it, is really built up on the assumption that the love of Lancelot and Guenevere is throughout sensual. The very achievement of the Sangreal depends on the birth of a child of Lancelot; and except on such an assumption the result is rendered impossible. Lancelot is entrapped by Elaine, because he supposes that he has been summoned to Queen Guenevere. But this is not a solitary instance. The same incident is repeated when the daughter of king Pelles visits the court of Arthur; nor is it possible to mistake the nature of the colloquy between Lancelot and Guenevere when the knight tears away the bars from her chamber window.

It may be urged that these are later additions which mar the ancient purity of the myth; but in favour of such a notion there is little indeed to be said. It cannot be supposed that the romance-maker, who has drawn a perfectly consistent character in Galahad, would have allowed a series of incidents which involve a monstrous contradiction between the career and the character of Lancelot and Guenevere as he has drawn them. Galahad before his birth is destined to be the pure and spotless knight, and such he remains always. Not less earnestly are Guenevere and Lancelot made to declare that their love has never been of a kind to reflect the least dishonour on king Arthur; yet this solemn asseveration, made again and again, is contradicted by a series of incidents which they are compelled to keep out of Arthur's knowledge by a long course of equivocation and lying....

...It may be urged that the sensual fury displayed by Guenevere, when she finds that the very plan which she has laid to keep Lancelot by her side leads to his being again entrapped by Elaine while he sojourns in Arthur's court, is to be charged to the corrupt imagination of a later age; but it must be remembered that the very structure of the story which relates the career of Galahad utterly precludes this notion. Nay, Guenevere is not only a destroyer of many knights, as she might easily be on the hypothesis that though seemingly guilty she was really innocent: we have seen that in the case of Meliagrance she combines cruelty with her sensuality. As to Lancelot, who thus commits murder at her bidding, he avoids in this instance the utterance of a direct falsehood, because the partial knowledge of Meliagrance makes it possible for him to employ the tricks of a dishonest pleader.

Thus, then, we have treachery on the one side, and faithlessness on the other; and the taking away of Guenevere from the court of Arthur, who had cherished him as his friend, answers to the taking away of Helen from Menelaos by the man in whom he had placed a perfect trust. In short, the character of Lancelot precisely reflects that of Paris; and the words of Menelaos before the walls of Ilion are echoed in those of Arthur before the gates of Joyous Gard. 'Fie on thy fair speech; I am now thy mortal foe, for thou hast slain my knights and dishonoured my queen.' But in spite of all his efforts, the Christian sentiment of the romance-maker cannot disguise the nature of the materials which he was handling. If Arthur was the man so little extreme to mark what is done amiss, as he is here represented, so little disposed to think evil of another without due evidence, the persistence with which he follows up to the death a quarrel with his friend on a charge which, according to some portions of the story as we have it, is unproven, and even after the touching protestations of innocence which mark the restitution of Guenevere to her husband, becomes inexplicable....

We have now reached the ending of the great drama. The victory of the snake Ahi is a victory of the great worm of darkness, which slays the light of day; and thus in the Arthur myths also visions of snakes bring the foreboding of the end. The king dreams that he sits in a chair, fastened to a wheel, beneath which lies a deep black water full of serpents and noisome things, and that suddenly the wheel turns round and he is plunged into the infernal stream, where the serpents seize him by all his limbs. From this dream he passes into a half-waking state, in which he thinks that he sees the form of the dead Gawaine, and hears his voice warning him not to fight on the morrow, but to make a month's truce with Mordred, whose name (although little can be said of the names in these later compositions) seems to betoken him as the murderer, biter, or crusher. The king follows Gawaine's advice; but his doom is not thus to be averted. It had been agreed that if during the conference between Arthur and Mordred a sword should be raised on either side, this should be the signal for mortal battle. But while they are yet speaking, the snake again plays its part. An adder bites the heel of one of Arthur's knights, who raises his weapon to slay the venomous beast; and Mordred's people, taking alarm, rush upon their adversaries. The prophecy of Merlin is well-nigh accomplished. The father and the son are to die, each by the other's hand. In vain Sir Lucan warns Arthur to remember his dream; Arthur will not hear. He sees the traitor who has done all the wrong, and betide him life or betide him death, he is resolved to slay him. But Mordred, writhing like a snake along the spear which has passed through his body, smites Arthur on the temples with the sword which he holds in both hands, and the king falls back in a swoon. It is the old tale of the Fatal Children, of children born to be great, born to slay their parents. There is death everywhere; and the phrases which described the death of the day and the night, of the sun and the darkness, of the dawn and the dew, explain every incident of the closing scenes in the lives of the heroes or maidens who represent them in mythical stories. One feature more remains. With the death of the sun his rays cease to shoot across the heaven. The great being is gone who could wield the unerring spear, or bow, or sword; and his weapon must go with him. Hence Arthur's sword must no more be profaned by the touch of mortal hand; and as the sun rises from the eastern waters when Phoebus springs to life on Delos, and plunges into his sleep like Endymion or Odysseus in the western sea, so the sword Excalibur must be restored to the waters from which it had arisen.

Arthur himself, as we have seen, is borne away in the barge in which the weird sisters have long waited for him; but he departs, not to die, but only to heal him of his grievous wound in the valley of Avilion, the Latmian land in which Endymion takes his rest....

NOTE

1 Nothing can show more clearly or convincingly than this fact the artificial process by which the Arthur romance as we have it has been brought into shape. But this assertion cannot be twisted into a charge that unity of authorship is denied for compositions which have manifestly proceeded from a single poet or story-teller. The whole myth of Arthur might have been first put into its present form by Malory, although we know that it was not; but it would be none the less a fact that the stories of Arthur, Balin, Lancelot, Gareth, Tristram, of the Isoltes, and the Elaines, and Guenevere, repeat each other; that this likeness is inherent in the materials on which the romance writer worked; and that he was compelled in each episode to give the supremacy to the hero of that episode. If then into this episode the heroes of other tales be introduced, it follows inevitably that they must play in it a subordinate part.... inconsistencies, which are surely unavoidable

when independent myths are woven together, illustrate precisely the changes which pass over Lancelot or Arthur in those parts of the tale which bear no immediate relation to themselves.

35. Gaston Paris

1883, 1886

Gaston Paris (1839–1903), the great French scholar, published in 1883 in *Romania* an important article entitled 'La Conte de la Charrette'. Here he showed conclusively that Chrétien's poem was the direct source of the corresponding episode in the prose *Lancelot* and also discussed the relationship of the episode in Malory to these sources. The first excerpt is from that article; all but the last two paragraphs were translated by H. Oskar Sommer (see No. 41; *Morte d'Arthur*, III, 233–41.) The last two paragraphs are translated from *Romania*, XII (1883), 507–8.

The publication of the Huth *Merlin*, or *Suite de Merlin* as it is now called, in 1886, was a help to Malory source studies as the *Suite* contained numerous incidents which Malory had used but which did not appear in the known accounts of the Vulgate *Merlin*. Paris, with Jacob Ulrich, edited this text and Paris wrote the introduction from which the second extract is translated. *Merlin: Roman en prose du XIIIe siècle* (Paris: Firmin Didot et Cie, 1886; reprinted New York: Johnson Reprint, 1965), pp. lxix–lxxii.

(a) 'La Conte de la Charrette'

Besides *Chrétien's* poem, which is, as we have seen, the direct source of the episode corresponding to it in the Prose—*Lancelot*, we possess an entirely independent account of the carrying off and the deliverance of *Guenièvre* in a well-known English compilation, which has been hitherto too little utilised for studies of this kind, the *Book of Arthur*, inappropriately styled *Le Morte Darthur*, composed by Sir Thomas Malory (or Malorye, or Maleore) in 1469 or 1470, and printed for the first time by Caxton in 1485, and often afterwards.[1] In Malory's book, which requires a special study, two elements can at once be distinguished: incidents more or less identical with those found in the known French romances, and others not to be found in these. It would be premature to look upon these latter as the outcome of the English compiler's imagination; many stories, formerly attributed to this origin, can now be identified with French episodes, unknown at the time, and it is highly probable that Malory has throughout confined himself to translating, abridging, and now and then modifying his source, or sources. Such is also the case with the nine first chapters of the nineteenth book, where he relates with considerable variations the adventure forming the subject of the *Conte de la Charete*. Here follows a *résumé* of these chapters.

. . . .

The author himself seems to divide his story into two distinct parts when he tells us, after having mentioned the surname of Lancelot, Chevalier du Chariot: 'and so leve we of this tale le Chevalier du charyot and torne we to this tale.'[2] It seems, indeed, to me that he has drawn from two distinct sources: the second part, in despite of the differences which separate it from the second part of *Chrétien*'s poem, may, after all, derive its origin more or less directly from it,[3] and I shall not occupy myself with it any longer. But such is by no means the case with the first part. Here we find particular facts, drawn most probably from a source independent from *Chrétien*'s.

Certain, indeed, of these traits are authenticated by various Welsh texts as having belonged to old Celtic stories. It requires no long argumentation to establish that Méléaguant, who carries off Guenièvre in the two French poems, *Chrétien*'s and the one Malory followed in his first part, is no other than the Maelwas or Melwas[4] of the Breton[5] tradition... who also carries off Arthur's wife. This carrying off is celebrated in Welsh poesy, and the allusions to it there show that in its primitive form it resembled Malory's much more than Chrétien's account of it.... William Owen, in his *Cambrian Biography* (London, 1803 (not 1813)), says in the article *Melwas*, 'He arrayed himself in leaves, to lie in wait for Gwenhwyvar and her attendants, who, according to custom, were out on May morning to gather birch for garlands to welcome the summer, and by means of that disguise he carried her away.'[6]

It is difficult to decide the exact value of this passage. Owen does not indicate his authorities; he may well have guessed, without saying it, the identity of Melwas and Méléaguant, and simply taken from Malory the incident of the maying. But the passages of David ab Gwilym, however obscure they may be, leave no doubt upon one point: Melwas, according to the old Welsh stories, carried the wife of Arthur away into a wood, disguised, as it would appear, in a garment of leaves. The lost French poem followed by Malory represents the carrying off in the same way; Méléaguant's disguise is not mentioned, but this trait seems to have disappeared by inadvertence, as the reader is prepared for it by the queen's order that all her companions should be arrayed in green; on their return they are completely covered with herbs and leaves, as is also the ravisher, doubtless in order that he might be taken for one of the maidens, and thus more easily carry off the queen. The fight which in Malory replaces this stratagem does not, therefore, belong to the primitive story, and was perhaps only inserted by the compiler to join (by the story of the wounds) the second part of the episode to the first.

The French poem of which I postulate the existence as the source of the first part of this episode has perhaps left traces elsewhere than in Malory. The *Crone* of Heinrich von dem Türlin alludes to an adventure of Guenièvre with Méléaguant which I had at first, without more closely examining it, connected with Chrétien's poem, but which now seems to me to have relations with a story differing in some respects from and similar in others to that of Malory. . . .

The poem which Heinrich von dem Türlin knew narrates . . . the carrying away of Guenièvre by Méléaguant. Lanzelet, doubtless informed in the same way as in Malory, followed her; his horse was killed, and he advanced with great difficulty among the bushes and thickets surrounding the ravisher's castle. Disabled by fatigue, he resigned himself to entering a cart in order to continue his way. He crossed a river to enter Méléaguant's land, and found him without doubt at the river-side; he gave him battle, and overcame him, took back the queen and Ké the seneschal, who also intended to deliver her, but was thrown out of the saddle, wounded, and carried off as prisoner. Lanzelet accomplished this feat in his quality of faithful servant to Arthur and of valiant knight; there existed no intimate relation between him and Guenièvre.

Such too, I hold, was Lancelot's part in the poem which served Malory as source for the first part of his account. This compiler[7] has suppressed the combat of Lancelot with Méléaguant, thinking it enough to bring them face to face once; and this took place in the second part; he also suppressed the river crossed by Lancelot, and did away with Ké's special part, joining to Lancelot nine other knights; we may well believe that, in his source, prowess and fidelity were the sole motives of Lancelot's enterprise, and that, in representing the facts otherwise, he was influenced by the Prose-Lancelot, from which he borrowed so much of his compilation.

Also, an analogous poem must have served as the basis for Chrétien's, and nothing prevents the belief that it is the first one to introduce Lancelot as the lover beloved of Guenièvre. I say an analogous poem—not precisely the one that Malory followed and that Heinrich von dem Türlin perhaps knew. Indeed, the differences are too great. They can be explained, to be sure, if one admits what I believe very plausible, that there was between the original Anglo-Norman and Chrétien a purely oral transmission. Probably the Countess of Champagne had told him this story that she had herself got from some English knight. Daughter of Eleanor of Poitiers, she was in constant touch with her mother and with the English, as witness Walter Map being received at her court in 1179 with great hospitality. Passing thus by word of mouth, the story of the kidnapping of Guenièvre no doubt could only have reached Chrétien greatly altered, and one must take careful account of this circumstance in evaluating his work.

But on the other hand, the poem by Chrétien offers some features which do not seem to be found in the version followed by Malory and which, being certainly very ancient, point without any doubt to an Anglo-Norman poem first and, through that, to Celtic sources.

SELECTED NOTES

1 I use the edition of Macmillan, 1868, though it is 'revised for modern use;' this is of no importance here.
2 Le Morte Darthur, p. 780, ll. 121–2, book xix. chap. v.—H.O.S.

3 The differences are great, but may nevertheless be the work of a skilful abbreviator and arranger. Thus the trap which Méléaguant uses is happily substituted for the obscure story of the dwarf; the stake on which Guenièvre is to be burnt, which makes the conclusion more tragical, is met with in several analogous stories; Lancelot's generosity towards Méléaguant in the final combat (no less than Guenièvre's nodding to him) is already in the Prose-Charete, though without the strange addition of the English romance, a fact which proves that Malory's story has passed through the Prose-Lancelot; moreover, this generosity is an imitation of that which shows in *Chrétien* towards the knight who has insulted him, and which the prose-writer has repeated. But it is not quite clear why Méléaguant, once delivered from Lancelot, sends Guenièvre back. The compiler, not having at his disposal Bademagu, who was unknown to the poem which furnished his first part, did not know how to overcome the difficulty.

4 The *w* had to pass through *gu* to arrive at *g*; that is why I have preferred the spelling *Méléaguant*.

5 'Breton' means here *Welsh*, M.G. Paris using 'Breton' indifferently of Wales and modern Brittany, a usage to which exception is taken by Prof. H. Zimmer....—H.O.S.

6 It is strange that the author of this short notice does not state how the queen was taken away from Melwas.

7 In thus expressing myself, I do not intend to especially refer to Malory; we do not know what is his own in his work, and what that of his original or of his French originals.

(b) Introduction to the Huth *Merlin*

...As for the literary value of the original portion of this compilation [the *Suite de Merlin*], it has none really noteworthy, and we have already indicated above the weakness of certain episodes. The story of Balin is the best; the denouement, which certainly appears to belong to our author, is truly pathetic. For the rest, it is a series of tales which are much like all the others of the same genre, with this lesser quality—that the heroes in it are, for the most part, characters who do not interest us, and whose adventures, banal variants of adventures better told elsewhere, tire us more than the originals by their monotonous improbability. Our author did not have the fertile and sometimes really poetic imagination of the authors of *Lancelot* and *Tristan*, and in our opinion, he cannot even be placed in the same class with his rival, the pseudo-Robert de Boron, who gave to the *Merlin* its best known continuation. In preferring this latter work to the one which the Huth manuscript preserves for us, the audience of the Middle Ages has in short judged it as probably it would be judged again.

... Despite its mediocre success, our romance has not been as neglected as it seems at first approach. We have two translations, one in English, the other in Spanish.

The English translation is extensively and most successfully abridged. It is part of the vast compilation of the romances of the Round Table put into English in 1470 by a person otherwise unknown named Sir Thomas Malory, printed in 1485 by the celebrated Caxton, and often reprinted since.[1] The *Morte d'Arthur* (to use the title, however inexact, that Caxton gave to the book) borrowed its first four books almost entirely from a manuscript analogous to ours. Malory, who wished to tell a complete history of Arthur and the Round Table, omitted the *Joseph* and the greater part of the *Merlin* of Robert de Boron. He begins his books with the loves of Uther Pendragon and Igraine, which he relates very briefly; it seems that he is materially lacking something at the beginning of his book, for he introduces us to Merlin all of a sudden, referring in the work to his supernatural power, without our knowing who he was or from whence he got this power. The first four chapters of Book I are drawn from Robert de Boron; then, for chapters v–xvi, Malory turns to the ordinary *Merlin*. With chapter xvii, he begins to follow our text,[2] and except for a few modifications or additions that we need not be concerned with and especially except for some heavy abridgement, he does not leave it until the end of Book I. He takes it from the beginning and ends his Book I... with the episode of the children put out to sea.

Book II, whose beginning is rather odd and seems a beginning to the entire work, is devoted to the story of Balin (called Balin le Sauvage); it covers nineteen chapters.... Book III, comprising fifteen chapters, relates the marriage of Arthur, the revival of the Round Table, and the triple adventure of Gawain, Tor, and Pellinore ... but the ending is much shortened on the one hand; on the other, it contains some details which are missing in our manuscript.

Book IV, divided into twenty-eight chapters, includes all the rest of the Huth manuscript and in addition to it, as we have noted above, the denouement of the triple adventure of Iwain, Gawain, and the Morholt.

With Book V, Malory returns to the ordinary *Merlin*, and in Book VI, he is in the middle of the *Lancelot*; he appears to have been lacking the entire first part.

The redactor of the *Morte d'Arthur* does not seem to have had before him the third part of our compilation. [This *Merlin* is assumed to be part of a larger compilation.] One finds nowhere in his book the murder of Pellinore and Aglovale by Gawain, nor other events announced beforehand in the missing part of the text or in the *Queste du Saint Graal* incorporated into this compilation; these events are no longer to be found in any surviving version. As we have already said, the *Queste*, altered and appended to the *Lancelot*,[3] displaced the older *Queste* written under the name of Robert de Boron which formed the third part of our romance.

SELECTED NOTES

1 The most faithful (except for a few pages which were lacking in the text followed) is the one that Southey published in 1817. The easiest to read, because the language is discreetly modernized, is the edition produced for Macmillan in 1868 by Sir Edward Strachey. A new edition has been announced by the Early English Text Society. [See headnote to No. 25, above.]

2 Already in chapter XVI there is a blending with out text; but we will limit ourselves to some cursory indications, leaving the business of a detailed comparison to a future editor of Malory.

3 It is this later *Queste* which has been followed by Malory in Books XIII–XVII of his compilation.

36. Ernest Rhys

1886

Ernest Rhys (1859–1946), author and, from its beginnings in 1906, editor of the Everyman's Library for J. M. Dent, introduced and edited two versions of the *Morte Darthur*. The first volume of the earlier edition, abridged and expurgated, appeared in 1886 as the first book in the Camelot Series published by Walter Scott and intended to 'help a little in making the higher literature really responsive to everyday life and its need's. This was one of Rhys's first projects upon settling to a literary life in London; in these extracts, he admires the prose style and other aspects of the *Morte Darthur* in rather vague terms while expressing reservations about its construction; his cutting and arrangement will give the story 'greater coherency'.

The introduction, here much abridged, is extremely discursive, as Rhys attempts to trace the development of English prose through and beyond Malory and to discuss the development of Arthurian material from Welsh bards through the French romances up to Malory. (See also No. 46A.)

The extracts are from *Malory's History of King Arthur and the Quest of the Holy Grail* (London: Walter Scott, 1886), pp. v–xxxv.

This book of King Arthur and his noble Knights of the Round Table, that sets out adventurously in modern guise to-day, has capital claim to be made herald of the great company of prose-writers. This, not so much for its own inherent quality, unique as that is, as for its bearing on the splendid aftergrowth of letters, and its touch of an event which, though compassed bloodlessly amid the rumours and fierce presence of war, was really revolutionary. It was the revolution of Caxton—so peacefully begun in the silence of Westminster; and yet so tremendous, as we see it now. And Sir Thomas Malory's *Morte D'Arthur* was one of the books most directly called into being by Caxton's introduction of printing in the Fifteenth Century.

It is natural to dwell on this link of the literary evolution first; the whole question of the popular approach to letters naturally makes us inclined to think with great interest on Caxton's deliverance. If we pursue this thought now, however, let us not forget the more inward side of things, and the place of the *Morte D'Arthur* on that side. For the inward significance of the book is not slight, and examining it more closely we shall find how typical it is in both matter and method, and how suggestive. Especially we at this time ought to be interested in it, for this prose outcome of the fascinating Middle Age sentiment has direct bearing on the order of prose writing tyrannically most in vogue with us,—Tale-telling! Across the naive pretence of the word HISTORY printed on its title-page we find *Romance* seductively scribbled, as it were; and indeed no more tempting by-way into English prose literature could well be found for the uninitiated than this first of all favourite English romances....

In Sir Thomas Malory—to whom we must leap now, the literary path being more familiarly known after Chaucer—the want of the more perfect art is not felt so much, the same demand not arising in narrative prose. At the same time one cannot read far in the *Morte D'Arthur* without feeling the inadequacy of the modes of expression; awkward confusions and repetitions abound. Happily Malory does not attempt anything in the way of rhetorical demonstrations; he is so simple and natural that the faults themselves have often a certain archaic effect, not unpleasing. The virtues of his style are on the other hand unique in their way, and despite their French derivation in part, merit a better tribute than critics have as a rule paid to them; in one popular and generally admirable account of English literature, indeed, he is scarcely so much as named. Remembering that the *Morte D'Arthur* was largely a translation and a collect from foreign sources, after all deductions are made, there is much with which Malory must be credited that is of the highest importance in prose. He had the literary instinct and genius without a doubt. It is partly for this very reason of its foreign derivation, moreover, that his work is so significant. In no sense of the word absolutely original, translated from sources in probably three different tongues, medley of history and myth, tradition and true report, as it is; the book is eminently typical of English prose generally, with its foreign foster-parentage and its constant foreign modification. The French influence is of course especially dominant in the book, in detail as well as in general treatment. The very idiom of the quaint old romances that Malory drew upon is copied and repeated, often indeed with charming effect. Some of the passages one could not imagine altered in any way so as to be improved. Here, for instance, is one touched with the simplest pathos, describing King Arthur's sorrowful reproach to the Knights on their leaving the court at Camelot on the Quest of the Holy Grail.... Such passages abound, but as we have to return to the book later it is best perhaps to resist the temptation to go on quoting now. Of course we do not look to it for many qualities which perfect prose must have, but in its own way, succeeding simply and naturally in that way, the *Morte D'Arthur* is admirable. In the history of prose it is most valuable indeed, as showing the attainment of a taking manner of tale-telling, which has greatly influenced later romancists, not to mention the poets who have been captivated by it....

This first voice, this romance of King Arthur and his Knights, may fairly serve as a test for those to follow. For although the *Morte D'Arthur* has had a certain vogue in time past, it has been found rather diffuse and incoherent as a rule, perhaps, by the modern reader who has turned to it. The present version therefore, revised and divided so as to give it greater coherency and make the leading lines of the romance clearer, may well serve as a test of the acceptance of old books in a new guise.[1] We have dwelt incidentally already on the place of Sir Thomas Malory among our prose-writers, but we must consider the *Morte D'Arthur* apart from pure literature merely if we wish to get at its full significance. The book's history is so remarkable as to seem itself like a romance. The curious parallels in some of its leading incidents with the ancient myths of the Eastern world suggest its genesis in the minds of the remote forefathers of the Welsh who invaded Britain centuries back. Dating back in an indistinguishable degree as far as the Sanskrit *Mahabharata* and other remote records, the story of King Arthur, the Prince who, fatefully environed, sinned his way as it were into heroism and kingdom, won shame and highest honour, and became the romance-type in his weakness and strength of all humanity, has never ceased to fascinate the story-tellers and the people. Its trace is continual in other languages, but especially in our own its history is interwoven, appearing and reappearing, as it does, in a hundred guises, altered in art-form as the literary custom of the day demanded, so that it serves in fact as a sort of touchstone of the different periods. In each version it was modified and added to, and the letter in especial violently revised; but in spite of a hundred re-shapings, the spirit of the book remains virtually the same....

...Since Caxton first issued Malory's English transcript, we know how the book has enthralled the popular heart. Milton, we know, hesitated for long whether he should not make it his life work, instead of the *Paradise Lost*. Its spirit lives in Spenser's *Faery Queen*. Even the Eighteenth Century felt its fascination, and attempted to adapt it to itself, with what unsuccess need hardly be said. The Nineteenth has been more successful, and it is indeed remarkable how the Arthurian and allied romances have affected modern art of all kinds, not only in England, but elsewhere. Tennyson's *Idylls of the King* naturally occur first to us, and in these poems, nobly perfect in themselves, we see at once an ominous sign of the times in that what has been called our English prose epic should lose its high epic proportion, and its fateful coherency, in the daintier loveliness of an idyllic presentment....

The book is a romance rather than a history, we have said, but to most of us this is no reproach. Some historians have indeed doubted altogether the existence of King Arthur, but such a doubt to your true reader will always be blasphemous....

If the exact letter of the book be doubted, its spirit is happily secure in our hearts for ever. The biography of the material King Arthur will never be catalogued possibly, but the ideal Arthur lives and reigns securely beyond time and space, in that kingdom of old romance of which Camelot is the capital. In Malory's account he is not immaculate; he errs and sins and suffers, is defeated and shamed often, and for that reason appeals more closely to the human heart. And so with all his knights, except Sir Galahad, whose honour was without reproach or stain. It is the flower of chivalry which King Arthur typifies, grown in the garden of romance, full of poetic and spiritual symbolism, which charms us to-day, a flower of incomparable setting. The beauty of this setting, so simple, so effective, with all its crudity, is really beyond analysis. How, for instance, this presentment of Merlin in one of his many disguises, pictures him as he came one wild February day to King Arthur at the Castle of Bedegraine, in the forest of Sherwood....

There is wonderful picturesqueness and colour in Malory's descriptions, and the feeling for the environment of the untiring action of the book is of the highest order of romance. What could be more effective than the episode of the Brachet and the White Hart in the Book of Queen Guenever, or of the Fair Maid of Astolat, so exquisitely reset by Tennyson, or of the Vision of Sir

Launcelot in the book we have named after him? The account of Sir Launcelot's death in the last chapters of the last book is full of sorrowful beauty, and contains too the most remarkable prose passage in the *Morte D'Arthur*, that eloquent moral appeal beginning—'Oh, ye mighty and pompous lords!' [See No. 2 above.] There is an heroic elevatedness about the last book—the Book of the Morte D' Arthur—throughout, that specially marks it. Malory's practice in the earlier books seemed to have taught him a greater mastery of the means at his command. But in truth, wherever we turn, memorable passages occur tempting us to quote. Here, almost at random, is one from the Book of Balin le Savage, touched with most pathetic grace,—a passage once heard never to be forgotten.

[Quotes 'two hearts in one body' passage after death of Lanceor.]

... the damsel only comes to kill herself with her lover's sword, and her fatal fidelity is characteristic of the tragic consistency of the *Morte D'Arthur* episodes throughout.

The whole story of the Quest of the Holy Grail, again, is full of beauty, with its spiritual significance and mysticism woven most imaginatively into the main woof of the book. Walter Map, when he added this, giving coherency to the diffuse insertion of the various romances, showed true poetic perception. Before it was a mere testament of chivalry,—a chivalry of animal heat and energy; but now upon the knights fell the strange allurement of the Holy Ghost, and following its mystic impulse, they set forth on their new quest with passionate heroism and devotion....

Altogether the romance may be trusted to charm us to-day as it charmed its readers in Caxton's first edition. Its spirit of adventure, the spiritualised reflex of an age of animal energy, is a salutary one to move in our too reflective, critical modern order of literature. There is nothing of the latter-day morbid sentimentalism in it; throughout it is as fresh and breezy as the first west wind of spring. As a romance it is mainly significant; it bears especially upon the processes of tale-telling, and touches the root of the vexed question of romance and realism which is so exercising the present writers of fiction. From a purely literary point of view, it is in this respect that it chiefly commands attention; there is a potent fund of suggestion for the tale-teller in its simple methods and effects. Idealistic and realistic presentment; place and folk interest; dramatic movement:

there is curious lore to be learnt in these things from the book.

As collated by Malory, the epic interest of the *Morte D'Arthur* was not kept very strictly in mind, and a certain diffuseness and repetition resulted which have done much to deter the general reader from it. Malory's *Book* really resolves itself into three great divisions: first, the history of King Arthur proper; second, the romances of Sir Launcelot and Sir Tristram de Lyoness, which, chronicling the feats of arms of these two, the most famous of all the knights, become really the story of the long duel in knighthood and chivalry betwixt them; and third, the Quest of the Grail. In the present version it has been thought well to omit the second of these two divisions, which it is proposed to afterwards issue as a volume by itself, complementary to this of King Arthur and the Quest of the Grail. By this alteration the fateful epic consistency of the book is, it is believed, enhanced, and the tragic movement of the story on through the mysteries of the Holy Grail to the death of Arthur by the hands of Mordred is thrown into clearer outline. What other alterations it has been thought wise to make are explained in the notes at the end of the book, in which will be found, too, other information throwing light upon the present edition. . . .

NOTE

1 Of the *Morte D'Arthur* as prepared by Malory, seven out of the twenty-one Books have been here omitted, in order, as was explained in the Introduction, to throw the Arthurian history proper into clearer and more coherent form—the history, that is, as complemented by the Quest of the Grail. The omitted books, dealing chiefly with pure knight-errantry, as in the romances of Sir Launcelot, Sir Beaumains, Sir Tristram, and other of the knights, it is intended to publish shortly as a companion volume of the CAMELOT CLASSICS. One book, however, dealing with Arthur's Roman War, being neither history nor good romance, is cast aside altogether; and the Book of Sir Bors in the portion dealing with the Quest of the Holy Grail, though interesting in itself, being largely a repetition of adventures chronicled of other knights also, is reserved for a still further use in the series.

37. Brief references

1886-90

A. Frederic Harrison

1886

Frederic Harrison (1831–1923), author, popular lecturer, professor of jurisprudence, wrote prolifically on a variety of historical and literary subjects. In *The Choice of Books* (1886), Harrison provides some commentary and background information for favourite works of literature; in the extract below, he briefly compares the *Morte Darthur* and *The Cid* and later justifies calling Malory's work poetry.

Extracts are from *The Choice of Books* (London: Macmillan, 1925), pp. 43–5.

...Spain and the Celtic race of Western England and Western France have two great epic cycles, which cluster round the names of the Cid and of Arthur.

Whilst the Spanish Cycle is the more national, heroic, and stirring, the Arthurian Cycle is the best embodiment of chivalry, of romance, of gallantry. The vast cluster of tales which envelop King Arthur and his comrades is the expression of European chivalry and the feudal genius as a whole, idealising the knight, the squire, the lady, the princess of the Middle Ages. For all practical purposes, we English have it in its best form; for the compilation of Sir Thomas Malory is wrought into a mould of pure English, hardly second to the English of the Bible.[1]...

Methinks that the tale of the death of Arthur, Guinevere, and of Lancelot, as told by Malory, along with the death and last death-march of the Cid, as told in the Chronicle, may stand beside the funeral of Hector, which closes the Iliad—[2]

233

NOTES

1 It will be seen that in the original text of Malory about 98 per cent of the words are pure English, without Latin alloy.

2 In nothing has the revival of sound critical taste done better service than in recalling us to the Arthurian Cycle, the dayspring of our glorious literature. The closing books of Malory's Arthur certainly rank, both in conception and in form, with the best poetry of Europe; in quiet pathos and reserved strength they hold their own with the epics of any age. Beside this simple, manly type of the mediaeval hero the figures in the Idylls of the King look like the dainty Perseus of Canova placed beside the heroic Theseus of Pheidias.

It is true, as Mr. Matthew Arnold has said, that poetry and prose are perfectly distinct forms of utterance. But the line which marks off poetry from prose is not an absolutely rigid one, and we may have the essentials of poetry without metre or scansion. In Malory's Death of Arthur and Lancelot, or in Chapters of Job and Isaiah in the English Bible, we have the conceptions, the melody, the winged words, and inimitable turns of phrase which constitute the highest poetry. We need a term to include the best imaginative work in the most artistic form, and the only English word left is—poetry.

B. Alfred Trübner Nutt

1886, 1888

Alfred Trübner Nutt (1856–1910), publisher and scholar, produced in 1888 in his *Studies on the Legend of the Holy Grail* the first carefully researched consideration in England of the tangled and perplexing questions surrounding the origin and development of the Grail legend. Much of his pioneering work and certainly his central hypothesis regarding the Celtic origin of the Grail have become the 'givens' of much modern Grail scholarship.

His opinion of Malory's artistic skills is not high, but he admires the style. The first extract is taken from a review of Rhys's 1886 edition of part of Malory (see No. 36); it appeared in *Academy*, 29 (20 March 1886), 195–6. The review anticipates similar points to be noted in the second extract,

from Nutt's book (London: David Nutt, 1888, reprinted
New York: Cooper Square, 1965), pp. 235–6.

(a)

This edition of Malory's 'most pleasant jumble or summary of the
Arthurian legends,' to use Mr. Furnivall's telling words, deserves,
and will doubtless meet with, a cordial welcome....

Mr. Rhys has printed, broadly speaking, those portions of
Malory's work relating to Arthur's youth, to Lancelot and his love
for Guinevere, to the Grail Quest, to Modred's rebellion, and to the
final woe. He has followed Caxton's text in the main faithfully,
contenting himself with modernising the spelling, with occasional
substitution of newer for archaic words and expressions, and with
omission or alteration of phrases 'which the squeamishness of the
day might object to.' He has provided an introduction explaining
the general scope and aim of the Camelot Classics series, and
dwelling upon the genesis and spirit of Malory's work. On this
head Mr. Rhys has little to say that is new. He can hardly be
blamed, however, for following the current English text-books,
instead of attempting an independent study of the Arthur cycle. In
few departments of literary history is the temptation greater to
accept the opinion of others. And yet, in view of the immense
importance of the Arthurian romance in the history of European
literature, it seems desirable to trace the main outlines of its growth
more definitely than has hitherto been done.

[Outlines early developments from ballads and short tales (now lost)
to cycles and later romances including relationships among several
Grail and Lancelot romances.]

  Towards the end of the twelfth century a new Quest of the Grail,
differing profoundly both in spirit and in the general conduct of the
story from that of Crestien, yet obviously based in part upon his or
upon an allied version, was tacked on to the Lancelot, in its turn
revised to bring it into harmony with its new sequel. This new
Quest substituted Galahad for the original hero Percival, whom,
however, not daring entirely to banish, it relegated to the second
place. As it followed the Lancelot, it was naturally ascribed to the
same author, Map. Later still, another writer took Borron's poem as

a ground-work, added largely to it by the introduction of episodes copied bodily from, or designed to bring it into harmony with, the pseudo-Map Quest, and thus produced the work known as the Grand St. Graal. In reality a second draft of Borron's poem, it came naturally enough to be ascribed to him by the copyists. It reads as the natural prologue to the pseudo-Map Quest; hence, in the MSS. it often immediately precedes it. The revised Lancelot, with the pseudo-Map Quest woven into it, seems to have been an especial favourite in England. Together with portions of the Tristram cycle and the Arthur-sage, it forms the staple of Malory's compilation, which thus dealt with but a small portion of the existing Arthurian romance, and with that in its latest shape and when it had been revised for harmonising purposes. An artificial air of unity is thus obtained, rendered more striking in the present volume by the elimination of all that belongs to the Tristram cycle.

Mr. Rhys's statements (Introduction, p. xxix.) may now be examined.

[Points out inaccuracies in Rhys's tracing of the development of romances before Malory.]

These questions have not a mere antiquarian interest. There can be no sound aesthetic criticism of the Arthurian romances until the place of each in, and its relation to the other members of, the whole cycle have been determined. Mr. Rhys refers several times to the 'fateful epic consistency' of Malory's work, and speaks thus of the 'Idylls of the King':

> In these poems, nobly perfect in themselves, we see at once an ominous sign of the times in that what has been called our English prose epic should lose its high proportion and its fateful coherency.

If what I have said is correct, Malory's work is, in no sense of the word, an epic; it is a combination of some among the latest forms of an immense body of romance literature which originally had no real connexion one with the other. Never was Lord Tennyson better inspired by his genius than when he resorted to the idyllic presentment in his retelling of the Arthur stories. Their true charm and beauty, the charm and beauty of Celtic literature generally, lie in felicity and picturesqueness of style, in exquisite rendering of detail, in a subtle fairy-like glamour found nowhere else. Much of this charm still clings to the pages of Malory, and ensures him his enduring place among English classics. But we must look elsewhere for 'epic' merits and characteristics. The unhappy nature of the 'epic' estimate of Malory is shown by reference to the Grail episode. We are told that this gives 'coherency to the diffuse insertion of the various romances.' Now, were Malory's work really an epic, the introduction of the Grail Quest would constitute the most deplorable of anti-climaxes. The achievement of the Quest in no way affects the fate of Arthur. It does not even affect the after-life of Lancelot, who plays such a prominent part in it. Nor is the episode more satisfactory if considered solely with reference to its chief hero. Galahad achieves at last the adventure there is no reason he should not have achieved at the outset, dies—'et praeterea nihil'; the 'epic' goes on as if nothing had happened. Nor can I look upon the enthusiasm (re-echoed by Mr. Rhys) about its 'spiritual significance' as justified. Mystic fervour cannot be denied to many passages; but our favourable verdict is probably influenced by the glamour cast backwards upon the romance by those perfect lines in which the Laureate has distilled, as it were, whatever it contained of pure and lovely. But we must not let ourselves be blinded to the real spirit of the work. Mr. Furnivall finds in it 'that deep seated reverence for woman which is the most refining, and one of the noblest sentiments of man's nature.' It may be added—and one the least likely to have occurred to the author of the Quest. Physical chastity is therein exalted, with the grossness peculiar to asceticism, not because woman was reverenced, but because she was abhorred. Carnal sin is condemned because committed with her through whom sin first came into the world. This sentiment may be admirable or not; but it should not be confounded with our modern ideal of chastity. It is hardly too much to say that the morality, such as it is, of sinful Lancelot is truer, more human, and therefore more progressive, than that of sinless Galahad. Malory, it is true, occasionally tones down the grossness of the first draft; and for this, as well as for his swift, clear, and vivacious narrative (compared, that is, with so much of the Arthurian romance), his work will always remain the best introduction to the cycle at large. But it must not be forgotten that it is a late attempt at fusing into some sort of whole a number of independent, often discordant, stories. And whoever would learn the utmost artistic capabilities of the Arthurian legends as exhibited in mediaeval literature, who would rightly estimate the wealth of passionate human interest, of profound moral thought, which lie therein embedded, must put Malory aside and turn to Gottfried von Strassburg and Wolfram von Eschenbach.

(b)
In England the Grail-legend is hardly known save in that form which it has assumed in the Queste. This French romance was one of those which Malory embodied in his *rifacimento* of the Arthurian cycle, and, thanks to Malory, it has become a portion of English speech and thought.[1] In our own days our greatest poet has expressed the quintessence of what is best and purest in the old romance in lines of imperishable beauty. ... And yet of the two main paths which the legend has trodden that of Galahad is the least fruitful and the least beautiful. Compared with the Perceval Quest in its highest literary embodiment the Galahad Quest is false and antiquated on the ethical side, lifeless on the aesthetic side.

NOTE

1 Malory is a wonderful example of the power of style. He is a most unintelligent compiler. He frequently chooses out of the many versions of the legend, the longest, most wearisome, and least beautiful; his own contributions to the story are beneath contempt as a rule. But his language is exactly what it ought to be, and his has remained in consequence the classic English version of the Arthur story.

C. Henry Morley

1890

Henry Morley (1822–94), author, editor, lecturer, teacher, began a comprehensive biographical and critical literary history of England in 1864, but completed only two volumes (down to Dunbar) before allowing the project to lapse. In 1873, he brought out in a single volume *A First Sketch of English Literature*, which went through more than a dozen editions. In the 1880s he returned to the larger project of the

1860s and produced ten volumes of *English Writers* down to Shakespeare.

These volumes are often cited through the period; however, Morley's romance criticism is, for the 1880s, old-fashioned, little altered if at all from the work done some twenty years before. His remarks on Malory are somewhat incidental to his longer discussion of Caxton, but he does notice the structural problem of the Tristram section.

From *English Writers*, VI (1890), third edition (London: Cassell & Co., 1896), 330–1.

Little is known of Sir Thomas Malory, from whom Caxton obtained his prose version of the 'History of Arthur,' which gave the main incidents in the cycle of Arthurian romance arranged in their due order. ... He has certainly retained the spirit in which Walter Map arranged the sequence of the tales, with the romance of the Graal set in their midst to blend with the tales of earthly love and war a heavenly inspiration. The very soul of mediaeval Christianity breathes out of the story of the Quest of the Graal as told with simple directness by Sir Thomas Malory. The great popularity of the romance of Tristram and King Mark's wife, the fair Isolde, made it impossible that Malory should have thought of omitting that. But in some sense Tristram is to Isolde as Lancelot to Guinevere. The romance of Tristan was an early offshoot from the sequence planned by Walter Map, and a reader of Sir Thomas Malory's 'History of Arthur' might get a better impression of the sequence of adventures, as Map had arranged them, by omitting from the first reading those chapters which interweave the tale of Tristram and Isolde. They were inseparable from the Arthur Legend of Sir Thomas Malory's time, but they break the harmony of the first arrangement by burdening one part of it with variations on its motive.

38. Edward R. Russell

1889

Edward, Lord Russell (1834–1920), knighted in 1893 and elevated to the baronage in 1919, was the long-time editor of the *Liverpool Post*. In addition, he published a number of pamphlets on Shakespeare and essays on Marlowe, Garrick, Irving, and Ibsen. He was widely known for his lectures on these playwrights and actors as well, and contributed articles and reviews on these and other topics to numerous periodicals. His pamphlet *The Book of King Arthur* (Liverpool, 1889) was originally a paper read before the Literary and Philosophical Society of Liverpool.

Russell finds that the *Morte Darthur* has charm but no great merit; his generally low rating of its appeal to the intellect of enlightened nineteenth-century man makes the more impressive his praise of the portrait of Lancelot.

Extracts are from *The Book of King Arthur* (Liverpool: D. Marples, 1889), pp. 4–7, 17–22, and 25–36. A number of pages of plot summary and lengthy quoting have been omitted.

... Caxton recognised in a Shakspearian spirit the mingled character of the scene and the personages: 'chivalry, courtesy, humanity, friendliness, hardiness, love, friendship, cowardice, murder, hate, virtue and sin. Do,' said he, 'after the good and leave the evil'....

To this admirable teaching must be at once appended the statement, afterwards to be attested more at large, that the sermon is not in every sense warranted by the text. While the finest and supreme ideal of the book, associated with the pursuit and achievement of the Holy Grail is uncompromisingly pure, almost to the edge of miracle, the ordinary and working standard hypothesis of virtue is in one point, most essential in human life, extremely low; much lower than is now professed or, it may be hoped, practised. Significantly enough King Arthur himself, though nearly as good as men are made, is not brought into the quest of the Holy Grail at all. The one man who achieves it is almost miraculously as free from stain as the Saviour of the world himself. And unquestionably the finest type of intelligent and conscious virtue presented except Arthur, Galahad and Percivale, is that of a man who lives his active life through in deliberate and permitted, but always on one side of it, faithful sin—the knight of whom Tennyson in one of the most perfect and pregnant of epigrams says, that—

> His honour rooted in dishonour stood,
> And faith unfaithful kept him falsely true.

In all such comments now and throughout the paper I am not troubling to find fault. It is superfluous. We have but to observe. The morals here mirrored are the morals of Errant Knighthood— errant in a double sense. The interest lies in this as an historical phase of evolution in ethics—in the curious place which it held in point of time—and in the question (too large for our debate) how far such toleration is a necessary element in the highest imaginative literature: possibly in all generous judgings of human life.

To what extent the moral atmosphere of Morte D'Arthur was that of Sir Thomas Malory's time—the time of Edward the Fourth; to what extent it was merely the moral atmosphere attributed to mythical times and scenes in earlier and cruder romances—to what extent it accurately represented the moral atmosphere of chivalry, when chivalry actually existed—each must decide for himself. ... In a vast proportion of cases the formal worship of ideals artistically blended with Christian ideas was carried on along with free indulgence in enjoyments which were not chaste at all, and where a special degree of virtue was attained and maintained it was rarely that of continence, but only that of continuance in one faithful long protracted *liaison*. When all else of chivalry except this and belligerent personal bravery had died out, we can well imagine that Sir Thomas Malory would know of much in his own times which would enable him to give point and effect to everything that he had to say of the relations of men and women in framing from the old French stories and any other materials the epic of King Arthur.

That it is a prose epic, and that he did so frame it, I shall assume without discussion. The chronology appears to be something like this: King Arthur—a King Arthur of some sort—lived and did deeds of kingly (if not knightly) prowess about the beginning of the sixth century. Three centuries later the stories of King Arthur began to take form in various writings of chivalry, and these composed in bulk a quite considerable literature. Scholars say that Sir Thomas Malory used these materials very much as we know Shakspeare to have used his—improving the stories, and adding bright touches of nature, of pathos, of grace, and of moral interest. Sir Edward Strachey calls him a Shakspeare-like or Homeric man. We know little, perhaps, of how Homer composed his epic, but if we are of opinion that Homer wrote Homer we can imagine that in an infantile manner, and with children material, Malory did in prose for a chivalry literature spreading over centuries, and having supposititious roots in ages of myth, what Homer did for the material which tradition had accumulated for him. And here again we must be struck with what I have already hinted at—the curious position of these legends, whether as written by Malory or as prepared in the rough from the ninth century downwards—their curious position in point of time. Childish they are in comparison with the adult majesty, and scope, and pregnancy of Homer written two thousand years before. Infinitely greater is the contrast between their childishness and the perfected, the God-like man-hood of Shakspeare, written about a hundred years after Malory was composed and printed. ...

If the sentimental occupation of the Knights was love, their actual business was adventurous fighting. An enormous proportion of Malory's Book is taken up with narratives of their combats, in which there is little merit, and what there is is spoilt by being repeated, and repeated over so large a surface. One can well understand how a bored world may well have sighed for a Cervantes to deliver it by caricature from such endless and bald repetitions of the same old mauling about. Indeed if those ages had by miracle prophetically sighed for a Mark Twain it would not have been by any means wonderful, under such dire and wearisome provocation. The old language and the men being encased in knightly armour of course makes a difference, but intrinsically there is no more intellectual interest in those slashings, and staggerings, and buffetings, and piercings than in an account of prize fighting in *Bell's Life*, and they are entirely devoid of that ingenuity and invention of cant synonyms which made *Bell's Life in*

London fifty years ago a respectable precursor—well, no—but a lively precursor of the most slangy American journalism.

The accounts of knightly struggles given in Sir Thomas Malory's work may almost be said to be drawn in a common form. There is just a little variety in the terms in which the knights challenge each other and vaunt themselves, and in the manner in which they behave when their opponents are completely at their mercy. ... The average fight of two knights is incessantly repeated *ad nauseam* in the absolute identity of phraseology. First they come on the field like thunder. Then they feuter their spears and come upon each other with a great crash. One usually unhorses the other. Then the knight still on horseback requires the knight who is afoot to yield. He always refuses, and in quite a large proportion of cases shouts out what on the first occasion of its use may have seemed a witty and original saying—that he has been betrayed by the son of a mare, but is not going to give in to the son of a woman. Then they avoid their horses and pull out their swords, and lash together as men that are wild and courageous, and often their shields fly in cantels, and the place all around streams with blood. Then they leave their strokes and foin at their breathes and visors. When they see that that may not avail them, they hurtle together like rams to bear either other down. Both are wounded passing sore that the blood runs freshly from them to the ground; but one waxes more fresher than the other, and better winded and bigger; and so with a mighty stroke he smites the other on the helm such a buffet that it goes through the helm, and through his coif of steel, and through the brain pan, so that the sword sticks so fast in the helm and in the brain pan that the victor knight pulls thrice at his sword or ever he may get it out from the other's head; and then the conquered knight falls down on his knees, the edge of the other's sword left in his brain pan.

This palls. Once or twice one may bear with it. When it is multiplied indefinitely with only a little bit of separate character to refresh the wearied reader it forfeits all claim to be literature, and becomes mere traces of customs and tastes, which if they cannot be got out of civilisation are at least unworthy and incapable of being glorified by good writing. ...

The noblest and most interesting struggle in the Book is that in which Arthur himself fights Sir Accolon and successfully resists for many hours both the bravery and skill of his antagonist, and the acts of the wicked Morgan le Fay, by which the antagonist has been feloniously armed. . . . It is clear that the literary merit of the book rises here, because there are novelty and scope in the incidents. It is not mere fighting. The rival enchantments, the heroic defiance of an extraordinary fate, the fearsome failure of the better knight's weapon, the noble continuance of the battle disarmed, and the dramatic recovery of Excalibur make up a splendid scene and story, and the language in which they are presented is such as may well fill any literary Englishman with reminiscent pride and fervent gratitude.

In the vein one degree removed above the mere fighting level, but consisting largely of fighting detail, is the story of Tristram— the knight of sorrowful birth but very cheerful life. No part of it, either in narrative of conflict or any other element, rises to the point of interest attained in the combat between Arthur and Accolon; and the whole creation is infinitely below the standard of moral interest sustained throughout the story of Sir Launcelot of the Lake. Tristram had no conscience to speak of on the subject of marriage and connubial fidelity. He does not appear, however, to have had any wayward or merely animal passions, and he was a fine, manly, trusty, courteous, cordial, powerful and unconquerable knight errant. La Beale Isoud, another knight's wife, was 'the causer of his honour,' and to her he was always true; and without any of the qualms and scruples and crises by which Sir Launcelot's love for Guenever was chequered. In the general run of the lives, and especially in his going mad, there was a considerable parallelism between the two careers. With Launcelot he was immediately compared by every one who knew them both, and the reader finds that this instinct is soon bred in him as naturally as it existed among the knights and ladies of Arthur's society. Launcelot himself recognised the supreme knightly merit of Tristram. It was one of Launcelot's noble qualities always to be generously just. Tristram's open and admirable knightliness is thrown up into high relief by the dark and sinister meanness of his enemy King Marke. The fact that he was the known lover of Marke's queen did not derogate from his popularity in Arthur's or probably in Malory's time— when the only penalty of a knight's adultery was that he was not considered fit to be one of the two knights in all the world who found the Holy Grail. Even in our day the very treacherous manner in which King Marke behaves wins sympathy for the successful paramour and provokes disgust towards the injured husband. The love of Tristram and Isoud is, however, common-place. It is just a noble-hearted man and a loving woman. Anything else has to be read into it by modern poetry or composed upon the rude theme of it by modern music. . . .

Of Guenever's great sin nothing is to be said here; first, because this is not a sermon; secondly, because it could not be spoken of in due reprobation without going out of the tone of the book we are criticising. The morality must be taken as it is. Allowing for different periods and manners, it is that which is supposed to be the morality of the French novel. The only commandment which was greatly respected at King Arthur's and King Marke's courts was that which forbids being found out. Nor can I agree that, except in the most conventional way, and in reference to sins that knighthood had no mind to, the writer endeavours to distinguish between vice and virtue. All that is written about the quest of the Holy Grail is as solemn as it is superstitious. When set to Wagner's unparalleled music it is capable of obtaining the most profound command over the heart. It is touching too to find Launcelot, noblest of men, prevented from succeeding in the quest by the Divine cognisance of his sin. The transparent beauty of the virgin Sir Galahad and Sir Percivale must also live luminous for ever in the imagination of mankind. But it is impossible not to feel that, according to the view of Sir Thomas Malory and of knighthood, purity is a virtue 'too bright and good for human nature's daily food.'

Our review would be too long if discrimination were made between the characters of the knights; and though very distinct and interestingly distinguishable, the majority of these personages are not important enough to demand detailed description. But it is due to the literary and dramatic excellence of the work to recognise that much as they are necessarily alike each is different from the other as real man must differ from real man.

The story and character of Launcelot are probably unique. Here we are in a separate atmosphere—an atmosphere which, so to speak, the hero carries about with him. Although it is an atmosphere of sin it is a nimbus of glory. It protects him not against the vicissitudes of a life not wholly pure. It shields him not from the searching penetration of omniscience. 'Thou God seest me' might be emblazoned upon the cloud by which Launcelot is environed—might be the text of all the sermons that good men preach him. But his sin is so glorious; his unfaith is so faithful; the single line of evil in his course is so arrow-straight and undeviating; even his treachery to his sovereign is so full of love and so devoid of any injury or malfeasance beyond the one great, continuous wrong of it; his recognition of his sweet guilt as inevitable is so solemnly and simply absolute; his reverence for abstract purity is so evidently genuine; his submission to spiritual verities is so heartfelt though inoperative; his final penitence is so loyal and yet so curiously and magnificently imperfect and unreal from the inconceivableness of his being stable in the avoidance of Guenever; and in every other respect and relation of life his character is so perfect and yet so free from pretention—so simply transparent, so strong and manly, so powerful in mind and body, so gracious and so ready in self-sacrifice, so easy in confiding, so frank and natural in forgiveness, that this sinner, this disloyal knight, this adulterer, this man unworthy to participate in Christian mysteries, stands among the very highest in the intuitive and indefeasible admiration of the Christian world. Launcelot is a sort of irresistible proof, put in evidence by a genius capable of establishing its creations indisputably in the credence of mankind—an irresistible proof that sin is not necessarily Satanic—that in the most damning guilt there may be no malignity—that, explain it how we may, sexual guilt (perhaps any guilt) does not always 'harden all within and petrify the feeling.' The subtleties of sin have often been tracked and dissected, but never with such classic simplicity—never with such restraint of diction—never with such a marvellous combination of sharpness and tenderness in the analysis—never with so perfect a perception under rudimentary forms of the good that abides in evil—never with so perfect an avoidance of the mawkish—never with such unconscious and gospel-like literary severity. When one remembers how plain, unadorned, uncomplicated and unsophisticated the story of Launcelot is, one feels almost ashamed to have used so many words in praising it; but the very simplicity of a great work of art may demand copiousness and detail in the criticism of it. In sum, what must be said of the story of Launcelot in the Book of King Arthur is that its classic merit is incomparably superior to everything else in Malory's work, and that, elementary as are its style and scope, it places its author among the six or seven really great 'makers' of the world—with Homer, with Shakspeare, with Cervantes, with Goethe, with Sterne, with Thackeray, and with George Eliot.

It is the story of the problems and passages of a knightly life, in which one darling sin is not resisted, but takes the place of virtue. From the beginning of the Morte D'Arthur the singular power of this conception exhibits its hold alike upon the author and upon his personages. The nobleness of Launcelot is alway prominently mentioned. Early in the book Merlin the enchanter constructs a bed in which no man shall ever lie without losing his wits; but it is interpolated that Launcelot 'fordid that bed through his nobleness.' That is to say, he lay in it and did not go out of his mind. He is never mentioned without, as it were, a bating of the breath, part admiration, part sorrow. Other knights were as knightly, and by any standard of chivalry Sir Tristram would be accounted his equal alike in prowess and in character; yet about Tristram's peccadilloes and great sin neither author nor personages seem to be troubled. The moment Launcelot comes in sight the minds of author, personages, and readers become attuned to a sad yet delightful sympathising melancholy. Although the judgment perforce condemns him, it is only by a positive moral effort that one can wish him other than he is. He is made so pathetic a figure by his devotion to Guenever; by his impeccable persistence in that devotion, from which in spirit he never falters, and only degenerates from it in act, under magical influences which persuade him of the identity of other women with the queen; by the sufferings which he undergoes in consequence of his loyalty to his illicit but romantic love; by the curt and pettish, if not harsh, treatment which he receives from Guenever without moulting a feather of his devotion; by the noble courtesy of the unmoved indifference with which he receives the affectionate demonstrations of other ladies whose hearts are set upon him; and by the pensive resignation with which he accepts, as a proper and just disability, that exclusion from the highest spiritual privileges that falls upon him in consequence of his sin, although he is admitted to be the noblest and best knight among sinful men.

While it may be allowed that on the whole Tennyson's Launcelot is a fine and sympathetic version of the character, it must be added that in labouring and refining upon it the modern poet has detrimentally changed its precise effect upon the reader of Sir Thomas Malory's book. And the numerous living persons who are acquainted with the Arthurian stories only through Tennyson, need also to be told that King Arthur, excellent husband as he is, shows no sign of making himself understood by Guenever, or of carrying her along with him, from first to last. They agree. They perform their royal functions in harmony. Their mutual demeanour and relations correspond with the conceptions most of us have of the probable life of husbands and wives in very high places. They never wrangle. Arthur, we are told, from the time he first saw her never loved any other woman. But there is not much sign that ever Guenever loved him except in a very matter-of-fact way; and Arthur was too serious and too seriously occupied to worry himself about the precise complexion and temperature of her love. Probably he thought it was all right, though everybody else knew it was all wrong, and whenever his queen's honour was impeached he confidently and warmly committed the defence of her honour to Launcelot. Launcelot was certainly the knight most bound to defend her, though the last upon whom, if he had known everything, King Arthur would have called. He did not know everything. In fact, the trouble was to get him to know anything. Repeatedly, Launcelot's strong arm re-established the queen's honour according to the absurd fashion of the time. She was fortunate in having a lover of such prowess. And at last, when under circumstances of glaring scandal, King Arthur had to recognise his wife's guilt and to break with Launcelot, it was made evident by his swoonings and his laments that the loss of his friend was the greater trouble of the two.

The simplicity of Sir Launcelot's character was most remarkable. He appears never to have had a double thought. His hold upon the affections of those around him was complete. He is not described as having any of the arts of a squire of dames, and so far from laying himself out to captivate them, his thoughts were ever on Guenever, but one after another fell desperately in love with him. None did he encourage. To all he was sweetly kind. It cannot be said that he made any real effort to break the golden chains of his infatuation, though his sense of deprivation when not allowed to behold the Holy Grail appears to have been none the less severe. But he was told on all hands, what was true, that he was 'feeble of evil trust and good belief.' He was a man of evil faith and poor belief. He trusted more, and his heart was more set on an earthly good, and that by no right his, than on the great mystic verities of which he yet had a stronger feeling, as became the depth of his nature, than any other knight. He made his prayer to a cross after being encouraged to hope that he might see the Sancgreal; but he was ever unstable in the one matter, and this infected his otherwise beautiful life. He all but saw the Holy Grail in a vision, and lay in a consequent trance many days; and when he awoke and 'saw folk he made great sorrow, and said "Why have ye wakened me, for I was better at ease than I am now. Oh! Jesu Christ, who might be so blessed, that might see openly the great marvels of secretness, there where no sinner may be."' But he was never stable, so the Book says, or always stable, as you may say if you prefer it. 'By his thought he was likely to turn again,' even when, as was rare, he resolved, or rather prayed, to avoid the besetting frailty which had become his very life. It was after this that he indulged with the queen in the amour at the castle of Sir Meliagraunce, and indeed there never was a question whether he would yield or not when her fascinations were around him. To think most highly of him, you must observe how it was only she that ever could lead him from the true path of moral loyalty—how faithful he was to her—how exquisitely gentle—how firm as a rock he was in holding off other women—how gracious and self-sacrificing he was in his jousts and in his deadliest combats—how he worshipped the King he was daily wronging, and would have fought for him with entire self-abnegation, as always so to the close, had not his and the Queen's love, as she expressed it, 'come to a mischievous end.'

With the breach between Arthur and Launcelot ended the glory and dominion of the King. The fall of Arthur's kingship, his mysterious passing away, and Launcelot's single hearted melancholy compose the climax of the epic. 'Alas!' said Sir Launcelot, 'this is the heaviest tidings that ever came to me.'

It is easy to imagine—it is diffcult not to imagine, when you have surrendered yourself to Launcelot's beautiful and subtle though primitive story—the half puzzled brooding into which his mind would be thrown by the ruin brought upon those he most loved by a sin the heinousness of which he had never realized, even under the sharpest Divine reproofs, and which even then he would have resumed if opportunity had been afforded him. It is a sufficient literary vindication, if this is true, to some phases of human nature, as well as finely done. I hold that it is both, and that the achievement is a remarkable one.*

Scarcely less remarkable is the extremely delicate portraiture of

King Arthur. That a husband so egregiously trustful, and so perpetually deceived, should be clearly and uncompromisingly exhibited in this character in a rough age, and never be subjected to a word of despite or contumely, or made a butt for ridicule, is extraordinary. When one of Guenever's acts of infidelity is rudely exposed by uncouth knights, it is finely said that King Arthur would not have displaced her curtains. Alike to men and women, this mirror of chivalry always presented a surface at once true and smooth. He was never untrue of his promise, never deficient in charity, never failed in courtesy, never misdoubted a seeming friend.

Any general observations that I can offer in conclusion must be confused and complicated by a profound difficulty which I feel in reasonably making out the place of the Book of King Arthur in literary development. For those who accept Tennyson the question is easier. His Idylls are at once more capable of being sympathised with by rational readers of this century, and more what we should expect a thousand years after the coming of Christ. Even they are below the level of moral manhood reached in the educated life of Greece and Rome fifteen hundred years before. And though the roots of Tennyson are in Malory we cannot be sure, and in fact we feel it to be most unlikely, that anything like Tennyson grew from them until centuries of cultured imagination had imbued them with a higher life not their own. Thus we are landed with what seems a problem—the existence in the thousandth year of Christianity, and amidst a full provision of Christian ordinances, almost exactly corresponding with those existing to-day, of a state of society most elementary and primitive, infinitely less advanced in its reasons and motives than the society of ancient Greece and Rome. Is it or is it not true that an ordinarily cultivated man of to-day finds his mind moving freely about with Thucydides, Plato, Livy, Tacitus and Pliny, while he can only take a perfunctory interest in the manners, doings, and modes of thought of the period of the Round Table? Regarded seriously the Book of King Arthur is very much as if men had descended to become interesting dumb animals, even lacking the wistfulness under limitations which is seen in dumb animals by those who understand them....

If the Nineteenth Century has any perplexities which can be solved by the problems of Camelot, it must be in a very babyish condition. Some of the ideals of knighthood have been very properly discarded. Others have been developed into high and spiritual perfection, so that the Nineteenth Century has no need to recur to the beggarly elements of the Tenth or the Fifteenth....

I must say that I shrink from these conclusions as much in the philosophy of religion as in the evolution of literature. And in both we have the great encouragement of experience for a contrary opinion. Simple incidents and simple emotions alike in religion and in literature must always have their place and power. In all ages they have retained their place and power. But that they might do so it was never necessary that the play of the intellect should be limited to the mere rudimentary thoughts and feelings which are identified with the most childish forms of literature and the most ceremonial types of religion. The primitive composition of Sir Thomas Malory, having bequeathed the fair and noble music of its language to the English of the future, was soon followed by the translation of Utopia, by the authorised version of the English Bible, by the Essays of Lord Bacon, by the History of Sir Walter Raleigh, and by the wonderful productions of the Elizabethan age in almost every region of human thought. Theology and spiritual life never relinquished the basis upon which the religious part of Sir Thomas Malory's book was built; but in successive ages great divines and preachers have substituted for the bald and almost blind devotion of a monastic cult and of miraculous legends a vast range of inspiring contemplations and exhortations, in which the spirit of man expatiates not by means of the lowest and most abject, but through the highest and most soaring of his faculties. And from this height there should be no declension in the operative and working mind. What I mean is, that although it may be good and interesting to read and even study the stories of King Arthur or any other memorials of an inferior past, there should be no taking them or their spirit for serious guidance....

... The Book of King Arthur treats of a mythical age, and deals with mythical people in a manner which would be easy enough to understand if it dated from an earliest age. Written about 1480, and narrating supposed events of from 800 to 1100, it puzzles us, as to how such a period could have been so mythical, and as to how the ethical spirit of such an age can have become so elementary. The charm of it must be admitted; the value of it is but moderate. Its simplicity and primitiveness are part of a great enigma—the decay of literature and intelligence during the first thousand years of

Christianity. In the rapid advance of literature and intelligence from Sir Thomas Malory's point of time—an advance so much more rapid than any that followed the productions of Chaucer—we may perhaps detect an illustration, not only of the value of printing, but of that extraordinary action of prose language in exploiting and generating mental power which has still to be taken into due consideration in accounting for the beginnings of civilisation.

39. Frederick Ryland

1888–9

'The Morte d'Arthur', *English Illustrated Magazine*, 6 (1888–9), pp. 55–64 and 86–92.

Frederick Ryland (1854–1902) lectured at University College, London, and published student manuals on logic and psychology. He also edited Swift, Locke, and Johnson, and drew up a *Chronological Outline of English Literature* presumably as an aid to memorization for students; the work went through numerous editions.

In the article below, besides noting some of Malory's alterations to his Vulgate sources, Ryland points out that Malory and other medieval authors cannot be judged by neo-classical standards. (See Introduction, pp. 22–4.) His lengthy passages of quotation and paraphrasing from Malory have been omitted.

For the reference to the popularizing efforts of Rhys, see No. 36; B. Montgomerie Ranking was the editor of *La Mort d'Arthur: The Old Prose Stories Whence the 'Idylls of the King' Have Been Taken* (London: John Camden Hotten, 1871), a book of selections from Malory and the *Mabinogion*.

Sir Thomas Malory's *Morte d'Arthur* is one of the many books whose fate is to be more talked about than read. Most educated men would be ashamed to own they knew nothing of it, but very few could give any account of what took place at the Chapel Perilous and in the Castle of Damsels, or indicate the exact relationship between Sir Ector de Maris and Sir Galahad. The work is accessible in a cheap and readable form; but boys fight shy of it, preferring apparently the quasi-scientific romance of Jules Verne and his imitators, while girls are given over to the seductive delights of the love story. Mr. Montgomerie Ranking and Mr. Ernest Rhys have done something to popularise it by their volumes of selections, but the fact remains that the original is not a book with a large audience of young people. Among elder folk, popular scientific works, biographies of third-rate politicians, and flimsy histories of the last half-century occupy the leisure of the more serious; while the frivolous have sensational tales, or at best the somewhat rarified novels of the American gentlemen who have proclaimed themselves the successors, and superiors, of Dickens and Thackeray. They would never think of turning for instruction and amusement to a fifteenth century recension of a set of twelfth century romances. What of speculation or of conduct is to be learnt from men who believed in all sorts of superstitions, persecuted the Jews, and knew nothing of evolution and electrical lighting? Or what pleasure is to be got from a work of fiction without plot and without psychological analysis, and wholly innocent of realism, whether after the manner of Mr. Howells or the manner of M. Zola? Not a single library edition has been published since Southey's quartos in 1818, unless Wright's reprint of 1858 can be so-called, and every publisher I have asked has told me that such an edition would not sell.

The *Morte d'Arthur*, which is certainly the most important piece of English prose written before the age of Elizabeth, is a compilation and translation, more or less free, of certain selected romances in the Arthurian cycle. The chief of these are the *Joseph d' Arimathie* and *Merlin* of Robert de Boron, the *Tristram* of Luces de Gast, with the continuation by Hélie de Boron, the *Lancelot*, *Sangrall*, and *Morte d'Arthur* of Walter Map, and the *Perceval* of Chrestien de Troyes. These in turn were connected, harmonised, and enlarged forms of legends, written or unwritten, mainly of Celtic origin, but perhaps in some degree traceable to the classical stories of Troy and Thebes, of Jason and Alexander. The first to give a literary shape to these old-world stories had been Geoffrey of Monmouth, in his *History of British Kings*, written about 1140; but the form he chose was an imitation of authentic history. De Boron and his followers were more happy. They boldly adopted the form of romance. Their stories necessarily often overlapped, and many discrepancies in incident, character, and moral tone appeared. The Welsh knight, or (it may be) priest, Sir Thomas Malory, pieced together the best of the various French romances, and thus produced what Mr. Furnivall somewhat slightingly calls his 'pleasant jumble,' the *Morte d'Arthur*, in 1470. His share in the work must not be overlooked. There is no real evidence of any French compilation followed by Malory, who must be assumed to have selected, compressed, and arranged, as well as translated. He deserves at any rate the honour which is due to patient editing. He often leaves out unsatisfactory passages, and sometimes shows considerable judgment in his selection of incidents. In the earlier part of the book he follows De Boron; but he does well to omit the unpoetical and unpleasant details with which De Boron decorates the story of the diabolical origin of Merlin. He shows again true artistic sensibility in following Map rather than De Boron in the legend of the Sangraal, and by dropping the prosaic account of the origin of the graal, he leaves it clothed in a haze of mystery and spiritual suggestion.

Of a connected and coherent story there is small trace.

[Plot summaries.]

In all this there is of course a lack of such interest as proceeds from the involution and solution of difficulties, the suspended explanation of incidents, and the convergence of separate trains of action. The nearest approach to plot interest lies in the element of prophecy, chiefly, though not entirely, due to Merlin. Many prophetic utterances are introduced only in order to be immediately fulfilled: but others serve a more artistic purpose by raising our expectation of fulfilment, and by introducing a bond of unity, however slight, into the chaos of incident. Such are the repeated predictions about the Siege Perilous—'There shall no man sit but one, and if there be any so hardy to do it, he shall be destroyed, and he that shall sit there shall have no fellow'; the prediction about the dolorous stroke which Sir Balin should give; and that about the great battle near Salisbury which Mordred should fight against Arthur. The accomplishing of the sinister oracle in Mordred, the incestuous offspring of the king, although containing all the features of a classical tragedy such as that of Oedipus, is not dwelt on sufficiently to compel our interest and stimulate our continued expectation.

There is thus a long succession of incidents of an episodical nature, with little other connection than the fact that they occurred to the same set of persons; not as a rule rising out of each other, or proceeding from the characters of those who are concerned in them, and having no claim to that coherence and development which are needed to constitute the most elementary plot. Herein we have a curious contrast to the Homeric poems. Whatever may have been the origin of these, they have been worked into a homogeneous whole. The traditional material is everywhere assimilated, and the adequacy, consistency, and economy of the story are remarkable in a very high degree. Malory, translating and piecing together his originals, has taken no pains to evolve a well-defined plot for his epic. He leaves it a beautiful wilderness in which a man may wander all day without understanding how the several parts lie with regard to each other.

The *Morte d'Arthur* is in fact a very typical product of the art of the Middle Ages, which always tends to subordinate form to matter, rejoicing in rich multiplicity of detail, in beautiful luxuriance of colour, and in unspeakable wealth of ornament. This naive indulgence of feeling and constant play of fancy are characteristic of mediaeval architecture, painting, dress, conduct and ritual. We are still perhaps inclined to forget that in art there is something worth attaining besides form, and that form may sometimes be legitimately sacrificed to it. In spite of the work of the romantic school, we are still prone to apply conceptions derived from a study of Greek art to the criticism of art wholly different in spirit, method, and aim. Intelligibility, symmetry, and logical consistency are instinctively sought for, and if they are wanting the picture or the poem is contemptuously dismissed. Some of the best mediaeval work sets such attempts at defiance. Like nature, its infinite variety cannot be summed up in a few formulas. Its unity is often lyrical rather than logical. A common emotional tone, like a pedal bass in old music, harmonizes the diverse incidents and characters. In any case it loses much more than classical art when we abstract and summarise, and fix our attention on the whole by withdrawing it from the parts, because the work exists for the sake of the parts, and not the parts for the sake of the whole.

The constant use of the episode as an aesthetic form is an example of this. In the most characteristic Greek work digression is sternly repressed; everything is strictly subordinated to the central idea. Mediaeval art is as spontaneous and unrestrained as nature herself. It is essentially excursive and episodical. The episodes find their justification not only in their individual interest, but in the impression of splendid profusion which they produce, and in the increased volume of the prevailing emotional tone. In the art of music we have a certain parallel; for here too the whole is subordinated, and the chief effect is due to the beauty of the parts rather than the coherence of the entire work. The melodic phrase is the unit, and the process of construction is essentially synthetical. This is especially true of modern music, with its frequent changes of key and its subtleties of rhythm. The episode is constantly employed. Schumann's *Novelletten* bear a considerable analogy to the romances and buildings of the Middle Ages.

We ought not so much to say that the *Morte d'Arthur* contains episodes as that it consists of them. They are jewels set in a framework whose real *raison d'être* is to hold them. The story of Arthur, which is the central *motif* of Tennyson, appears here only as the 'enveloping action' which binds together the various parts.

It cannot be denied that the interest of the book suffers from the great similarities of incident. Battles and single combats of the most bloodthirsty description, the latter often waged for hours, until 'all the ground there as they fought was all bespeckled with blood,' recur with a regularity less stimulating to the modern reader than to the contemporaries of the author. Through four mortal chapters we are pitilessly told the details of the great battle fought between Arthur and the eleven kings, which, like all the other battles that succeed it, is mainly a series of contests between individual champions. When nearly all the heroes are, even for the most attentive reader, mere names, it will be readily conceived that there is a strong temptation to skip. But it would be a pity to miss such a vigorous bit of description as this from the combat between Beaumains (Sir Gareth) and the Knight of the Red Lawns:—

And thus they fought till it was past noon, and never would stint till at last they lacked wind both, and then they stood wagging and scattering, panting, blowing and bleeding, that all that beheld them for the most part wept for pity. So when they had rested them a while, they went to battle again, tracing, racing and foaming as two boars. And at some time they took their run as it had been two rams, and hurtled together that some time they fell grovelling to the earth: and at some time they were so amazed [stunned], that either took other's sword instead of his own. Thus they endured till evensong time, that there was none that beheld them might know whether was like to win the battle; and their armour was so far hewn that men might see their naked sides.... And the red knight was a wily knight of war, and his wily fighting taught Sir Beaumains to be wise; but he abought it full sore ere he did espy his fighting.

And so on, with a particularity worthy of *Bell's Life* in the palmy days of the prize-ring.

The similarity of incident is not confined to the encounters of the knights. There is a considerable resemblance in the odd 'quests' which they undertake, in the extraordinary 'customs' which they abolish, and the amours in which they engage. Both Arthur and Galahad take a sword from a marble stone in which it is fixed, and from which other knights are unable to remove it; while Balin alone succeeds in drawing from its scabbard the fateful sword borne by the damsel of the lady Lile of Avelion. Both Lancelot and Tristram go mad for love of their ladies. Both Bors and Percivale are tempted by a devil in woman's likeness. Two kings lie wounded, unable to recover health save at the hands of Galahad.

Perhaps one seldom realizes how much of the pleasure derived from a story is due not to its dynamical aspect, the actual progress of the action, but to its statical aspect, the situations. They afford resting-places for the attention, the details are filled in by the imagination, and they dwell long and pleasantly in the memory, so that we return to them with satisfaction when even the main outline of the tale has faded away. One or two clearly seen figures will often stand with their appropriate background as the sum and essence of a whole romance. The story may indeed never have been known to us, but the situation suggests a dim set of possibilities, a hypothetical history, on the threshold of which we linger lovingly. . . .

This element of artistic effect is constantly present in the *Morte d'Arthur*, which is full of beautiful and strange pictures. . . .

Everywhere in the *Morte d'Arthur* we walk through a land full of forms as ill-defined and strangely impressive as those which to children's eyes hide in the intricacies of ancient tapestry. Many of the characters are little more than romantic names, in themselves suggestive of mystery. What may not we expect from champions called Sir Frol of the Out Isles, Sir Graciens le Castlein, Sir Tor le Fise Aries, or Sir Carados of the Dolorous Tower? Others have a sense of irrationality and inexplicableness attaching to them— something which by defying our power of explanation, sets us guessing and wondering. Why should Sir Palamides, the chivalrous and gentle paynim, ever pursue Glatisant, the questing beast? How are we to account for the merciless cruelty of Sir Bruce *sans pitie*, or of Sir Garlon, the knight who rides invisible? The arbitrary 'customs' which are kept up in various castles, and which are so often done away by the courage of the knights of the Round Table, add to the sense of bewilderment, for their irrationality is so obvious and so gratuitous. As in all early poetry and romance, persons appear suddenly without description or explanation, for the primitive story-teller assumes that his characters are known to his audience, and need no formal introduction. A fresh knight is present, and we know him though we have never seen him before; then he disappears, leaving no trace behind. Folk seem to change before our eyes like the images of a dream. The old man in a bed richly dight is now Joseph of Arimathea, and now King Evelake, and now King Pelles. Sir Kay receives knighthood the year before Arthur becomes king, and yet has been one of Uther's most trusted knights.

This sense of mystery is not necessarily connected with the supernatural and impossible. *Jack the Giant Killer* contains elements quite as impossible as the *Morte d'Arthur*; but no sense of mystery attaches to it. These strange incidents set you marvelling, as though you stood before some half-understood hieroglyph. The adventure of the Chapel Perilous just referred to is an example of this as well as of other characteristic qualities of the book. Here is another from the story of Balin and Balan, which the Laureate has lately told as an additional *Idyll*, and for once marred in the telling.

[Balin, Pellam, and the Dolorous Stroke.]

The vision of the strange and beautiful chamber situated at the end of the long series of untenanted rooms, with its wonderful contents, the unburied body of the expectant saint, and the lance which consummated the passion of the Incarnate God, capable of inflicting a wound such that it could only be healed by the sacred blood itself, is full of weird and fascinating mystery. Then there is the marvel of the siege perilous, the seat at the Round Table which was reserved for the best knight of all, and Merlin's prophecy connected with it. . . .

Allied with this and running through the book there is a hint of spiritual allegory which becomes increasingly important in the latter part of it. There seems to be no set allegorical purpose, 'shadowing Sense at war with Soul': the deeper meaning is temporary and evanescent, and nowhere obscures the artistic beauty of the story. But here and there underneath the fanciful words and deeds, we trace a spiritual suggestion. The last eight or nine books are much more earnest and more charged with this curious meaning than the earlier. The story of the Sangraal is full of suppressed eucharistic teaching. As in those romantic Madonnas of the early German painters, the poetical and the devotional are so interfused that we cannot separate them. The books which follow the quest of the Graal and tell the treason of Sir Lancelot and his war with Arthur, and the accusation in no way applies. Guided by prophecy and sign and speech from heaven, instructed by visions, and fed by the Lord's body, the champions live in a spiritual atmosphere, full of types and symbols. Sometimes the teaching of the allegory is explained, where Malory has the authority of Map to make clear *la sinefianche* of the story. Often it is left for us to guess at dimly.

[History of Grail romances.]

Whatever may have been the origin of this wonderful story, it became in the hands of Walter Map, the somewhat Rabelaisian archdeacon of Oxford, a spiritual romance of exquisite beauty. At the end of his *Quest of the Sangraal*, he informs us that the adventure of the Graal as told by Sir Bors, one of the three who achieved it, was put in writing by clerks and kept in the Abbey of Salisbury (where Map had once been a canon). . . . Malory did little else than turn Map's book into his own quaint and vigorous English.

Lord Tennyson seems to regard the quest of the Graal as a misfortune, the breaking away of the knights from ordered usefulness to follow visions and dreams. Notwithstanding the lofty dignity of his noble poem, a suggestion of what one may call, without intention of offence, the Broad Church tone of mind is perceptible in it; a hint of a superiority consciously tolerant in the presence of fanatical and superstitious enthusiasm. In Malory's work the quest of the Graal is the culmination of all. In the earlier part of the book prophecies and tokens point to it; what comes after it is distinctly the winding up of a history, the chief incident of which has been told. For him, as well as for many of his readers, it is 'a story chronicled for one of the truest and the holiest that is in this world.'...

One of the things that strike the reader most forcibly in the *Morte d'Arthur* is the clearness and consistency with which the characters of the different knights are drawn. When we consider how the book is pieced together from many and various sources, this distinctness is very remarkable. It is no doubt partly due to the natural good taste of the early Celtic singers, and the conservatism of their hearers, who would as a rule resent the insertion of what was in flagrant violation of the accepted character of a hero. Partly again, it is due to the harmonising efforts made by the more important compilers and inventors of the quasi histories and prose romances, such as Geoffrey of Monmouth and Walter Map, and finally Malory himself had a share in it. Here and there, as for instance in the case of Arthur, the traditional handling did not prevent the introduction of incidents difficult to reconcile with the general reputation of the persons who were supposed to take part in them; but on the whole the characters are harmonious and sufficiently marked off from each other.

As an example of this let us take Arthur's four nephews, Gawaine, Gaheris, Agravaine, and Gareth. They are the sons of King Lot of Orkney and of Morgawse. They are all brave knights, but except Gareth, they are all revengeful and cruel, and 'hate all the good knights of the Round Table for the most part.' Sir Gawaine is the eldest and most renowned. His natural disposition shows itself on his first adventure, undertaken on the very day he received knighthood from Arthur. At the wedding-feast of the king a white hart rushed into the hall at Camelot pursued by hounds, and fled away. To Gawaine was assigned the task of bringing it again. Accompanied by Gaheris, as his squire, he pursued the hart into a castle courtyard; and there a knight came forth and slew two of the hounds. Enraged at the loss of the hounds, Gawaine fought and conquered the knight; but when Sir Ablamor cried mercy and yielded him, Gawaine would no mercy have, but unlaced his helm to have stricken off his head. Meantime Sir Ablamor's lady had come down and thrown herself on his body, and so Gawaine by misadventure smote off her head. And in like manner throughout the story, Gawaine remains merciless and unforgiving. To his brothers, indeed, he is tender, especially to Gareth. Outside his family he cares for no one except Lancelot, to whom he is grateful for saving his life from Sir Carados of the Dolorous Tower: he refuses to quarrel with him for slaying Agravaine, on the ground that Agravaine had no right to interfere in the matter of Lancelot and Guenever; but when, a little later, in rescuing the queen, Lancelot slays Gaheris and Gareth, though unwittingly, Gawaine's friendship is turned to unchangeable hatred; 'from this day I shall never fail, Sir Lancelot, until the one of us have slain the other.' He is voluptuous, worldly, and ambitious; as Nacien the hermit tells him, he is 'of poor faith and wicked belief,' and fails in 'these three things, charity, abstinence, and truth, and therefore ye may not attain the high adventure of the san graal.' Sir Gaheris is a less forcible copy of Gawaine; but he has not the grateful admiration which redeems the character of his elder brother, and he surpasses all other pitiless deeds by the murder of his mother in consequence of her amour with Sir Lamorak de Galis. Sir Agravaine is a knight of less prowess than these two; he is more treacherous and suspicious, and his favourite companion is his half-brother, the traitor Mordred. It is these two who from hatred of Lancelot lay the trap for him and Guenever, which cost Agravaine his life; and this in spite of Gawaine's protest on the ground that Lancelot had several times saved them from death. Gareth is the noblest of the four—he is frank, courteous, and gentle. He shrinks from the society of his brothers; and when they secretly assassinate Sir Lamorak (by the way, it is by a nice adjustment of parts that Mordred gives the death-blow, and from behind), Gareth is indignant. 'Fie upon treason,' said Sir Tristram, 'for it killeth my heart to hear this tale.' 'So doth it mine,' said Gareth; 'brethren as they be of mine, I shall never love them, nor draw in their fellowship, because of that deed.' He is the companion of Lancelot, 'whom he loved above all men earthly,' and of Sir Tristram, and other knights of great worship. His death at the hands of Lancelot, who had made him knight and who loved him better than any of his own kinsmen, is one of the sad consequences of Lancelot's sin.

Arthur is a commanding figure, though less impressive than Lancelot. 'In his person the most manly man that liveth,' as the ambassadors tell the Emperor Lucius, there are few to equal him in prowess. He is brave, gentle, prudent, temperate and just. 'All knights may learn to be a knight of him,' says Sir Tristram; and Lancelot, even in the heat of his great quarrel, refuses to consider the possibility of the king's want of faith—'there was never yet man that could prove King Arthur untrue of his promise.' He has learned something of Merlin's self-control and indifference to the desires which shape the course of his knights and too often lead them astray. He returns their loyalty and admiration, and does them 'worship' in return for their services. Towards Lancelot he shows the most generous affection, and, by an excess of complaisance which cannot be reasonably excused, even overlooks his ambiguous relation to the queen; 'the king had a deeming [suspicion], but he would not hear of it, for Sir Lancelot had done so much for him and for the queen so many times, that, wit ye well, the king loved him passingly well.' It is unfair to call this, as some have done, a guilty connivance at adultery from fear of losing his best knight. Arthur is stern and fierce when he is certain of Lancelot's guilt; 'if I may get Sir Lancelot, wit ye well he shall have a shameful death.' Although a noble crown to a noble edifice, Malory's Arthur is by no means faultless. He can lay no claim to the impeccability of the Laureate's hero. The 'passing fair damsel Lionors' was not the only object of his attentions; and he fell into a shameful and horrible sin with his half-sister, Morgawse. Thus was Mordred born, the evil genius of Arthur. On the advice of Merlin, or at any rate acting on a prediction of the wizard's that 'he that should destroy him should be born on May-day,' Arthur emulates the infamy of Herod; for he orders all the children who have the ill-luck to be born on that festival to be put on board ship and sent to sea. 'And so by fortune the ship drove into a castle, and was all toriven, and destroyed the most part,' but Mordred escaped. No unpleasant consequences for Arthur seem to have followed immediately, though we hear that, not unnaturally, 'many lords and barons of this realm were displeased for their children were so lost.' These dark shadows however occupy a small space in

Malory's portrait. They had crept into the romances through the misplaced ingenuity of men who had no eye for character; or through the confusion of names and events, such as produced some of the most extraordinary and least edifying incidents in classical mythology. In the earliest forms of the Arthur legend, there was no mention of these horrors, nor of Guenever's infidelity. Once in the romances there was no getting them out again. Just as in the case of the legends of the saints, while addition was regarded as quite pardonable, subtraction savoured of heresy; so here—what was written, was written, and Malory will leave out nothing, although he may modify and soften. He finds them in his authorities and feels bound to insert them; but they are felt as incongruities. Putting out of sight these inharmonious details, his Arthur is a real flesh and blood king, with his faults and foibles, and not a model of consistent propriety. For instance, he is a little irritable at times; when a damsel who had presented herself at his wedding and made great dole, was suddenly carried off by a knight who rode armed into the hall, we read 'the king was glad, for she made such a noise.' But in Malory as well as in the old Welsh and English traditions Arthur stands out as the ideal king, 'to be remembered before all other Christian kings.' His conquest of Lucius, Emperor of Rome, forms the principal event in his career as related by Geoffrey of Monmouth, who also makes Arthur subdue the Saxons, Ireland, Iceland, Gothland, Norway, Dacia, Aquitaine, and Gaul. The account of the Roman expedition in the *Morte d'Arthur* is certainly the most extravagant and most tiresome part of the book....

Sir Lancelot is distinctly the most brilliant among the champions of the Round Table. Originally perhaps a reduplication of the character of Mordred, in so far as he is in a position of antagonism to Arthur, the lover of his wife, and the rebel against his crown, his reputation increased at the expense of Mordred's. (It is worth while to remark that Mordred's attempt to marry Guenever is rendered less extraordinary, if the original identity of the two characters, before Mordred was thought of as Arthur's son and nephew, is kept in view.) In the hands of Map, Lancelot became the incarnation of the knightly ideal. His physical strength and courage are greater than those of any other knight; he 'was never matched of earthly knight's hand.' He is merciful and gentle; he 'will never smite a felled knight,' and spares the life of Gawaine under the severest provocation; he is, as his brother Sir Ector de Maris declares, 'the kindest man that ever strake with sword,' as well as 'the sternest knight to his mortal foe that ever put spear in the rest.' To Queen Guenever he is a faithful lover; he has 'never failed her in right nor in wrong since the first day that Arthur made him knight.' To King Arthur, save in this one matter, and what flows from it when the sin is discovered, he is always loyal and full of hearty admiration; in the battle with Arthur before the castle of Joyous Gard, when Arthur sought to slay him, 'Sir Lancelot suffered him and would not strike again;' and after Arthur had been unhorsed by Sir Bors, 'therewithal Sir Lancelot alight off his horse and took up the king and horsed him again,' declaring, 'I will never see that most noble king that made me knight neither slain nor shamed.' To his fellows he is ever true and self-forgetful; he gives Sir Tristram his vote as best knight after the great tournament at Lonazep, and urges all to do the same. He is 'the goodliest person ever came among press of knights;' of high birth, his father being King Ban of Benwick (that is, Benoic, or Brittany), and himself eighth in degree from Jesus Christ. He is full of fine natural impulses, and of God's graces—sympathetic, humble, reverent, and pious. At the command of Arthur he miraculously heals the wounds of Sir Urre of Hungary; at first modestly refusing to attempt where 'so many kings and knights have assayed and failed,' he afterwards knelt down and held up his hands and invoked the Blessed Trinity, 'and forthwith all the wounds fair healed and seemed as they had been whole a seven year. Then King Arthur and all the kings and knights kneeled down and gave thanks and lovings unto God and to His Blessed Mother, and ever Sir Lancelot wept as he had been a child that had been beaten.' The Nemesis of his sin is complete. He slays unwittingly Sir Gareth, whom he loves with almost fatherly affection, and Sir Gawaine, his best friend. After the war with Arthur, when the king is suddenly called home to defend himself against Mordred, Gawaine, who is now Lancelot's bitterest enemy, writes to him and entreats him to come over and help the king. The letter is so interesting, as showing the essentially Christian character of the knightly ideal, that it is worth while to transcribe part of it....

The character of Lancelot is in fact a magnificent creation. It is highly complex, full of contradictory qualities, united and reconciled: gentleness and courage, loyalty and treachery, strength and frailty, 'passions of nobleness and aches of shame.' We get to know it by an infinity of separate touches, for the old romancer had not the short and easy method of formal analysis which the modern novelist employs. It was built up by many different writers, often ignorant of each other's work, but harmonized by the genius of Map. Nor must we overlook the share of Malory, whose fine insight and great constructive skill enabled him to select and arrange his allusions in such a way as to produce a portrait worthy to stand beside any in fiction—clear, gracious, and vivid.

A great deal of nonsense has been talked about the ethics of the chivalrous romances of the Middle Ages. Many writers have spoken of it as a terribly low and sensual reality, veiling itself under an unpractically lofty ideal. Ascham's often-quoted opinion of the *Morte d'Arthur* may be once more repeated here.... This is of course outrageously unfair; but not more so than the opinion of a clever writer of to-day, who speaks of the ethics of chivalry as 'an essentially aesthetic, unpractical system' and 'utterly incompatible with any real and serious business in life.' Now, the truth is that, although not absolutely perfect, the ethical theory of the Arthurian epos is a distinctly high one; and the practice does not fall short of the theory in a greater degree than we see among ourselves. Among the more conspicuous virtues are courage, love of justice and hatred of injustice, loyalty, fidelity to promises and to the unspoken obligations implied by friendship and brotherhood, self-control, and disregard of mere bodily ease. Clemency is held in the highest estimation; for as Gaheris told Gawaine when he strove to slay Sir Ablamor, 'a knight without mercy is without worship.' While the motive for action is often love of fame, the best knights are notable for their humility; and lofty self-respect is combined with almost child-like simplicity. Gentleness, generosity, and courtesy, among lesser excellences which go to make up the character of the gentleman, are there; and with them sincere reverence for God and man, the absence of which lies at the root of half our modern failures and follies. The influence of definitely Christian feeling is seen not only in the high place given to the virtues of mercy for the fallen and tenderness for the weak, but in the supreme importance attached to purity. The almost superstitious exaltation of bodily chastity is due to a vivid realisation of the beatitude which promises to the pure the vision of God. With this lofty ideal before them, the shortcomings of the knights are often lamentable; but it would hardly be correct to say that we have greatly improved in our practice, while in its reverence for purity the *Morte d'Arthur* is distinctly in advance of much of the popular fiction of to-day. The main ethical impulse is clearly love of honour; and, as Aristotle says, honour is the chief of all external goods. The desire for fame is something very different from mere love of applause, and if not the highest motive is at least superior to most of those which move 'the average sensual man,' such as love of money, pleasure, and position. It leads to a lofty self-respect, a shrinking from what is mean, contemptible, and cowardly, and to that 'chastity of honour which feels a stain like a wound.' If this is only an aesthetic motive of morality, it is one which has been sanctioned by Plato and Aristotle, not to speak of others; and when completed and spiritualised by Christianity, it gives us one of the most serviceable, as well as one of the most beautiful standards of conduct. The ethics of chivalry are a compromise between the ideal of the priest, the ideal of the warrior, and the ideal of the poet. That the result falls short of the very highest is no doubt true, but that is the way with compromises; and after all, is not our own work-a-day system of ethics a compromise, and is it always superior to Gareth's and Galahad's?

In the *Morte d'Arthur* we find, as Caxton promises in the preface, 'noble chivalry, courtesy, humanity, friendliness, hardiness, love, friendship, cowardice, murder, hate, virtue, and sin. Do after the good and leave the evil and it shall bring unto you good fame and renommee.'

40. Bernhard Ten Brink

1877–96

Bernhard Ten Brink (1841–92), the distinguished Dutch scholar, treated a number of Arthurian topics besides Malory's work in his *History of English Literature*. Sections on Geoffrey, Wace, Layamon, development of the Arthurian legend through French romance, the Tristan story, and

Chrétien are marked by thoughtful analyses and careful scholarship. His remarks on Malory, while less enthusiastic and considerably more qualified than others quoted in this volume, do grant Malory a degree of skill, even of art, and point out the need for additional work in several areas of Malory scholarship.

The first volume of this work was published in German in 1877, the third in 1892, after Ten Brink's death. English translations began appearing in 1883 (volume I), and the Malory references are from volume III, translated by L. Dora Schmitz (London: George Bell, 1896), 45–6.

Sir Thomas Malory was one of the first men of distinction—with the exception of Sir John Maundeville—to write works in English, and this was at a time when a Scottish king had already won his laurels as a national poet. It was a happy idea of Sir Thomas's to make King Arthur and the Knights of the Round Table the subject of his work; for Middle English poetry—not to mention prose— had by no means exhausted the theme, and the imperfect knowledge and contradictory statements that had been made about many of the personages and events connected with the legend, made it appear doubly desirable to possess a full and comprehensive account of them. In the year 1469, or at the beginning of 1470, Sir Thomas had finished his compilation, and fifteen years afterwards Caxton brought it within the reach of a large circle of readers, since which time, by means of numbers of reprints and new editions, it has more and more distinctly influenced the popular English idea of the Arthurian legend, and furnished important material for the classic poetry both of the great era and of our own time.

Where Malory himself obtained the materials for his narrative is well known upon the whole—or, at least, we think we know whence he took them. There is the 'Merlin' founded upon Robert de Boron's poem, the latter parts of which, at all events, were made use of, and two different continuations of it, the one appearing here to be interwoven with the other; there is 'Launcelotte' in its earliest form, together with the earlier versions of the Search for the Grail, and the Death of Arthur, which had been added to it before Malory's day; there is, finally, 'Tristan' also, which is again interwoven with 'Launcelotte'—all of them French prose-romances. In many passages, however, it is distinctly evident that Malory may have made use of earlier sources no longer accessible to us; and again, there are differences which though unimportant are difficult to account for; or there is extraneous matter, in the narrative, which shows that here, too, where everything appears plain and clear, problems still remain to be solved.

The 'Morte d'Arthur'—by which title the work is generally known—can in no way divest itself of the character of being a compilation: repetitions, contradictions, and other irregularities are by no means of rare occurrence. At the same time, it is, upon the whole, arranged with a certain degree of skill, for in spite of the abundance of episode, Malory has succeeded in producing a kind of unity, and even though some monotony in the variety was unavoidable, still the plan and style of the narrative do not allow our interest to sleep, or, if asleep, it is aroused at definite points. Above all, the terse style of the narrative, in simple, but by no means colourless language, produces a good effect; and it was this alone which made it possible to compress the mass of material within a space readily surveyable.

41. H. Oskar Sommer
1889–91

Heinrich Oskar Sommer (b. 1861), as a young German scholar, began his scholarly edition of Caxton in the late 1880s. The text appeared in 1889, followed by two volumes of commentary in 1890 and 1891. In the early twentieth century (1908–16), Sommer published texts of the Vulgate romances in eight volumes.

The first selection (a) is from a letter to *Academy* (4 January 1890, pp. 11–12), summarizing his findings and commenting on Malory's adaptive genius, as a sort of prelude to the publication of volumes II and III. It is in volume III of his

Morte Darthur that Sommer presents the first systematic study of Malory's use of specific sources; it is here that Sommer's evaluation of Malory's skill occurs, in close comparisons running well over 300 pages. Presented here (b) are representative extracts based on Sommer's comparison of Malory and the *Suite de Merlin*, the alliterative *Morte Arthure*, the prose *Lancelot*, the *Queste*, the stanzaic *Morte Arthur*, and the French *Mort Artu*. The last extract is Sommer's less favourable conclusion to volume III. (London: David Nutt, 1891, reprinted New York: AMS Press, 1973.)

(a) *Academy*

The result of my researches surpasses all my anticipations. I have been enabled to determine exactly Malory's position in the history of English literature. I can clearly show what were the versions of the sources he used, and how he altered and added to them to suit his purpose. There is no reason to suppose, as Leland is said to have done (though I cannot find any such passage in his works) that Malory was a Welshman; nor was he, as often asserted, a mere translator. He evidently endeavoured—and with no little measure of success—to weld into an harmonious whole the immense mass of French romance. After a comparison with the sources, his work gives the impression that he did not servilely copy his originals, but that he had read various versions, and that he impressed upon the whole the stamp of his own individuality. He certainly did as much as many of the French compilers, who only retold what they had heard or read in their own tongue, while Malory combined both English and foreign romances. Sir Walter Scott says of 'Le Morte Darthur,' that 'it is indisputably the best prose romance the English language can boast of'; I may add, also, that it is one of the most important and interesting, considering the great influence it has exercised not only on the formation of English prose style, but also on the subject-matter of English literature....

(b) *Le Morte Darthur*, vol. III

(i) Introductory (pp. 1–12)
... Generation after generation has read with interest and enthusiasm of the noble Arthur and his valiant knights; England's first

poets have not hesitated to make their verse a vehicle for the praise of this national hero. It is equally remarkable and interesting, that all that has been written in England on this subject, be it in prose or in verse, be it in English, Latin, or Norman-French, can be traced back to a common source, and forms, as it were, the links of one immense chain running throughout the history of English literature. Beginning with Nennius' Eulogium Brittaniae sive Historia Britonum and Geoffrey's Historia Britonum, the most important of these links are: Wace's Brut, Layamon's Brut, Langtoft's and Robert of Gloucester's chronicles, Huchown's Morte Arthure,[1] and English translations and metrical romances, by unknown authors belonging to the fourteenth and fifteenth centuries. Malory's work follows, and this, be its shortcomings what they may, is unique of its kind. It appeared at the most favourable moment, at a time when the taste for metrical romances, of which such numerous English and French specimens existed, had died out. . . .

Sir Thomas Malory 'reduced,' as Caxton tells us, his work from certain books in French, and, indeed, no less than fifty-six times in the course of the work are these sources referred to in terms such as 'the frensshe booke maketh no mencyon,'. . . 'as it telleth in the booke,'. . . 'for as the frensshe book saith,'. . . &c.

The term 'reduced' is to be taken literally, the materials worked up into 'Le Morte Darthur' being about ten times as long as the book itself. It has long since been recognised that these 'French books' must have been the different branches of the Arthurian romances referred to above, but how far this was so, and what particular versions were used, has not as yet been investigated. In two cases, at least, the French book is an English one, as we shall see hereafter.

Before entering upon the detailed critical examination of the relationship of 'Le Morte Darthur' to its different English and French sources, I think it well to point out the various versions made use of by Sir Thomas Malory, and to give a description of them.

The romance of 'Merlin' must be considered as the basis of the first four books. There exist three different phases of this romance—the prose-rendering of the 'Merlin' by Robert de Boron, the 'Ordinary Merlin,' and the 'Suite de Merlin,' wrongly attributed to Robert de Boron. . . . Chapters 1 to 18 of the first book are drawn from this version. By 'Suite de Merlin' is understood the unique text represented by the Huth MS., from fol. 75ᵃ to the end. It has to be remarked that the Huth MS. is not quite perfect, breaking off in the midst of the adventure of Gawayn, Vwayne, and Marhaus with the three ladies; thus we lack a positive source for the last few chapters of the fourth book, Malory's account being consequently the only known version extant.

The fifth book is not, as M. Gaston Paris supposes...drawn from the 'Ordinary Merlin,' but it is a rendering in prose of the English metrical romance, 'La Morte Arthure,' represented by the unique Thornton MS. in the library of Lincoln Cathedral, which has been several times printed, with occasional references to the English chronicles. This romance is the work of the Scotch poet, Huchown, as conclusively shown by Professor M. Trautmann, who must also be credited with having first pointed out that Malory made use of it, but his contemptuous reference to Malory as a 'Zusammenstoppler' is unjustified, as my studies will show.[2] The sixth book is taken from the 'Lancelot' as represented by...several MSS....and several printed editions of the beginning of the sixteenth century.

As to the seventh book, I can trace no part of its contents in the numerous MSS. I have studied. It cannot be denied that there exists some slight resemblance between the romance entitled 'Le beaus Disconus' and Malory's narrative, but it is not sufficient to establish any connection between them. This book relates the adventures of Gareth, a brother of syr Gawayn, how he came disguised to King Arthur's court, and was nicknamed by syr Kay 'Beaumayns.' The whole book has the character of a folk-tale, and differs greatly from the general run of Arthurian adventures. I am inclined to doubt its originally belonging to the Arthurian cycle, to which it may have been adapted by Malory, or by some unknown writer before him, from some now lost French poem. This conjecture is strengthened by the fact that in none of the versions which I have read, and which are represented in Malory's work, is any, even the slightest, reference made to Gareth's exploits on his way to the castle of Lady Lyonesse, or to this lady, her sister Lynet, her brother Gryngamor, or the five brothers whom Gareth overcame and sent to Arthur's court.

In the eighth, ninth, and tenth books Malory follows the prose-version of 'Tristan,' represented by MS. No. 103 of the

Bibliothèque Nationale and by several printed texts of the end of the fifteenth and beginning of the sixteenth centuries, copies of which are in the British Museum. This version, which is generally attributed to Luces de Gast, differs greatly from the so-called enlarged 'Tristan' by Hélie de Boron.... The chapters xxi. to xxviii. of the tenth book, however, are taken from 'The Prophecies of Merlin'.... These chapters narrate the adventures of Alysaunder le orphelyn and the great tournament of Surluse, and, as they are the only part of Malory's sources which has never been printed, I have edited them faithfully, and printed them in the Appendix to this volume.[3]

The eleventh and twelfth books are again drawn from the above-mentioned 'Lancelot,' save the last three chapters of the twelfth book, relating the fight between Trystram and Palomydes, which are not to be met with in any of the above-named versions of the 'Tristan.' At the end of the twelfth book Malory says, 'Here ends the second book of syr Trystram that was drawen oute of Frensshe, but here is no rehersal made of the thyrd book.' It is not quite clear what is meant by this third book, as the source which Malory follows for his whole account only consists of two books; therefore he must either refer to the so-called enlarged 'Tristan' ascribed to Hélie de Boron, or he knew another third part which we no longer possess. I believe that he meant the 'Tristan' as enlarged by Hélie de Boron, because the references he makes to Trystram's death in the eleventh chapter of the nineteenth and in the sixth chapter of the twentieth book, according to which Trystram suffered death from being stabbed by king Mark from behind, correspond exactly to the account given in that version....

The thirteenth to the close of the seventeenth book represent the Quest of the Holy Grail as it is found in the 'Lancelot'....

The eighteenth book follows apparently two versions: the 'Lancelot' and the English metrical romance 'Le Morte Arthur' as represented by Harl. MS. 2252. Here Malory greatly alters the sequence of events. Perhaps he knew a version which combined the peculiarities of both versions. The twentieth chapter of this book and the introductory lines of the first chapter in the twentieth book are, as well as some other passages in the two last books of 'Le Morte Darthur,' evidently Malory's own.

As to the nineteenth book, I agree with M. Gaston Paris... that

Malory, besides the 'Lancelot,' had another source from which he drew the first part of the episode of Malegeaunt and Gueneuer; or else that a previous version existed combining the two accounts. The last four chapters of this book, describing the handling of syr Vrre's wounds, cannot be traced. I believe Malory adapted them from some now lost French lay. The enumeration of all the knights who, at Arthur's request, handle Vrre's wounds is undoubtedly Malory's own; he seems, as I can prove from other instances, to have had a great predilection for such catalogues of names.

The twentieth and twenty-first books are a prose-rendering of the English metrical romance, 'Le Morte Arthur,' as given in the Harl. MS. 2252; the 'Lancelot' may occasionally also have been used.

It must, however, be observed that all the MSS. mentioned here as the sources of 'Le Morte Darthur' can only be styled thus in so far as they contain the same versions as those Malory actually had before him when compiling his work; in no case can we assert with certainty that this or that is the very MS., or even a faithful copy of it, which the compiler had before him.

After these general remarks, I now proceed to critically examine the sources, one by one, not as they are arbitrarily arranged in 'Le Morte Darthur,' but according to the great branches of Arthurian romances, to which the single parts belong....

(ii) Vulgate *Merlin* (Caxton's Book I, chapters 1–18), III, pp. 15–62

It is at once noticeable that Malory has considerably condensed the narrative of his source. This part of his work is not merely translated, but re-told and in the strict sense of the word 'reduced.'...Malory's account is thus 'reduced' to about a fifth of the original....

Malory modifies this story considerably. In order to have a beginning, he speaks of great wars which the king has made against the mighty duke of Cornwall, and of a peace arranged 'by the meanes of grete lordes.' The visit of the duke and his wife to the court as related by Malory gives the impression of a festival of reconciliation. In the 'Ordinary Merlin' both the duke and his wife are introduced into the story here for the first time. To facilitate the understanding of the narrative, and to throw light on various incidents not intelligible in Malory, I here give a brief *résumé* of the 'Merlin' up to the point where Malory takes it up....

This detailed narrative is thrown by Malory into the first chapter. All the main features of it are to be recognised in Malory's account. . . .

The second chapter of 'Le Morte Darthur' is a simple abridgment. . . . Besides one point of importance at the beginning, some slight variations are noticeable at the end. Malory states here, contrary to the version of the Huth, Add., Harl., and Cambridge MSS., that Ulfyns received the semblance of Brastias, and Merlin took that of Iordanus; those MSS. relate that Ulfyn became Iourdain, and Merlin took Bretel's semblance. Only the Auchinleck MS. agrees in this point with Malory. This fact shows that the MSS. which Malory and the poet of 'Arthour and Merlin' had before them had a common descent. . . . The modifications may therefore be either attributed to Malory or to the source from which he translated. . . .

The oath which Ector bids Kay take before telling all he knows of the marvellous sword, and Ector's attempt to pull out the sword, are Malory's additions. . . . Malory omits Arthur's council with Merlin, Autor, Ulfin, and Bretel, Merlin's advice to go to king Leodegan, the banner, &c., and modifies the first fight between Arthur and the rebels by greatly abridging it, thus omitting Nantres' proposal to kill Arthur and his attempt to carry it out. Malory, who is generally inclined to see things through the magnifying glass, says the sword which Arthur pulled out of the stone, i.e., Excalibor, 'gaf light like xxx torches,' whereas the Cambridge MS. has 'twenti tapres,' and Add. MS. 'doi chierge.' That Malory was not entirely master of his subject is shown by the fact that here, following the 'Ordinary Merlin,' he calls the sword which Arthur draws out of the anvil Excalibor, whereas. . . (book ii, chap. iii.), forgetting this, and following the 'Suite de Merlin,' he declares the sword which the lady of the lake gives Arthur is called Excalibor. Malory further omits the enchantment which Merlin casts upon the enemy, and the fire which he throws on their tents. He states that Merlin bids Arthur leave off fighting against them, contrary to the 'Ordinary Merlin,' and, on the other hand, he omits Arthur's distributing large gifts among the poor in order to gain the hearts of the people. . . .

Bretel and Ulfyn's journey to Ban and Bors is summarily told by Malory. . . . Malory skips the war between Claudas and the two kings entirely. . . . Contrary to his source, Malory states that the messengers receive large presents, and return first to Logres, the kings following soon. Malory then skips the means by which the two kings protect their country in their absence, thus omitting the ring, though he mentions it later on in two passages, where it is entirely unintelligible. . . . The appearance of Gryflet here is another proof how little Malory is aware that the 'Ordinary Merlin' and the 'Suite' contain contradictory accounts, for we shall find the same Gryflet, who fights here as a valiant knight, described later on, in the twenty-first chapter of the same book, as requesting knight-hood at Arthur's hands that he may go and fight the knight of the fountain. . . .

The twelfth to the eighteenth chapters recount the rather complicated events which make up the battle of Bedegrayne, and which are doubtless told with over-great length in the 'Ordinary Merlin,' requiring some reading to be thoroughly understood, but are nevertheless perfectly clear and intelligible. Malory's reproduction is, in many respects, a muddle. He discards the fine plan of the battle which the writer of the 'Ordinary Merlin' carries out in detail; he never tells us how Arthur's, Ban's, and Bors' men are divided, nor how their enemies arrange their forces, and omits, in addition to these prominent features, many others of hardly less importance. Had I to give an opinion on this portion of Malory's work, in so far as the reproduction of the 'Ordinary Merlin' is concerned, I should describe it as a poor specimen of re-telling a story. . . .

The end of the battle of Bedegrayne, in the first half of the seventeenth chapter, is Malory's own composition. . . . I had the pleasure of discovering that the incident of the forty knights was suggested to Malory from a much later passage of the narrative, forming, as it does, a prominent feature of the expedition of Arthur, Ban, Bors, and Leodegan against Rion and his allies. . . .

The words, 'and there hadde Arthur the fyrst syght of gweneuer the kynges doughter of Camylyard/and euer after loued her/After they were weddyd as it telleth in the booke,' are Malory's addition. He omits the version of Arthur's wedding to Gueneuer as told in the 'Ordinary Merlin,' in order to adopt, later on, the version of the 'Suite de Merlin.' The episode of the false Gueneuer which forms such a prominent feature of the 'Ordinary Merlin' is passed over in silence.

Arthur's parting with Ban and Bors, and Merlin's remarks upon the situation of the eleven kings, are made up by Malory. . . .

(iii) *Suite de Merlin*, pp. 62–148

Malory ... already alluded, at the end of chapter xviii., to the 'Suite de Merlin.' In order to have the means of joining the two versions, he begins the nineteenth chapter with the statement: 'After the departyng of kyng Ban and kyng Bors,' and adds that Lot's wife comes, or is sent, 'to aspye' Arthur's court. This is not in the Huth MS. His account of Arthur's dream is so much curtailed that it is difficult to recognise the original in it. ...

The latter part of this episode [the revelation of Arthur's parentage] is much weakened through Malory's condensation, and deprived of its most prominent features. Ulfyn accuses Igrayne directly. Merlin's stratagem arranged with Ector and Ulfyn, Arthur's feigned ignorance of and surprise at the whole story, Merlin's disguise, and the final denouement of the situation when it has come to its climax through Merlin's story and his demanding the child from Ector, to whom he had given it, and Ector's pointing out Artus, are all points omitted by Malory. The festival arranged in the celebration of this joyful event, according to Malory, lasts, not fifteen, but only eight days. ...

The twenty-fifth to the twenty-seventh chapter in Malory are an even more shortened reproduction of the source than before. ...Merlin's suggestion that Arthur should postpone the fight with the knight of the fountain until he had a good sword, and Merlin's remark, when they approach the lake, that they will find a sword there, are omitted, but soon after Malory, forgetting this, makes Merlin say, 'yonder is that swerd that I spak of.' According to Malory the damsel is already upon the lake, and comes to Arthur, whereas in the 'Suite' she arrives from afar on a small black horse at great speed. The description of the lady's walking on the water and fetching the sword, and Merlin's following explanation of the enchanted palace and the invisible bridge, were, it appears, too improbable for Malory; with him the damsel simply bids Arthur take 'yonder barge,' and row himself over the lake to get the sword, which Arthur, with Merlin's help, really carries out, himself receiving the sword from the hand which holds it above the water. Arthur's reflections on the sword are suppressed by Malory, but come in somewhat later in a different form. ... Merlin's prophecy that Arthur shall lose the sword through his sister, &c., is omitted by Malory. The 'crafte' which, according to Malory, Merlin employs to render the knight of the fountain invisible to

Arthur and *vice versa*, is Malory's addition. The description of the enchanted lake, &c., is suppressed, as well as the wedding of Morgan and Vrien, and their rich endowment by Arthur.

Malory's abridging process in the three last chapters is carried to an extreme in the twenty-eighth chapter. Folios 96^a–99^a of the Huth MS., pp. 203–212 of the printed text, are represented by fifteen lines. . . .

The introductory lines of the second book . . . are Malory's addition; they form a sort of link between the first and second books. On the whole, Malory faithfully reproduces the account given in the 'Suite' [of Balin episodes and intervening material]. Now and then he alters slightly, and frequently shortens the French text. The knight who delivers the damsel from the sword is called Balyn by Malory from the moment when first mentioned, whereas in the source the name is only disclosed to Arthur by Merlin after he has left the court. Malory makes out of the French 'la dame de l'yle d'avalon' a proper name, viz., 'lady lylle of auelion.' . . . Sometimes, but comparatively rarely, the English is a literal translation of the French text. . . . Malory dealt with his text more freely than sagaciously, often reproducing incidents of secondary importance, and, on the other hand, omitting important facts, thereby often rendering his text obscure. . . .

The 'liaison' of Morgain and Merlin, the episode of the sheath, the knight loved by Morgain, &c., are omitted. Malory, evidently confounding this knight, unnamed in the 'Suite,' with the 'Accolon' mentioned later on in the 'Suite' and also in the fourth book of 'Le Morte Darthur,' gives him the name 'Accolon.' The birth of 'Ywain,' who, to judge from the 'Suite,' is Merlin's offspring, is not mentioned by Malory. . . .

In the nineteenth chapter Malory follows the 'Suite,' but adds the last eight lines . . . as the 'Suite' does not say that Merlin told Arthur about the end of the two brothers. . . .

The opening lines of book iii. are, like the last lines of book ii., Malory's own composition; by these links he seemingly endeavours to join the two portions of the narrative more closely than in the 'Suite.' The first five chapters represent summarily, and with many inaccuracies, modifications, and omissions, the corresponding section of the 'Suite.' The remarks Merlin makes with regard to Guenever . . . differ widely from those in the 'Suite;' Malory evidently misunderstood his text. . . .

In the next chapter, besides various omissions, Malory states that Merlin could find only 'xx & xiij' good knights; and a little farther on he declares the 'viij and xx' sat in their seats. These quotations are evidently based upon errors, for the number must be xxxxviij, as the 'Suite' states, and as Malory himself admits . . . 'But two syeges were voyde.' Merlin's prophecy regarding the perilous seat and his address to the knights of the round table are skipped.

As usual, Malory differs from the 'Suite' in mentioning at once the names Aries and Tor, and further alters the source by stating that Artus demanded Aries to bring his other sons before him, and that he found a great difference in them from Tor. Merlin's disclosure that Tor is son of King Pellinor and Aries' wife before her marriage is here anticipated by Malory from two later passages; in the 'Suite' it is made partly after Tor's return from his quest, partly after King Pellinor's. By this anticipation of events King Pellinor's arrival at Arthur's court is varied considerably from the account in the 'Suite;' Arthur already knows that Tor is Pellinor's son. Forgetting that he has already described the dubbing of Tor in the third chapter, Malory follows the 'Suite' in the fourth, and states: 'but Tor was the fyrst (knight) he made at the feest.'. . .

Malory's account of Tor's quest is not only, as is usual with him, greatly abridged, but, especially in the latter portion, presents several features not to be found in the 'Suite.'. . .

Lines 10–17, forming the conclusion of the eleventh chapter, are Malory's composition, probably intended as a substitute for Arthur and Merlin's conversation regarding Tor, Merlin's disclosures about his birth, and his announcement that Pellinor will return from the quest the same evening, and, finally, Arthur's wish to see Pellinor, Tor, and the wife of Aries side by side, and the order to Merlin to fetch this lady to the court—of which Malory, as I have mentioned... anticipated the substance in the third chapter of the third book....

... Malory links together the third and fourth books by the words: 'After these questys of ... It felle so,' &c. Merlin's love to Niviene, called either 'Nyneue' or 'Nymue,' is only briefly mentioned. Merlin's revelation to Arthur of his own approaching end, and warnings to the king to take good care of his sword and sheath, are partly additions, partly repetition, by Malory of an earlier passage of the 'Suite.'. . .

Merlin and Niviene's journey to Brittany, and all that takes place there, is either unnoticed by Malory save the episode at Trebe, where they see young Lancelot and his mother Elayne, or just hinted at in the words: 'Merlyn showed her many wonders.'

Merlin's death as related in the seven last lines of the first chapter is anticipated by Malory from a much later portion of the 'Suite.'... I am unable to say whence Malory drew the information for the line, 'And ther by the way he founde a braūche of an holy herbe that was the sygne of the Sancgraill/and no knyght founde suche tokens but he were a good lyuer;' it is not in the Huth MS. A passage to this effect may have occurred in the copy of the 'Suite' used by Malory, or he may have added it in imitation of analogous accounts in the Quest of the Holy Grail. Baudemagus' visit to the stone under which Niviene had placed Merlin by her enchantments, Merlin's great moan, and the fruitless endeavours to remove the stone are anticipated from a later part of the 'Suite.'...

Malory's account of the fight between Arthur and Accolon differs from that of the 'Suite' in so far that Arthur very soon suspects that Accolon has Escalibor, because 'at euery stroke that Accolon stroke he drewe blood on' him.

The appearance of Niviene, the lady of the lake, at the supreme moment, prepared for in the 'Suite' by various references in previous chapters, stands entirely by itself, and is thereby unintelligible, in 'Le Morte Darthur,' Malory having previously omitted Merlin's warning to Niviene about Arthur's danger, and the fact that Merlin returned with her to Great Britain at her request....

In addition to the characteristic features of Malory's work, as compared with the text of the Huth MS., which have been repeatedly noticed, such as abridgment, omissions, slight modifications, and the insertion of proper names where they are missing in the French text, this portion is peculiarly marked by additional incidents absent from the 'Suite' as represented by the Huth MS., and by a different order of the events. ...

Having now completed the critical examination of the 'Suite de Merlin,' as represented by the Huth MS., in its relation to Malory's 'Le Morte Darthur,' it is natural to ask if the MS. Malory used was a faithful copy of the Huth MS., and if we can attribute to the compiler all the variants between the English and French versions.

As long as the Huth MS. is the only known French text of this romance, it is obviously impossible to answer this question with absolute certainty; but even at present I am disinclined, after considering all the circumstances of the case, to ascribe all the variants to Malory, but rather hold that many were already present in the MS. of the 'Suite' which he used, especially the great number of proper names. . . . The Huth MS. and the one Malory used thus belong evidently to different stages in the development of the MSS., the Huth MS. being, I believe, of earlier date than that used by Malory.[4]. . .

(iv) The alliterative *Morte Arthure* (MA), pp. 148–75

For the fifth book of 'Le Morte Darthur' in Caxton's edition Malory principally used the 'La Morte Arthure' by the Scotch poet Huchown. . . . Now and then, however, Malory embodies facts into his narrative, in contradiction to Huchown, which he can only have found either in Wace's Brut, in Robert of Gloucester's Chronicle, in Layamon's Brut, or in the 'Suite de Merlin.' Malory has suppressed Huchown's ending, as it did not suit his purpose. . . . Certain variations are, however, noticeable, which it is difficult to explain.

Did M. intentionally alter MA., or did the copy of MA. he saw differ from the Thornton MS.?[5]. . .

The fourth chapter of book iv. in M. is, throughout, a prose-rendering of MA. . . . None of the other versions contains such a detailed description of the dream and its interpretation. . . .

The fifth chapter in M. follows still more servilely, if that be possible, the contents of MA. . . . indeed, almost every word of M. can be traced in MA. . . . In this last part of his account of Arthur's war against Lucius, M., though still following MA., condenses more than before, modifies the narrative, and repeatedly intercalates episodes of his own devising. . . . The episode of the christening of Priamus and his enrolment among the knights of the Round Table . . . is Malory's own invention, and is not recorded in MA. . . .

The end of the fifth book . . . is Malory's own invention. He states that the 'Romaunce telleth' that King Arthur was on a certain day crowned at Rome, but the romance tells nothing of the sort, nor does it record the fact that 'the duchye of Lorrayne' is given to Pryamous as reward for his assistance. M. suppresses the last part of MA., . . . in order to replace it in his twenty-first book by the version of Harl. MS. 2252, 'Le Mort Arthur.'

(v) *Lancelot* (PL), pp. 176–205

After mentioning (book iv. chapter i.), in accordance with the 'Suite de Merlin,' that, when Merlin and Niviene visit Benoyc, Queen Elayne, the wife of King Ban, showed them the young Lancelot, whose 'fyrst name was Galahad,' and after the reference to him, in accordance with the English metrical romance 'La Morte Arthure,' in chapter vii. of book v., Malory entirely skips his early life, and, without even mentioning his coming to Arthur's court, introduces him in the beginning of the sixth book with a few phrases of a very general character, not only as a knight of the Round Table, but as the knight who—

> in al turnementys and Iustes and dedes of armes for lyf and deth passed al other knyghtes / and at no tyme he was neuer ouercome / but yf it were by treson or enchauntement / so syr Launcelot encreaced soo merueyllously in worship and in honour / therfor is he the fyrst knyght that the frensshe book maketh mencyon of after kynge Arthur come fro rome / wherfore quene gweneuer had hym in grete favour aboue al other knyghtes, and in certayne he loued the quene ageyne aboue al other ladyes & damoysels of his lyf /

Though it cannot be denied that these few lines remind the reader versed in the early part of Lancelot's life of much therein, they convey hardly anything to the reader unacquainted with the events they hint at; and the supposition that Malory possessed no source for the early life of this most famous of all Arthur's knights can alone account for his not giving, at least summarily, some indications about him, and relating his arrival at Arthur's court.

I fail to see what Malory means by the French book which mentions Lancelot first after Arthur's return from his Roman expedition; it cannot be the 'Lancelot,' nor is it the 'Merlin,' in which Lancelot only plays a secondary part; the phrase seems introduced in order to make the abrupt introduction less noticeable.... After these general remarks, Malory relates how Lancelot, after having 'rested hym longe with play and game,' decides upon starting in search of adventures, and requests his 'neuewe' (!) Lionel to accompany him. The portion of the Prose-Lancelot in which these incidents are told differs much, and appears in quite another connection; it forms part of the second part of the 'Lancelot' proper. . . .

In P.L., after Lancelot's departure from the tournament, . . . there follow over forty folios before M. takes up the narrative again. . . . It is by no means impossible that Lancelot's passing the night with Baudemagus is a simple addition either by M. or by the compiler of the source whence he drew his information, intended to link together the two sets of adventures, which belong to quite different portions of the original. . . . [The] passage, in which the damsel advises Lancelot to marry, and Lancelot endeavours to explain to her the reasons why he can and will not do so, are probably Malory's invention, an hypothesis strengthened by the moralising tendency exhibited in other similar intercalations. . . .

. . . a paragraph mark and the general character of the contents of the then following lines—'And thenne he mounted vpon his hors & rode in to many straunge & wyld countreyes and thorou many waters and valeyes and euyl was he lodged / And at laste by fortune hym happend,' &c.—clearly indicate that the events which follow do not immediately join on to those told before the paragraph mark, but that either Malory, or the writer of the source whence he drew his information, broke away here from the thread of the Prose-Lancelot, and either inserted adventures from another source or invented them himself in imitation of the many similar episodes in other romances. Here I will only mention that I incline to think that, beside the Vulgate-Lancelot, there existed another version of the Lancelot, modified and enlarged, in the same manner as beside the Vulgate-Merlin there exists a 'Suite de Merlin,' or an enlarged Tristan by the side of the original Tristan, and that Malory knew this version, which we no longer possess. . . .

The old romance writers were apparently not very particular as regards time. According to 'Le Roman de Lancelot' as a whole, it seems as if the knights set out on the quest of the Holy Grail on the Whitsunday after Lancelot's return from the joyous island. According to the account [in P.L.], how Galahad remained at the abbey of nuns until his fifteenth year, we have to suppose that several years elapsed between Lancelot's return and the Whitsunday on which Galahad comes to Arthur's court.

The hermit tells Arthur that on the next feast of Whitsun the knight will come to his court who is to sit in the perilous seat, and who will bring to an end the Quest of the Holy Grail; therefore

Arthur should be sure to assemble all his knights at that feast. On his return to court, Arthur at once takes the necessary measures to ensure the next feast of Whitsun being one of the finest, in every respect, ever held.

M. omits most of these details—*e.g.*, Galahad's being taken to the nunnery—so that, at the opening of his thirteenth book, one cannot understand how Galahad came to the abbey. . . .

(vi) *Queste* (R), pp. 205–20

Malory has shortened his original in this portion of his *rifacimento* less than in any other, and has in many cases limited himself to translating it. . . .

. . . These two chapters [Bk 13, chap v–vi], except a few additions, agree almost literally in M. and R. In M.'s fifth chapter Galahad adds, after saying he was sure of finding a sword, and therefore brought none with him: 'For here by my syde hangeth the scauberd.' Farther on occurs a passage relating to the sword attributed to Galahad:

> that somtyme was the good knyghtes Balyn le saueage / and he was a passynge good man of his handes / And with this suerd he slewe his broder Balan and that was grete pyte for he was a good knyghte / and eyther slewe other thorou a dolorous stroke that Balyn gaf vnto my graūte fader / kynge Pelles / the whiche is not yet hole / nor not shal be tyl I hele hym.

It is impossible to say whether M. added this passage on his own account, as recapitulating Merlin's prophecy in the 'Suite de Merlin,' or whether the MS. he possessed contained it. The latter seems to me the more probable; I think it will be found one day that the Balyn story and the 'Queste,' in which Galahad is the hero, hang together. . . .

. . . In the tenth and in the three following chapters M. relates with fair accuracy, though greatly abridging them, the contents of . . . the printed 'Queste.' . . .

The greater part of the fourteenth chapter, in which one of the monks expounds Melians' adventure to Galahad, is much shortened. . . .

. . . M. omits the long description in R. of the three chief tables which were to come after Christ's birth—first, the table at which

Christ often had his meals with the disciples; secondly, the table of the Holy Grail which Joseph brought to England; and, thirdly, the Round Table, which Merlin constructed in imitation of the second table. All this is related with great detail in R., M. only mentions the Round Table, and of this also he omits many particulars. . . .

In the fifteenth book the adventures of Lancelot are continued. M. here attains his purpose of 'reducing' his source more by omission than by condensation, as is shown by the fact that eight pages and a half of the Caxton correspond to twenty-eight pages of the printed 'Queste.'. . .

M.'s sixteenth book is a very faithful reproduction of the corresponding part of R.; though a little 'reduced,' no incident of importance is omitted, nor are modifications noticeable. . . .

In the seventeenth book M.'s account of the incidents of the quest presents more variants from R. than in the preceding one, and the process of abridging the source is carried to a greater extent. This book shows clearly how little consistent is the division of the matter in 'Le Morte Darthur' which Caxton in his Preface owns to having introduced. . . .

The concluding twelve lines of the twenty-third and last chapter of this book, and of the 'Quest of the Holy Grail,' are M.'s own composition.

(vii) Vulgate *Morte Artu* (PL) and stanzaic *Morte Arthur* (MH), pp. 220–72

The last books of 'Le Morte Darthur,' excepting the nineteenth book, relate the events which take place after the return of the knights of the Round Table from the quest of the Holy Grail until the deaths of King Arthur, Queen Guenever, and Lancelot, and correspond to the fourth part of the Prose-Lancelot, entitled 'La Mort au roi Artus,' a name very inappropriately given either by Malory himself or by Caxton to the whole compilation. The nineteenth book relates an episode which forms the subject of Chrétien de Troyes' 'Roman de la Charrette,' and is told in the first part of the Prose-Lancelot (in the second volume of the edition of 1513).

A close examination of the last portion of Malory's compilation shows that he cannot have derived his account from the Prose-Lancelot, to which, however, it is equally certain that his source was intimately related. Malory's source is thus either derived from the Prose-Lancelot, or both come from a common original. In the English metrical romance 'Le Mort Arthur,' as preserved in the unique Harl. MS. 2252, we possess a version which stands in the same relation to Malory's source as that does to the Prose-Lancelot; and of this Malory was aware, for, in his last two books, he often makes free use of the very words of the English poem. But Malory, or rather the author of his source, has altered the sequence of events in this section; whilst, in the Prose-Lancelot and in the English poem, the tournament at Winchester and Lancelot's meeting the fair maiden of Astolat precede the queen's dinner, the incident of the poisoned apple, Mador's accusation of Guenever, and Lancelot's fighting for the queen, Malory in his eighteenth book observes the reversed order. Owing to this alternation of the sequence of incidents, many modifications became necessary; and there are, besides, feats described in Malory's account which are entirely absent from the Prose-Lancelot. The twentieth and twenty-first books follow the 'Lancelot' on the whole; but, whilst many incidents are added, others are omitted. I have treated the nineteenth book in this section on account of its relation to the eighteenth and twentieth books, though I should have treated it more properly in the beginning of the section entitled 'Lancelot, or the Later History of King Arthur,' as its contents are told in a portion of the 'Lancelot' which precedes all that Malory relates of him. . . .

Of all the books of 'Le Morte Darthur,' book xviii. is at once the most interesting and the most difficult for a critical examination, as the alteration in the sequence of incidents has caused many complicated modifications. . . .

Before comparing in detail the various episodes of book xviii. in M. with the corresponding ones in P.L., it will be necessary to look at the whole structure of the section. The first question which naturally offers itself, is: Why has the writer of M.'s source not preserved the same sequence of incidents as in P.L.? The eighteenth book in itself contains no clue to this engima, but, if we consider books xviii. and xix. together, I think it is not difficult to find an answer. The subject of book xix., though different in many points, agrees with the episode of Guenever and Mador de la porte in two characteristic points: Guenever's danger, and her rescue by Lancelot as her champion. Had the writer of M.'s source—who intercalated the contents of book xix. from a much earlier portion of P.L.—preserved the sequence of incidents in P.L., the two episodes would have immediately followed one another, and the one would have thus weakened the effect of the other. ...

Whether chapter xxv. was part of M.'s source, or whether he added it himself, is difficult to say; it is not in P.L. I incline to believe the reflections on love are Malory's own. ...

[Quotes at length the remarks of Gaston Paris on the relationship between Chrétien's *Lancelot*, the prose *Lancelot*, and Malory's Book XIX. See above, No. 35.]

I thus think M. Gaston Paris' suggestion, that Malory, or, rather, the writer of the source he used, may well have adapted the Prose-Lancelot version for his account, more than probable; the only point which is unintelligible in Malory's account, Meleagant's sending Guenever back after having got rid of Lancelot, indicates, as M. G. Paris remarks, 'that the compiler, not having at his disposal Bagdemagus, who was unknown to the poem which furnished his first part, did not know how otherwise to overcome the difficulty.' I hold the opinion that Malory found the account he sets forth in his xix[th] book ready made in a French source, which was derived from the Prose-Lancelot + a lost French or Welsh poem.

The incidents related in the third part of book xix., *i.e.*, chapters x–xii, which relate the arrival of a wounded knight, syr Vrre of Hongry, at Arthur's court, the handling of his wounds by all the knights of the court, his final healing by Lancelot, and the festival given in celebration of it, are not to be met with in any known French or English romance. I incline to believe that Malory adapted to his purpose some lost poem, most likely a French one.

The catalogue of names in chapter xi. is evidently Malory's own; one can trace almost all the groups of names in previous chapters. ...

The English metrical romance 'Le Mort Arthur' is of greater importance for the critic of the Arthurian romance than has hitherto been supposed, based, as it is, on two French sources, which in some points contradict each other. ... The Vulgate-Lancelot (P.L.) is the source for the first part, ... whereas for the remainder of the poem, . . . the poet used the same source as did M. for the two last books of his *rifacimento*.[6] . . . The opening lines of M.'s book xx. are his own composition. Neither MH. nor P.L. contains anything similar to these few general phrases, which introduce the subsequent events. . . .

The contents of chapter vi., the allusions to syr Trystram and to his murder by King Mark, are not in P.L.

MH. agrees in this portion with M., except that the former omits the long conversations, first between Guenever and Lancelot, and later on between Lancelot and his companions, as well as the enumeration of knights.

Several pasages of MH. are again literally reproduced by M. . . .

. . . In this section M. does not forget himself so far as to copy the very words of MH., though his phraseology often unmistakably suggests his use of that poem. . . .

. . . Many passages of M. suggest that, while writing his account, he had a copy of MH. before him. I only mention a few where the evidence is clear. . . .

. . . The portion of P.L. which corresponds to the last chapters of M.'s book xx. is one of the weakest parts of the whole romance. Dialogue, which plays an important part in all the French prose-romances, and is the cause of their inordinate length, is extremely prevalent; episodes which are absolutely out of place, and only produce a ridiculous effect, such as Arthur's defeat of the Roman emperor after being himself defeated at the siege of Gannes, produce the impression that the writer simply wished to fill a given number of pages.

M. and P.L. have features in common in this portion, which form, as it were, the framework upon which the episodes are built, but they often differ widely. . . .

In MH., ll. 2500–2951 correspond to M.'s chapters xix.–xxii., and both versions agree, not only in all incidents, but M., on various occasions, incorporates words, phrases, and even whole lines of MH. in his own text, whilst generally, as if to conceal the fact and mislead the reader, adding that the 'Frensshe book' says so. . . .

A minute examination of M.'s twenty-first book compared with the last ten folios of P.L. discloses many and great differences, but also here the ground-plan of the two accounts is the same, and the incidents common to both establish beyond doubt an intimate, though indirect, relation between the two versions; this fact points out either that the sources of both are derived from a common source, or that P.L. itself is the source of the French romance used by M....

In M. the [final] battle comes about quite differently. Whilst Arthur and Mordred, accompanied by their knights, are treating for a month's truce, a knight, stung by an adder, pulls out his sword, and this incident is the signal for the battle. The battle itself and Arthur's and Mordred's wounding each other to death vary considerably. P.L. then continues thus....

M. deviates from this most extraordinary account in several points. First of all Arthur does not, as in P.L., remount his horse after being mortally wounded, ride a considerable distance, stay a long time in a chapel praying, and then still retain so much force as to kill Lucans in his embrace. In M., Arthur is able to walk no more, and the death of the grievously wounded Lucans is caused by carrying his king. The part of Girflet is taken in M. by Bedwere, the former's name not being even mentioned. Both M. and P.L. agree that Arthur asks Bedwere (Girflet) to throw his sword into a lake, that Bedwere (Girflet) deceives Arthur twice before carrying out this wish, and then sees a hand rise out of the water, receive the sword, brandish and disappear with it. In P.L., Girflet first throws his own sword into the lake, then the sheath of Excalibor....

...The remainder of chapter vi...is apparently M.'s composition, the mention of the names of Morgan, the Queen of Northgalys, the Queen of the 'waste landes,' and 'Nynyue' being another example of his repeatedly noticed predilection for such lists. The opening lines of chapter vii. are also M.'s addition; the line: '*His iacet Arthurus Rex quondam Rex que futurus,*' occurs at the end of the Thornton MS. 'La Morte Arthure.'...

Comparing M. with MH., we find that both versions agree very closely in this portion, save for...insignificant variations.... MH. omits the letter which, according to M., Gawayne writes to Lancelot before his death, and states that Gawayne was found dead in the boat. M.'s text suggests throughout that MH. was before him during the compilation of it, but in this part he comparatively rarely forgets himself so far as to reproduce the very words of MH., but passages of the latter sort occur....

... The last six chapters of M. have but few points in common with the last folios of P.L. The former contains many incidents entirely absent from the latter.... In both versions Lancelot returns with his faithful knights to England. Save some points in the description of Lancelot's death M. and P.L. have nothing more in common after this....

Comparing this last section of M. with the conclusion of MH. we find many incidents common to both, but also some in M. absent from MH.—*e.g.*, Lancelot's going to Gawayne's tomb and the offering he makes there. Further, whilst in M. Lancelot buries Guenever himself at Glastonbury, in MH. she is only buried there after his death. But on the whole both versions tally closely, nay M. in many cases servilely copies the words and phrases of MH....

The last part of the final chapter of book xxi. contains I think incidents of three different kinds; those invented by M., as Ector's praise of Lancelot and the enumeration of the knights who return to their own land; those which M. has in common with the Thornton MS. 'La Morte Arthure,' such as the succession to the throne of England by 'Constantyn that was syr Cadores sone of Cornwayl'; lastly those M. must have borrowed from some French source we no longer possess, such as the statement, that Bors, Ector, Blamour, and Bleoberis undertake a pilgrimage to the Holy Land....

(viii) conclusion, pp. 293—4

...M. Gaston Paris speaks of Malory's work as 'a well-known compilation hitherto too little utilised for critical studies.' I think I may fairly claim that it has now been utilised, and that, altogether apart from its interest as prose literature, it has been shown to occupy a most important place in the criticism of the Arthurian cycle.

The researches of M. Gaston Paris, of Professor W. Foerster, of Professor H. Zimmer, and of Professor Rhys[7] have drawn the attention of the learned world afresh to the Arthurian legend and to the innumerable difficulties which it presents to the investigator. I claim that henceforward no researches can be regarded as exhaustive which disregard Malory's compilation, and, further, that his work is by far the best guide to the Arthurian romances in their entirety.

It may, I trust, be considered as finally settled that for several portions of the cycle Malory is our only authority. These are:

1. The last part of book iv.
2. The whole of book vii.
3. The lost 'Suite de Lancelot.'
4. The lost 'Tristan' trilogy.

On the other hand, my examination of such portions of Malory as are common to him and to his sources will, I trust, enable students to discriminate what in him belongs to the older stratum of the Romance-cycle and what are his own additions and modifications. It need hardly be pointed out how important this is in the case of investigations which deal with early Celtic heroic and mythic legend. Conclusions might otherwise be based upon what is simply a fact of Malory's own invention.

The most important critical result is, I need hardly say, the reconstruction of the 'Suite de Lancelot.' Although I have provisionally treated this as a modification and a development of the Vulgate-Lancelot, it is quite possible that it may contain older as well as younger elements. I would also direct the attention of future investigators to the Tristan form of the 'Quest of the Holy Grail.'

As regards the special features of Malory's compilation, I trust I have succeeded in clearly exhibiting his merits and demerits as a writer. I have shown that he sometimes added small episodes of his own composition, though, as a rule, he contented himself with welding into one the diverse materials that were at his disposal, and that not infrequently he literally translated entire passages from his French, or made large transcripts from his English, sources.

We owe the worthy knight a deep debt of gratitude both for preserving the mediaeval romances in a form which enabled them to remain an integral portion of English literature, and for rescuing from oblivion certain French versions of great value to the critical student. But truth demands that we should not rate him too highly. To put it mildly, his work is very unequal—sometimes he excels, but often he falls beneath, oftener still, he servilely reproduces his originals. Nor can his selection of material be unreservedly praised. Difficulties in procuring certain MSS. may possibly have occurred of which we have nowadays no idea; yet, giving him the full benefit of this supposition, we must still say that he left out many of the most touching and admirable portions of the French romances, and that he has incorporated others of inferior quality.

The most marked and distressing instance is his preference of the trivial and distasteful version of the Merlin and Niviene episode as found in the 'Suite de Merlin' to the exquisite version of the Vulgate-Merlin, which, in its mingling of wild romance and delicate sentiment, is perhaps the most beautiful and characteristic story of mediaeval literature. Be this as it may, Malory must always be counted as an English classic. I shall be satisfied if what I have done be considered not unworthy his merits and his position in English literature.

EDITOR'S NOTES

1 The alliterative *Morte Arthure* was often ascribed to this author. See also section (b. iv) below.

2 *Anglia*, I (1878), 143–6. *Zusammenstoppler* may be translated as 'one who clumsily patches together'.

3 Much later discoveries have located the Alexander episodes in various versions of the expanded prose *Tristan*; Sommer's hypothesis (developed later in this volume) that Malory had access to an expanded *Tristan* which included some Lancelot adventures as well as those of Alexander was essentially correct.

4 A subsequently discovered version of the *Suite de Merlin* suggests that Sommer was wrong on this point, that the changes he noted were more likely Malory's own.

5 This question has generally been answered affirmatively by more recent scholars; Vinaver, for example, believed that Malory had access to a better text than the one represented by the Thornton MS. (*Works*, III, 1366).

6 In Sommer's hypothesis concerning a lost 'Suite de Lancelot', the 'Suite's' author is supposed to have made precisely those changes that differentiate Malory's version from that of the Vulgate. Therefore (the reasoning goes) it must have been Malory's source as well as the source of the stanzaic *Morte*.

7 Gaston Paris—see No. 35 above.

   John Rhys, *Studies in The Arthurian Legend* (Oxford, 1891). In 1893 Rhys also wrote the introduction to a new (modernized) edition of Malory edited by F. J. Simmons and illustrated by Aubrey Beardsley; this introduction presents much of the Welsh background to Arthurian romance.

   W. Foerster had by this time published his editions of Chrétien's *Cligès*, *Yvain*, and *Erec*.

Heinrich Zimmer, professor of Sanskrit, and later of Celtic, at Berlin, had recently (1890) introduced his view that the transmission of Celtic Arthurian matter had reached French trouvères not through the Welsh but from the Bretons.

42. Andrew Lang

1891

Andrew Lang (1844–1912), scholar, historian, folklorist, and versatile essayist, did perhaps his most important work on Greek literature; he collaborated on translations of the *Odyssey* and the *Iliad* and wrote three important books on Homer, arguing for unity. Like other classicists, he compares Malory and Homer and finds many similarities; although Malory's work seems 'structureless', it is nevertheless 'strong on the side of goodness'. In the essay below, Lang also discusses nineteenth-century adaptations of Malory and finds that neither Tennyson nor Swinburne has done him justice.

The essay was published as a preface to Sommer's volume III (London: David Nutt, 1891), pp. xiii–xxv.

The learning about Malory has been so fully dealt with in this edition by an expert, that the comments of one who merely reads Malory for enjoyment may be confined to the enjoyable elements in his work. His, as Mr. Furnivall remarks, 'is a most pleasant jumble and summary of the legends about Arthur.' The knight was no great clerk in Celtic mythology, and perhaps no very discriminate judge of what was best to choose, what best to omit, in his 'French books.' He was content to tell of 'noble and renowned acts of humanity, gentleness, and chivalry. For herein may be seen noble chivalry, courtesy, humanity, friendliness, hardiness, love, friendship, cowardice, murder, hate, virtue, and sin.' These are the elements of our life, these are the *farrago libelli* which Ascham should not have reproached for containing mere 'bold bawdry and open manslaughter.' In the very first page we meet Igerne, 'a passing good woman,' who 'would not consent unto the king,' though hers, after all, was Alcmena's fate. Malory is throughout strong on the side of goodness. The Laureate talks of his book as 'touched with the adulterous finger' of the time of Edward IV. But assuredly, if we compare the popular romance of that day with the popular romances of any other, we might consider that a golden age which found its favourite reading, and its ideals of conduct, in the 'Morte d'Arthur.' Men and women will be men and women; but here, even if the passion be sinful, it is still passion, ardent, constant, and loyal to the grave.

There is no more strange fortune in literature than that which blended wild Celtic myths, and a monastic theory of the saintly life, with all of chivalrous adventure, with all of courtesy and gentleness, that the Middle Ages could conceive, and handed it on to be the delight of the changing ages.

In this respect, in the mingling of remote, scarce decipherable legends with a high theory of human life, in the choice of what was feasible in Celtic legends, in its transmutation into the universally appropriate and excellent, the work of Malory may be compared to the Homeric epics. Both have their distant undiscoverable sources in the high far-off lands of a society to which we can never return. Both gain a mystery and a magic from early imaginings, both have been touched with the colour of many ages, both have the noble melancholy of great deeds done and great enterprises attempted, to end as all human endeavour ends, leaving only a song or a story in the ears of men yet to be born. Studying Malory and Homer together, we are struck by the resemblances and differences of life and of its ideals; we are impressed by the changes that Christianity and the temper of the North have brought into what may be styled the heroic and aristocratic theory of existence, of duty, of enjoyment.

The epic and the romance both start from the conception of the marvellous, the supernatural, but how strangely that conception varies in each under the influence of the new, the Christian, and the Northern ideas. The old capricious Gods have departed, of course, and made way for a deity of mercy and justice. But magic is as powerful in Malory as in Homer. Merlin does such a craft that Pellinore saw not Arthur, as Apollo lightly hides Agenor or Aeneas in a mist. In Nimue, one of the ladies of the lake, we have Malory's Circe, whose wiles are too cunning even for his Odysseus, Merlin. The wide world to the knights, as to the adventurous Ithacan, is an unsubstantial fairy place, and Malory's castles are as enchanted as the isles of the unsailed Homeric seas. The vividness of Malory's pictures has that element of surprise which waits for us as we go up to Circe's house, through the oak coppice and the wild wood. The knight rides over a bridge that is old and feeble, and, coming into a great hall, sees lying a dead knight that was a seemly man, and a brachet licks his wounds, and there comes a lady weeping. Across the moors, and through the darkness of the forests, Arthur rides after the mysterious Morgan le Fay, who shapes herself, by enchantment, into a great marble stone. But in Malory the adventures lead to no end till the Graal has to be won; the knights ride forth for the mere pleasure of the unknown, for the mere interest of what may befall them. One sleeps below an apple-tree, and lo! there come four Queens, and look on his face, and know that it is Lancelot, and contend for his love. Then Morgan le Fay carries him to the enchanted Castle Chariot, and they lay him 'in a chamber cold,' and tell him that, though no lady can have his love but one, and that Queen Guinevere, 'now thou shalt lose her for ever, and she thee, and therefore thee behoveth to choose now one of us four.' The knight is more loyal to his love than Odysseus to his wedded wife: 'lever had I die in this prison with worship, than to have one of you to my love, maugre my head. .... And as to Queen Guinevere, she is the truest lady unto her lord living.' But all these adventures among chapels perilous, and valleys where stand pavilions of red sandal, are, unlike the Homeric adventures, without an end or aim. The slight unity that we find in the earlier parts, before the Graal becomes an aim and end, before the love of Lancelot brings a doom on all, is in the character and position of Arthur. ...

Different as are their ideas of love, and of pure fidelity and constancy unshaken in a man, Homer and Malory draw near each other in their pictures of their great ladies and lovers, Helen and Guinevere. Ruinous they both are, but each might say to her singer and her romancer, in the words of Helen to the dead Hector, 'Never yet heard I evil or despiteful word from thee.' Both romance and epic are chivalrous here; neither Homer nor Malory preaches nor rebukes, like the Arthur of the 'Idylls of the King.' But different are the repentances of the fateful ladies, the sorrows of the North and South. 'At the last,' says Helen, 'I groaned for my blindness that Aphrodite gave me, when she led me to Troy from mine own country, forsaking my child and my bridal chamber, and my lord, that lacked not aught, either of wisdom or beauty.' In heroic Greece, the shame is over and past; in Elysium, in the Avalon of Argos, Helen and Menelaus are destined to endless joy. But the spirit of Christianity and of the North, that gave us the passion of Brynhild, demand from Guinevere another penance. 'She let make herself a nun, and great penance she took, as ever did sinful lady in this land, and never creature could make her merry, but lived in fasting, prayers, and alms deeds, that all manner of people marvelled how virtuously she was changed.' In that last meeting of Lancelot and Guinevere, when she might have gone with him to her own Elysium of Joyous Garde, she cries, 'As well as I have loved thee, mine heart will not serve me to see thee; for through thee and me is the flower of kings and knights destroyed.' So she parts from 'the truest lover of a sinful man that ever loved woman,' 'then he sickened more and more and dwined and died away; .... sometime he slumbered a broken sleep, and ever he was lying grovelling on the tomb of King Arthur and Queen Guinevere.'

Helen and Guinevere are both children of the old world of dreams; both born in the land of myth, each is a daughter of Gods, or a daughter of the moon, as the old story fabled of Helen, or 'the white ghost,' as Guinevere's name is interpreted; they are not born of men nor of mortal seed: they are as the vision of Beauty on earth among the passions of men. But between the years that sang of Helen and the years that told of Guinevere what a change has come, and how readily the Greek wins to her rest in her home by Eurotas, and how hardly does Guinevere attain to hers. Guinevere is never in later time to be worshipped and sainted, like Helen, for her very beauty's sake. 'Une immense espérance a traversée la terre,' a hope that brings with it pain and sorrow, and an array of new passions and desires that never vexed or rejoiced the older faith, the older time. In all this conclusion of the faithful and disloyal love,

Whose honour rooted in dishonour stood,

Malory has penned the great and chief romance of his own age and of ours, the story that must endure and must move the *lacrymae rerum* till man's nature is altered again. Homer knows wedded love, which no man has praised with nobler words than he puts in the lips of Nausicaa; and he knows light loves of chiefs and captives. But that great charm of a love which is constant as it is sinful, of Lancelot and of Guinevere, does not come into his ken, nor can we fancy him alluring and saddening us with the passion of Clytaemnestra and Aegisthus, 'with sheer doom before their eyes,' the doom that they drew on them 'beyond what was ordained.' Nor does Homer know, or care to dwell on, a hopeless passion like the mortal love of Elaine for Lancelot. We may see one touch of such an affection in the words of Nausicaa when she bids Odysseus a last farewell, a passage the more deeply moving for its reticence. But of Nausicaa we learn no more; tradition even is not busy with her; while the last voyage of the Maid of Astolat is an enduring possession of romance. And yet more remote from Homer, of course, is the chastity of the Sangraal legend. Mr. Rhys has very ingeniously tried to account for the purity of Galahad and Percival, as if it were the inheritance from solar heroes, who had been of much prowess before the age of the passions began. But we may far more plausibly attribute the purity of Galahad to monastic influence in part, and in part to the Germanic chastity of which Tacitus tells, arising from a lofty respect for women. We may contrast it with those views of Thetis, so frankly heathen, which disconcert Mr. Gladstone in the 'Iliad.' Malory's ideal in this matter was probably very far from being attained by his readers, yet it remains an attractive picture of a manly purity associated with strength and courage.

Among the many differences of temper which distinguish this great romance of the Middle Ages from the great epics of prehistoric Hellas, perhaps the strongest is to be found in the various theories of courage. In Homer, courage is a very varying quality. When Hector challenges the Achaean princes, dismay and silence fall on them. No man is eager to volunteer. In battle even Achilles (perhaps in an interpolated passage) is adread. Agamemnon is eternally despondent and anxious for flight. Only Odysseus, when cut off by a crowd of Trojans, dares to stand his ground, unaided and alone. 'For I know that they are cowards, who flee the fight, but whosoever is a hero in war, him it mainly behoves to stand stubbornly, whether he be smitten, or whether he smite.' Even Hector, in his last stand at the Scaean gate, deliberates about making shameful terms with Achilles, though Asteropaeus has just set him the example of a gallant and glorious death. Neither Greek nor Trojan fights a losing battle well; and when Homer makes Hector actually run for his life, he gives us a scene which no romancer nor saga-man dared to write about a hero. Other is the temper of Lancelot in the Queen's chamber, naked and unarmed, and beset by overwhelming numbers: 'Wit you well, Madam, I shall sell my life as dear as I may:—And now I had liever than to be lord of all Christendom that I had sure armour upon me, that men might speak of my deeds or ever I were slain.'

We cannot doubt that Homer sang to men who shared his theory of courage—who, like him, believed that the bravest had their fighting days, as Paris says of himself, and their days when fighting was not dear to them. All this is doubtless true enough to human nature. But not to believe it, not to acknowledge it, to resist and defy the whispers of fear, is true to the Northern nature, and this creed has given us many an unsung Thermopylae.

The Celtic legends, passed through the French mind, and rendered in Malory's English, have, what Homer lacks, the charm of mystery and distance, the background of the unknown. In Homer all is beheld in the clearest and most delicate air; about Merlin and Morgan le Fay, and the ladies of the lake, and the strange swords and cups, there is a mist of enchantment. They are relics of an older world, not understood even by the narrators. It is, probably, not the Celtic, but the mediaeval fancy which introduces another element of the romancer, much suppressed in Homer— that of broad conventional humour. The epics know of no such warrior as Dinadan among their many types of character. He satisfies the rude mediaeval taste in jokes; he preserves the romances from becoming too sentimental. He sets a dish of fish before 'the haut prince' because the haut prince 'had a custom he loved no fish.' So comic is this excellent Dinadan that Lancelot 'may not sit in his saddle when that spear hitteth him,' that spear with which the humorous knight smote his friends in the ribs. 'Then laughed the queen and the haut prince that they might not sit at their table,' so 'tickle of thes ear' are those beings, children of the mist and of the night as they are.

Thus Malory's book is a very complete and composite picture of a strangely inherited ideal; it is, indeed, 'a jumble,' but, of all jumbles, the most poetic and the most pathetic. Structureless as it seems, patchwork as it is, the 'Morte d'Arthur' ends as nobly as the 'Iliad,' deserving the praise which Shelley gives to Homer, and dying away in 'the high and solemn close of the whole bloody tale in tenderness and inexpiable sorrow.' It is well called 'La Morte d'Arthur,' for the ending atones for all, wins forgiveness for all, and, like the death of Roland, is more triumphant than a victory. Like the three damoysels, Malory is skilled 'to teach men unto strange adventures,' to instruct in all courage, chastity, endurance, and true love, nor can we estimate what his influence must have been in training the fathers of Elizabeth's Englishmen. Thus it has somehow befallen that the Arthurian legends, in their third descent, are infinitely more dear and familiar to Englishmen and English boys than the original French romances are to the French, or to any foreign people who borrowed them from the French. In France, the romances are the special possession of scholars only; in England, Malory's 'Morte' is a favourite in most school-rooms, and has been the inspiration of our greatest poet since our great poetic age. It is characteristic of our mixed race that we have nothing at all like an ancient Germanic epic in our popular and living literature. 'Beowulf' is far too remote from us in every way; we are not fortunate enough to possess anything corresponding to the 'Song of Roland.' We owe our national romance first to the Celts, then to the French; but the form and, to a great extent, the spirit are English, are Malory's.

The style of Malory is, of course, based on the fresh and simple manner of his French originals. For an English style of his age, it is particularly fluent. Periods of considerable length and intricacy, especially in speeches, do not give him any trouble. As examples, we might take the dialogue (book xx. chapter iii.) of Lancelot and the Queen when he is surprised in her chamber. The daring, chivalry, and self-restraint of the knight are here admirably and suitably expressed. Perhaps it is just because he does follow a French copy, and so is familiar with words derived from the Latin, that Malory possesses his fluency and facility. The constant advice to use only 'Anglo-Saxon' in modern composition is erroneous, and is ungrateful to those great makers of our language, the writers from Spenser to Shakspere. Malory is, of course, much less Latinised than they; such a phrase as

The multitudinous seas incarnadine

cannot be expected from him. But he is almost as remote from the
'Wardour Street English' which stands in a false following of the
Icelandic. If we take his famous chapter on true love and the month
of May, we see how much his language owes to the Latin, or to the
Latin through the French (book xviii. chapter xxv.). Here we have
such Latinised words as 'flourisheth,' 'constrain,' 'divers causes,'
'gentleness,' 'service,' 'negligence,' 'deface,' 'stability,' 'virtuous,'
'endure,' 'accord,' and so forth, all in half a page. The language has
slipped away from its monosyllables, and is becoming more rapid
and more fluent. Here, too, Malory offers examples of a trait
common in him—the sudden change to the second person, as if in
livelier and more actual address: 'There never was worshipful man
or worshipful woman but they loved one better than another, and
worship in arms may never be foiled, but first reserve the honour
to God, and secondly the quarrel must come of thy lady. . . . Therefore all ye that be lovers call unto your remembrance the month of
May, like as did Queen Guinevere, for whom I make here a little
mention, that while she lived she was a true lover, and therefore she
had a good end.' In ordinary spelling, the words all remain good
current English. Almost the only obsolete word in the chapter is
'lycours.' Even when the carter 'drove on a great wallop' Malory
needs no glossary. His language always explains itself; for example,
in the picturesque expression, 'I sawe no thynge but the waters
wappe and waves wanne.' Malory's chief mark of childlike
simplicity is in his conjunctions; his narrative is stitched with 'so's'
and 'and's,' though this is, of course, less marked in his dialogue
and in his reflective passages. The childlike character becomes
almost Republican in such a passage as this: 'he landed wyth seven
kynges, and the nombre was hydous to beholde.' On the whole, it
may be said of the narrative manner that it is well fitted to the
wandering tale; just old enough and quaint enough to allure, and to
mark the age, without disturbing or delaying even the youngest
reader of the noble and joyous history. Readers enough Malory
has, and is likely to have, more probably than any other ancient
English author, more even than Chaucer, whose language and
prosody offer more difficulty, and who has the perennial disadvantage of writing in verse. Maundeville, probably, can never be
popular, in spite of his entertaining matter. Ascham only attracts

scholars and the curious. But the manner and matter of Malory make him the most generally known of all old authors, except, of course, the translators of the Bible.

The name of Arthur has been unfortunate when borne by English princes, and the fame of Arthur has not always been happy in the hands of Malory's successors. Many have been moved to write an Arthuriad, but a kind of blight always fell on their intentions. Spenser's is but an Arthur of allegory and fantasy, not a living character in real romance. Milton never carried out his long-cherished design, nor did Dryden 'raise the Table Round again.' In Malory's narrative, poets have felt that more was meant than met the ear. The myths of one age naturally become the symbols of the next, and Arthur's wars, passing from myth into romance, and touched by religion, were especially destined to end in the symbolical. This their third stage has, of necessity, the least tangible motive. As the Laureate declares, his 'Idylls' are:

> New-old, and shadowing Sense at war with Soul,
> Rather than that grey King, whose name, a ghost
> Streams like a cloud, man-shaped, from mountain-peak,
> And cleaves to cairn and cromlech still; or him
> Of Geoffrey's book, or him of Malleor's, one
> Touched by the adulterous finger of a time
> That hover'd between war and wantonness,
> And crownings and dethronings.

This is a hard judgment on Malory's book, in which the evil is not triumphant, nor sympathetic beyond the true bounds of human sympathy. It is not so much the fault of the Laureate's genius, as of literary necessity, that the 'Idylls' are almost too obviously allegoric. The Arthurian traditions remain purely romantic in his early 'Lady of Shalott,' and in that sweet vernal piece, 'a fragment,' 'Sir Launcelot and Queen Guinevere.'... This and the magical 'Lady of Shalott' are indeed poems of 'the boyhood of the year,' unclouded by inevitable, but not wholly appropriate reflection. The 'Idylls,' on the other side, have a purpose, a purpose which the ancient romance unavoidably suggests, but which is not of a piece with the legend. New wine is put into old bottles. It may be doubted whether a poet is well advised when he deliberately treats the theme of another age in the spirit of to-day. Even in the first noble fragment of 1842, 'The Morte d'Arthur,' the strain of thought and speech are modern. King Arthur is, indeed, what the poet dreams that he is to be, 'a modern gentleman of stateliest port.' Admirable as his words are for wisdom and music, and imperishable in our memories, the voice is not the voice of the Arthur whom we knew. The knight has become a type; a type he remains, through the cycle of the 'Idylls of the King.' It is not our Arthur who preaches to the repentant Guinevere: the King has become the Conscience. All this, we may say, was not to be avoided. We can scarcely take an old theme of the dead world, and tell the story again in verse, without bringing, in one way or other, the new kind of thought. The new kind of expression, his own, the noble sort of conceits in which he is an inimitable master, also mark the Laureate's 'Idylls.'...

... This is remote from the tone of the romance we know and love; beautiful in itself as it is, we cannot but feel that it is as inconsistent as the wisdom and mildness of the Greek in Mr. Bridges's 'Achilles in Scyros.' Or is this feeling only part of our haunting archaeological pedantry, which, content with the heroes in the garb of their day, is vexed to find them familiar with our own more involved speech, and more involved thought? Every reader must judge for himself. Poetry is always turning back on her only valuable material, that which she does not and cannot make, that which was bequeathed to her in the youth of our race, when man wandered in worlds not realised, and explained them by his fancies. In spite of the cry for poetry of our own day and our own life, great poets have all turned to tradition for their materials. They may use tradition in two ways—frankly appropriating it, never dreaming that its people were in any way other than those they know; or clearly knowing the difference, and making the ancient persons mere *personae*, masks through which the new voice is uttered. The first method is that of Homer, of Chaucer, and, to a great extent, of Shakspere. Homer's men, Chaucer's men, when Chaucer deals with the remote past, are frankly Homeric and Chaucerian. The tragedians, on the other hand, place the ideas and the problems of Athenian thought in the mouths of mythic heroes and heroines, Agamemnon and Alcestis, Helen, Clytaemnestra, and Odysseus. But the tragedians themselves are so remote that only fanatical adorers of Homer are conscious of any travesty, and that travesty they can pardon. So, too, in Shakspere, Hamlet is no heroic Dane, but a man born after the Renaissance and Reformation. This use of far older legends and persons by the great poets of the past is so masterful, so imaginative, that it conquers us, and subdues us to belief. In the 'Idylls of the King' we believe less, either that the sentiments are too peculiarly modern, or that the dramatic force is less vigorous, or that the veil of long familiarity is absent. They remain a wonderfully wrought series of pictures, gorgeous as the Gate of Camelot with its mystic sculptures, visionary and magnificent and unreal:

> New things and old co-twisted.

The age has seen many other Arthurian revivals. Mr. Morris has given us the 'Defence of Guinevere,' his most imaginative work, but this, too, has a fantasy, an 'intensity' that is alien to the leisurely romance. It is pictorial in another way, full of the colour of the fourteenth century. Like Guinevere—

> We gaze upon the arras giddily,
> Where the wind set the silken kings asway.

Mr. Swinburne's poem of 'Tristram of Lyoness' merely showed that, among Mr. Swinburne's many gifts the gift of narrative is not one. The story was clogged and covered out of sight by the heavy splendour of the style. Events and characters were lost in vast digressions of description. In Mr. Arnold's brief poem of the death of Tristram the passage which haunts us is all his own, owes nothing to Malory or the French books, the beautiful passage on the children of Iseult:

> But they sleep in sheltered rest
> Like helpless birds in the warm nest
> On the castle's southern side, ...

Thus the cycle of Arthur has not failed to enrich our modern poetry, nor our poetry to enrich it; but a new epic it has not given us, because a new epic is an impossibility. Far hence, in the untravelled-future, the echo of the tumult of an age dimly heard, faintly understood, may become a song in the ears of men unborn. But we have not the epic spirit; ere that can come to birth, the world, too, must die and be born again.

43. Reviews of Sommer's edition of Malory

A. Lionel Johnson, *Academy*

20 September 1890, pp. 237–9

Lionel Johnson (1867–1902), the poet, went from Oxford to London in 1890 to establish himself in a literary career. During the early 1890s, he supported himself by writing book reviews for *Academy* and a number of other periodicals, bringing a well-furnished mind to the consideration of a number of topics.

Johnson reviews volumes I and II only of Sommer's work, and much of his review, omitted here, concerns the text, the previous editions, and Sommer's comments on Malory's syntax. Vernon Lee, referred to below, was the pen name of Violet Paget, and the reference is to a comment in her book *Euphorion: Studies of the Antique and the Medieval in the Renaissance* (London, 1884). Her point there was that the passionate love of some troubadour lyrics had been considerably softened; she also referred to Malory's version as 'our expunged English "Morte"'.

It is difficult to exaggerate the services, and the wrongs, done to English literature by German scholars. On the one hand, there is such admirable work as that of Lessing. Nowhere have we a more just and subtile appreciation of Milton and of Shakspere than in the *Laocoon* and the *Dramaturgie*. On the other hand, there is no need to name those German scholars who have wandered from learni into pedantry; and who have found in English literature a f the display of wild and precarious theories. A ba scholarship, by a German scholar, is the most sig saying, 'Corruptio optimi pessima'; so tha misgiving that we approach a great and English classic by a German editor a

But to the confusion of English scholarship, and to the praise of German, we have in Dr. Sommer the very type and example of sound and judicious learning, conscientiously employed in research, and prudently applied in composition. *Le Morte Darthur* is the earliest classic of English prose, and of English printing; and yet no book has met with such neglect from English scholars, nor been treated with such carelessness as this. It has been reserved for Dr. Sommer to edit a genuine text, to write bibliographical and philological studies, to compile laborious indices. Nor is this all; for we are promised a third volume upon the sources of Malory, by Dr. Sommer, who has secured in Mr. Andrew Lang an accomplished man of letters to deal with Malory as a writer of prose and a master of style. . . .

The next study of general importance is a collection of notes upon the language of *Le Morte Darthur*, and it is here that we most cordially thank and congratulate Dr. Sommer. His notes make no pretence to completeness, to a systematic study of Malory's English; but they help the reader to appreciate at once the differences and the resemblances between that English and ours. In one way Dr. Sommer has done to English literature a service, possibly undesigned: he shows plainly that in countless idioms and usages of syntax Malory wrote just such English as the more correct and pure among our modern writers. There are many habits of speech to be found in the writing of 'purists,' ˄nd undeniably correct, which are laughed at by the dailv ⌐ t which abound in Malory, in Bacon, in Addisⁿ ˄ Arnold. The tradition of fine English ⌐ ised, but the fine writers are
ᵌˡ⁻ to each other than to their
ago, Mr. Justice Kay was
ˀg down the sound and
ˀf 'Lewis' is 'Lewis',' not
Malory 'names terminat-
. A few more instances
⌐eats as archaic usages
ɔod modern English.
ˀel; so would, and so
vrite with euphony.
knyght so good as
⌐ue to say that the
ɔr the accusative.
English in Dr.

43. Reviews of Sommer's edition of Malory

A. Lionel Johnson, *Academy*

20 September 1890, pp. 237–9

Lionel Johnson (1867–1902), the poet, went from Oxford to London in 1890 to establish himself in a literary career. During the early 1890s, he supported himself by writing book reviews for *Academy* and a number of other periodicals, bringing a well-furnished mind to the consideration of a number of topics.

Johnson reviews volumes I and II only of Sommer's work, and much of his review, omitted here, concerns the text, the previous editions, and Sommer's comments on Malory's syntax. Vernon Lee, referred to below, was the pen name of Violet Paget, and the reference is to a comment in her book *Euphorion: Studies of the Antique and the Medieval in the Renaissance* (London, 1884). Her point there was that the passionate love of some troubadour lyrics had been considerably softened; she also referred to Malory's version as 'our expunged English "Morte"'.

It is difficult to exaggerate the services, and the wrongs, done to English literature by German scholars. On the one hand, there is such admirable work as that of Lessing. Nowhere have we a more just and subtle appreciation of Milton and of Shakspere than in the *Laocoon* and the *Dramaturgie*. On the other hand, there is no need to name those German scholars who have wandered from learning into pedantry; and who have found in English literature a field for the display of wild and precarious theories. A bad book of scholarship, by a German scholar, is the most signal case of that saying, 'Corruptio optimi pessima'; so that it is with some misgiving that we approach a great and weighty edition of an English classic by a German editor and critic.

But to the confusion of English scholarship, and to the praise of German, we have in Dr. Sommer the very type and example of sound and judicious learning, conscientiously employed in research, and prudently applied in composition. *Le Morte Darthur* is the earliest classic of English prose, and of English printing; and yet no book has met with such neglect from English scholars, nor been treated with such carelessness as this. It has been reserved for Dr. Sommer to edit a genuine text, to write bibliographical and philological studies, to compile laborious indices. Nor is this all; for we are promised a third volume upon the sources of Malory, by Dr. Sommer, who has secured in Mr. Andrew Lang an accomplished man of letters to deal with Malory as a writer of prose and a master of style. . . .

The next study of general importance is a collection of notes upon the language of *Le Morte Darthur*, and it is here that we most cordially thank and congratulate Dr. Sommer. His notes make no pretence to completeness, to a systematic study of Malory's English; but they help the reader to appreciate at once the differences and the resemblances between that English and ours. In one way Dr. Sommer has done to English literature a service, possibly undesigned: he shows plainly that in countless idioms and usages of syntax Malory wrote just such English as the more correct and pure among our modern writers. There are many habits of speech to be found in the writing of 'purists,' and undeniably correct, which are laughed at by the daily press, but which abound in Malory, in Bacon, in Addison, in Newman, in Arnold. The tradition of fine English may be ignored and vulgarised, but the fine writers are always the same, always more like to each other than to their vulgar contemporaries. A few weeks ago, Mr. Justice Kay was ridiculed in the newspapers for laying down the sound and scholarly rule that the possessive case of 'Lewis' is 'Lewis',' not 'Lewis's'; Dr. Sommer tells us that with Malory 'names terminating in *s* remain unchanged' in such a case. A few more instances may be mentioned where Dr. Sommer treats as archaic usages forms of phrase and syntax common to good modern English. Thus Malory always wrote *myn* before a vowel; so would, and so does, any living writer who has the courage to write with euphony. Again, '*He* stands for hymself: "He weneth no knyght so good as he."' This is correct, though it is more strictly true to say that the verb is dropped than that the nominative stands for the accusative. Soon after this occurs the only piece of bad English in Dr.

Sommer's voluminous work: '*That what* is rendered by *that that.*'
Neither Malory nor any other Englishman ever wrote 'that what,'
though the modern 'that which' is certainly an improvement upon
'that that,' an ugly, yet not an obsolete, usage. Dr. Sommer also
says: 'In many cases the relative pronoun is entirely omitted, an
infrequent usage in modern English.' To name no others, Milton
and Browning, learned masters of the English grammar and
language, use it upon every page. And is it quite correct to say that
'*together*' or '*to gyder*,' in the following phrases merely stands for
'each other'?—'They loved to gyder,' 'They kyssed to gyder.'
Surely this is a little prosaic, as is the amusing observation that 'the
substantive *love* is treated as a masculine noun.' It would be well to
amend the rule thus: In *Le Morte Darthur*, 'Love is a god.' It is true
that 'many abstract names only used in modern English in the
singular occur in the plural'; but *wronges*, *advyses*, *ententes*, *buryels*,
are not examples of them. And such an expression as '*fourty
pounde*,' singular for plural, is common enough all through English
literature. Ascham, in his great invocation of 'Master Cicero,' has
'sixteen hundred year, after you were dead and gone.' Dr. Sommer
adds that the addition of the indefinite article is still more remarkable; but we all know 'John Gilpin,' and how

> He carries weight! he rides a race!
> 'Tis for a *thousand pound!*

Once more, 'many verbs are treated as reflexive which are no
longer such nowadays'; but to *rest*, *bethink*, *arme*, *defende*, *byhave*,
are constantly so used in good English. Many more cases occur
in which Dr. Sommer has abandoned, as out of use, excellent and
sound usages of modern English. Not that he has done amiss in
collecting examples of these extant words; they serve to remind us
how good English still survives and may be written. But to brand
them as archaic is to help forward the debasement of the language.
Otherwise, this brief sketch of Malory's language is useful and good.

Dr. Sommer's next performance demands the gratitude and the
admiration of all scholars. It is a collation of Wynkyn de Worde
with Caxton, giving a complete list of *variae lectiones....*

... To discuss the sources of Malory, or to approach in any way
the Arthurian legend, would be premature at the present time,
when we are expecting the publication of Dr. Sommer's volume
upon the former question, and that of Prof. Rhys upon the second.
The excellence of Dr. Sommer's work now before us, and the

unrivalled reputation of the Oxford Professor of Celtic, lead us to believe that in the two works we shall have a complete treatment of the mythology, history, and literature of King Arthur and of his legend; so that the Celtic hero will take his place, whether in fact or fiction, as definitely as the Frank Charlemagne and the Scandinavian Sigurd, or the Gothic Siegfried, have taken theirs. But there are certain considerations, possibly worth a little notice, upon the Celtic, or Arthurian, tradition in English literature. It is commonly said that a care for things Celtic, a recognition of the Celtic element in our life and literature, is of recent date; and if by this be meant that past generations knew little about Celtic philology and the like, it is very true; but it is not true to say that past generations were not profoundly attached to the Celts—Cambro-Britons, as they were fond of calling them. In Malory's time there was an immense interest in such things; witness Caxton's account.... Doubtless they knew little about the real Celts; what they relished was the romantic and chivalrous air thrown over those original legends, the courtly, knightly, and Christian charm of the story, as presented by those 'two Archdeacons,' upon whom Buckle poured such scorn. To Walter of Oxford, and to Geoffrey of Monmouth, is due the popularity in England, as distinct from Welsh tradition and folk-lore, of the familiar stories of Brute the Trojan and so forth. The whole history, with its curious narratives, in which occur Trojans, and Joseph of Arimathaea and other discordant persons, was accepted for truth; nor was anyone bold enough to question it till Polydore Virgil did so, to the indignation of everyone. That ingenious but over-fluent writer, Vernon Lee, speaks of 'the colourless respectability of the collection made by Sir Thomas Malory.' The literary value of Malory is a question which we may leave aside; certainly his work represents an increasing concern for the ancient histories and traditions of Britain. Gradually there seems to have sprung up an appreciation of the 'Britons' as the earliest genuine ancestors of the English: an uncritical instinct, true in the main. This most strongly is seen in Drayton; *Polyolbion* is, for the most part, a long chaunt in praise of Wales. He defends the traditional story 'Our Geffray had his Brute,' and he invokes the bard who

> Of famous Arthur told'st, and where he was interred;
> In which these wretchless times had long and blindly erred,
> And ignorance had brought the world to such a pass,

306

As now, which scarce believes that Arthur ever was.
But when King Henry sent, th' reported place to view,
He found that man of men: and what thou said'st was true.

Drayton was indignant at the scepticism; and there are some thirty
passages in his poems where he breaks out in praise of Wales and of
Arthur. He has one reference in his *Eclogues* which I can only
interpret as an allusion to Wynkyn de Worde's edition of Malory.
One shepherd exclaims to another called Winkin:

'What, may'st thou be that old Winkin de Word?
    ★ ★ ★ ★ ★ ★
Come, sit we down under this Hawthorne Tree,
The Morrowe's Light shall lend us Day enough,
And let us tell of Gawen or Sir Guy,
Of Robin Hood, or of old Clem a Clough.
Or else some Romant unto us areede,
By former shepheards taught thee in thy youth,
Of noble Lords and Ladies gentle deede,
Or of thy Love, or of thy Lasses truth.'

Spenser, as all know, loved the legends of King Arthur, and
'moralised his song' by their help. Milton is full of gorgeous
passages about them. It was reserved for Sir Richard Blackmore
and for Lord Tennyson to attempt what was intended, but not
done, by Milton and by Dryden. The loss of Milton's projected
epic is irretrievable; he alone could have given us all the grandeur
and the beauty of old romance, without renouncing his classical
perfection. Dr. Sommer has quoted the passage in Ascham, where
that delightful scholar falls foul of Malory for his vicious influence;
and I may add Ben Jonson to the number of ill wishers to King
Arthur. In his *Underwoods* he execrates Vulcan for burning his
MSS. He could have spared anything, he says, but that. He would
have thrown on the fire.

        the whole sum
Of Errant Knighthood, with the Dames and Dwarfs;
The charmed Boats, and the inchanted Wharfs,
The *Tristrams*, *Lanc'lots*, *Turpins*, and the *Peers*,
All the mad *Rolands*, and sweet *Oliveers*;
To *Merlin's* Marvails, and his *Caball's* loss
With the Chimaera of the *Rosie Cross*.

Again, an interest in early British legend led Shakespere to go thither for his *Cymbeline* and *King Lear*. In short, what I may call British things, as distinct from Celtic, always kept a fascination for our older men of letters. I might mention the Wartons, and especially the younger's poems; and Gray, who here, as in much else, caught the modern spirit, and was a Celtic scholar for that age. In our own time the pre-Raphaelite movement found a singular occasion of success in these Arthurian stories. Malory, writes Mr. William Rossetti, had 'a great influence upon Rossetti's mind.' Mr. Pater has told us how wonderfully Mr. Morris touched the old legends; and, besides Mr. Swinburne's *Tristram of Lyonnesse* and the Laureate's unsatisfactory *Idylls*, there is Arnold's great poem, *Tristram and Iseult*. In Germany there is Wagner's magnificent drama, *Parzifal*; in France. M. Verlaine, with his sensuous mysticism, has written upon the same theme. Characteristically enough, Mr. Walt Whitman exclaims, 'Away with old romance!' because 'Arthur is vanished with all his knights.' Arnold's lectures upon Celtic literature contain the finest and most subtile things yet said upon the Celts, unless the beautiful essay of M. Renan be held their equal. And, finally, we have Prof. Rhys to keep before us the facts of science, of philology: not to destroy poetry, but to explain its original in these old myths; to tell us that Merlin is 'the Brythonic Zeus,' for example, and not an inexplicable 'Ambrosius.' Let me add that it is discreditable to Mark Twain that he should have spoiled his reputation for humour by the foolish scurrilities of his burlesque upon Malory. I have touched upon these illustrations of the influence, and of the popularity, won by the legends, of which Malory, as de Quincey said, is the Herodotus; because to do so emphasises the value of Dr. Sommer's great undertaking. There is no English classic of equal fame and worth so poorly and neglectfully treated hitherto. Now, at last, a scholar not of our nation has given us a final and a nearly faultless edition. For the first time we can read, in its most perfect form, the mediaeval version of that national legend.…

B. Unsigned reviews in the *Nation*

2 January 1890, pp. 15–16 and 21 January 1892, p. 58

The American periodical the *Nation*, founded in 1865, was a weekly journal concerned with politics, literature, science, and art. Its criticism of books was as important as its liberal politics; during the remainder of the nineteenth century, its editors drew upon a more imposing staff of contributors than that assembled by any other American periodical. The reviews, all unsigned, were undertaken by such persons as Charles Eliot Norton, George Perkins Marsh (see No. 23 above), William Francis Allen, and a number of other university professors prominent in a variety of fields.

Selection (a) below is from the 1890 review of Sommer's volume I; (b) is from 1892 and reviews volume III.

(a)

The 'Morte Darthur' is the most familiar by name of all early English books; perhaps the most familiar to the general reader of our time of all prose romances before those of Walter Scott. But it has been one of the rarest of well-known books. It is but a few years since it was not known at the New York libraries that there was a copy in America. Now, however, the one perfect copy of the original edition in the world is owned by Mrs. Abby E. Pope of Brooklyn, N.Y.... A good edition in its way, by Thomas Wright (1858), and a later Globe edition made the old romance accessible to general readers who read for the story and the style. But for students who wish to be sure of the exact words, the spelling and punctuation, and all that, it has remained inaccessible. Here at last is the very thing that was wanting—a faithful reprint of the original of Caxton, page for page, line for line, word for word. ...

This book is a sort of Iliad of Chivalry. The adventures in it had been separately told in ballads and metrical romances, and chanted in baronial halls, for two or three centuries. Coleridge said that he would engage to compile twelve books with characters as distinct and consistent as those in the 'Iliad' from these metrical ballads and other chronicles about King Arthur and the Knights of the Round Table. It was safe to say. It had been done already by Sir Thomas Malory in the 'Morte Darthur.' There is very much such a plot and unity in it as in the 'Iliad.' Arthur grows up, the Round Table is fitted with knights who have glorious adventures of fighting and of love, then the sin of Launcelot and Guenever sets the knights against each other, and they perish in two bloody battles. The 'passing of Arthur' after the battle is familiar to every one in

Tennyson's versification of it. Every one who likes it there should read it in Malory. The Queen and Launcelot retire to houses of 'religion' and die in the odor of sanctity. 'So whan syr Bors & his felowes came to his bedde they founde hym starke dede & he laye as he had smyled & the swettest sauour aboute hym that euer they felte.' Like the 'Iliad,' the 'Arabian Nights,' and all great folk stories, the 'Morte Darthur' has its interest for persons at any age. A boy is ready for it when he is in the early foot-ball stage, reading the 'Lay of the Last Minstrel,' and 'Ivanhoe,' and 'Tom Brown.' There is rushing and tackling of the most vigorous kind at almost every turn. This is the way Sir Gareth and Sir Ironside go on:

> And thus they foughte tyl it was past none and neuer wold stynte tyl att the laste they both lackt wynde, and thenne they stode wagging, staggering, panting, blowing, and bleeding, so that all that beheld them for the most part wepte for pytie. So whan they had restyd them a whyle; they yede to battle againe, tracing, racing, and foyning as two bores. And at sometime they toke their renne as hit had ben two wild rammys, and hurtled to gyders that somtyme they felle to the erthe groveling; and their armour was so sore hewen that men might see their naked sydes.

Most of the jousts and encounters of adventure do no more damage than a university foot-ball game. Sir Launcelot in one of his adventures 'had the better hand of five hundred knights, and yet,' exults the chronicler, 'there was none slain of them'; to be a murderer, to kill men in jousting, is the greatest shame that a knight may have. The knights can bear any amount of 'smiting, racing, tracing, foyning,' and the like. Sir Launcelot, for example, fights all day with a spear-head in his side, smites and pulls down more than thirty knights, and then rides off and gets well in a few days. The leeches are often women, and do wonderful cures. The attention of the young reader is held by a rapid succession of adventures, told in the briefest, simplest, and most realistic fashion. If there is any way in which a knight, or a knight and his horse, can be turned 'up-so-down,' or otherwise put *hors de combat*, which is not here described, it must be some later evolution. The variety of wounds can hardly be matched from Homer. There are some combats with monsters and giants, mostly in foreign countries. When Arthur was subduing the Romans, he met the giant Galapas: 'He shorted hym and smote of bothe his legges by the knees, sayenge, Now arte thow better of a sise to dele with than thow were.' And he does not leave him to fight upon his stumps like Witherington, in similar doleful dumps, in 'Chevy Chase,' but smites off his head forthwith; 'and the body slew six Saracens in the falling downe,' says Wright's edition, but that was not known to Caxton. Sir Servause is contemptuously described as one 'that had neuer courage nor lust to doo batail ageynst no man, but yf it were ageynst gyants & ageynst dragons and wylde beestes.' There are also a thousand and one love stories, and as many tricks of magic, and much mystic lore of religion, especially in the quest of the holy grail.

It must be confessed that to an unsympathetic reader there may be something monotonous in the succession of adventures, and the knights and their combats seem all alike, as babies do to bachelors. The shifting figures have something of the Punch and Judy aspect. All the world is a stage—no seasons, no weather, no nature; everybody is always in character, serious—no humor, no laughter, except now and then, when a knight is tumbled up-so-down in jousting, the 'queene' or the 'haute prince,' perhaps, will laugh so sore that they may not stand. But if the old critic, or the philosophic student, is not fascinated by the stories, the book has other charms. It is a vivid picture of the ideals, the characters, the manners, the life of the age of chivalry. Courage, strength, size, activity are primary heroic qualities. 'Sir Tristram was called the strongest and biggest knight of the world, for he was bigger than Sir Launcelot, but Sir Launcelot was better breathed.' Meekness and gentleness are eminent moral qualities; Sir Launcelot was 'the meekest man and the gentlest that ever eate in hall among ladies.' Sir Galahad is 'demure as a dove.' Truthfulness and hatred of treason are among the vows of knighthood and continually shown in remarkable ways. Every knight should be a lover. 'Why,' said La beale Isoud, 'are yee a knight and bee yee no lover? It is a shame unto you.' The knights are all fair riders. 'What is a knight,' says Sir Launcelot, 'but when he is on horseback?' Sir Tristram is a 'curious harper.' They learn hawking, hunting, chess playing, carving. Surgery, medicine, magic, and music are common accomplishments of the ladies; they sometimes compound love potions, but they are wholly unversed in coquetry; they speak their love right out for the heroes who please them. Chastity is the crowning virtue of a knight. Sir Galahad needs be a 'pure maide' to win the holy grail. A gentle piety pervades the book, a contrast with 'Piers Ploughman' or Chaucer. The men of 'religion,' often hermits or 'white munks,' are pious, good leeches, good confessors. The language of piety is simple and tender: 'Faire, sweete Father, Jesu Christ,' 'Mild mother Mary,' 'Faire father God.' Nice touches abound. Sir Gareth 'knightly ate his meat and egerly'; he had 'the fairest and the largest hands that ever man saw.' 'The King wept and dried his eyes with a handkercher.' 'These Britons brag as though they bare up all the world,' says the Roman Emperor's cousin.

For the student of language no English book is more fascinating. It is packed with the most expressive words and idioms just strange enough to stimulate interest, piquant, picturesque, gentle, as well as queer combinations of words which offer grammatical problems as inviting as the particles of Homer. But to the discussion of such matters we shall be introduced by the apparatus of the second volume.

(b)

... It was well known that our Iliad of Chivalry was made from earlier romances. Caxton tells us in his preface that 'Syr Thomas Malorye dyd take it oute of certeyn bookes of frensshe and reduced it into Englysshe.' Malory, also, in the text itself, frequently reminds us that he tells the tale as the French book says. French books and English books telling similar adventures of the same heroes have been long familiar. Dr. Sommer has attempted to trace in detail the whole series of adventures, tell us where the original of each is found, and set the original before us by description and quotation, so that we can make out clearly what credit belongs to Malory. Thus he finds that the first seven chapters of book first run parallel with the 'Merlin' of Robert de Boron. He therefore gives a *résumé* of this 'Merlin,' with quotations of considerable passages, stopping at every turn to point out in what particulars, if any, Malory varies from the original. It is accompanied, of course, with much collateral information, such as the thorough student desiderates, about other texts, the bibliography, and the like, and makes a pretty long chapter—more than twice as long as the Malory.

The result of it, however, is to give a distinct picture of Malory's manner of working. In the first place, the De Boron story is more than five times as long as Malory's. The materials worked up in the whole 'Morte Darthur' are ten times as long as the book. Then this brevity is not gained by dropping descriptive particulars, and reducing all to a thread of narrative, or an outline of adventures, but by modification of the series of events and persons, omitting such as do not suit the adapter. What he does tell he tells with minute realism, often adding fresh particulars. These Dr. Sommer sometimes finds in other versions, sometimes credits to Malory's invention. Changes are not infrequently made to adjust matters to different forms of the story which Malory has accepted in the later books. He is not merely collecting by whim a jumble of good stories. He has a plan. His diction also is seen to be his own. Sometimes he translates literally, sometimes not; but he never goes far without showing vital signs. So that, on the whole, Malory writing his 'Morte Darthur' from De Boron, is quite like Shakspere writing a scene of 'Julius Caesar' from North's 'Plutarch.'... The seventh book is the adventures of Gareth and Lynette, with which Tennyson begins his Round Table series. Dr. Sommer can trace no part of this book, nor can he find anywhere the slightest reference to Gareth's exploits on this adventure, or to the Lady Lyonesse, her sister Lynet, her brother Gryngamor, or the five brothers whom Gareth fought and overcame. He suggests that it is a story not belonging to the Arthurian cycle, but adapted to it by Malory, or by some unknown author whose version has been lost. Malory speaks of his 'frensshe book' as usual in this narrative, but the style is perfect Malory—Malory delighted with the unwonted humors of his personages. He evidently relished the later lively fabliaux; possibly this may be one of his own making. To the general reader it is like one of Shakspere's comic scenes in a tragedy: it gives a delightful laugh; and now that Tennyson has repeated it we may safely say that its introduction shows high art in Malory. Tennyson closes:

> And he that told the tale in older times
> Says that Sir Gareth wedded Lyonors
> But he that told it later, says Lynette.

So far as appears in Dr. Sommer's 'Sources,' all the old books say 'Lyonors,' that is, 'Lyonesse.' It is Tennyson who says 'Lynette,' that is, 'Lynet.'

So far as the statistical setting forth of the immediate antecedents of Malory's book is concerned, Dr. Sommer's volume is of great value. He has completed a work of immense labor....

44. 'An Arthurian Journey', unsigned essay, *Atlantic Monthly*

65 (June 1890), 811–29

This essay begins with an account of the writer's visits to Arthurian localities with descriptions of such sites as Tintagel and Glastonbury interspersed with chunks of Malory's narrative. In the extract which follows, however, the writer has shifted to an appreciation of the *Morte Darthur*; despite the effusiveness of the style, the writer manages to suggest that Malory uses a variety of descriptive details and that he moves deliberately from the lighter tone of the beginning episodes to the darker tragedy of the conclusion, although the writer finds the construction faulty along the way. Much plot summary has been omitted, along with the descriptions of Arthurian sites.

... The earlier portion of the Arthuriad, after the preliminary incidents are disposed of and the leading personages have been introduced, is pervaded by a bright freshness as of the breeze and sunshine of morning. The knights and ladies are young; the swords are unworn though not unproved, the shields untarnished; love, faith, hope, ambition, and belief in life are warming the veins and lifting the hearts. There are bursts of joy and recklessness, born of animal spirits and the exuberance of youth. There are springs of tenderness in these dauntless souls, not yet dried by the length and drought of the day. Even King Mark, the meanest and most abject of the throng, finding the bodies of an Irish knight, killed in combat by Balin, and of his lady-love, who stabbed herself on seeing him fall, lays them together in a rich tomb within a beautiful church. The friendship of the brute creation and its part in the life of man give rise to many touching incidents. The most important of them is the adventure of the lady of the white hart and her knight, who kills Gawaine's hounds to avenge the pet creature's death. 'Why have ye slain my hounds?' said Sir Gawaine. 'They did but after their kind, and lever had I ye had wroken your anger upon me than upon a dumb beast.' The death of the hart and hounds brought about the death of the knight and lady, for which Gawaine was tried by Guinivere's court of ladies, and rebuked by his younger brother and squire: 'Ye should give mercy to them that ask mercy, for a knight without mercy is without worship.' Percivale, on a lone mountain-side, beset with foes and danger, rescues a lion's whelp from a serpent; the lion kills the snake, carries the whelp to a safe place, and comes back to fawn on Percivale like a spaniel. The knight, in the loneliness of his peril, stroked him 'on the neck and on the shoulders and gave thanks to God for the fellowship of the beast.' The little hound given by Tristan to Yseult plays his humble part in their drama, he alone recognizing his lord through the rags and strangeness of a lately past insanity. Horses and their faithful service are not forgotten. When Launcelot nearly lost his life in an ambush, and his horse was shot under him, the devoted creature followed his master, with forty arrows in his flanks and his entrails dragging, until he fell dead. Even birds have their place in this largely drawn plan of an ideal world. Launcelot got into one of his worst scrapes by climbing a tree to release a falcon entangled in her jesses. 'When she would have taken flight she hung by the legs fast, and Sir Launcelot saw how she hung and beheld the fair perigot and was sorry for her.' Arthur has the largest share of this compassion, the high-minded, great-hearted king, who was subject to a sacred rage in the fray, was pitiful and courteous to any woman, child, serf, or beast that cried for help.

Woods and flowery fields were favorite resorts of the brotherhood, in the prime of their errantry; they were addicted to sitting by forest wells and springs, a practice so well known of them that a heart-whole fellow, passing where a knight lay watching the bubbles in a fountain, taxed him at once with being of the court and with his lovelorn state. Launcelot's grief after a night of bitter repentance is assuaged by hearing the birds sing at dawn. Feeling for nature, so vehemently claimed as a development of modern sensibility, belongs not only to Sir Thomas Malory, but to the old romances, which abound even more than he does in picturesque details and descriptions. They are sprinkled with little poems in prose on springtime and summer.... Malory has a lovely interlude on May, wherein 'true love is likened to summer,' as introduction to How Queen Guinever rode on Maying. These softer strains run through the gladsome measures of hunting, tilting, and going to battle. Only the predictions of Merlin rise from time to time, like the chill breath on a cloudless day foretelling a change of weather. Gradually the morning music dies away, and exultation gives place to murmurs, wrangling, recriminations, care, and remorse. Under the changefulness of fortune and the fickle heart of man, the bonds of loyalty slacken, those of love and friendship chafe, the lustre of the Round Table grows dull. In this transition Malory shows his knowledge of life and human nature as well as his genius; no modern analyst has a finer touch for the intricacies of the heart. . . . Merlin, the sage, after leading his long life with credit and dignity, when he was an old man 'fell on a dotage' of the youthful Vivien, with what disastrous result is known. He remains the type and warning of amorous graybeards. When three knights, Marhaus, Gawaine, and Uwaine, or Evan, met three damsels, and agreed to spend a year in their company, seeking adventures, the eldest knight chose the youngest maid; the young squire, who had not won his spurs, took the elderly damsel, who discreetly guided him to renown. The modification of temperament and character by time and circumstance is indicated with consummate skill, yet with absolute simplicity of method.

The art of bookmaking was not understood in those days, however. The prose Morte d'Arthur is a patchy bit of work; the edges of the scraps seldom meet exactly. It is easy to recognize different versions of one story in several adventures which are narrated as happening at distinct times and places. Even by its own system of chronology and geography there are discrepancies and contradictions; it is full of clumsy translation, while the bloodthirstiness of some episodes and the tender chivalry and piety of others show that the original documents must have been of widely different dates. But the same spirit animates the whole book, and that was infused by Sir Thomas Malory.

As natural vicissitude was bringing the court and fellowship to a turning-point, the St. Grail appeared. This had been foretold long before by Merlin, and it came to pass when the youth Galahad saw the vision of the sacred chalice in hall and vowed to follow the summons. The other knights saw it at the same time in different manifestations, and all swore to follow; the gay Gawaine, who was the first to swear, was the first to weary of the search. From this climax there is a change of tone in Malory's recital, which can be explained only by supposing a different and deeper meaning in the old romance whence he took the quest of the Sangreal from those which furnished him with the histories of Merlin and Arthur, and the previous adventures of various knights. It has a strange and solemnizing effect on the rest of the story. In the choosing of Arthur as king, in spite of his doubtful birth and humble rearing, and the setting him over the heads of petty kings and powerful chieftains, there is a Scriptural significance, which reappears faintly from time to time during the epic. This, however, may be merely the glimpsing up of eternal moral truths underlying the curse of events in history and human life, of which romance and fiction are but rearrangements. But after the quest of the St. Grail is proclaimed, the fabulous color of the adventures gives place to an allegorical one. There is a mystic elevation, a religious fervor, in the moods of the knights and in their pursuits; they vow themselves to the service of Christ instead of to their lady's; their sins find them out and bring them to repentance. A gentler code prevails in their encounters; they are content to prove their prowess by overthrowing an adversary without slaying him. Hermits and holy women begin to play important parts; white birds and beasts and flowers and white-robed visitants haunt the visions of the knights; the personages themselves become conscious that they are carrying out an allegory, as when the anchorite expounds to Gawaine that the captives in the Castle of Maidens typify 'the good soules that were in prison afore the incarnation of Christ.' Sir Bors sees a pelican feed its starving young and die, and recognizes it as a symbol. The marvelous is transmuted into the miraculous. Dreams have a spiritual interpretation, temptations are of the same character, and a foreshadowing of the end falls across the minds of the brotherhood. Arthur, more than the rest, is burdened by the presentiment, and it weighs heavily on the queen, who tries to stir up the king to forbid the knights to follow the St. Grail, as they had taken their oath when he was not in hall. He will not interfere, and they set out on the morrow, after hearing mass in the minster with the king and queen, a sad and solemn farewell rite. The knights then armed and rode away, commending themselves to the queen, with a clash, tramp, and sound of departure that reverberates through the blood as one reads. This is one of the very few passages in which Tennyson has enfeebled the old narrative, instead of enriching it and making it more beautiful. His picture of Guinivere riding by Launcelot, weeping and wailing before all the people who had come out, sorrowing, to see the fellowship go forth, lacks the dignity and poignancy of the other version. She was mastered by her emotion, and withdrew to her chamber. Launcelot missed and followed her. "'Ah, madam! I pray you be not displeased, for I shall come again as soon as I may with my worship." "Alas!" said she, "that ever I saw you! but Hee that suffered death upon the crosse for all mankind bee to you good conduct and safetie, and to all the whole fellowship."' ...

The conclusion is prolonged by Sir Thomas Malory with a diversity of magnanimous and affecting incidents, in which the nobility of the chief actors comes to light in a final glow. . . .

. . . One of the finest touches of the conclusion is the relentless purpose of Gawaine, once the lightest trifler of the court, yet a true knight and prince, under the tragic stress of the exigency and his vindictive grief for his brothers. . . All this and much that follows is eminently pathetic, and in place in a romance; but Lord Tennyson's abridgment is at once more poetical and more dramatic. Both he and Sir Thomas Malory lead the way to Salisbury. . . .

. . . There is no more tragical or majestic queen in fiction than Guinivere as she appears at the last; there is no page in literature more palpitating with high-wrought passion than Sir Thomas Malory's recital of the parting and death of Launcelot and his royal lady. . . .

45. Strachey again

1891

Sir Edward Strachey rewrote parts of his 1868 introduction (No. 28 above) for an edition that appeared in 1891 following the publication of Sommer's critical edition. As Strachey notes, his own evaluation of Malory's genius is higher than Sommer's, and this evaluation is expressed more positively and more expansively than in his remarks of 1868. A similar response to Sommer's somewhat disparaging remarks may be noted in subsequent selections, especially in the essays of George Saintsbury (see No. 51 below). After Sommer called attention to Bale's earlier passage on Malory (see No. 3B above), critics became more attentive to problems of biography; Strachey here expands the previous biographical account.

Much of the text of 1868 is retained in the 1891 version, but the excerpts that follow are new additions. (London: Macmillan, 1923, pp. ix–xxviii.)

... But to Sir Thomas Malory he [Caxton] gives all the honour of having provided him with the copy which he printed. And ever since, for more than four hundred years, successive generations have approved the fitness of Caxton's choice. For it is Malory's book, and not the older forms of King Arthur's story which we still read for enjoyment, and for the illustration of which scholars edit those earlier books. Only a true poem, the offspring of genius, could have so held, and be still holding its ground, age after age. It may be said that it is chiefly with boys, and with men who have formed the taste by their boyish reading, that the book is so popular. But is not this so with the Iliad too? Men of mature intellect and taste read and re-read the Iliad with ever new discoveries, appreciation, and enjoyment; but it may be questioned whether there are many, or even any, of them who did not begin those studies at school, and learn to love Homer before they knew that he was worthy of their love. And they who have given most of such reading, in youth and in manhood, to Malory's Morte Darthur will be the most able and ready to recognise its claim to the character of an Epic poem.

MALORY A POET

Malory wrote in prose, but he had 'the vision and the faculty divine' of the poet, though 'wanting the accomplishment of verse'; and, great as that want is, we may apply Milton's test of 'simple, sensuous, and passionate,' and we shall find no right to these names more real than is Malory's. Every incident, the description of every event, is 'simple,' that is to say, complete in itself, while making a part of the whole story. The story is 'sensuous,' like that of Homer, and as every true poem must be, it is a living succession of concrete images and pictures, not of abstractions or generalized arguments and reasonings. These are the characteristics of the book, from its opening story of Igraine, which 'befell in the days of Uther Pendragon,' down to the death of the last four remaining knights who 'went into the Holy Land, there as Jesus Christ was quick and dead,' and there 'did many battles upon the miscreants or Turks, and there they died on a Good Friday for God's sake.' And for 'passion,' for that emotion which the poet first feels in a special manner, and then awakens in his hearers, though they could not have originated it in themselves, with the adventures of the Round Table and the San Greal, or the deaths of Arthur, of Guenever, and of Launcelot, we may compare the wrath of Achilles, its cause and its consequences, or the leave-taking of Hector and Andromache. It would, indeed, be hard to find anywhere a pathos greater than that of Malory's description of the death or 'passing' of Arthur, the penitence of Guenever, and her parting with Launcelot, or the lament of Launcelot over the King and Queen, and of Sir Ector over Launcelot himself. The first is too long to quote, but I may say that Malory has re-cast the old story, and all the poetry is his own. I give the two last:—

Truly, said Sir Launcelot, I trust I do not displease God, for He knoweth mine intent, for my sorrow was not, nor is not, for any rejoicing of sin, but my sorrow may never have end. For when I remember of her beauty, and of her noblesse, that was both with her king and with her; so when I saw his corpse and her corpse so lie together, truly mine heart would not serve to sustain my careful body. Also when I remember me, how by my default, mine orgule, and my pride, that they were both laid full low, that were peerless that ever was living of christian people, wit you well, said Sir Launcelot, this remembered, of their kindness and mine unkindness, sank so to my heart, that I might not sustain myself.

And again:—

Ah, Launcelot, he said, thou were head of all christian knights; and now I dare say, said Sir Ector, thou Sir Launcelot, there thou liest, that thou were never matched of earthly knight's hand; and thou were the courtiest knight that ever bare shield; and thou were the truest friend to thy lover that ever bestrode horse; and thou were the truest lover of a sinful man that ever loved woman; and thou were the kindest man that ever strake with sword; and thou were the goodliest person ever came among press of knights; and thou was the meekest man and the gentlest that ever ate in hall among ladies; and thou were the sternest knight to thy mortal foe that ever put spear in the rest.[1]

The former passage is all Malory's own: the beauty of the latter is enhanced, if we set by its side the old version which he follows:—

> Alas, sir [said] Bors, that I was born,
> That ever I should see this indeed,
> The beste knight his life hath lorn,
> That ever in stoure [fight] bestrode a steed,
> Jesu, that crowned was with thorn.
> In heaven his soul foster and feed.[2]

Humour is akin to passion; and it may not be out of place to notice here Malory's vein of humour, as shown, for instance, in the way in which he tells the adventures of La Cote Male Taile, and of Beaumains; the pranks of the braver knights with Dinadan and Dagonet; the story of Arthur's wedding feast, when a lady who 'cried and made great dole,' was forcibly carried out of the hall by a strange knight, and Arthur 'was glad, for she made such a noise,' and was thereupon rebuked by Merlin for thinking so lightly of his royal and knightly duties; or that of the usurper Mordred and the Bishop of Canterbury, when after each had defied the other, the bishop 'did the curse in the most orgulous wise that might be done,' and then retired to live 'in poverty and holy prayers, for well he understood that mischievous war was at hand.'

THE BOOK EPIC IN PLAN

In the Drama the action is present, actually unwinding itself and going on before our eyes. The Epic is the story of the past, a cycle of events completed, while through the one and the other may be traced a thread of destiny and providence, leading either to a happy triumph over circumstances, or to a tragic doom, which, too, is in the end, a triumph also. Thomas Hughes, the early Elizabethan dramatist, in his 'Misfortunes of Arthur,' concentrated and deepened the horror of such a tragedy by transferring the guilt of Launcelot to Mordred the son of Arthur and his unknown sister. He would better have recognised and followed the finer art of Malory. For though the motive of Malory's epic is less gross and exaggerated than that of Hughes's drama, the thread of guilt and doom which runs from first to last through the former is not less real than in the latter. The crime of Uther Pendragon, with which the story opens, leads to the concealment of Arthur's parentage from himself, and this to his illicit love for her whom he does not know to be his sister, and so to the birth of Mordred. Then comes the prophetic doom:—'Ye have done of late a thing that God is displeased with you: and your sister shall have a child that shall destroy you and all the knights of your realm.' Arthur tries in vain to prevent the fulfilment of this doom by the only cruel deed of his life: and then—after another warning of the woe which his marriage with Guinevere will bring on him, through her guilty love for Launcelot—these germs of tragic destiny remain hidden through long years of prosperity. Arthur, aided by his fellowship of the Round Table, reduces universal anarchy into order: and not only 'gets into his hand' all England, Wales, and Scotland, but by his march to Rome makes himself emperor, and the head of all the kingdoms as well as of all the chivalry of Christendom. . . .

MALORY'S USE OF THE OLD ROMANCES

. . . Twenty-three years ago, I ventured to assert Malory's claim to epic genius: and now this claim may be farther tested, and as I think, established, by help of the learned researches of Dr. Sommer. . . . We may now see how Malory's Morte Darthur was fused into its actual form out of crude materials of ten times its bulk, and that while he often translated or transcribed the French or English romances as they lay before him, on the other hand he not only re-wrote, in order to bring into its present shape the whole story, but also varied both the order and the substance of the incidents that so he might give them that epic character, and that beauty in the details, which his book shows throughout. Malory was no doubt a 'finder' as well as a 'maker,' but so, I repeat, was Shakespeare, and so was every other great poet. But the quarry and the building are not the same thing, though the one supplies the rough stones with which the other is raised up. We see that there is much that is rude and inartificial in Malory's art. He has built a great, rambling, mediaeval castle, the walls of which enclose rude and even ruinous work of earlier times, and not a Greek Parthenon nor even an Italian palace of the Renaissance. Still, it is a grand pile, and tells everywhere of the genius of its builder. And I ask, as Carlyle once asked me, Who built St. Paul's? Was it Wren, or the hodman who carried up the bricks? But while supporting my conclusions as to Malory's art by the evidence of Dr. Sommer's facts, it is right to add that the conclusions are my own rather than those of this learned critic. His estimate of Malory's genius in the choice and treatment of his materials falls far short of mine: and I can believe that Malory may have judged rightly, for his own purpose, when he did not take that form of a legend which was in itself the most beautiful. . . .

INFLUENCE OF THE BOOK ON ENGLISH LETTERS AND LIFE

The influence of Sir Thomas Malory's book upon English literature, and so upon English life, upon our thoughts, morals, and manners, has been great and important. I have spoken of its claims to be considered an Epic poem; but it is not the less true, that it is our first great work of English prose, the first in which the writing of prose was shown to be one of the fine arts for England. Malory's style is often inartificial: he is not always able to master the huge masses of his materials, and fails to fuse and mould them into a perfect whole. But we must confess the like of Milton, whose grand periods of magnificent English are often followed by others which are confused and cumbrous in form, if not in thought. It has taken many workmen, through many generations, to make our prose writing what it is: but there is an infant beauty in Malory's style which is full of promise of the perfect manly form that is to be. The passages which I have already quoted are instances of this inartificial beauty of style. The thoughts and images spontaneously utter themselves in words without any attempt at rhetorical balance and arrangement. Thus in the lament of Sir Ector over Sir Launcelot, Malory does not ask himself whether there is a logical connection between courtesy and bearing a shield, or between true friendship and bestriding a horse, as a modern writer would have done, and so brought those sentences into a more finished though more monotonous correspondence with the rest. The flow of feeling is true, direct, and simple, and that is enough. Dr. Sommer, in his notes on the language of 'Le Morte Darthur,' points to the indications, in grammar, spelling, and other usages of words, of its transitional place between the language of Chaucer and that of Shakespeare; while Southey says that it was composed in the best possible time for making it what it is: and Mr. J.A. Symonds (whom I am permitted to name) says:—'The Morte

Darthur was written at a lucky moment in our literary history, when the old Saxon fountain of speech was yet undefiled, and when printing had not introduced stereotyped forms or enforced the laws of a too scrupulous grammar; at the same time the language is truly English—rich in French and Latin words, as well as Saxon, and not so archaic as to be grotesque or repulsive.'[3]

And if in these things Malory was happy in the opportuneness of the times in which he wrote, not less was he so in that he lived in a day in which (as we see from Caxton's Preface) men could still believe in the marvellous adventures of knight-errantry. A hundred years later, the spirit of chivalry had so departed from the old forms that Spenser could only use them as materials for allegory, while Cervantes, himself full of the old spirit, could only treat the belief in knight-errantry as the fantasy of a crazed though generous mind. But Malory was still able to embody the ideals of chivalry in actual and serious personages, and so to influence the national character and manners of his countrymen in the best way. His book is a possession for all times. The old stock is still putting out new leaves and fruits for ourselves.

The Morality of the Book

In morals as well as in language (though more obscurely, since the subject of morals is so much more complicated than that of philology), we may find signs of a transition from the times of Chaucer to those of Shakespeare, and of progress no less than transition. The suppression of the Lollards—hated alike by the Church and the feudal lords, the War of the Roses, and the licentiousness of the court and courtiers, must, in the days of Edward IV, in which Malory wrote, have cut the moral and social life of the country down to its roots. Yet even in Malory's book there are signs of the new moral life which was coming, and which in the days of the Reformation reached a power and expansion never before known. It would be absurd to pretend that Malory had greatly advanced in morality from the position of Chaucer and his age towards that of the Elizabethan period. Roger Ascham, indeed, while admitting that 'ten Morte Arthurs do not the tenth part so much harm as one of these books made in Italy and translated in England,' protests against the demoralising effect of the literature of which he takes this book as the example, 'the whole pleasure of which,' he says, 'standeth in two special points—in open manslaughter and bold bawdray. In which book those be counted the noblest knights that do kill most men without any quarrel, and commit foulest adulteries by subtlest shifts.' I remember Dante's story of the sin and doom of Paolo and Francesca—

Galeotto fu il libro, e chi lo scrisse—

and recognise a real though only half truth in Ascham's strictures. But he greatly over-states the evil, while he altogether omits to recognise the good in the book. Caxton's estimate of the moral purport of the whole book, gives not merely the other side, but both sides of the case. Much more than half the 'open manslaughter' is done in putting down cruel oppressors and bringing back kingdoms from anarchy to law and good government; and the occasions call forth all the knightly virtues of gentleness, forbearance, and self-sacrifice, as well as those of courage and hardihood. And though it is far from possible to deny the weight of Ascham's other charge, yet we must not, in forming our estimate of the book, forget the silent yet implied judgment which is passed upon lawless love by its tragic end, nor the ideal presented in the lives of the maiden knights, Sir Galahad and Sir Percivale. For the purpose of a due estimate of Malory's 'Morte Darthur,' we may fairly take Caxton's Preface as an integral part of the book. The Preface gives the tone, the motive, to the whole book. The morality of 'Morte Darthur' is low in one essential thing, and this alike in what it says and in what it omits: and Lord Tennyson shows us how it should be raised. The ideal of marriage, in its relation and its contrast with all other forms of love and chastity, is brought out in every form, rising at last to tragic grandeur, in the *Idylls of the King*. It is not in celibacy, though spiritual and holy as that of Galahad or Percivale, but in marriage, as the highest and purest realisation of the ideal of human conditions and relations, that we are to rise above the temptations of a love like that of Launcelot or even of Elaine; and Malory's book does not set this ideal of life before us with any power or clearness....

... a transformation has, indeed, been effected for us by Lord Tennyson in his *Idylls of the King*. He who has been familiar with the old Morte Arthur from his boyhood, must consent to let the poet transport him into a quite new region of the imagination, and must in a manner and for the time forget the old before he can read the *Idylls of the King* without a somewhat sad feeling that these are not the old knights whom he has always known. I have already likened Malory's work to a mediaeval castle, and, if I may be allowed to vary my parable a little, I would say this: There are some of us who in their childhood lived in, or can at least remember, some old house, with its tower and turret stairs, its hall with the screen, and the minstrel's gallery, and the armour where it was hung up by him who last wore it: the panelled chambers, the lady's bower, and the chapel, and all the quaint rambling passages and steps which lead from one to another of these. And when in after years he comes to this same house, and finds that it has all been remodelled, enlarged, furnished and beautified to meet the needs and the tastes of modern life, he feels that this is not the very home of his childhood, and that a glory has departed from the scenes he once knew: and yet, if the changes have been made with true judgment, and only with a rightful recognition of the claim that the modern life should have full scope for itself while preserving all that was possible of the old, though not letting itself be sacrificed or even cramped and limited, for its sake: if he is thus reasonable, he will acknowledge that it was well that the old order should yield place to the new, or at least make room for it at its side. And such are the thoughts and sentiments with which the lover of the old Morte Arthur will, if he be also a student of the growth of our national character and life, read the new *Idylls of the King*.

Sir Thomas Malory

Of Sir Thomas Malory himself we know nothing more than can be inferred by probable conjecture from his book. His name occurs in it three times, and with the three variations of Malorye, Malory, and Maleore. These variations are not singular, for the spelling of proper as well as of common names was very much at the fancy of the writer; and we know that Shakespeare, Marvell, and Pym, wrote their own names in various forms. Sir Thomas Malory tells us that his book was ended in the ninth year of the reign of Edward IV, or 1470 A.D.; and at that time there was an old and important Yorkshire family of the name at Hutton Coniers and High Studley, near Ripon; for Leland, early in the next century, speaks of the ancestors of Malory[4], and in 1427 and 1472 the death or burial of two persons of the same name is recorded at Ripon.[5] Andrew Mallorie of Middlesex *armiger* is among the contributors to the funds for defence against the Spanish Armada (1588).[6] At the beginning of the seventeenth century we find Sir John Mallory of Studley, and son of Sir William Mallory, M.P. for Thirsk and Ripon, and a subscriber to the second Virginia Charter:[7] in 1622 Burton speaks of the pedigree, arms, and lands of Sir Thomas Malory in Kirby-Malory, Winwick, Newbould, and Swinford in Leicestershire;[8] and about the same time two scholars of the name were elected to Winchester College;[9] and reasonable conjecture may connect our author with these Malorys, although no links of actual pedigree have been found.

The *Biographia Britannica* (article 'Caxton') says:—

'If this Sir Thomas Malory was a Welshman, as Leland and others after him assert, he was probably a Welsh Priest.'

[See Nos 3A and 6.]

But no references are given as to where this supposed assertion by 'Leland and others' is to be found; in fact, it is not to be found in any of Leland's writings. And the origin of the statement remained an unexplained puzzle, until Dr. Sommer has now apparently discovered the key to it in a passage which he quotes from Bale's *Illustrium Maioris Britanniae Scriptorum*, &c., first edition, folio 208.

[See No. 3B.]

I have not myself verified these references, but I infer from what Dr. Sommer tells us, that Bale, perhaps writing from an imperfect recollection, supposed that he had the authority of Leland for a connection between Mailorius, and the Welsh place of the like name: and then the writer of the *Biographia Britannica*, still more inaccurately, converted the possible suggestion of Bale into the direct statement that Leland had asserted Malory to be a Welshman, while Bale himself is referred to as 'the others.' Nor is there any reason to suppose from Malory's own book that he was a Welshman. Though Caxton tells us that there were books in Welsh about Arthur and his Knights, Malory never quotes any but the French and English books. He shows no acquaintance with Welsh legends or traditions, unless it be with those in Geoffrey of

Monmouth, who wrote in Latin, nor of any local knowledge of Welsh places. Then as to the fanciful and inconsequent conjecture that he was a priest, he himself tells us that he was a knight, and thus implies that he was not a priest, while the words that 'he is the servant of Jesu by day and by night,' which suggested the notion that he was a priest, are evidently put into that form in order to give a rhythmical ending to the book. Nor did the priest's usual title of 'Sir' make him a knight. What we may say of Sir Thomas Malory is that he was probably of an old English family: that he was a knight both in rank and in temper and spirit, and a lover alike of the gentle and the soldierly virtues of knighthood. He was a man of genius, and a devout Christian: he wrote for gentlewomen as well as gentlemen, believing that they would read his book 'from the beginning to the ending,' and that it would call forth in them a sympathy which would properly express itself in prayers for the pious writer.

SELECTED NOTES

1   A brave soldier never couched lance,
         A gentler heart did never sway in court.
                            First part of *Henry VI*, iii, 2.

2 *Le Morte Darthur*, edited from the Harleian MS. 2252, in the British Museum, by F. J. Furnivall, 1864.

3 'Pall Mall Gazette,' of June 23, 1868.

4 'There be 2 Lordshipps lyenge not very far from *Ripon* ... *Malory* hath *Hutton Coniers*. Thes Lands cam to their Aunciters by two Dowghtars, Heirs generall of that *Coniers*. *Malory* hath another place called *Highe Studly*, a litle from Fountaines.' Leland's Itinerary, viii. 2. p. 55. Hearne, 1712.

5 These two dates are obligingly given me by G. W. Tomlinson, Esq., Secretary of the Yorkshire Archaeological Society.

6 Noble's Spanish Armada List, 1886, p. 42.

7 Brown's Genesis of the United States, 1890. Vol. I, p. 211; Vol. II, p. 940.

8 Burton's Description of Leicestershire, pp. 140, 262.

9 Kirby's Register of the Wardens, Fellows, and Scholars of Winchester, 1888, quoted by Mr. L. Johnson in the Academy, September 20th, 1890.

46. Other nineteenth-century editors after Sommer

A. Ernest Rhys
1892

Ernest Rhys, like Strachey, though less extensively, changed his introduction to the *Morte Darthur* when, in 1892, he brought out a complete two-volume edition using Wright's text of the Stansby edition. Having read Sommer, Rhys, too, is interested in biographical questions, although he would prefer to believe that Malory was a Welshman.

Included here are the major portions which differ from the Camelot Series introduction of 1886 (see No. 36 above). Volume I, in which the introduction appears, is called *The Noble and Joyous History of King Arthur* (London: Walter Scott, c. 1892), pp. vii–xiii.

Of Malory and his *Morte d'Arthur*, and the wider field of romance into which the book leads us, so much has been abstrusely written in the last four or five years, that the simple critic, delighting in the thing for its own sake, had needs hesitate where so many of authority have been before him. Since the present writer first wrote on the subject, with more enthusiasm, it may be owned, than science, many contributions have been made to it. The legends embodied by Malory have been learnedly dealt with, in terms of folk-lore, philology, and the like, by Professor Rhys and Mr. Alfred Nutt. Still more to the purpose, last year saw the completion of Dr. Oskar Sommer's monumental edition of the *Morte d'Arthur*, whose scholarly accomplishment it needs almost a special education to appreciate. To Dr. Sommer's three volumes, those who come to Malory, not for pleasure, but for exact knowledge, must be referred. Those, however, who come to him with the careless instinct of romance, as to a delightful tale-teller, will be differently and more easily satisfied. There is one book for the scholars and doctors of literature; there is another for the whole congregation.

At the end of the *Morte d'Arthur*, Malory tells us that the book was finished in 'the ninth year of the reign of King Edward the Fourth.' This roughly corresponds, as a note in Dr. Sommer's edition tells us, to the year 1469. The book was published by Caxton in 1485; and these two dates give the only exact points that can be verified in Malory's history. Caxton refers to him in a way that leads us to suppose him still living in 1485; and as he was probably not a young man at the completion of his work in 1469, we may fairly conjecture that his period ranged from about 1420 to 1490. Beyond these dates, the only direct news, so to speak, of Malory, that can certainly be added is also due to Dr. Sommer, who discovered at the last moment an extremely interesting account of him in Bale's *Illustrium Maioris Britanniae Scriptorum* .... There are Malorys in Wales, on the Dee, Bale says further, quoting Leland; but there is no localising of Malory himself beyond this vague general statement. The tradition that he was a Welshman is so agreeable to one's feeling about him as a worker in half-Welsh romance, that it is hard, for a Welshman at any rate, to refuse it credit. Dr. Sommer mentions a family of Malorys that lived in Yorkshire in Leland's time; and another, or perhaps the same, in Leicestershire. Commenting upon this, Mr. Lionel Johnson referred, in a review in the *Academy* (September 20, 1890), to other occurrences of the name in the annals of Winchester College. The tombs, I may add, of the Mallorys of Mobberley, who were all ecclesiastical, and whose usual Christian name was Thomas, may be found in the churchyard of Mobberley, Cheshire. A later member of the family, also a Thomas, was rector of Northenden, and died in his house near there in 1671. Further research would seem to tend to identify these with Leland's Yorkshire branch; and the missing clue to our author, though we may be a little nearer it by these references, is, it is clear, yet to be found.

The history of Sir Thomas Malory's book is fortunately much fuller than that of himself; and there is no more interesting study in literary origins, perhaps, in all the range of English literature. The parallels, discovered by Professor Rhys and others, between some of its episodes and certain others in the ancient myths of the East, carry us back to the very first beginnings of folk-lore. These lead us to the folk-tales told by the remote forefathers of the Welsh, who afterwards so delighted, as in the Mabinogion, in retelling them in later Arthurian form. The after traces of these legends are continual, if often disguised by the varying colour and form of the different languages in which their original germs took root. . . . We are come now to the point where Malory intervened, turning to France in the course of that search 'through all the remnants of scattered antiquity,' of which Bale tells us, and so making the 'selections from various authors concerning the valour and victories of the most renowned King Arthur,' which seem likely to stand as the final popular form of the Arthurian anthology.

One of the most important of these sources of the *Morte d'Arthur*, as thus collated and reshaped by Malory, is to be found in the famous sequence of Merlin-romances by Robert de Borron and his followers. Dr. Sommer, in his second volume, has given us a most exhaustive analysis and comparison of the different versions of the 'Merlin,' showing exactly how far Malory followed in the steps of these predecessors. Diffuse as Malory often seems, and careless in his work, it is surprising to find how great an art of concentration he nevertheless used in dealing with his material. It may prove interesting to quote here a passage from the fourteenth century English translation of the French 'Merlin,' relating the beginning of the familiar sword episode, as similarly told in the first book of Malory:—

Some of the peple yede oute of the cherche where ther was a voyde place; and whan they com oute of the cherche thei sawghe it gan dawe and clere, and sawghe before the cherche dore a grete ston foure square, and ne knewe of what ston it was; but some seide it was marble. And above in the myddill place of this ston, ther stode a styth of Iren that was largely half a fote of height, and thorugh this stithi was a swerde ficchid into the ston.

For comparison, here is the corresponding passage in Malory, as Caxton originally gave it:—

And whan matyns and the first masse was done, there was sene in the chircheyard ayest the hyghe aulter a grete stone four square lyke vnto a marbel stone. And in myddes thereof was lyke an Anuylde of stele a foot on hyghe, and theryn stack a fayre swerd naked by the poynt. . . .

The further pursuit of Malory's French originals may be commended as an exciting one to all those who take your true student's interest in such things. Here, however, is no be-quarto'd opportunity for such literary adventures. Since the Mabinogion have been referred to let us be content, instead, to quote from that fascinating treasury of the less confused Welsh sources of Arthurian romance. The opening of the first Mabinogi in Lady Charlotte Schreiber's delightful translation, 'The Lady of the Fountain,' may serve to compare with the opening of more than one similar scene in Malory. ...

Many further Arthurian passages might be given from the Mabinogion, both to show the Welsh treatment of Malory's subject-matter, and to prove how exquisite a kind of romance those early Welsh romancers could tell in their own tongue. ... But we must leave now, as Malory would say, and turn to our matter,— turning from other romancers to Malory himself. Since Caxton first issued the *Morte d'Arthur*, we know how the book has enthralled poets and men. ... This various reflection in modern art may perhaps serve to show in these times of realism, healthy and morbid, how the artistic spirit will still repair to the ideal, trying, as it were, to solve the problems of nineteenth century life by a reference to mediaeval romance. It clearly shows again, if nothing else, the extraordinary vitality of the book.

B. Unsigned review of Simmons's edition

(5 April 1894 *Nation*)

In 1893 (volume I) and 1894 (volume II), F. J. Simmons produced a complete edition of the *Morte Darthur* based on the Southey edition with some reference to Sommer's text, but with modernized spelling and punctuation. This edition was widely circulated after 1906 when it became the Everyman's edition published by Dent. Both the original edition and the one issued by Everyman's Library had an introduction by John Rhys; it is not quoted here because Rhys's remarks on Malory and the *Morte Darthur* are neither extensive nor novel. The major interest of this introduction lies in its tracing of the legendary/historical Arthur through early Welsh literature.

Simmons's edition also featured illustrations by Aubrey Beardsley; the reviewer, like many of his contemporaries, did not like them. The unsigned review appeared in the *Nation* (see headnote to No. 43B above), 58(5 April 1894), pp. 255–6.

Sir Thomas Malory has no reason to complain of the 'iniquity of oblivion.' To be sure, he has been pretty well obscured in person—for the editors and critics have not made up their minds whether he was an Englishman or a Welshman, sir knight or sir priest—but his book has had a vogue that he little dreamed of. The causes of this popularity it would be interesting to investigate. So far as they coincide with merits in the book itself, they have been often set forth; but there are other causes which one must suspect have been no less potent though less talked about. In the first place, the 'Morte Darthur' 'met a demand,' 'filled a long-felt want.' Caxton tells us that he was urged by many noble gentlemen to publish some account of King Arthur, and that, when his scruples as to the historical reality of that 'King and Emperor' had been in some sort removed by the citation of Gawain's skull and Cradock's mantle, and the tomb at Glastonbury, and other pieces of extant testimony, he consented. How much of this entertaining preface is mere publisher's flourish, it is hard to say, but one thing is certain: the 'Morte Darthur' met with immediate success. It was very convenient for all kinds of readers to have a body of the scattered Arthur romances at hand in a single volume and in the vernacular, and the work became at once for Englishmen the orthodox version of the whole 'matter of Britain.' Few inquiries were made as to the taste with which Sir Thomas had selected his materials, or the fidelity with which he had reproduced his French originals. An interested and uncritical public was waiting for some such compilation, and a welcome was ready for it in advance.

In the pseudo-classical period Malory's renown suffered eclipse. His subject was too 'romantic' for the classicists, and his language and sentiments were too 'rude.' But even the pseudo-classical influences have contributed indirectly to his subsequent fame. They made the whole Arthurian matter seem so remote that, when the dawn of the Romantic revival appeared, few Englishmen were tempted to search beyond Malory for older forms of these stories. The 'Morte Darthur' emerged again into the light of popularity, and regained without an effort its position as the orthodox version. Even to-day, when the Old French romances have lost something of their remoteness, Malory's compilation, whether immdiately or through the adaptations of Tennyson and others, is the main source of our ideas about the Round Table and consequently of many of our literary conventions about the middle ages.

The language in which the book is written is no doubt another cause of its popularity. Archaic enough to be attractive, and not too archaic to be readily intelligible to cursory readers, Malory's diction has flattered many excellent persons into the belief that they were masters of Old English—and that has been no small recommendation for it. This is not a dignified ground for admiring a piece of literature, but it has none the less had its part in calling forth the somewhat extravagant praise which the 'Morte Darthur' has met with. Apart from its antique flavor, Malory's style has no doubt a charm of its own; but this charm, we suspect, would not have prompted such epithets as 'incomparable' and 'unapproachable' but for the titillation of the reader's vanity just refered to. However, we have no wish to run a tilt at the highly decorative figure of the old knight that modern critics have done their best to keep in the lists. The 'Morte Darthur' is indisputably a classic, and we should be sorry to see it despised. It may be hoped, notwithstanding, that tract of time will bring about a somewhat more discriminating regard.

The scholar has many quarrels with Sir Thomas Malory—but those are private affairs to be fought out at a distance from newspaper publicity. The lover of literature has his quarrel, too, and that of a more serious nature and not to be compounded without great argument. Malory is perhaps to be credited with having kept the Arthur stories alive in the knowledge of modern English writers; but his deserts in this direction, however considerable, are almost counterbalanced by a very special demerit. Selecting his materials (and perhaps forced to select them) without much discrimination, he has reproduced and made almost exclusively current various late and bad versions of excellent old stories, and—what is worse—various scandalous misrepresentations of heroic personages. The vogue of the 'Morte Darthur' has been so great that the moderns have too seldom gone beyond it for literary material, and, as a result, the book has impoverished our literature only less than it has enriched it. The most flagrant offence of this kind is the case of Sir Gawain.

In the earlier romances of the Arthur cycle Gawain is a most amiable and charming person. He is invincible in the field and in the lists, but he is even more remarkable for his courtesy. This courtesy is of the true ring; it is not hollow, it is not acquired, it is a part of the man's nature, and finds expression in every word he says and every deed he does. His faith is unblemished; his generosity and the nobility of his heart are unwavering. This is the Gawain of the old French verse romances—the Chevalier au Lion, the Perceval, and the rest—and this is the Gawain of the fourteenth-century romances in English. He is seen at his best in the beautiful 'Gawain and the Green Knight,' by an unknown contemporary of Chaucer.

This, however, is not the Gawain to whom Malory introduces us. Following late French prose romances which had systematically debased Gawain to exalt Lancelot, he has represented the paragon of the Round Table as a pitiful, treacherous creature—a blusterer and a bully. Tennyson follows Sir Thomas, and so we have the flower of Arthurian chivalry maligned in such verses as these:

> Light was Gawain in life, and light in death
> Is Gawain, for the ghost is as the man.

> The hall long silent till Sir Gawain—nay,
> Brother, I need not tell thee—foolish words—
> A reckless and irreverent knight was he.

> To this the courteous prince
> Accorded with his wonted courtesy—
> Courtesy with a touch of traitor in it!

And hence, too, we have the unforgivable libel of 'Pelleas and Etarre.' We cannot help thinking that this degradation of Gawain, which has robbed modern literature of a figure that it very much needs—an Arthurian hero with no nonsense about him—is a heavy charge on the soul of Sir Thomas Malory.

But, whatever our grudges against Malory, and however much we may feel inclined to protest against the superlatives so often applied to him, we must extend a cordial welcome to the present edition. It is, of course, not meant for specialists, whose needs have been competently met by the elaborate volumes of Dr. Sommer. It is not intended to be studied, but to be read—for it is beautifully printed in large type and with commendably black ink—and to be looked at, for it is a rather sumptuous book and has an abundance of pictures. The text is Southey's, with some corrections. The spelling and punctuation have been judiciously modernized, but the grammar and phraseology have not been interfered with. There are glosses—rather scanty, it must be admitted, and not always exact—at the foot of the page. There is an interesting preface by Prof. Rhŷs, which occupies itself chiefly with Arthur in Welsh literature, but, of course, settles nothing. The volume before us contains nine books of the 'Morte Darthur'; a second volume will complete the work.

The designs with which Mr. Aubrey Beardsley has embellished this volume are frankly decorative rather than illustrative. The ladies are very lank and often snaky-haired, the knights are seldom athletic in appearance, and there is a vast deal of posing. But on the whole the full-page pictures assist one to enjoy the book, and the headpieces of the chapters, as well as the borders which adorn the first page of each of the larger divisions, are almost uniformly successful. At three things, notwithstanding, we must enter a protest: the hideous caricature labelled 'Merlin,' which should be relegated to the forest of Broceliande as soon as possible; the ugliness of some of the ladies' faces, which makes the sense ache at them; and the Ethiopian cast of countenance given to Morgan le Fay and La Beale Isoude.

C. Israel Gollancz

1897

Israel Gollancz (1864–1930), the distinguished scholar and editor of a number of medieval and Renaissance texts, was the first lecturer in English at Cambridge upon the establishment of the English programme there in 1896 and later held the chair of English language and literature at King's College, London. He was the general editor of the Temple *Shakespeare* and of several other series including the Temple Classics for which he brought out an edition of the *Morte Darthur* in 1897. The four-volume modernized edition, based on Sommer, has no introduction; the comments below appear in a note at the end of volume I (a) and a 'Bibliographical Note' in volume IV (b) (London: J.M. Dent, 1897), I, n.p.n., and IV, 313–17.

(a)

The present text of *Sir Thomas Malory's* 'noble and joyous book entitled *le morte Darthur*' is substantially that printed by Caxton.... except in so far as its spelling and punctuation have been modernised. By the fairly consistent retention of archaisms (verbal, grammatical, and syntactical) it is hoped that a somewhat successful compromise has been effected between an absolute reproduction of the 'editio princeps' and a thorough modernisation. As little as possible of the charm of the original edition has been sacrificed; its typographical characteristics and vagaries of spelling are not for the general reader, and they may now be studied in Dr. Sommer's excellent reprint.... they do not constitute any part of the abiding interest in the famous book.

(b)

[Gollancz traces the printing history of the various editions.]

...in 1889–91 Sommer's monumental reprint marked an epoch in the history of the work; it is a conscientious and successful attempt to give students a trustworthy text, together with the necessary apparatus (though the glossary is sadly defective); in 1894 the publishers of the present volumes issued, in two stately quartos, a modernised reprint of Caxton's text, embellished with many original designs by Aubrey Beardsley, and with an introduction by Professor Rhys.

Caxton's text has again been used as the basis for the present edition.... a considerable number of Caxton's misprints and other errors (more than have hitherto been pointed out) have been removed, and it is hoped that the difficult task of hitting the mean between a mere reprint and an absolute modernisation may have been accomplished, though the correctness of many passages may still be questioned.

It is beyond the scope of this Note to deal with the question of Malory's Sources.

[Summarizes Sommer on main sources.]

(It is noteworthy that Spenser's *Faerie Queene* owed much of its general plan to Malory's story of the adventures of Gareth, as well as to the minstrel's song of *Le Beaus Disconnus*.)

As regards the origin of the whole cycle of Arthurian stories and romances, the student should consult the introduction by Prof. Rhys to the edition of *Le Morte D'Arthur* mentioned above, and the books and articles there referred to, more especially the treatises of Dr. Zimmer, who believes the romances to be based on stories of Breton rather than of Welsh origin, while Prof. Rhys' researches have led him to the two-fold conclusion that, while the older romances relating chiefly to Arthur and his men are of Breton rather than of Welsh origin, the reverse is the case with the Grail romances. The *Historia Brittonum* (a Latin history of Arthur's deeds and the origin of the Britons) associated with the name of Nennius was put together probably as early as the end of the ninth century; on this work Geoffrey of Monmouth, in the twelfth century, founded in great part his new *Historia regum Britanniae*, the main source of all our poetry inspired by British Legend and Arthurian Romance. In mediaeval times the West of England was fittingly the home of the poets who cherished this ancient lore; here arose the venerable Layamon, who, at the beginning of the thirteenth century, first sang the story of Britain in English verse....it is pleasant to think that in all probability Sir Thomas Malory was also 'a Western man'; little is known of his history, but such evidence as exists seems to point to a Welsh origin.

Malory's picturesque prose, its very simplicity and unaffected quaintness suggestive of so much mystery, must have done more than any other work to nationalise the ancient story of Arthur and his Knights; a long succession of poets, from Spenser to Tennyson, have yielded to its irresistible fascination, though the latter poet, like old Roger Ascham, passes a somewhat severe judgment on 'Malleor's' Arthur,

> Touched by the adulterous finger of a time
> That hovered between war and wantonness;

Caxton perhaps foresaw the possibility of some such criticism, when he wrote in his Preface:—'For herein may be seen noble chivalry, courtesy, humanity, friendliness, hardiness, love, friendship, cowardice, murder, hate, virtue, and sin. Do after the good and leave the evil, and it shall bring you to good fame and renown.' Tennyson's Arthurian allegories, 'new-old, and shadowing Sense at war with Soul,' have called forth a number of works dealing with the different treatments of these myths in English literature; perhaps the most useful, more especially its introductory discourse, is Mr. MacCallum's book on *The Idylls of the King.* [See No. 48.]

Finally, the student's attention should be called to Mr. Andrew Lang's brief but penetrating essay, introductory to vol. iii. of Dr. Sommer's edition of *Le Morte D'Arthur*; it illumines many aspects of the problem. [See No. 42.]

D. A. W. Pollard

1900

Alfred William Pollard (1859–1944), librarian, bibliographer, editor, Shakespeare scholar, collaborated in editing the Globe *Chaucer* and a number of other medieval texts before beginning the work in bibliographical and textual criticism of Shakespeare's plays which challenged then current ideas and changed the direction of modern textual criticism of Shakespeare. His edition of the *Morte Darthur* for Macmillan in 1900 was reprinted numerous times and was one of the most widely read of the several modernized versions based on Sommer's edition. In the introduction, he includes then recent announcements of new biographical information about Malory; A.T. Martin's identification of Malory, mentioned here, was soon eclipsed by Kittredge's publications on the subject. (See Introduction, pp. 35–6, and Kittredge's short essay in Mead's introduction, No. 49 below.)

The next-to-last paragraph suggests a reaction, like those of Strachey and Saintsbury, to Sommer's underrating of Malory's genius. The extract is from Pollard's introduction (London: Macmillan, 1900), pp. v–viii.

... Caxton's story of how the book was brought to him and he was induced to print it may be read farther on in his own preface. From this we learn also that he was not only the printer of the book, but to some extent its editor also, dividing Malory's work into twenty-one books, splitting up the books into chapters, by no means skilfully, and supplying the 'Rubrish' or chapter-headings. It may be added that Caxton's preface contains, moreover, a brief criticism which, on the points on which it touches, is still the soundest and most sympathetic that has been written.

Caxton finished his edition the last day of July 1485, some fifteen or sixteen years after Malory wrote his epilogue. It is clear that the author was then dead, or the printer would not have acted as a clumsy editor to the book, and recent discoveries (if bibliography may, for the moment, enlarge its bounds to mention such matters) have revealed with tolerable certainty when Malory died and who he was. In letters to *The Athenaeum* in July 1896 Mr. T. Williams pointed out that the name of a Sir Thomas Malorie occurred among those of a number of other Lancastrians excluded from a general pardon granted by Edward IV. in 1468, and that a William Mallerye was mentioned in the same year as taking part in a Lancastrian rising. In September 1897, again, in another letter to the same paper, Mr. A. T. Martin reported the finding of the will of a Thomas Malory of Papworth, a hundred partly in Cambridgeshire, partly in Hunts. This will was made on September 16, 1469, and as it was proved the 27th of the next month the testator must have been in immediate expectation of death. It contains the most careful provision for the education and starting in life of a family of three daughters and seven sons, of whom the youngest seems to have been still an infant. We cannot say with certainty that this Thomas Malory, whose last thoughts were so busy for his children, was our author, or that the Lancastrian knight discovered by Mr. Williams was identical with either or both, but such evidence as the *Morte Darthur* offers favours such a belief. There is not only the epilogue with its petition, 'pray for me while I am alive that God send me good deliverance and when I am dead pray you all for my soul,' but this very request is foreshadowed at the end of chap. 37 of Book ix. in the touching passage, surely inspired by personal experience, as to the sickness 'that is the greatest pain a prisoner may have'; and the reflections of English fickleness in the first chapter of Book xxi., though the Wars of the Roses might have inspired them in any one, come most naturally from an author who was a Lancastrian knight.

If the *Morte Darthur* was really written in prison and by a prisoner distressed by ill-health as well as by lack of liberty, surely no task was ever better devised to while away weary hours. Leaving abundant scope for originality in selection, modification, and arrangement, as a compilation and translation it had in it that mechanical element which adds the touch of restfulness to literary work. No original, it is said, has yet been found for Book vii., and it is possible that none will ever be forthcoming for chap. 20 of Book xviii., which describes the arrival of the body of the Fair Maiden of Astolat at Arthur's court, or for chap. 25 of the same book, with its discourse on true love; but the great bulk of the work has been traced chapter by chapter.... As to Malory's choice of his authorities critics have not failed to point out that now and again he gives a worse version where a better has come down to us, and if he had been able to order a complete set of Arthurian manuscripts from his bookseller, no doubt he would have done even better than he did! But of the skill, approaching to original genius, with which he used the books from which he worked there is little dispute.

Malory died leaving his work obviously unrevised, and in this condition it was brought to Caxton, who prepared it for the press with his usual enthusiasm in the cause of good literature, and also, it must be added, with his usual carelessness. New chapters are sometimes made to begin in the middle of a sentence, and in addition to simple misprints there are numerous passages in which it is impossible to believe that we have the text as Malory intended it to stand. After Caxton's edition Malory's manuscript must have disappeared, and subsequent editions are differentiated only by the degree of closeness with which they follow the first....

47. Craik's *English Prose Selections*

1893

A. W. P. Ker

Walter Paton Ker (1855–1923) wrote the general introduction to volume I of *English Prose Selections*, edited by Henry

Craik; this volume covered the fourteenth to the sixteenth century. It is one of Ker's earlier publications, preceding by some four years *Epic and Romance*, the work that established his considerable scholarly reputation. His argument, though briefer, is much like Mead's (see No. 49 below): Malory deserves great credit for having done something very difficult in good and sometimes splendid prose. (London: Macmillan, 1893, pp. 12–18.)

In the fifteenth century there is something more than repetition of old forms. There are two argumentative books which are fresh and new—Bishop Pecock's *Repressour* and Sir John Fortescue on the *Governance of England*. It is a relief to come to these books which require thinking, after all the homilies and moral treatises which require merely to be listened to. The great prose achievement of the fifteenth century, and indeed of the whole time before the *Advancement of Learning*, is a book in many ways less original than those of Pecock and Fortescue. But Sir Thomas Malory's *Morte D'Arthur*, antique though its matter be, is singular in its qualities of style; and if the books of the Bishop and the Judge are remarkable for the modern good sense of their arguments, the *Morte D'Arthur* has its own place apart from them in a region of high imaginative prose.

Many things about the *Morte D'Arthur* are perplexing and even irritating. It is a free version of some of the finest stories ever made, and is based on versions of the multiform Arthurian romance, which in some respects are beyond comparison the best. Yet Malory has rejected some of the best things in the 'French book' which he followed. There is nothing in Malory corresponding to the truth and the dramatic sincerity of the first interview between Lancelot and the Queen—the passage which Dante could not forget. Malory never rises, as his original here does, out of romance into drama. His refusal to finish the story of Tristram is as hard to understand as to forgive, and as hard to forgive as the *Last Tournament*. But when all is said that the Devil's advocate can say, it all goes for nothing compared with what remains in Malory untouched and unblemished by any hint of dispraise.

Malory accomplished one of the hardest things in literature. He had to rewrite in English some of the finest of medieval French prose, full of romance, and of the strangest harmonies between the spirit of romance and the spirit of confessors, saints, and pilgrims. What could be done in those days by adapters and abridgers one knows well enough. Caxton himself tried his hand on some others of the Nine Worthies; they did not fare as Arthur did. To know what Malory really is, it is enough to turn to Caxton's *Lyf of Charles the Grete* or *Recuyell of the Histories of Troy*. Malory kept in English all the beauty of the *Queste del St. Graal*, that strange confusion of Celtic myth with Christian dreams, the most representative among all the books of the thirteenth century. The story suffers no wrong in the English version; there as well as in the French may be heard the melancholy voices of the adventurers who follow the radiance of Heaven across the land of Morgan le Fay. The time in which Malory wrote was not favourable to pure imaginative literature—poetry was all but extinguished—yet Malory was able to revive, by some wonderful gift, the aspirations and the visionary ardour of the youth of Christendom—little in agreement, one might fancy, with the positive and selfish world described in the Paston letters. He did more than this also, as may be seen by a comparison of the French book, or books, with his own writing. The style of his original has the graces of early art; the pathos, the simplicity of the early French prose at its best, and always that haunting elegiac tone or undertone which never fails in romance or homily to bring its sad suggestions of the vanity and transience of all things, of the passing away of pomp and splendour, of the falls of princes. In Malory, while this tone is kept, there is a more decided and more artistic command of rhythm than in the Lancelot or the Tristan. They are even throughout, one page very much like another in general character: Malory has splendid passages to which he rises, and from which he falls back into the even tenour of his discourse. In the less distinguished parts of his book, besides, there cannot fail to be noted a more careful choice of words and testing of sounds than in the uncalculating spontaneous eloquence of his original.

Malory has been compared to Herodotus, and in this the resemblance may be made out; while, in both authors, the ground-work of their style is the natural simple story-teller's loose fabric of easy-going clauses, in both there is a further process of rhetoric embroidering the plain stuff. Neither Herodotus nor Malory can be taken for the earliest sort of prose artist. Both of them are already some way from the beginning of their art, and though in both of them the primitive rhetoric may be found by analysis, they are not novices. Though they have preserved many of the beauties of the uncritical childhood of literature, they are both of them sophisticated; it is their craft, or their good genius, that makes one overlook the critical and testing processes, the conscious rhetoric, without which they could not have written as they did. Malory's prose, and not Chaucer's, is the prose analogue of Chaucer's poetry; summing up as it does some of the great attainments of the earlier Middle Ages, and presenting them in colours more brilliant, with a more conscious style, than they had possessed in their first rendering. The superiority of Chaucer's *Troilus* over the early version of the Norman *trouvère* is derived through Boccaccio from a school that had begun to be critical and reflective. Malory, in a similar way, rewrites his 'French book' with an ear for new varieties of cadence, and makes the book his own, in virtue of this art of his. Much of the 'French book' has the common fault of medieval literature, the want of personal character in the style; like so many medieval books, it is thought of as belonging to a class rather than a personal author, as if it were one of many similar things turned out by a company with common trade methods. This is the case with some, not with the whole, of Malory's original; it is not the case with Malory. He is an author and an artist, and his style is his own.

Malory, in much the same way as Chaucer, is one of the moderns. He is not antiquated; he is old fashioned, perhaps—a different thing, for so are Bacon and Jeremy Taylor old fashioned, and Addison, and Fielding. The modern and intelligible and generally acceptable nature of Malory's book may serve to prove, if that were necessary, how very far from true or adequate is the belief that the beginning of the modern world was a revolt against the Middle Ages. The progress out of the Middle Ages had its revolutionary aspects, as when Duns Scotus was torn up in the New College quadrangle, and Florismarte of Hyrcania delivered to the secular arm in Don Quixote's backyard. But in literature, as a general rule, progress was made in a direct and continuous line, by taking up what was old and carrying it on. This at least was the method of Ariosto and Spenser, of Shakespeare and Cervantes, and their predecessors in this were Chaucer and Malory. It is impossible to draw any dividing line. There was no Protestant schism in literature. One cannot separate the *Morte D'Arthur* from the old romances on the one hand, nor from the Elizabethans on the other. Malory is succeeded by Lord Berners with his *Froissart* and his *Huon of Bordeaux*, and Lord Berners is a link with Thomas North, *Euphues*, and Sir Philip Sidney. Innumerable classical and foreign influences went to make the new world, but among them all the old currents from the old well-springs kept on flowing....

B. John W. Hales

John W. Hales (1836–1914), Professor of English Literature mainly at King's College, London, co-edited with F.J. Furnivall *Bishop Percy's Folio MS.* (1867–8) and edited or wrote books on Shakespeare, Milton, and Chaucer. Hales' introduction to the selections from Malory's work is shorter than Ker's section on Malory in the general introduction, but he does include a generous sampling of the prose of the *Morte Darthur*, selecting early passages beginning with Arthur and Merlin getting Excalibur, through Balin and Balan killing each other, and Tristram and Isond drinking the potion; in addition, he includes more than half of Caxton's Book XXI.

[Beyond what is stated by Caxton in his Preface to the *Morte d' Arthur* and in his Colophon, and what Malory himself says at the end of his compilation, we know nothing of the authorship or of the author of this the most popular English work of the closing Middle Ages.

[Quotes from Caxton's preface and Malory's concluding colophon.]

There is a village called Kirkby Mallory in Leicestershire, about five miles north of Hinckly; and we know, on Leland's authority, that a family of the name held property at Hutton Conyers and also at High Studley, both places near Ripon in the West Riding of Yorkshire. In the north transept of Ripon Cathedral is a monument to the Mallorys of Studley Royal. But with neither of these occurrences of the name can he be certainly connected. His description of himself as the servant of Jesu both day and night might very well mean, and has been taken to mean, that he was in 'Holy Orders'; but more probably it simply expresses what all his work illustrates, viz. that he was of a sincerely religious spirit.]

Sir Thomas Malory's *Morte d'Arthur* is of high distinction in many ways. It is the largest and completest collection of the Arthurian romances; it is arranged with remarkable skill and judgment; it is written in a style of wonderful simplicity and of wonderful effectiveness; it has been ever since the favourite hand-book of all students, poetic and other, who have felt any interest in the Arthurian story and in chivalrous romance.

It is, in fact, a complete Arthuriad. What so many great writers designed, Malory has in his own way accomplished. He tells the tale of the old king from the beginning to the end. There are many episodes, but these are subordinate to the main theme. No doubt he takes his material from the French; but he takes it from various sources, not from any single work which had already done what it was his special purpose to do. So to translate and abridge and to correlate numerous French works that treated of the Table Round in prose and in poetry was an achievement demanding a real artistic sense and power. And, in fact, to this day the only Arthurian epic our literature has to show is this work of Malory's. For Spenser never reached the properly Arthurian part of the *Faerie Queen*; Milton never actually took in hand the Arthurian legends, though they so long and so late attracted him; Dryden's opera *King Arthur* just serves to remind us that he never wrote the heroic poem on Arthur which, wisely or unwisely, he for many years meditated; Tennyson himself warns us against looking to him for an epic, when he entitles his Arthurian pieces 'Idylls.' Thus our one Arthurian epic is in prose. Some critic has regretted that Malory did not attempt verse; but we may be sure that Malory's judgment was sound in this respect. He understood well his own limits and the limits of his time, as also his own genius and the genius of his time. A different age would have filled him with a different inspiration. But the latter part of the fifteenth century in England was probably incapable of any high poetic form. And an attempt on Malory's part to assume a poetic form would probably have been scarcely less disastrous than had Bunyan produced his famous allegory in such couplets as compose its Preface, instead of in the admirable prose which, with his other gifts, has given him a place amongst English classics. The prose of Malory too is admirable. It is spoilt by no tricks or affectations; it is not always thinking of itself, so to speak, or wishing to be thought about. It aims merely at doing its duty as a rendering of its master's thought. What particularly distinguishes it is its thoroughly idiomatic character. Malory displays a fine instinct in his use of his mother-tongue. It is wonderful to see how this subtle sense led him to the choice of phrases that were to remain always part of the vernacular, his choice, no doubt, improving their chance of remaining so; for there was no more popular book in the sixteenth century than the *Morte d'Arthur*. Above all, Malory's language and style exactly suit his subject. In no work is there a perfecter harmony—a more sympathetic marriage—of this kind. This chronicler of knighthood is himself a knight. His heart is devoted to the chivalry he portrays, and his tongue is the faithful spokesmen of his heart.

48. Mungo MacCallum

1894

Mungo W. MacCallum (1854–1942), who held the chair of Modern Literature for some thirty years and was then Chancellor at the University of Sydney, published *Tennyson's Idylls of the King and Arthurian Story from the XVIth Century* in 1894. As the title suggests, the emphasis is upon Arthurian-based literature from the Renaissance through Tennyson, and the last four chapters are devoted exclusively to the *Idylls*. However, a section of the introductory chapter is entitled 'Malory's Compilation and the English Ballads', and it is from this section that the extract is drawn. (Glasgow, 1894; reprinted New York: Books for Libraries Press, 1971), pp. 85–101.

Not surprisingly, MacCallum here prepares for his discussion of Tennyson's achievement by comparing Malory and Tennyson, to the advantage of the latter.

... In the fifteenth century there was a reversion to the Middle Ages in several important respects; the Lollard heresy was repressed, the real authority of Parliament declined, the Wars of the Roses restored the anarchy of feudalism. In that atmosphere the interest in Arthurian stories ran high, and at last the task of compilation was seriously set about in the reign of Edward IV., that king who rose to power with the help, and recovered power by the fall, of the 'Last of the Barons,' and under whom the new principles of society began obviously to declare themselves. It is characteristic that just at the final gasp of the Middle Ages, the work of welding the mass of Arthurian story was undertaken. And the *Morte Darthur* shows traces of this in the circumstances of its authorship and its literary position. The concluding words of the book are framed on the well-known medieval formula; 'I praye you all, Ientyl men and Ientyl wymmen, that redeth this book of Arthur and his knyghtes from the begynnyng to the endyng, praye for me whyle I am on lyue that God sende me good delyueraunce, and whan I am deed, I praye you all praye for my soule; for this book was ended the ix yere of the reygne of Kyng Edward the Fourth by Syr Thomas Maleore, knyght, as Jhesu helpe hym for his grete myght, as he is the seruaunt of Jhesu bothe day and nyght.' There is a medieval accent in these devout words of the knightly author. On the other hand, it is no less typical that his book proceeded from Caxton's press at Westminster, and was among the first fruits of that art of printing that has done so much to make the new times what they are. And Malory in style and diction is very near ourselves, in some aspects having a good claim to be considered the father of modern English prose.[1] ... Malory's language is in prose the direct descendent of Chaucer's in verse; his book was still popular and influential in the latter half of the sixteenth century; and even now with all its apparent artlessness and want of rule, his style has a quaint and stately charm that school boy and critic can feel and respect. Indeed, Malory has a claim to be called a genius, though a minor one, in virtue of his graphic narratives, especially of tournaments and fights; his swift descriptions, as of the coming of

the Grail; his appeals to the feelings, as in his famous encomium on
Sir Lancelot. The following passage is of a kind less frequent in his
book but not less characteristic.

[Quotes from the healing of Sir Urre down to 'and euer Syr
Launcelot wepte as he had ben a child that had ben beten.']

Even in his subject matter, Malory, however closely he follows his
sources, is entitled to the credit of independence, and, it might be
said, of originality; for a compiler must select and connect; in
selecting he must use his judgment, and in connecting he must
appeal to his own imaginative presentiment. Moreover, the mere
conception of a unity in the straggling wilderness of Arthurian
romance was genial and large-hearted. Besides, in a matter of this
kind, the judgment must, to a great extent, depend on the results.
Malory's predecessor, Rusticien of Pisa, and his later contemporary, Ulrich Fürterer, have apparently, to all intents and purposes,
been without influence on literature, but the *Morte Darthur* is both a
landmark and a fountain-head of literature. Of course Malory's
work is by no means beyond criticism. He is capricious in his
insertions and in his omissions; we well could spare the story of
Alisander and Anglides to find room for Erec. He often leaves a
history half told, notably in the case of Sir Tristram, where besides
he follows a poor version of the legend. His dexterity in mosaic is
so small that he frequently contradicts himself in detail, and his
arrangement is very confused. But he 'means right,' and he has
succeeded in the grand lines of the history. He has told the tale of
Arthur, so that none of the pathos and terror is lost. The son of the
devout Uther and the chaste Igraine, he is yet the fruit of a lawless
amour. Though chosen and hallowed by heaven, in his youthful
passion he violates the common instincts of mankind, and,
ruthlessly but vainly, by an attempted massacre of children, seeks
to escape the consequences of his guilt. Nevertheless for long all
seems to go well with him. He weds the fair Guinevere, who
brings him Uther's Round Table as her dowry. He fills its seats
with knights of unmatched prowess, some of whom even excel
himself; and he and they do their part manfully to purge the world
from ill. Yet, amid all his pomp and magnificence, his weird is
slowly fulfilling itself. Lancelot, his best knight, his best friend, is
but his dearest foe. As Arthur's truant passion has its fruit in

Modred born to be the scourge of the order by his villainy, so Lancelot, in his involuntary breach of faith to the Queen, becomes the father of Galahad, born to be its scourge by his holiness. For this holiness attracts once more the Holy Grail to the haunts of men; and the fellowship wrecks itself on the quest that is only for the virgin knight. Soon the discovery of Lancelot's guilt ensues to divide it against itself. While Arthur is warring with him over sea, Modred seizes the kingdom and Queen, avenging his origin with equal wrong. And, though Arthur returns to take vengeance on this baser treason, vengeance does not mean redress. In the ruinous battle that takes place through a mere accident and blunder, the great king and his nephew son fall at the hands of each other.

Thus the Arthurian stories, after expressing the beauty and fulness of chivalry, ended by expressing its dissolution, and the tragic catastrophe is what gives its name and unity to the *Morte Darthur*, the cyclic work composed at the end of the fifteenth century. That this ultimate phase was necessary both in the ideal and in its literary reflection we may see, if we recall what chivalry was and how it found utterance in song. It sought to establish a compromise or equipoise between the opposing forces of religious monastic theory and irreligious lay life. The scales dip to the clerical side in the song of Roland, and to the mundane in the lay of Alexander. Only in the career of Arthur, supplemented in the adventures of his knights, do we find anything like an exact balance. But since in chivalry there was mere adjustment and no real fusion of the opposing elements, it was at best in unstable equilibrium, difficult to attain and liable at any moment to be destroyed. It begins in the Romance of Tristram with an over-accentuation of the secular, it proceeds in the Romance of Percivale to an over-accentuation of the spiritual. In the reconstruction of the story, which makes Arthur in his own person represent the conflicting forces, and Lancelot and Galahad follow them out to the uttermost, the whole contrivance breaks up.

And this was the fate of chivalry, because, as a guiding principle, it was unequal to the problem which it undertook, and men soon saw that it merely professed to give the answer. Yet, like every great attempt to reconcile the two sides of man's nature, it retains a perennial interest for mankind; and the fictions which were fostered under its shadow possess a certain capability of meaning that not only makes them immortal, but endows them with a living inspiration and challenges the world to treat them anew. And Malory's compilation, which supplies as it were the last word and classic form to the medieval conception, has justly enjoyed most popularity and exercised most influence in after times. Later writers may draw here on a Welsh story and there on a separate romance; but generally and essentially it is to Malory, with or without supplementary hints from Geoffrey, that the greatest English poets have recourse. And this is specially true of Tennyson, chief of the subsequent singers of Arthur, and the only one on whom falls Malory's mantle, in so far as the encyclopaedic character of the work is concerned.

Tennyson so obviously hews most of his material from this quarry, that comparisons between the *Morte Darthur* and the *Idylls of the King* are inevitable. Further, as Tennyson's indebtedness is at first sight very great, such comparisons have often led to his being described as a copyist, and even a bad copyist, under whose hands the grand features of the story are weakened or obliterated. The examination of Tennyson's work belongs to a later portion of this essay, but it may be well to protest in advance against such views. Tennyson has often followed Malory very closely in plot, in idea, even in expression, but in the same way as he has followed Raleigh for his *Revenge*. Many of his excellences are annexed, but they gain new lustre from their new position, they are heightened and strengthened under his touch; and the most and the finest are his own; while the method of treatment is entirely original. A most instructive comparison may be made between the fifth chapter of Malory's twenty-first book and the *Passing of Arthur*. The general course of the story is the same in both, and the similarity extends even to minute details. Malory's Arthur says to Bedivere: 'But yf thou do now as I byd the, yf euer I may see the, I shal slee the with myn owne handes'; where *but if* means *unless*. Tennyson keeps the expression, though it has now a different force and he must give a new turn to the sentence to make it relevant:—

> 'But, if thou spare to fling Excalibur,
> I will arise and slay thee with my hands.'

It is not often, however, that Tennyson's loans are merely verbal. Generally we are struck quite as much by the difference as by the resemblance between them and the original. 'Syr,' says Bedivere in the prose, 'I sawe no thynge but the waters wappe and the wawes wanne'; which in the poem becomes the famous couplet:—

> 'I heard the water lapping on the crag,
> And the long ripple washing in the reeds.'

When the king is put on board the barge, Malory says: 'And there receyued hym thre quenes wyth grete mornyng'; which is to Tennyson's lines as a diagram is to a picture:—

> And from them rose
> A cry that shiver'd to the tingling stars,
> And, as it were one voice, an agony
> Of lamentation, like a wind that shrills
> All night in a waste land, where no one comes,
> Or hath come, since the making of the world.

The description of the place, the broken chancel with a 'broken cross' upon 'the strait of barren land' between the two expanses of water, and of Sir Bedivere striding over the ice-bound cliffs, is all Tennyson's own, with hardly a hint from Malory. It is the same if we consider the psychological motives. The adapter leaves his authority far behind. In Malory, Sir Bedivere on his first errand 'behelde that noble swerde that the pomel and the hafte was al of precyous stones, and thenne sayd to hym self; "Yf I throwe this ryche swerde in the water, therof shall neuer come good, but harme and losse."' And the same idea is repeated on his second expedition. Tennyson does not neglect this hint:—

> There drew he forth the brand Excalibur,
> ....
> ...all the haft twinkled with diamond sparks,
> Myriads of topaz-lights, and jacinth-work
> Of subtlest jewellery.

But this is preliminary. On the second occasion it is care for the king's own honour that makes him fail:—

> 'What record, or what relic of my lord
> Should be to aftertime, but empty breath
> And rumours of a doubt? But were this kept,
> Stored in some treasure-house of mighty kings,
> Some one might show it at a joust of arms,
> Saying, "King Arthur's sword, Excalibur,"'...

Or, again, for profundity of conception, compare the king's last words in the two versions. In Malory it runs: 'Comfort thyself and doo as wel as thou mayst, for in me is no truste to truste in. For I wyl in to the vale of Awylyon to hele me of my grevous wounde. And yf thou here neuer more of me, praye for my soule.' Contrast with this the farewell greeting in Tennyson:—

> 'The old order changeth, yielding place to new,
> And God fulfils himself in many ways,
> Lest one good custom should corrupt the world.'

Surely there is a depth of meaning in these and the following lines for which we should vainly look in Malory's ringing prose. And significance combined with workmanship cannot fail to bring with them artistic arrangement. In this respect, Malory, as we have seen, hardly succeeds in carrying out what was in his mind. A glance at Tennyson's Idylls shows that he has cut and carved and reconstructed the order of Malory's stories. Malory tells of the birth of Arthur, of Balin and Balan, of the king's marriage and acquisition of the Round Table, of Merlin's fate, of Pelleas and Ettard, of Arthur's expedition against Rome, of Gareth, of Tristram, of Lancelot and Elaine, of the Sangrail, of the Maid of Astolat, of the discovery of Guinevere's infidelity, and of the death of Arthur. Tennyson, on the other hand, begins with the coming of Arthur, his wars with the Saxons and the rebels, his founding of the Table, his marriage and his contest with Rome, in the introductory poem. Then he proceeds to Gareth and Lynette, to the companion poems which he interpolates from the *Mabinogion* on Geraint and Enid, to Merlin and Vivien, to Lancelot and Elaine, and thus reaches the Holy Grail: then come in order Pelleas and Ettarre, the Last Tournament with Tristram for centre, Guinevere, and the Passing of Arthur. Even before the exact meaning of this arrangement has disclosed itself, it is obvious that the order is no haphazard one, but is adopted intentionally on a plan that is distinct from Malory's. And further, it is evident that here there is a gradual transition from light to dark as the guilt of Lancelot and Guinevere deepens and works out its bitter fruits. There is no hint of such an artistic sequence in Malory's fortuitous jumble; and this, as we shall find, is only one indication of Tennyson's reorganisation of the story according to the requirements of contemporary thought.

NOTE

1 In his book of specimens Mr. Saintsbury very fitly assigns him the first place. [See No. 51 below.]

49. W. E. Mead

1897

William Edward Mead (1860–1949), scholar and professor of English, in addition to books on composition and rhetoric and numerous contributions to literary reviews and philological journals, wrote the lengthy introduction to the Early English Text Society's edition of the English prose *Merlin*; this scholarly addition to the printed text appeared in 1899. The extract included here is from Mead's introduction to *Selections from Sir Thomas Malory's Morte Darthur*, which he also edited, for the Athenaeum Press Series in 1897. This work provides a good example of American scholarship toward the end of the nineteenth century, the more so as the section on Malory's biography was written by George Lyman Kittredge (1860–1941), professor of English at Harvard University, presenting the now familiar identification of Malory that has been almost universally accepted until very recently (see Introduction, pp. 35–6).

Mead takes an objective view, acknowledging some defects in the *Morte Darthur*, but defending it against many of Sommer's strictures and on the whole finding it a remarkable achievement for its time. Mead's introduction is divided into seven sections, some of which are merely summarized here (Boston: Ginn & Company, 1897, pp. ix–lxii.)

I.

The 15th century has had its full measure of condemnation as an unproductive period in English literary annals. Its barrenness is often contrasted unfavorably with the comparative richness of the century that preceded it, and particularly with the marvellous fecundity of the age of Elizabeth. Taken as a whole, the literary output of the 15th century must be acknowledged to be small in quantity and mediocre in quality. Yet, singularly enough, the 15th century produced one writer who shares with Chaucer the distinction of being read to-day by the general public. Sir Thomas Malory is, by popular consent at least, the greatest master of prose before the Revival of Learning.

The popular verdict, which has marked the *Morte Darthur* as worthy of the attention of the modern reader, while allowing all other early English prose—with the possible exception of the pseudo-Mandeville's *Travels*—to remain the undisturbed possession of scholars, may not be the surest test of the merit of the book as a piece of original composition. Some other names rank high in any survey of 15th-century literature, such as Fortescue and Fabyan and Capgrave and Pecocke. To take a single instance, Fortescue's *Treatise on the Difference between Absolute and Limited Monarchy* was, in its way, more original than the *Morte Darthur*, and was probably quite beyond the powers of Malory. Yet the nature of the topics that Fortescue discussed must have made his readers few even in his own day. Malory, on the other hand, could appeal at the outset to a widespread interest in his subject, and he knew how to awaken interest where it had not existed.

The 15th century was doubtless not an ideal time for a writer or a student. The utter neglect of English letters under Henry V, the selfishness and greed of the turbulent nobles who crowded the court of Henry VI and took advantage of his helplessness to make gains while they could, the wasting of England under the armies of York and of Lancaster, fighting for—men hardly knew what, took away much of the inspiration for original literary production.

Yet, as Emerson somewhere says, 'every age has a thousand sides and signs and tendencies'; and one who lives in the age itself cannot always tell whither it is drifting. In the 15th century the feudal system was tottering to its fall. The forms still survived, and the pomp and glitter of feudal life were present at every turn. But the times were evil, and they seemed to contain the promise of evil. In such an age, men who saw the troubled state of their own time, but who were not skilled as prophets, may well have dreamed of the olden days when the institutions which were rapidly going to decay had been vigorous with a new life. It is not strange, therefore, that when Malory cast about for a subject he turned away from the intrigues and petty quarrels of court factions to the deeds of an ideal king and an ideal court in a far-away age.

We know indeed very little about the influences that shaped a writer in the turbulent 15th century. Some of them may have been more favorable than we commonly think. We may freely admit that the poetry, except that produced in the North, could hardly be worse. Hobbling, uninspired doggerel most of it is, as inane as it is formless. But the prose, taken as a whole, is surely better than any that England had produced since the Norman Conquest. There are modern readers who even prefer the simple, natural style of Malory and his contemporaries to the tortuous indirectness of much of the Elizabethan and early 17th-century prose. Malory opened new paths for the prose writer, and showed how men to whom the gift of song was denied might still write a rich and beautiful prose. Possibly his age was the most unfavourable in which a writer's lot could be cast, but those who hold that opinion are bound to give all the more credit to Malory for rising above the dead level of his time. . . . The state of literature in England, though surely bad enough, was not so decidedly worse than that of the rest of Europe as one might at first imagine. The soil was preparing for the great outburst of the following century.

Malory, however, belongs to the older order. Scarcely a ripple of the great Renaissance movement had touched England when he began to write. He was himself entirely uninfluenced by it. He lived wholly in the Middle Ages, and breathed their very spirit into his great book of romances. Yet there must have been signs enough, even in Malory's time, that a new spirit was rising, and that the days of the old order were numbered. Tradesmen were acquiring political power and social recognition. The towns were rapidly growing in wealth and population and influence. The people were gaining more than the privileged classes. Each new turn of events that brought the king out of harmony with his great nobles threw him into the hands of the people, and they did not fail to profit by the opportunity. The new common soldiers were a match for the knights and gentlemen. War abroad and civil strife at home had reduced the number of the nobles and made still easier the progress of the social revolution. In a generation or two more, chivalry was the theme for a jest, and its glory had departed forever.

II.[1]

In any attempt to identify the author of the *Morte Darthur* with an historical Sir Thomas Malory, one must not look for demonstration. Probably no direct evidence on the subject exists. Public records and business papers of the 14th and 15th centuries may be expected to supply information about estates and offices and military service, but they are not likely to mention literary works.[2] A high degree of probability may, however, be arrived at. If, amongst the various Malorys of the 15th century, but one can be found who satisfies all the conditions of the problem, we may reasonably claim for him the authorship of this famous work, though no direct evidence of his connection with it be procurable.

What the required conditions are may be seen from three places in the *Morte Darthur* which mention Malory:

(1) Caxton's Preface, in which he says he has printed 'after a copye vnto me delyuerd, whyche copye Syr Thomas Malorye dyd take oute of certeyn bookes of frensshe and reduced it in to Englysshe' (Sommer, p. 3).

(2) The concluding words of the last book: 'I praye you all Ientyl men and Ientyl wymmen that redeth this book of Arthur and his knyghtes... | praye for me whyle I am on lyue that god sende me good delyueraunce | & whan I am deed I praye you all praye for my soule | for this book was ended the ix yere of the reygne of kyng edward the fourth | by syr Thomas Maleore knyght as Ihesu helpe hym for hys grete myght | as he is the seruaunt of Ihesu bothe day and nyght |' (Sommer, p. 861). These are obviously not the words of Caxton, as Dr. Sommer takes them to be, but the words of Malory himself.

(3) Caxton's colophon, which says that the book 'was reduced in to englysshe by syr Thomas Malory knyght as afore is sayd[3] | and by me deuyded in to xxi bookes chapytred and enprynted | and fynysshed in thabbey westmestre the last day of Iuly the yere of our lord |M| CCCC |lxxxv|' (Sommer, p. 861).

From these passages it appears that any Sir Thomas Malory advanced as the author of the *Morte Darthur* must fulfill the following conditions: (1) He must have been a knight;[4] (2) he must have been alive in the ninth year of Edward IV, which extended from Mar. 4. 1469, to Mar. 3, 1470 (both included); (3) he must have been old enough in 9 Edward IV to make it possible that he should have written this work. Further, Caxton does not say that he received the 'copy' directly from the author, and his language may be held to indicate that Malory was dead when the book was printed. In this case he must have died before the last day of July, 1485, and we have a fourth condition to be complied with.

Up to the present time[5] but one Thomas Malory has been discovered who fulfills these three imperative conditions, and this person satisfies also the fourth condition, which, as we have seen, is not entirely imperative. We may, therefore, accept him as the author of whom we are in search and insert his biography in our literary histories, at least until a better candidate offers. That such a candidate is likely to appear the present writer is not inclined to believe, for obviously, the number of knights named Thomas Malory and living at any single time must, of necessity, be small; and, in the attempt to apply as rigid a test as possible to this identification, the pedigree and alliances of the several Malory (Malore) families have been carefully scrutinized.

This Sir Thomas Malory[6] was (1) certainly a knight. (2) He survived the ninth year of Edward IV, dying Mar. 14, 1470 (10 Edward IV). This fits the closing passage of the *Morte Darthur*. (3) He was not under fifty-seven years of age when he died, and he may have been seventy or above. (4) The *Morte Darthur* was not printed until some fifteen years after his death.

The birth, circumstances, and education of this Sir Thomas Malory appear, so far as we can discover them, to fit well with his authorship of this work. He belonged to that class to whom the Arthurian stories directly appealed: he was a gentleman of an ancient house and a soldier.[7]

His ancestors had been lords of Draughton in Northamptonshire as early, apparently, as 1267–68, and certainly earlier than 1285; and the Malores had been persons of consequence in that county and in Leicestershire from the time of Henry II or Stephen. Sir Peter Malore, justice of the common pleas (1292–1309) and one of the commission to try Sir William Wallace, was a brother of Sir Stephen Malore, the great-grandfather of our Sir Thomas,—that Sir Stephen whose marriage with Margaret Revell brought the Newbold estates[8] into the family. Thomas's father, John Malory, was sheriff of Leicestershire and Warwickshire, Escheator, Knight of the Shire for Warwick in the Parliament of 1413, and held other offices of trust. It is not to be doubted, then, that Sir Thomas received a gentleman's education according to the ideas of the 15th century, which are not to be confounded with those of an earlier, illiterate period. That he should learn to read and write French, as well as to speak it, was a matter of course.

Sir John Malory seems to have died in 12 Henry VI (1433 or 1434), and Sir Thomas succeeded to the ancestral estates. We have, however, some information about Sir Thomas in his father's lifetime: when a young man he served in France, in the military retinue of Richard Beauchamp, Earl of Warwick,—a fact to which I shall soon revert. In the twenty-third year of Henry VI (1445) we find him a knight and sitting in Parliament for Warwickshire. Some years later he appears to have made himself conspicuous on the Lancastrian side in the War of the Roses, for in 1468 'Thomas Malorie, miles,'·is excluded, along with 'Humphry Nevyll, miles,' and several others, from the operation of a pardon issued by Edward IV. We know nothing of the matter except this bare fact. Whether or not Malory subsequently obtained a special pardon cannot now be determined. If he did not we must suppose that he was relieved by the general amnesty of 1469, since, on his death in 1470, there seems to have been no question as to the inheritance of his estate. Malory died, as has been already noted, Mar. 14, 1470, and when Dugdale wrote his *Warwickshire* (about 1656) lay 'buryed under a marble in the Chappell of St. Francis at the Gray Friars, near Newgate in the Suburbs of London.' He left a widow, Elizabeth Malory, who lived until 1480, and a grandson, Nicholas, about four years of age. This Nicholas was alive in 1511. He died without male heirs.

The most interesting of these biographical fragments is the association of Sir Thomas Malory with Richard of Warwick. Dugdale states the fact in the following words: '*Thomas*; who, in K. H. 5. time, was of the retinue of *Ric. Beauchamp* E. *Warr.* at the siege of Caleys, and served there with one lance and two archers; receiving for his lance and 1. archer xx. *li. per an.* and their dyet; and for the other archer, x. marks and no dyet.' I can find no siege of Calais in Henry V's time. Perhaps the agreement was merely to serve *at Calais*. In that case the likeliest date for Malory's covenant is perhaps 1415, when Warwick indented 'to serve the King as Captain of Calais, until *Febr. 3. An.* 1416 (4 *Hen. 5*). And to have with him in the time of Truce or Peace, for the safeguard thereof, Thirty Men at Arms, himself and three Knights accounted as part of that number; Thirty Archers on Horsback, Two hundred Foot Soldiers, and Two hundred Archers, all of his own retinue.... And in time of War, he to have One hundred and forty Men on Horsbak,' etc.

In our uncertainty with regard to the year of this service we can draw no solid inference as to the date of Malory's birth. We have already seen that he was probably of age and over in 1433−34: if he served with Beauchamp in 1416, he was doubtless born as early as 1400, but not much earlier. This would make him seventy years old at the time of his death.

The service of Malory with Richard of Warwick is, however, peculiarly significant in view of the well-known character of the earl. No better school for the future author of the *Morte Darthur* can be imagined than a personal acquaintance with that Englishman whom all Europe recognized as embodying the knightly ideal of the age. The Emperor Sigismund, we are informed on excellent authority, said to Henry V 'that no prince Cristen for wisdom, norture, and manhode, hadde such another knyght as he had of therle Warrewyk; addyng therto that if al curtesye were lost, yet myght hit be founde ageyn in hym; and so ever after by the emperours auctorite he was called the Fadre of Curteisy.'[9]

The history of Warwick's life, as set down by John Rous, chantry priest and antiquary, and almost a contemporary of the great earl, reads like a *roman d'aventure*. One exploit in particular might almost have been taken out of the *Morte Darthur* itself.[10] 'Erle Richard,' we are told, '... heryng of a greet gaderyng in Fraunce, inasmoche as he was capteyn of Caleys he hied him thidre hastely, and was there worthely received; and when that he herd that the gaderyng in Fraunce was appoynted to come to Caleys, he cast in his mynde to do sume newe poynt of chevalry; wheruppon,' under the several names of 'the grene knyght,' 'Chevaler Vert,' and 'Chevaler Attendant,' he sent three challenges to the French king's court. 'And anone other 3 Frenche knyghtes received them, and graunted their felowes to mete at day and place assigned.' On the first day, 'the xii day of Christmasse, in a lawnde called the Park Hedge of Gynes,' Earl Richard unhorsed the first of the French knights. Next day he came to the field in another armor and defeated the second French knight, 'and so with the victory, and hymself unknown rode to his pavilion agayn, and sent to this blank knyght Sir Hugh Lawney, a good courser.' On the third day the earl 'came in face opyn... and said like as he hadde his owne persone performed the two dayes afore, so with Goddes grace he wolde the third, then ran he to the Chevaler name[d] Sir Colard Fymes, and every stroke he bare hym bakwards to his hors bakke; and then the Frenchmen said he was bounde to the sadyll, wherfor he alighted down from his horse, and forthwith stept up into his sadyll ageyn, and so with worshipe rode to his pavilion, and sent to Sir Colard a good courser, and fested all the people;... and rode to Calys with great worshipe' (Strutt, *Horda*, ii, 124, 125).

This romantic adventure cannot be dated with any certainty. The *days* are settled by the text of Rous: they are January 6, 7, and 8 (Twelfth-Day and the two days following), but the *year* is not easily fixed. By a process of elimination we may arrive at the date 1416 or 1417, either of which may be right. One likes to imagine Thomas Malory as serving in Warwick's retinue on this occasion, and I know of nothing to forbid our indulging so agreeable a fancy.

It may, I think, be safely asserted that we have before us a Sir Thomas Malory who, so far as one can see, fulfills all the conditions required of a claimant for the honor of having written the *Morte Darthur*. There is absolutely no contestant, and until such a contestant appears, it is not unreasonable to insist on the claims of this Sir Thomas.

III. [Editions of the *Morte Darthur*]

IV.

Malory's purpose in the *Morte Darthur* is sufficiently evident to one who runs through the Table of Contents. He evidently tried to bring together, as compactly as he could without sacrificing the beauty of the originals, those Arthurian stories which had best pleased him. The title is indeed misleading, and its insufficiency is felt by Caxton, who presents an excuse for it in his colophon to the book: 'Thus endeth thys noble and Ioyous book entytled le morte Darthur/Notwythstandyng it treateth of the byrth/lyf/and actes of the sayd kyng Arthur/of his noble knyghtes of the rounde table/theyr meruayllous enquestes and aduentures/thachyeuyng of the sangreal/& in thende the dolorous deth & departyng out of thys world of them al.'

The aim of the author, then, was to furnish for English readers a compendium of the Arthurian stories, and to give in a rough chronological order the history of the life and times of Arthur, together with the chief exploits of his most famous knights. Some critics, in their enthusiasm for Malory's work, have fancied that the *Morte Darthur* deserves to be called an epic in prose. We may grant without hesitation that Malory has a vein of poetry, and that his feeling for style is exquisite. We may find somewhat of the epic breadth of treatment in parts of the story. But the book as a whole lacks the unity and the continuity of an epic; and we hardly gain in clearness of critical estimate by claiming for Malory what he would probably have been the first to disavow. If one wishes to hold that Malory wrote an epic in spite of himself, or chooses to dignify by the name of epic what is more exactly described as a collection of charming stories rather loosely tied together, there is no serious ground for a quarrel.

How Malory would have succeeded if he had tried to connect the parts of his book more closely, and had subordinated the episodes to one great central conception, we can hardly venture to say. What success he would have had with verse is also an idle question; but there is reason to fear that if he had attempted to versify the *Morte Darthur*, he would have added one more to the list of now forgotten books, of which the 15th century produced such an appalling number.

Malory's apparently simple task was far more difficult than we sometimes think. If he had worked upon originals that agreed with one another or that had been brought together according to a consistent plan, he could have proceeded mechanically to reduce their size by mere excision and then to translate what was left. But the French romances were not the work of a single author, and consequently they could not show unity of conception in delineation of character or agreement as to the relative importance of the various knights of the Round Table. The romances were produced in different periods and under different influences. Futhermore, the original romances, when once written, were so freely handled by copyists who omitted and added material at will that the final versions which lay before Malory presented contradictions not to be entirely overcome except by rewriting the whole according to a clearly conceived plan. It is not surprising, therefore, that here and there in the *Morte Darthur* a knight who has been suitably buried should reappear somewhat later as though the experience had done him no harm. Malory's success in avoiding the pitfalls that lay in his path must be evident even to the casual reader; but it can be fully realized only by one who compares the *Morte Darthur* with its sources.

Malory's purpose in writing his great romance was somewhat different from that of most of his predecessors who had attempted to tell Arthurian stories in English. For the most part, the earlier writers had contented themselves with translating or adapting a single French Arthurian romance or episode. From the beginning of the 13th century this Arthurian literature had been steadily growing, until in the course of two centuries and a half it included large tracts of Arthurian story. That it was of very unequal merit and of varying degrees of originality is exactly what we might expect. We cannot easily characterize in general terms productions so diverse in character as Laymon's *Brut*, the *Merlin* in verse, the *Merlin* in prose, the *Tristram* in verse, the exquisite *Sir Gawain and the Green Knight*, and the notable poems on the death of Arthur. This list is, of course, not complete; but, even when it is supplemented by all of the minor pieces, it is far from including the immense volume of Arthurian romance. Moreover, none of the pieces in prose or verse, nor all of them together, gave a connected view of the legends as a whole. Each romancer or translator presented an episode or group of episodes without caring much whether the separate stories could be harmonized. Then, too, the English versions were made at a time when the language was rapidly changing, and when dialectic differences threw real obstacles in the path of a reader. The fact that the versions were rare and scattered, and that the difficulty of communication presented a serious problem in the 15th century and greatly hindered acquaintance with books in a remote district, must also be taken into account in our endeavor to estimate what may have influenced Malory in his undertaking. Furthermore, the Arthurian literature in French was far too extensive to allow a reader, unless very favorably situated, to get acquainted with any considerable part of it. The MSS. cost much money and were out of the reach of any but the favored few. Yet the Arthurian stories had been for generations an important factor in the education of a gentleman; while, on the other hand, the earlier general familiarity of English gentlemen with French was daily becoming rarer, and a large number of those readers who would most appreciate the old stories could not read the original French versions. Malory had, then, many special incentives to encourage him in his work, and he could not well have had a fairer field in which to try his powers.

Whatever may have influenced Malory, he produced a book which cannot safely be neglected by the student of mediaeval life and manners, to say nothing of the reader who is interested in the *Morte Darthur* on purely literary grounds. One can hardly understand the spirit of the Middle Ages without giving much attention to the romances, and one can find no romance in English to compare with the *Morte Darthur*. Even though the life there depicted is neither English nor French, and though the narrative has little or no basis in reality, the picture which the romance presents has just enough resemblance to the real society to be highly suggestive. Of course the picture needs interpretation and modification, yet it presents in a vivid light the ideals of what we somewhat vaguely call chivalry, and is steeped in the spirit of the great feudal society. This spirit it was, we may well believe, that made the book popular in its own time, and this will doubtless win for it favor in centuries to come.

V.

We cannot properly estimate the originality of Malory's work without studying the materials that he used, and we ought therefore, if we had the space, to make a survey of the various forms of Arthurian literature existing at the time when Malory wrote, and also to consider the various theories concerning the origin of the romances. Yet the field thus opened is so vast, and the opinions on matters of detail are so divergent, that I can here do no more than indicate briefly what some of the problems are.

A glance at Caxton's Table of Contents to the *Morte Darthur* suggests that the book is a composite of several different romances. A careful reading of the book itself proves that there is no vital connection between the stories about Merlin and Balin and Tristram and Launcelot. A slight study of the older French literature enables us to see that the *Morte Darthur* is but a small part of a vast cycle of Arthurian romances. These romances have a common tie in that they all introduce Arthur and the Round Table; but many of them have so slight a connection that they require but little investigation to prove their independent origin.

We cannot here consider the source and development of the various branches of Arthurian romance represented in the *Morte*

Darthur, and we must therefore leave untouched the origin of the Launcelot and Tristram stories, as well as the questions connected with the legend of the Grail. The primary question, and the one which has most occupied the students of Arthurian romance, relates to the legends connected with Arthur himself.

[Discusses Breton and Welsh sources of Arthurian romances, Geoffrey, Wace, Chrétien, French prose cycles.]

VI.

After this brief study of the original materials of which the *Morte Darthur* is composed, we may well glance at the history of the book since its first publication and note the influence it has exerted upon later literature. There is some difficulty in tracing the influence of a great book like Malory's, for the suggestions that come from it may be so indirect that they cannot be followed. Yet the wonderful thing about the *Morte Darthur* is that, so far as we can follow it, we find it has been a perennial inspiration to poets, and that it has furnished the material, and even a part of the diction, of more than one exquisite poem. No other English book has called into being such a library of poetry as has the *Morte Darthur*. The bulk of this poetry is work of the 19th century, but traces of Malory's influence are not lacking in earlier centuries.

What sort of reception was given to Malory's book in his own century we do not precisely know, since we have no data concerning the size of the edition printed by Caxton and no contemporary allusion to it. Yet the fact that a second edition of so large a work was published within thirteen years may be taken as evidence of public favor. The continued popularity of the *Morte Darthur* throughout the 16th century is proved by the publication of four editions, and by the complaint of that sturdy old moralist Roger Ascham that people were reading the *Morte Darthur* when they might be better employed.[11]

When we consider with what infatuation aspiring scholars and the reading public in general greeted the newly discovered Latin and Greek classics in the period of the Revival of Learning, we may well be surprised that the *Morte Darthur* won favor while most of the other literature of the Middle Ages was being rapidly forgotten. In the early part of the century the versions of *Artus de la Bretagne* and of *Huon of Bourdeaux* by Lord Berners divided with Malory's book what interest was left for mediaeval literature, but they gradually lost their hold on the reading public, and seem to have been almost destitute of influence upon the later development of the literature. Malory indeed so far eclipsed his rivals that his is almost the only one of the early English Arthurian romances known even by name to the average modern reader.

Malory's popularity in the great transitional period of the 16th century is certainly remarkable, but the influence of his book was not strong enough to allure many English poets to enthusiastic original work in the Arthurian cycle. Most of the Arthurian literature of the 16th century is poor in quality and not remarkable for quantity. The single drama[12] on Arthur is hardly readable, and most of the other forms of literature touch the Arthurian cycle only incidentally. Writers seem to have felt that the old machinery of tournaments, and knights rescuing ladies, the killing of dragons, and the fulfillment of fantastic vows was worn out.[13] Satire and parody had begun to make the old conceptions ridiculous.[14] The writers who represented the popular taste turned for themes to Spain and to Italy, to Greece and to Rome, and to less hackneyed subjects suggested by real or legendary national history. Attention was also drawn more and more to the absorbing questions of the Reformation. Little wonder is it, then, that the *Morte Darthur* and other romances were, as living forces in literature,[15] simply crowded out.

The great apparent exception is Spenser's *Faerie Queene*. This does indeed borrow motives in great abundance from mediaeval chivalry and from Arthurian romance, but it contains only a few passages that suggest an acquaintance with Malory. We must believe that the *Morte Darthur* gave some inspiration to the poet, yet we find that the larger portion of the Arthurian material is drawn from Holinshed and from Hardyng.[16] The *Faerie Queene* was born out of due time, and although it is the noblest poetic achievement of the 16th century, it is, so far as external structure goes, in the strictest sense artificial, a literary *tour de force*.

The 17th and 18th centuries were, as a whole, out of sympathy with the spirit of Arthurian romance. A single edition of the *Morte Darthur* (1634) supplied the demand of the reading public up to the year 1816. We cannot say positively that the book was disliked, but we may be sure that it was little read. Neither Cavaliers nor Puritans knew much about the Middle Ages, and they cared less. Here and there an antiquary or a poet delved into the literature of the pre-Reformation period, but the attention of the public, and even of men of letters, was given to other matters. The men who wrote society verse and scribbled indecent plays for the delight of Charles the Second's court had no interest in Arthur or Launcelot or Galahad. Milton did indeed think of writing an Arthurian epic, and Dryden actually wrote an Arthurian opera, but they stood well-nigh alone. The epic was produced by the well-intentioned but long-winded Dr. Richard Blackmore, whose *Prince Arthur*, published in 1695, actually ran through several editions. No more convincing proof is needed of the difference in spirit between the age that produced Malory and the age that produced Blackmore. The sweet simplicity of the *Morte Darthur* is replaced by an ambitious combination of hobbling verse and moralizing twaddle. The prosing doctor was an estimable man, but he should have kept his hands off an Arthurian epic.

We cannot regard Blackmore's attempt and his tolerable vogue in his own day as evidence of Malory's popularity in the 17th and 18th centuries. There was no modernized edition of the *Morte Darthur*, and the prose of the 15th century, simple as it is in Malory's pages, doubtless presented just enough difficulty to repel readers who brought a languid interest to an old and partly forgotten book. The writers of the older period were too childishly simple to suit a hard-headed, matter-of-fact age such as the early 18th century. Naturally enough, then, the prevailing opinion concerning the older literature was that it was the product of a barbarous time and not worthy the attention of readers.

The gradual change in taste which marked the close of the 18th, and the beginning of the 19th, century, placed the Middle Ages in a truer light, and even led to an overestimate of the value of their artistic and ethical ideals. But along with the extravagances of Romanticism, there was a quick appreciation of the essential beauty of the Age of Chivalry, and a desire to adapt what was best in it to the needs of modern life. Yet Malory appears to have had comparatively little to do with the development of the Romantic movement in the latter part of the 18th century. Several of the poems of unknown age in Percy's *Reliques* (1765), such as *King Arthur's Death*, *The Legend of King Arthur*, *King Ryence's Challenge*, and *Sir Lancelot du Lake*, make considerable use of the *Morte Darthur*; but others, such as *The Boy and the Mantle*, *The Horn of King Arthur*, *The Grene Knight*, *Carle of Carlile*, and *The Marriage of*

Sir Gawaine, are based upon material not found at all in Malory. Both Percy and Warton had a tolerable acquaintance with the *Morte Darthur* and its relation to other literature, but there is little evidence that many other 18th-century scholars troubled themselves with the book at first hand.

The revival of interest in Malory during our own century is in marked contrast with the neglect of him in the 17th and early 18th centuries, and appears in many quarters. The publication of Southey's edition of Malory is a fact of great significance in the literary history of the last three generations. Southey wrote the introduction, but left the text of Malory to shift for itself,—somewhat to the disadvantage of the text. Yet the importance of his edition is not to be measured by its accuracy or philological value. Its significance lies in the fact that it appeared just at the time when the rediscovery of the Middle Ages had prepared young poets to read it and to be filled with its spirit. The impulse which it gave to the writing of poems based directly upon it or upon material connected with the Arthurian cycle has lasted down to our own day.

I shall not undertake in this rapid sketch to mention, much less to discuss, all the Arthurian poems that have appeared in our century. The proper treatment of the theme would require more detail than is possible here. A few of the best-known names may serve to indicate how deeply the Arthurian story has appealed to the poetic sense of our own time....

Of *The Idylls of the King* all but one are based upon Malory's *Morte Darthur*. The material is in some of the pieces treated very freely: *The Last Tournament*, for example, is an expansion of a few hints suggested by Malory, but in many poems the borrowing extends to words and phrases, transferred with a slight change of order to the new setting. Tennyson does indeed transform the spirit of some of Malory's stories so that familiar acquaintances appear new and strange, but he retains enough of his original to indicate where he went for his inspiration.

[Discusses Bulwer, Arnold, Morris, Hawker, Swinburne's *Tristram*.]

Swinburne's most recent work, *The Tale of Balen* (1896), follows closely the second book of *Le Morte Darthur*, and yet breathes a spirit of high poetry. Swinburne is far truer to his original than Tennyson is in his *Balin and Balan*, and, in the opinion of many readers, will seem no less effectively than the laureate to have mastered the lost art of the old romancers, the art of telling a story objectively but with the closest sympathy. In tender grace and simplicity nothing that Swinburne has written surpasses *The Tale of Balen*. On the other hand, nothing better demonstrates the essentially poetic character of Malory's *Morte Darthur* than the fact that it can be turned with little change into the form of noble poetry....

How much of this mass of poetry is in one way or another due to Malory we have already seen. So often, indeed, is the original hint or the actual source to be found in the *Morte Darthur* that we may at least raise the question whether the actual preservation of the Arthurian story as a living force in modern English literature is not largely due to Malory. The Arthurian ballads in Percy's *Reliques* have been almost destitute of literary influence. The vast Arthurian literature of the Middle Ages was, till recently, buried in unpublished MSS., and the recollection of it had utterly perished from the minds of the people. Popular traditions about Arthur have lingered with singular tenacity in remote districts, yet these traditions have not had sufficient vitality of power of attraction to bring the poets to utilize them in verse. The transmission of the Arthurian story is literary rather than popular. The legends cannot grow except by intentional deviation from the inherited forms. And these forms will doubtless continue to be most familiar in the shape which Malory gave them in *Le Morte Darthur*.

VII.

We have seen that *Le Morte Darthur* has held a remarkable place among the notable books of the last four hundred years. We have yet to consider how it is to be ranked as a piece of literature, and whether its importance is more than merely historical. Criticisms of various sorts have been passed upon the book, some ignorant and captious, some unmeasured in enthusiasm. Those readers who dislike it call it a dry, inartistic compilation, based upon ill-chosen originals; those who admire it call it a prose epic, the best romance in the language, a model of style, and one of the treasures of English literature. Evidently one who bases an opinion of the *Morte*

369

Darthur on what is written about it is very much at the mercy of the critics.

We may clear the ground at the outset by freely admitting that Malory's part is, in the main, that of a translator and adapter of French originals,[17] which he abridged and otherwise shaped to his purpose. Our estimate of his originality is made somewhat more difficult by the fact that we do not know what MSS. he had before him, and whether they were mutilated or complete. Sommer has made a laborious investigation of Malory's relation to his sources, and shown how largely he is dependent upon them. But even yet we have to face the possibility that gleanings in other MSS. still undiscovered would prove that some details now confidently claimed as Malory's invention are really due to his original.[18]

As was remarked in an earlier section, Malory's task looks to a modern reader much easier than it really was. The enormous mass of the Arthurian romances, doubtless greater in Malory's time than in our own, made anything like a comprehensive survey almost impossible. All the books were in MS., many of them difficult of access, if not inaccessible; they differed widely in the versions they presented, and were in many cases incomplete. A mere general acquaintance with the Arthurian cycle would have required years of time, and the mere translation of as large a book as the *Morte Darthur*, even had there been no attempt to give it literary form, must have involved an expenditure of long-continued effort. That Malory now and then went wrong in his choice is not to be wondered at; but it is gratuitous to assume that he deliberately rejected a good version for a bad one, and that he would not have taken the best if he could have got it.[19]

If we are tempted to think slightly of his work on the ground that it is a mere translation, we must remember that translation such as Malory's is exceedingly rare. Any one who imagines vigorous, idiomatic translation to be easy has evidently never attempted it. Malory is the peer of the greatest of the Elizabethan translators, and he enjoys the distinction of being yet read. How immeasurably he surpasses the modern scholars who now and then attempt a version of a piece of Old French may be seen by any one who will take the trouble to make the comparison. Real translation, that is, a transfer, not only of sense, but of spirit,[20] is quite as difficult as original composition. We may count on the fingers of one hand the English translators of prose before the year 1500 who deserve to be mentioned beside Malory. We naturally think first of Chaucer and Wyclif, the pseudo-Mandeville and Caxton, and of nameless writers like the translator of the prose *Merlin*. Single passages doubtless occur in the work of all of these men worthy to be placed beside that of Malory. It is when taken in the mass that Malory's superiority is evident.

But Malory was more than a mere translator: he realized that there was something to omit. Nearly all the other reproducers of French romances had slavishly followed every turn of the original. This is the method of the prose *Merlin*, of Herry Lonelich's metrical *Merlin* and *Holy Grail*, and of scores of other works. If the original were Holy Scripture there could hardly be more anxiety to preserve the *ipsissima verba*.

Omission is, in some cases, rather delicate work, too delicate even for Malory. And here, in the opinion of some critics, he mangles his material so badly as to make the original story at times almost unintelligible. Here and there Malory did bungle somewhat, if he really tried to reproduce one story and, in spite of himself, succeeded in telling quite another. This charge may be made to some extent against his treatment of the French prose *Merlin*. Yet there is in Malory's condensed version a lightness and rapidity of movement painfully lacking in part of the original, picturesque and interesting though much of that is.

The real question is this: What ought Malory to have done with the material at his disposal? The answers will vary according to individual preference. The chief fault found with the *Morte Darthur* as an artistic work is that its artistic purpose is too timid. It lacks complete unity, and does not move with a steady, undeviating sweep from beginning to end.[21] The episodes are too frequent and too long, and, though interesting, they have too little to do with the main current of the narrative. It is urged that Malory might have joined the whole more closely. Instead of making abrupt transitions from one part to another, and actually beginning some books as though they were entirely independent, he might have produced a great Arthurian epic conceived as a whole, with due subordination of parts and a central motive sufficient to carry the story to a natural conclusion. In other words, Malory ought to have done either more or less than he did: he ought to have used the French versions as crude material to be wrought into a new artistic creation, or else he ought to have proceeded more cautiously and have reproduced as exactly as possible the original stories.

It is, however, by no means certain that the separate parts would have been greatly improved by being made over into something new. The episodes are exquisite, and they have perhaps as much right to exist thus as have the separate poems in Chaucer's *Canterbury Tales* and *The Legend of Good Women*, or in Longfellow's *Tales of a Wayside Inn*. Doubtless a little more oiling of the machinery would have been possible, and, to modern notions, desirable; but there is at least a question whether a book constructed according to 19th-century ideals would have suited Malory's time better than the one he actually produced.

If we turn from the *Morte Darthur* to the French originals we see where the real difficulty lay. The primary defect of the French romances is a loosely constructed plot—or none at all—and an insufficiency of motive. All the characters are somewhat superficially conceived, and they do such strange and unnecessary things that orderly progression in the narrative is impossible. The unexpected constantly happens. If, then, Malory was to follow his original with any fidelity, he could not avoid faults of construction inherent in the French romances. In the embarrassment of choice he decided to reduce to convenient proportions the romances most suitable for his purpose, and to translate his story instead of attempting to create it. The contradictions in his work are in part those of his originals, made somewhat more glaring here and there from the fact that he attempted to combine into one book material scattered through several independent romances. The original stories were not made to be fitted together. The surprising fact is that they are combined in the *Morte Darthur* as well as they are.

If, then, the *Morte Darthur* falls short of the highest artistic excellence, in that it lacks unity, coherence, and proportion, it is nevertheless written in a style of singular charm and beauty, not indeed free from technical defects, but remarkable for freshness and vigor and the power of engaging attention. This last quality I have more than once tested by reading passages aloud to hearers who had no previous acquaintance with early English literature, and invariably finding that Malory won an interested hearing where other mediaeval writers were languidly received.

The technical defects in Malory's composition, judged by modern standards, are indeed obvious enough. His paragraphs are formless and are constructed on no discoverable principle,—even of length. Some of them hold closely to a single topic, but they are as likely as not to wander in several directions at once. Malory is, of course, in this matter no greater sinner than other early writers. Paragraph construction is a modern art, and Malory is hardly to be blamed for failing to do what nobody else thought of. Moreover, narrative is not so easy to divide into paragraphs as writing of another sort. Possibly, too, Caxton or his printers made the divisions, which are surely as mechanical as if they had been made by accident.

Malory's sentences are not entirely above criticism. Some are as halting and clumsy and disjointed as though they had followed every turn of expression in the original and had never been revised. Indeed, the fact that Caxton divided the work into books and chapters and passed the whole through the press as an editor makes it unlikely that Malory ever saw the printed pages. But Malory or somebody is apparently unable to decide exactly when a sentence should end. He ignores 'regularity, uniformity, precision, balance.' He runs on through half a page, introducing new clauses with *and* and bolstering them up with more clauses beginning with *for*.[22] Modern punctuation helps the matter somewhat, but not altogether.

Syntax, in the sense of subordination of parts, is scarcely known; parataxis is the characterisitc form. Now and then he writes a sentence that is a mere chaos of cross-purposes, defying all analysis. Like the early writers in the Old English Chronicle and the authors of the Icelandic sagas, he changes the construction[23] without warning, and turns from indirect discourse to direct and back again within the limits of a single sentence. Like careless writers of our own time, he introduces dependent clauses with *that*, and before he gets to the end of his sentence repeats[24] the word so as to make sure that the reader is following him. He is careless of his arrangement, of his emphasis, of his concords. His pronouns choose their antecedents by a process of natural selection. In short, he is now and then guilty of well-nigh all the sins that the grammarian bids us shun.

In all this Malory deserves no special reprobation. He shares the faults of the writers of his time. What makes his work notable is that notwithstanding these defects his style instantly impresses its charm upon the reader. Its very carelessness lends an added grace and beauty. It has an air of perfect breeding and courtly distinction and yet the elastic ease of polished conversation. Even the sentences that abound in faults of construction are as clear as a mountain brook. The musical quality of the phrases, which nevertheless generally avoid the rhythm of verse,[25] is marvellous. Malory's style has the simplicity of genius; it is always perfectly adapted to its object, and so is perfectly natural. It never strives for effect; it has no forced antitheses, no mere smartness of phrase, no tricks of alliteration and euphuistic affectation. In other words, it is an honest style, the transparent medium through which we see the writer's thought.

In nothing does Malory's excellence so plainly appear as in the color and freshness of his diction. He proved that the homely phrase of the street or the camp or the hunting-field might be the most picturesque instrument of literary expression.

As might be expected from the fact that in his pages the expression is closely fitted to the thought, the proportion of native English words is unusually large.[26] Yet Malory is no purist. He borrows French words without hesitation when he can make his expression more effective. Hence he very successfully avoids any appearance of bookishness. He is as natural as if he were talking to his friends. Nothing indicates the self-consciousness of a man who has decided to create a masterpiece—if he can. He acts like a plain man who has a plain task,—to reduce a set of French romances to portable form, and to suppress his own personality as much as possible.

Yet Malory is no mere machine through which the French romances pass in order to become English. He is keenly alive to the beauty of the scenes he describes, and his words vibrate with the emotion he feels. He is perhaps at his best in passages that describe something high and holy. When the Grail sweeps through Arthur's hall amid cracking and crying of thunder, and every knight looks in dumb surprise at his fellow, when Launcelot bows before the altar where the Grail is kept and feels his body shot through with fire, when the dead Launcelot rests in the solemn choir of Joyous Gard and the lament breaks from the lips of his brother Ector, the expression rises to a poetic beauty not surpassed in early English prose. In pathos Malory's exquisite tact never fails him. He chooses the simplest words, and suppresses all rhetoric and all impertinent reflection. His story of Balin and Balan, of Elaine, of the death of

Arthur, and of the wasting away of Guenever and Launcelot is told so artlessly that we forget the writer and have no thought except for the mournful tale.

The charm of mediaeval naïveté Malory shares with other writers of the pre-Renaissance period. What is remarkable in his work is an individuality that can be felt, but hardly expressed in words. There is a personal note in the *Morte Darthur*, evident enough to the attentive reader, notwithstanding the fact that the writer never obtrudes his personality upon us. For this very reason Malory's style is forever lost to us. Our age is steeped in a different spirit. We think in different forms. Our childhood has gone, and we can never bring back the childlike grace that belongs to a departed age.

Yet Malory shows no signs of decaying popularity. No more enthusiastic praise has been given in any century to the *Morte Darthur* than in our own. The book has outlived a half-dozen literary fashions, and bids fair to survive as many more. As marking the high-water level of 15th-century prose, as containing the source of some of the recognized classics in our literature, as being filled with the life and spirit of a deeply interesting age, and pervaded with the more enduring qualities of our common humanity, the *Morte Darthur* can hardly fail to claim in years to come its circle of admiring readers. Students of literature will read it for its historic importance; the poets will continue to find in it the themes of verse; and the general reader who goes to literature for rest and entertainment will not refuse to the *Morte Darthur* a place among the books of perennial interest. If all this be true, it must be admitted that the *Morte Darthur* holds a unique place. Exactly what is its relative rank among the great books of English prose, we need not be greatly concerned to know. Malory's *Morte Darthur* is assuredly one of the golden links that unite our age to his. If its beauty is lost upon a modern reader, there is little use in trying to force his admiration: if its beauty is felt, there is no need of further argument.

SELECTED NOTES

1 This section on Sir Thomas Malory and his family is contributed by Professor George Lyman Kittredge of Harvard University.
2 The reader will remember that the public records which furnish us with

so much information about Chaucer say not a word about his poetry.

3 That is, in Caxton's Preface.

4 'Sir *priest*' is out of the question, though some have absurdly suggested it (see the reference in Sommer, ii, 2, n.1).

5 This chapter is in part a reprint of an article entitled 'Who was Sir Thomas Malory?' published in 1897 in the Harvard *Studies and Notes in Philology and Literature*, iv, 85–105. The reader is referred to that article for the details of the evidence as well as for a discussion of the baseless theory that Malory was a Welshman. The conjectural identification discussed in the present chapter was made public by the writer Mar. 15, 1894, at a meeting held at Columbia College in honor of Friedrich Diez (cf. *Mod. Lang. Notes*, April, 1894, ix, 253). It was put on record by the writer in a brief article on Malory published in 1894 in vol. v. of *Johnson's Universal Cyclopaedia* (p. 498). In July, 1896, Mr. T.W. Williams, who had, very naturally, not seen the brief article in *Johnson's Cyclopaedia*, suggested (*Athenaeum*, No. 3585) that the author of the *Morte* might be a 'Thomas Malorie, miles' whom he had found mentioned in a document of the eighth year of Edward IV, but concerning whom he had no information except the single fact furnished by the document itself. Mr. Williams's Thomas Malory and the writer's are probably one and the same person.

6 The name is variously spelled, but was always trisyllabic.

7 Cf. Caxton's Preface: 'Many novle and dyvers gentylmen of thys royame of England camen and demaunded me many and oftymes wherfore that I have not do made & emprynte the noble hystorye of the saynt greal and of the moost renomed crysten kyng...kynge Arthur.'

8 In Warwickshire.

9 John Rous, *Life of Richard Earl of Warwick*, as printed from MS. Cotton. Julius E. IV, by Strutt, *Horda Angel-cynnan*, 1775–76, ii, 125, 126. Rous died Jan. 1492; Beauchamp, May 31, 1439.

10 For similar incidents in romance, see Ward, *Catalogue of Romances*, i, 733 ff., with which cf. Malory's *Morte Darthur*, Bk. vii, chs. xxviii, xxix, Sommer, i, 257 ff.

11 Ascham's remarks have been often quoted, but they are too important to be passed over with a mere reference. [Quotes Ascham, No. 4A.]

12 Thomas Hughes's *Misfortunes of Arthur* (1587). This owes little or nothing to Malory. Printed in *Dodsley's Old Plays*, ed. Hazlitt, iv, 249–343. Hathway's play on *The Life and Death of Arthur, King of England* is mentioned in Henslow's *Diary*, Apr. 11, 12, 1598, but is not otherwise known.

13 It is at least possible that the *Morte Darthur* suggested some of the characters that played a part in the festivities at Kenilworth in 1575 [see above, Nos. 4B and 8], only five years after Ascham's complaint...that

the book was too much read. In *The Princelye Pleasures at the Courte at Kenelwoorth*... we learn that the Lady [of the Lake] had been compelled to remain in the Lake by 'Sir Bruse, sauns pittie, in revenge of his cosen Merlyne, the Prophet, whom for his inordinate lust she had inclosed in a Rocke.' No such relationship is hinted at in the *Morte Darthur*, and no exploit exactly like this is assigned to Breuse saunce pyte, who is, nevertheless, frequently mentioned. Breuse is credited with several villainous performances in the *Morte Darthur*, such as following a lady to slay her... and killing a lady's brother and keeping her at his own will.... He may, therefore, have seemed to be a suitable character to be pressed into such service as was desired at the festivities. Literal reproduction of the Arthurian legends was not desired, for novelty was the chief aim in the whole entertainment; but the romantic motives and the names were as likely to have been suggested by the *Morte Darthur* as by any Arthurian literature that has come down to us.

14 A marked instance of the spirit in which the old romances were regarded is seen in Beaumont and Fletcher's *Knight of the Burning Pestle* (1610), which was evidently suggested by *Don Quixote* (1605). Rabelais's burlesque of the extravagances of chivalry appeared as early as 1532.

15 Robert Chester's *King Arthur*, printed in *The Annuals of great Brittaine*, London, 1611 (ed. Grosart), pp. 34–80, shows considerable acquaintance with Malory's book, particularly in the address To the courteous Reader, p. 35, and in the first division of the poem.

16 For a list of references to the passages in the *Faerie Queene*, where the Arthurian story principally appears, see Littledale's *Essays on Tennyson's Idylls of the King* (London, 1893), p. 17. Spenser's chief sources for the poem as a whole were, of course, Ariosto and Tasso.

17 If we could count Bk. vii as Malory's own composition, his originality would have to be rated much higher than it commonly is. No source has yet been found.

18 This, as is well known, is the result of the searching study of Chaucer within the last twenty-five years. This, too, was my own experience in studying the French sources of the Middle-English prose romance of *Merlin*. In two cases, in particular, I had decided that the translator had inserted a considerable amount of matter of his own, but somewhat later I found in other MSS. the original of the supposed additions.

19 A word on the *Tristram* fragment may not be out of place. Malory is sometimes blamed for not finishing his version of the *Tristram*. The story is developed through four books (viii, ix, x, xii), but it is not concluded in Bk. xii, and yet is not again taken up. There is indeed an artistic incompleteness in the unfinished work, but we cannot be sure that Malory is to blame. He may not have had a complete copy of the

French *Tristan* at hand; he may have worked at the story as long as his original held out and then turned temporarily to another part of the work till he should be able to get the missing original. Caxton, as we know, divided the *Morte Darthur* into books and chapters. He may have received the whole complete from Malory's hands, and for some reason have thrown out a portion of the Tristram story. Furthermore, we do not know in what chronological order Malory translated the various parts. He may have left the Tristram story till the last, and death may have overtaken him in the midst of his work. The entire lack of biographical detail makes easy an endless range of conjecture. In short, the same excuses that we may make for Chaucer failing to complete the *Canterbury Tales*, or for Spenser for failing to complete the *Faerie Queene*, or for Macaulay for failing to complete the *History of England*, may possibly be made for Malory.

20 It must not be forgotten that the praise bestowed upon the English Bible as a piece of unequalled musical prose, is bestowed upon a translation.

21 The story of Balin and Balan (Bk. ii) does not grow out of the book that precedes it. The story of Tristram calls for a violent transition, and it is at best but a fragment. The tale of Beaumayns (Bk. vii) is exceedingly attractive, yet it might be omitted without any one's suspecting the loss. And so on throughout the book.

Nothing, indeed, can well be more unlike the modern novel with its carefully interwoven plot, its well-grounded motives, its subtle analysis of character, than the *Morte Darthur*, with its simple story, its artless movement from one thing to another without any very sufficient reason, and its transparent characters, who, in any given situation, may always be expected to act in a particular fashion. Moreover, the story here and there drags a little. A reader must have a well-developed appetite for unimportant detail who can take in the entire description of a mediaeval battle without wincing.

22 Yet we cannot hold Malory responsible for all the *ands* and *fors*. A glance at his originals reveals *car* and *et* in abundance.

23 The abrupt change from indirect discourse to direct is too common to require illustration. The following are good instances of Malory's broken constructions. [Gives several examples.]

24 This sort of repetition is common in the oldest English.

25 Malory's choice of diction seems, however, to have been half unconscious; otherwise he would perhaps hardly have left such jingles as the following: 'alle the estates were longe or day in the chirche for to praye.' [Cites several examples.]

26 Marsh... [see No. 23] comments upon the small percentage of French words in Malory....

50. G.H. Maynadier
1907

Gustavus Howard Maynadier (1867–1960), professor of English at Harvard University, wrote introductions to novels of Defoe, Fielding, and Smollett, and also published a book on sources and analogues to the 'Wife of Bath's Tale'. The work quoted below, *The Arthur of the English Poets*, grew, he says in its preface, from a course for his Harvard and Radcliffe students begun in 1900. Maynadier notes, too, that MacCallum's book (No. 48) was then the only one on the subject that was both 'accurate and readable'. Maynadier's range is wider than that of MacCallum, and his discussion of pre-Renaissance Arthurian literature much more extensive.

Maynadier begins the chapter on Malory with a summary of Kittredge's biographical findings (see No. 49 above) omitted here. His assessment of Malory's talent stresses characterization and style over construction, but he does call the work epic and gives Malory some credit for originality. The book is a Riverside Press Edition (Boston: Houghton Mifflin, 1907), pp. 218–46.

Remarkable as it is that the author of so important a work as the *Morte Darthur* should till recently have been known only by name, such is nevertheless the case. You will search the *Dictionary of National Biography* in vain for definite information about him. It remained for Professor Kittredge of Harvard University to discover, not many years ago, the few facts that are known regarding this writer of the most popular mediaeval romance. In setting them forth I cannot do better, for the most part, than quote directly from Professor Kittredge's article, *Who Was Sir Thomas Malory?* [See No. 49]...

As Professor Kittredge says, this Malory was just the man to write the *Morte Darthur*. His birth, education, and training fitted him to do so. Excluded from the pardon issued by Edward IV, he had to keep out of public life, even in his native Warwickshire.

Under such conditions an elderly gentleman with the literary taste which Malory must have had, would have been likely to seek literary diversion. It is difficult not to agree with Professor Kittredge's conclusion that 'we have before us a Sir Thomas Malory who, so far as one can see, fulfils all the conditions required of a claimant for the honor of having written the *Morte Darthur*. There is absolutely no contestant, and until such a contestant appears, it is not unreasonable to insist on the claims of this Sir Thomas.'

Fortunately for English literature, Malory, so well fitted to produce the *Morte Darthur*, lived at a time which demanded it. We have seen that about the middle of the fifteenth century the Arthurian stories were very popular in England. And yet, outside of the chronicles, which omitted many of the most romantic and interesting adventures in the Round Table stories, there was in English nothing like a comprehensive history of Arthur and his knights. Malory, doubtless long familiar with most of the stories, decided now to write such a history. Accordingly he set to work, we may imagine, to acquaint himself with stories which he did not know, and to make selections for his new compilation from French romances and English, chiefly from the former....

Malory was not the first to collect disconnected Round Table stories in one volume. The prose *Lancelot* and the prose *Tristram* of the thirteenth century made in their later forms some attempt to bring various Arthurian stories together. In the latter part of the same century, Rusticiano da Pisa made a still more comprehensive collection of Round Table stories—that Rusticiano, who, finding himself in a Genoese jail in 1298, took down from the lips of a fellow prisoner, Marco Polo, the famous story of his adventures in Tartary and China. Rusticiano's Arthurian compilation, which included several of the most important tales of the Round Table, is said to be one of the most stupidly composed of the whole cycle.[1] It is full of signs of haste; the different stories are so badly joined that adventures of Tristram's maturity are followed by adventures of his father's youth. Yet Rusticiano's work, both in French, in which it was originally composed, and in Italian, into which it was translated, had considerable literary influence. Prior to Malory's richer compilation, it was the most important Arthurian work of its kind.

More than in his plan, Malory was original in the execution of it.

He was original in emphasising Arthur as the central figure of his tale. Though he takes the Merlin legend for the source of his first books, he does not go back to the very beginning, as many mediaeval writers would have done, and tell what happened to Merlin and Vortigern long before Arthur was born. Instead he begins with the meeting of Uther Pendragon, king of all England, and the lady Igraine, whom he loved, and on whom—in the shape of her husband, the Duke of Cornwall, assumed by Merlin's magic aid—he begot the mighty Arthur. And after the great King's death, Malory delays his conclusion only to narrate the death of Guinevere in the nunnery at Almesbury and her burial beside the king, and Lancelot's death in the monastery at Glastonbury and his burial at Joyous Gard. It is no violation of unity thus to bring these two, like every fair lady and brave knight, to the grave, for the interest of the book is in them as much as in the King.

Malory showed some originality, too, in the selection of his stories, and of the incidents in them—an originality not always commendable. Though it is impossible to know how wide his acquaintance was with Arthurian romances, it is reasonable to suppose that he had knowledge of more than he included in his compilation. Either through choice or ignorance he left out some very good stories, like that of the Green Knight; and he sometimes made use of the poorer versions of those which he included, as in narrating the death of Tristram, who, according to Malory, was treacherously slain by Mark while harping before Iseult. Besides, when he took his *Morte Darthur* out of 'certain books of French and reduced it into English,' he did not 'reduce' enough. There are too many inconsequent adventures, too many tournaments and single combats of similar nature. When one chapter is headed 'Yet of the same battle,' it seems unnecessary to follow it by two, each headed 'Yet more of the same battle.' But a critic should remember the difficulties that confronted Malory, and the perplexing number of stories and the confusion of the long, rambling narratives from which he had to select.

In still another way Malory was original, though not conspicuously so, because he was but doing what others had done before him. All the English Arthurian writers had Anglicised their Celtic-French material. Malory, at the end of the line of mediaeval romancers, was near enough to our own time to make the England of his Arthur, when not altogether unreal, something like the

England we know. The Archbishop (or Bishop, as Malory calls him) of Canterbury plays as important a part as he might play in the reign of an historical English sovereign. Queen Guinevere's excuse to put off her nuptials with Mordred, that she had to go up to London 'to buy all manner of things that longed unto the wedding,' makes her almost a bride of to-day.[2] Then her conduct when once in London, throwing herself into the Tower and sustaining a siege from Mordred, recalls Margaret of Anjou, who, in Malory's own time, had shown herself a woman of similar martial spirit in opposing the forces of Edward IV. And as the climax of Malory's realistic Englishing, there is that beautiful English Maying of immortal freshness: 'So it befell in the month of May, Queen Guenever called unto her knights of the Table Round, and she gave them warning that early upon the morrow she would ride on maying into woods and fields beside Westminster'.

[Quotes from Bk xix, chaps 1 and 2.]

I have quoted this not only for its fresh English treatment of nature, but also for its liveliness and picturesque mediaeval vividness—qualities which go far towards making Malory's *Morte Darthur*, more than four centuries and a quarter after its composition, a book which publishers find profitable to bring out. No one can read Malory long without feeling that vividness is one of the distinguishing qualities of his style. Not that he paints realistic pictures on a large scale; only small ones he could paint well: but with distinct little pictures his *Morte Darthur* is filled. I do not mean the conventional pictures, such as you find in the narration of single combats;—how the two knights come together like thunder so that their horses fall down, how they avoid them lightly, and then rush at one another like boars, racing, tracing, and foining, either giving other sad strokes the while, till one knight is overcome. This may seem vivid the first time you read it, but it is less so the second, and not at all so the twentieth time. There are other miniatures, however, always vivid, never monotonous, because, besides being as specific as the formula just cited, they are individual. 'And in the midst of the lake Arthur was ware of an arm clothed in white samite, that held a fair sword in that hand.' 'Now...speak we of Sir Launcelot du Lake that lieth under the apple tree sleeping. Even about the noon there came by him four queens of great estate; and, for the heat of the sun should not annoy them, there rode four knights about them and bare a cloth of green silk on four spears, betwixt them and the sun, and the queens rode on four white mules.' 'Sir Tristram ... came a soft trotting pace toward them.' 'Queen Guenever ... let make herself a nun, and wore white clothes and black, and ... lived in fastings, prayers, and alms-deeds, that all manner of people marvelled how virtuously she was changed.' Such concrete bits, though making Malory's *Morte Darthur* a succession of wonderfully vivid little pictures, nevertheless do not make it real as a whole. The Britain which it presents has reality here, and again there, but never continuous, logical reality like Homer's heroic Greece, or Dickens's middle-class England, or Hawthorn's Puritan New England. Britain with Malory, as with the Arthurian writers before him, is after all a romantic nowhere.

The characters in this nowhere, like the background, are real only at times, but then very much so. Lancelot, for instance, is thoroughly alive when, on one of his visits to a well in Windsor Forest, where he liked to 'lie down, and see the well spring and bubble, and sometime he slept there,' he is unfortunate enough to encounter a lady of no more accurate aim than many others of her sex. While he slept one day, this lady, who, Malory says, was 'a great huntress,' aiming an arrow at a hind, by misfortune overshot the hind, and 'the arrow smote Sir Lancelot in the thick of the thigh, over the barbs. When Sir Lancelot felt himself so hurt, he hurled up woodly, and saw the lady that had smitten him. And when he saw that she was a woman, he said thus, Lady or damsel, what that thou be, in an evil time bare ye a bow, the devil made you a shooter.' When Iseult was tired of disputing with Palamides, 'then La Beale Isoud held down her head, and said no more at that time.' When Lancelot had overcome Meliagrance, and looked to Guenever to see what she would have done with the caitiff, 'then the queen wagged her head... as though she would slay him. Full well knew Sir Lancelot by the wagging of her head that she would have had him dead.' And often these knights and ladies speak as well as move like real people, though never with marked indi-viduality.

Yet with all their external reality, Malory's characters are only partially alive, for Malory had but little psychological interest in them and but little invention. Accepting his people as he found them, he did not develop them further. One result of thus taking them from his sources unchanged, is that his characters are full of incongruities. Such is Malory's Gawain, who, in his attitude toward Guinevere and Lancelot, is more like the noble Gawain of the twelfth-century French romances and of the Gawain poems of northwestern England, than that Gawain in the earlier pages of Malory, who is as base to Pelleas, in his relations with Ettard, as Tennyson's Gawain.

But though Malory's characters are more or less contradictory, though you may read for pages without feeling one character distinct from another, yet when you get to the end of the *Morte Darthur*, you find that the most important have taken on some individuality. Especially is this true of the three chief personages— Arthur, Lancelot, and Guinevere. Of them Arthur is the least distinct: though he takes shape as a right kingly king, he is conventionally so. He spends most of his time sitting on his throne, presiding at his feasts, cheering the knights who are about to start on their quests, or welcoming those who return. When he is active himself, he seems often less a free agent than a puppet in the hands of his advisers, as in his war against Lancelot. Only now and then is he independently active, as in his young days, when he so boldly asserts and confirms his right to his father's throne. Afterwards he seldom wins our sympathy, except occasionally when he flings out at some one in righteous rage, as at Sir Bedivere when he tells the King falsely that he has thrown Excalibur into the lake. . . .

Lancelot is more individual than Arthur and more human, the strong man of noble feelings, in whom rages the conflict which will not end; the knight whose word is ever truth, save when he declares that Guinevere has always been a true wife to Arthur; the knight of greatest honor and greatest dishonor, for he was false to the friend who trusted him. And yet Malory's Lancelot is not so much to be condemned as Tennyson's, for though Arthur esteems Lancelot in the *Morte Darthur* as the first of his knights, there is not that remarkable love between the two which is one of the noble things in the *Idylls of the King*. Apart from his great fault, Malory's Lancelot like Tennyson's, is all but faultless. With all his prowess, he has that virtue of humility which his son Galahad lacked, as witness the story of Sir Urre of Hungary. . . .

Then, too, Lancelot is remarkably patient towards Guinevere. Without blaming the Queen for her whimsical tyranny, the natural result of her uncertain relations with Lancelot, we cannot help feeling that at times her knight had much to bear. When the Queen, for instance, at one moment upbraided him for having loved the maid of Astolat, and almost the next for not having loved her, we could have pardoned Lancelot a harsh reply instead of the gentle reproof. . . .

And there is Guinevere herself, who, were she known nowhere else than in Malory's *Morte Darthur*, would be one of the great epic queens of the world. Of her it may be said, as of so many other women whose lives go to wreck, that had she but had children to take her love and attention, the tragedy might have been averted. Proud and passionate, unreasonable in her demands on Lancelot, vindictive, as when she wags her head to have Meliagrance killed, she can be, and generally is, sweetly gracious, womanly, and queenly. We can understand that Sir Pelleas, Sir Ozanna le Cure Hardy, and the rest were willing to risk their lives fighting for her in the forest against the greater force of Meliagrance; not only was she their queen, but a woman who in the best womanly way would requite them for their services. When, sore wounded, they were captives, like Guinevere herself, in the castle of the craven prince, 'in no wise the queen would not suffer the wounded knights to be from her, but . . . they were laid within draughts by her chamber, upon beds and pillows, that she herself might see to them, that they wanted nothing.' And when finally shame and sorrow came, she was not only courageous in her resistance of Mordred, but also firmly self-sacrificing in her refusal to live her last days in love at Joyous Gard with Lancelot. . . .

Poor lady, who never found peace in her palaces of Westminster and Cardigan, Carlisle and Camelot, she found something of it finally, after she took her last leave of Lancelot, in this nunnery at quiet Almesbury, there to the southeast of Salisbury Plain in the valley of the Wiltshire Avon, with its stately trees, green fields, and low hills rising all around, where nothing seems to move but the cool, quick-flowing little river.

One reason that Malory's characters are only partially real is that he lacked the humor essential to the best realism. Such as he had is general, conventional, and broad. Lancelot, for example, like Fielding's equally chivalrous but less romantic Parson Adams, gets into the wrong bed, where he is surprised by the arrival of a knight, who takes him for quite a different person. It is in short the humor of the practical joke, like that of so many of Shakspere's Falstaffian scenes, and of some in *Don Quixote* and most in *Peregrine Pickle*, though far less amusing. When Sir Dinadan, overthrown at jousting by Sir Lancelot disguised as a maid, is dressed in woman's garments and brought before Queen Guinevere, she laughs till she falls down; and the same knight often diverts La Beale Isoud to a like degree; but a modern reader can scarce smile faintly at his fun.

More intellectual humor is almost wholly wanting. Though Malory makes much of the lay which Eliot the Harper composed at the instigation of Sir Dinadan to sing before King Mark, to the vast entertainment of all Mark's enemies who heard it, he never quotes so much as one word of the lay, which, had he been really a humorist, he would probably have quoted entire.[3] In fine, Malory gives no delicately humorous touches to his narrative, with one or two possible exceptions. When the Bishop of Canterbury 'does' his threatened curse on the incorrigible Mordred, with book, bell, and candle, it is 'in the most orgulous wise that might be done.' Were this in Chaucer, we should think it a hit at the self-importance of a haughty church dignitary; but, being in Malory, the passage is probably amusing not by intent, but only on account of its quaint expression. This brings us to the cause of much that seems humorous in Malory to-day. For instance, Arthur's reply to King Ryence, who sends the extraordinary message that he wishes Arthur's beard given him to trim his mantle, is humorous chiefly because of its archaic language: ' "Well," said Arthur, "thou hast said thy message, the which is the most villainous and lewdest message that ever man heard sent unto a king; also thou mayest see my beard is full young yet to make a trimming of it. But tell thou thy king this: I owe him none homage, nor none of mine elders; but or it be long he shall do me homage on both his knees, or else he shall lose his head, by the faith of my body, for this is the most shamefulest message that ever I heard speak of." ' Here the serious acceptance of an absurdly impossible situation, not less than the phrasing, amuses the modern reader; and it is these, his odd phrasing and his unnecessary seriousness, that produce one of Malory's charms, his quaintness.

Mere quaintness is not enough to keep a book alive for centuries; and since both the characters and the background of Malory's narrative have only partial reality, one naturally asks, what is it further which has given the *Morte Darthur* its long life? It cannot be excellence of plot, for we have already remarked that Malory, in 'reducing from French to English,' by no means got rid of all superfluous material, a fault which to some extent spoils the unity of his work. And yet when one considers that nearly every adventure is brought into some connection with Arthur, one must say that the book fails not so much in unity as in coherence. The chief trouble is that Malory has too many stories to tell, all of which he is so anxious to work in that he is seldom off with one before he is on with another. The result is often extreme confusion. Now and then, to be sure, a story stands out distinctly, as the tale of those unfortunate brothers, Balin and Balan, or that of the young knight, Gareth, and the scornful damsel, Linet; but for the most part, no uninterrupted tale runs through a whole book. I myself do not altogether mind this weaving together of many threads. Though most of us are agreed, I suppose, that the secret of art is selection, there may be so much selection as to produce an effect of simplicity which no human being is likely to experience after childhood, and then only rarely. Malory is guilty of no such simplicity. In the suddenly interrupted companionships and friendships and loves of his knights and ladies, in their continual meetings with the unexpected, a reader who will may see something of the confusion of actual life. Indeed, Malory has that without which the highest art does not exist—a sense of the mystery of life. He is as far from being confined by fact as most writers of the eighteenth century were from getting beyond it. From the beginning of his tale, with the love of Uther Pendragon for the Lady Igraine, to its conclusion, the death upon a Good Friday in the Holy Land of the last four knights of the Round Table, who have gone thither to do battle 'upon the miscreants or Turks,' Malory is never unconscious of the poetic wonder of this world, of the truths which we feel rather than know.

For a wider circle of readers a great charm of Malory's story is its rapidity; there is scarcely ever a cessation of action. From the first sentence, which tells of the war between Uther and the Duke of Tintagil, to the author's valedictory,—'Here is the end of the whole book of King Arthur ... and ... I pray you all pray for my soul,'—something is always happening. Sometimes the action is too rapid; it takes your breath away; but on the whole it is refreshing in these days when morbid introspection and hesitation too often prevent doing.

After all, though, the most potent charm of Malory is his style. It is not a style suited to the essay, as may be seen by looking at his childishly and delightfully ingenuous little chapter on true love and the month of May, which begins: 'And thus it passed on from Candlemas until after Easter, that the month of May was come, when every lusty heart beginneth to blossom and to bring forth fruit; for like as herbs and trees bring forth fruit and flourish in May, in likewise every lusty heart, that is in any manner a lover, springeth and flourisheth in lusty deeds;' and soon runs its brief, illogical course, concluding: 'Therefore all ye that be lovers call unto your remembrance the month of May, like as did Queen Guenever. For whom I make here a little mention, that while she lived she was a true lover, and therefore she had a good end.' After which comes the account of Guinevere's Maying, to which this chapter is leading up.

Now and then the style is tangled and inorganic, as in the sentence which tells of Sir Tristram's death:—

> Also that traitor king slew the noble knight Sir Tristram, as he sat harping afore his lady La Beale Isoud, with a trenchant glaive, for whose death was much bewailing of every knight that ever were in Arthur's days: there were never none so bewailed as was Sir Tristram, and Sir Lamorak, for they were traitorously slain, Sir Tristram by King Mark, and Sir Lamorak by Sir Gawaine and his brethren.

But what if Malory sometimes writes sentences which would keep a boy from passing his college examinations? What if he is hopelessly unreasonable in the use of the connectives 'and' and 'so'? In Malory's prose, as in that of few other authors, is there beautiful rhythm. Besides, he is dignified, simple, and generally direct; excellently specific, as we have seen; and now, after the lapse of years, charmingly quaint. It is the excellence of his style, in fact, that makes Malory the earliest English prose writer of whom we can read many pages at a time with pleasure. Except for the Book of Common Prayer, the *Morte Darthur* is the best known English prose before the King James Bible, whose style it frequently suggests; and when you have added to these three the *Pilgrim's Progress*, you have virtually all the English prose before Queen Anne's day which is still widely read.

In fine, Malory lives because he is a great epic writer. He has the three epic traits which Matthew Arnold justly ascribes to Homer—

swiftness, simplicity, nobility. Like Homer, he has swiftness only in detail; he does not hurry us to the final catastrophe. Often he takes us aside, rather than ahead, but only for the moment; he leads us after all pretty steadily towards his end. And always he is simple and noble in diction, and generally simple and noble in thought. If you will see Malory at his best, read the chapter which tells of Arthur's departure for Avalon. ...

Tennyson's *Passing of Arthur*, which this chapter inspired, is not nobler.

SELECTED NOTES

1 Paulin Paris, *Manuscrits Français*, Paris, 1838, ii, 358.
2 Both this excuse and the Bishop of Canterbury's hostility to Mordred appear in the octosyllabic *Morte Arthur*, but without seeming so real as in Malory.
3 The lay, to be sure, is not given in detail in the French prose *Tristram*, nor do we get any definite idea of its contents, though enough is said about it to excite our interest.

51. George Saintsbury

1885, 1898, 1912

George Edward Batemen Saintsbury (1845–1933), historian, influential literary critic, reviewer, and successor to David Masson's Chair in English Literature at Edinburgh from 1895 to 1915, was a prolific writer, producing dozens of books and having had some part in more than four hundred. A convenient source of information on Saintsbury's life and works is Walter Leuba, *George Saintsbury*, Twayne English Authors Series (New York, 1967).

Saintsbury's remarks on Malory are drawn from three sources, spaced over some twenty-five years and reflecting an increasing critical appreciation of Malory's genius and art. In 1885, Saintsbury chose selections from the *Morte Darthur* to begin his *Specimens of English Prose Style from Malory to*

Macaulay, but he led off with the interpolation from the edition of Wynkyn de Worde (see No. 2), and his remarks in the preface and headnote are not markedly enthusiastic. By 1898, however, in *A Short History of English Literature*, he is calling the *Morte Darthur* a 'great and original book' and rebutting neo-classical strictures on Malory's ineptness as an organizer with an important question: rather than ask what Malory might have done had he written to the standards of a later age, we are to ask whether Malory did what he *meant* to do and whether he did it well. In *A History of English Prose Rhythm* (1912), Saintsbury adds to the defence of Malory with an analysis of Malory's prose style and comments on its influence.

(a) *Specimens of English Prose Style* (London: Kegan Paul, Trench & Company, 1885), pp. xviii and l

For reasons obvious enough, not the most or the least obvious being the necessity of beginning somewhere, we begin these specimens with the invention of printing; not of course denying the title of books written before Caxton set up his press to the title of English or of English prose, but simply fixing a term from which literary production has been voluminous and uninterrupted in its volume. In the earlier examples, however (up, it may be said, to Lyly), the character of the passages, though often interesting and noteworthy, is scarcely characteristic. All the writers of this period are, if not actually, yet in a manner, translators. The work of Malory, charming as it is, and worthy to occupy the place of honour here given to it, is notoriously an adaptation of French originals. Latimer and Ascham, especially the former, in parts highly vernacular, are conversational where they are not classical.

It was not till the reign of Elizabeth was some way advanced that a definite effort on the part of writers to make an English prose style can be perceived. . . .

Nothing is known of the life of Sir Thomas Malory or Maleore. He is said to have been a Welshman and not Sir Knight but Sir Priest. He finished his work in the ninth year of King Edward the Fourth, and it was printed by Caxton in 1485. Compilation as it is, it has caught the whole spirit and beauty of the Arthurian legends, and is one of the first monuments of accomplished English prose.

(b) *Short History of English Literature* (New York: Macmillan, 1924 imprint), pp. 195–7

Practically nothing is known of the author of the greatest of all English romances, prose or verse—of one of the great romances of the world—a book which, though in mere material a compilation, and sometimes cleaving rather closely to its multifarious texts, is, despite the occasional misjudgment of unhappy criticism, a great and original book. Caxton, the printer—who, instead of, like most early printers, giving us early editions, and mostly bad ones, of the classics, which were quite safe, gave us, to the infinite advantage of England, early models of composition in English, and preserved to us, in this instance at least, an English text which might but for him have perished—tells us that the *Morte Darthur* was translated in the ninth year of King Edward IV. (that is to say, in 1470, fifteen years before he himself published it) by Sir Thomas Malory, Knight. Caxton's follower, Wynkyn de Worde, in the second edition of 1496, makes the name 'Maleore.' Malory or Mallory is both a Yorkshire and a Leicestershire name, but there are absolutely no materials for identifying Sir Thomas; the later suggestions that he was a Welsh priest, not an English knight, are baseless guesses, and we do not know in the very least why, when, or where he executed his book. What we do know, from the verse *Morte* and from Lonelich, is that a strong revived interest in the Arthurian Legend came in about the middle of the century, and this is to all appearances one of the fruits of it.

If so, it is incomparably the most precious. It is probable that, though among the laborious and respectable, but rather superfluous, inquiries into origins, none has yet been discovered for the 'Beaumains' story and for a few other things, Malory 'did not invent much.' The fifteenth century was not an inventive time, and there was much better work for it to do than second-rate invention. Then and then only could the mediaeval spirit, which was not quite dead, have been caught up and rendered for as with a still present familiarity, with the unconscious but unmistakable touch of magic which approaching loss reflects, and in English prose, which, unlike English verse, still had the bloom on it—the soon-fading *beauté du diable* of youth and freshness.

Criticisms have been made on Malory's manner of selecting and arranging his materials—criticisms which, like all unsuccessful exercises of the most difficult of arts, come from putting the wrong questions to the jury—from asking, 'Has this man done what *I* wanted him to do?' or 'Has he done it as *I* should have done it?' instead of 'Has he done what *he* meant to do?' and 'Has he done this well?' Malory might perhaps, though in his time it would have been difficult to get all the texts together, have given an intelligent *précis* of the whole Arthurian Legend, instead of which he selected his materials rather arbitrarily, and indulged in what looks to some critics like incomprehensible divagation, and not much more comprehensible suppression. He might have arranged a regular epic treatment of his subject, instead of which it is often difficult to say who is the hero, and never very easy to say what special contribution to the plot the occasionally inordinate episodes are making. What he did do consists mainly in two things, or perhaps three. He selected the most interesting things with an almost invariable sureness, though there are one or two omissions; and he omitted the less interesting parts with a sureness to which there are hardly any exceptions at all. He grasped, and this is his great and saving merit as an author, the one central fact of the story—that in the combination of the Quest of the Graal with the loves of Lancelot and Guinevere lay the kernel at once and the conclusion of the whole matter. And last (his great and saving merit as a writer) he told his tale in a manner which is very nearly impeccable.

There is one practically infallible test by which all but the dullest and most incompetent can be convinced of Sir Thomas's skill in this last direction, the comparison of his narrative of the last scenes of all with that in the verse *Morte d'Arthure* above mentioned, which was in all probability his direct original, and which was certainly written just before his day. Take the death of Arthur itself, or the final interview of Lancelot and the Queen, in both; compare them, and then remember that Malory has been dismissed as 'a mere compiler.' It is possible that his art is mostly unconscious art—it is not much the worse for that. But it is nearly as infallible as it is either unconscious or thoroughly concealed. The pictorial power, the musical cadence of the phrase, the steady glow of chivalrous feeling throughout, the noble morality (for the condemnation of Ascham and others is partly mere Renaissance priggishness stupidly condemning things mediaeval offhand, and partly Puritan prudery throwing its baleful shadow before), the kindliness, the sense of honour, the melancholy and yet never either gloomy or puling sense of the inevitable end—all these are eminent in it. It has been said, with perhaps hardly too great whimsicality, that there is only one bad thing about Malory—that to those who read him first he makes all other romances of Chivalry disappointing. But the fancy may at any rate be fairly retorted, for if any one is so unfortunate as to find other romances of chivalry disappointing, there is Malory to fall back upon. Merely in English prose he is a great figure, for although his medium would not be suitable for every purpose, it is nearly perfect for his own. Merely as the one great central storehouse of a famous and fertile story his place is sure. But apart from all these extrinsic considerations, it is surer still in the fact that he has added to literature an imperishable book.

(c) *A History of English Prose Rhythm* (London: Macmillan, 1912), pp. 80–93

... In Pecock's younger contemporary, Caxton, on the other hand, we find, perhaps for the first time, the conscious research of style. Again and again he tells us how, in that process of study and translation through which he went before devoting himself to the great accomplishment of popularising, through the printing-press, literature of the most diverse kinds in English, he had been struck and daunted by the inferiority of his English instrument, the difficulty of getting an adequate effect out of it, and the superiority of the 'fair language' of French. Except his production (how Heaven knows) of Malory, and his reproduction of Chaucer, nothing that Caxton printed is of the first value intrinsically. But all deserves the benefit of the definition of Goethe as to the duty of the scholar, that 'if he cannot accomplish he shall exercise himself.' And here at last he has the further benefit of our knowledge, due to himself, that he was exercising himself consciously.

It would not be exactly critical to say that these pains of Caxton's own brought him great profit as a translator from the point of view of style, or largely increased the treasury and pattern-storehouse of accomplished English prose. But they certainly show more than decent accomplishment; and by the variety of their subjects they must have exercised that subtle influence which has been so much dwelt on, while their direct evidence of conscious rhetorical study is invaluable. Moreover, for one thing that he did, if only ministerially, Caxton cannot be thanked too much or set too high. For the position which the fifteenth century (with its, in literature, necessary annexe of the first quarter or third of the sixteenth) bears in the history of English prose, is due to three persons—Malory, Fisher, and Berners; and the greatest of these three is Malory; and, so far as investigation has hitherto gone, we should have known nothing of Malory but for Caxton—which thing, if the sins of printers and publishers were twenty times as great even as they seemed to the poet Campbell or to my late friend Sir Walter Besant, let it utterly cancel and wash them away.

I do not know (or at least remember) who the person of genius was who first announced to the world that Malory was 'a compiler.' The statement is literally quite true (we may even surrender the Beaumains part and wish the receivers joy of it) in a certain lower sense, and exquisitely absurd as well as positively false in a higher. But it does not directly concern us. The point is that this *compilator compilans compilative in compilationibus compilandis* has, somehow or other, supplied a mortar of style and a design of word-architecture for his brute material of borrowed brick or stone, which is not only miraculous, but, in the nature even of miraculous things, uncompilable from any predecessor. Even if that single 'French book' which some have used against him from his own expressions, were to turn up, as it has never turned up yet, his benefit of clergy would still remain to him, for no French originals will give English clerkship of this kind and force. Moreover, as shall be more fully shown and illustrated presently, he had certainly English as well as French originals before him, and how he dealt with one at least of these we can show confidently, and as completely as if we had been present in Sir Thomas's *scriptorium*, in the ninth year of the reign of King Edward the Fourth, and he had kindly told us all about it.

'Original' in the only sense that imports to us, Malory can have had none—except perhaps the unknown translator or author of 'Mandeville,' on whom he has enormously improved. The *idée mère* of both styles—an idea of which in all probability both writers, and the earlier almost certainly, were quite unconscious— is the '*un*metring' without '*un*rhythming' of the best kind of romance style, with its easy flow, its short and uncomplicated sentences, and its picturesque stock phrases freed from verse- or rhyme-expletive and mere catchword. But the process, in Malory's case, had better be illustrated without further delay by comparison of the two passages cited above, from Malory's *Morte* itself and the verse *Morte*, which is almost certainly of the first half of the century if not earlier, and the verbal identities in part of which cannot be mere coincidence.

Abbess, to you I knowlache here,
That throw this elkè man and me,
(For we to-gedyr han loved us dere),
All this sorrowful war hath be;
My lord is slain that had no pere,
And many a doughty knight and free.

   . . . .

Ysett I am in suche a place,
My sowlè heal I will abide
Tellè God send[e] me some grace,
Through mercy of his woundès wide,

   . . . .

After to have a sight of his face
At Doomsday on his right side:
Therefore, Sir Lancelot du Lake,
For my love I now thee pray
My company thou aye forsake,
And to thy kingdom thou take thy way,
And keep thy realm from war and wrack,
And take a wife with her to play;

   . . . .

Unto God I pray, almighty king,
He give you together joy and bliss.

Through this man and me hath all this war been wrought, and the death of the most noblest knights of the world; for through our love that we have loved together is my most noble lord slain. Therefore, Sir Launcelot, wit thou well I am set in such a plight to get my soul's health; and yet I trust, through God's grace, that after my death to have a sight of the blessed face of Christ, and at doomsday to sit on his right side, for as sinful as ever I was are saints in heaven. Therefore, Sir Launcelot, I require thee and beseech thee heartily, for all the love that ever was betwixt us, that thou never see me more in the visage; and I command thee on God's behalf, that thou forsake my company, and to thy kingdom thou turn again and keep well thy realm from war and wrack. For as well as I have loved thee, mine heart will not serve me to see thee; for through thee and me is the flower of kings and knights destroyed. Therefore, Sir Launcelot, go to thy realm, and there take thee a wife, and live with her with joy and bliss, and I pray thee heartily pray for me to our Lord, that I may amend my misliving.

Now here, it will be observed, the verse is emphatically 'no great shakes.' It is not so bad as the contemporary exercitations of the abominable Herry [sic] Lonelich or Lovelich; but it has a great deal of the ever-recurring expletive, the flat and nerveless phrase, and the slipshod rather than flowing movement of the worst verse-romances. Still, it gives a fair 'canvas,' and this Sir Thomas takes, not even disdaining the retention of a few brighter stitches of his predecessor's, which he patches in, not fearing but welcoming, and mustering them into a distinct prose rhythm—treating them, in fact, just as Ruskin does his doses of blank verse. And so, out of the substance and the general procession of the verse, he has woven a quite new rhythm, accompanying and modulating graceful and almost majestic prose of the best type. There had been nothing in English prose before like the Queen's speech here; and it had been manufactured, as genius manufactures, out of a very commonplace web of English verse.

The Lancelot dirge, as has been said, may be a later composition, at a time when (*v. inf.*) definite rhetorical devices were attempted. It has at any rate no parallel in the verse, though this deals with the actual scene. But that, more famous than either of them, of the 'throwing Excalibur,' with its immensely interesting addition of Tennyson's re-versing from Malory himself, requires more notice.

The kynge tornyd hym there he stode
To syr Bedwere, *wyth* wordys kene,
'Have Excalaber, my swerd good,
A better brond was neuyr sene,
Go, Caste it in the salt flode,
And thou shalt se wonder, as I wene,
hye the faste, for crosse on Rode
And telle me what thou hast ther sene.'
The knyght was bothe hende and free;
To save that swerd he was fulle glad,
And thought, whethyr I better bee
yif neuyr man it After had;
And I it caste in to the see,
Off mold was neuyr man so mad.
The swerd he hyd vndyr A tree,
And sayd, 'syr, I ded as ye me bad.'
'What saw thow there? than sayd the kynge,
'Telle me now, yiff thow can;'
'Sertes syr,' he sayd, 'nothynge
But watres depe, And wawès wanne.'
'A now thou haste broke my byddynge!
Why haste thou do so, thow false man?
A-nother bode thou muste me brynge.'
Thanne careffully the knyght forthe Ranne,
And thought the swerd yit he wold hyde,
And keste the scauberke in the flode,
'Yif Any Aventurs shalle betyde,
There-by shalle I se tokenys goode.'
In-to the see hee lette the scauberke glyde;
A whyle on the land hee there stode;
Than to the kynge he wente that tyde
And sayd, 'syr, it is done by the Rode.'
Saw thow Any wondres more?'
'Sertys syr, I saw nought.'
'A! false traytor,' he sayd thore,
Twyse thou haste me treson wroght;

Therefore, said Arthur, take thou Excalibur, my good sword, and go with it to yonder water side, and when thou comest there, I charge thee throw my sword in that water, and come again, and tell me what thou there seest. My lord, said Bedivere, your commandment shall be done, and lightly bring you word again. So Sir Bedivere departed, and by the way he be held that noble sword, that the pommel and haft were all of precious stones, and then he said to himself, If I throw this rich sword in the water, thereof shall never come good, but harm and loss. And then Sir Bedivere hid Excalibur under a tree. And as soon as he might he came again unto the king, and said he had been at the water, and had thrown the sword into the water. What sawest thou there? said the king. Sir, he said, I saw nothing but waves and winds. That is untruly said of thee, said the king; therefore go thou lightly again, and do my command as thou art to me lief and dear, spare not, but throw it in. Then Sir Bedivere returned again, and took the sword in his hand; and then him thought sin and shame to throw away that noble sword; and so eft he hid the sword, and returned again, and told to the king that he had been at the water, and done his commandment. What saw thou there? said the king. Sir, he said, I saw nothing but the waters wap and the waves wan. Ah traitor, untrue, said king Arthur, now hast thou betrayed me twice. Who would have wend that thou that hast been to me so lief and dear, and thou art named a noble knight, and would betray me for the

That shall*e* thow rew sely sore,
And be thou bold it shalbe bought.'
The knyght than cryed, 'lord, thyn
ore,'
And to the swerd [*ẽ*] sone he sought.
Syr bedwere saw that bote was beste,
And to the good swerde he wente,
In-to the see he hyt, keste;
Than myght he see what that it mente;
There cam An hand, w*yth*-outen Reste,
Oute of the water, And feyre it hente,
And brandysshyd As it should braste,
And sythe, as gleme, A-way it glente.
To the kynge A-gayne wente he thare
And say, 'leve syr, I saw. An hand;
Oute of the water it cam All*e* bare,
And thryse brandysshd that Ryche
brande.'
'helpe me sone that I ware there.'
he leds hys lord vnto that stronde;
A rych*è* shippe w*yth* maste And ore,
Full*e* of ladyes there they fonde.
The ladyes, that were feyre and Free,
Curteysly the kynge gan they fonge,
And one, that bryghtest was of blee,
Wepyd sore, and handys wrange,
'Broder,' she sayd, 'wo ys me;
Fro lechyng hastow be to longe,
I wote that gretely greuyth me,
For thy paynès Ar full*e* stronge.'
The knyght kest A rewfull*e* rowne,
There he stode, sore and vnsownde,
And say, 'lord, whedyr Ar ye bowne,
Allas, whedyr wyll*e* ye fro me fownde?'
The kynge spake w*yth* A sory sowne,
'I wylle wende A lytell*e* stownde
In to the vale of Avelovne,
A whyle to hele me of my wounde.'

riches of the sword. But now go again lightly, for the long tarrying putteth me in great jeopardy of my life, for I have taken cold. And but if thou do now as I bid thee, if ever I may see thee, I shall slay thee with mine own hands, for thou wouldest for my rich sword see me dead. Then Sir Bedivere departed, and went to the sword, and lightly took it up, and went to the water side, and there he bound the girdle about the hilts, and then he threw the sword as far into the water as he might, and there came an arm and an hand above the water, and met it, and caught it, and so shook it thrice and brandished, and then vanished away the hand with the sword in the water. So sir Bedivere came again to the king, and told him what he saw. Alas, said the king, help me hence, for I dread me I have tarried over long. Then Sir Bedivere took the king upon his back, and so went with him to that water side. And when they were at the water side, even fast by the bank hoved a little barge, with many fair ladies in it, and among them all was a queen, and all they had black hoods, and all they wept and shrieked when they saw king Arthur. Now put me into the barge, said the king: and so he did softly. And there received him three queens with great mourning, and so they set him down, and in one of their laps king Arthur laid his head, and then that queen said, Ah, dear brother, why have ye tarried so long from me? Alas, this wound on your head hath caught over much cold. And so then they rowed from the land; and Sir Bedivere beheld all those ladies go from him. Then Sir Bedivere cried, Ah, my lord Arthur, what shall become of me now ye go from me, and leave me here alone among mine enemies. Comfort thyself, said the king, and do as well as thou mayest, for in me is no trust for to trust in. For I will into the vale of Avilion, to heal me of my grievous wound. And if thou hear never more of me, pray for my soul.

We may indeed note here how this 'compiler' succeeded, as to his mere matter, in compiling *out* Bedivere's silly compromise of throwing the scabbard the second time; but still more the real things—his fashion and manner of style and treatment. These are weaker in the verse than in the original of the Guinevere passage, and he hardly takes anything literal in phrase, altering importantly when he does take something, as in the feeble expletive 'deep.' But he weaves the whole once more into the most astonishing tissue of pure yet perfect prose rhythm. That it takes but little, as Tennyson showed, to make it once more into splendid verse of character as different as possible from the bald shambling sing-song of the early fifteenth-century man, is nothing against this. That you can get some actual blank verse or fragments of blank out of it is nothing again:

> That hast been [un] to me so lief and dear...
> And thou art named a noble knight...
> For thou wouldest for my rich sword see me dead...

For these (as such things in the right hands always do) act as ingredients, not as separable parts. They colour the rhythm, but they do not constitute it. They never correspond with each other.

It is not, however, to the great show passages of 'the death and departing out of this world of them all,' of the Quest of the Graal, of the adventures of Lancelot and the rest, that it is necessary to confine the search for proof of Malory's mastery of style and rhythm. One general symptom will strike any one who has read a fair amount of the *Morte* from our point of view. There are plenty of sentences in Malory beginning with 'and'; but it is not the constant go-between and usher-of-all-work that it is in Mandeville. The abundance of conversation gets him out of this difficulty at once; and he seems to have an instinctive knowledge—hardly shown before him, never reached after him till the time of the great novelists—of weaving conversation and narrative together. Bunyan, and certainly most people before Bunyan's day, with Defoe to some extent after him, seem to make distinct gaps between the two, like that of the scenes of a play—to have now a piece of narrative, now one of definite 'Tig and Tiri'[1] drama. Malory does not. His narrative order and his dialogue are so artistically adjusted that they dovetail into one another.[2] Here is an instance, taken entirely at hazard, not better than a hundred or a thousand others, and perhaps not so good as some:

And with that came the damosel of the lake unto the king and said, 'Sir, I must speak with you in private.' 'Say on,' said the king, 'what ye will.' 'Sir,' said the lady, 'put not on you this mantle till ye have seen more, and in no wise let it come upon you nor on no knight of yours till ye command the bringer thereof to put it upon her.' 'Well,' said King Arthur, 'it shall be done as ye counsel me.' And then he said unto the damosel that came from his sister, 'Damosel, this mantle that ye have brought me I will see it upon you.' 'Sir,' said she, 'it will not beseem me to wear a knight's garment.' 'By my head,' said King Arthur, 'ye shall wear it or it come on my back, on any man that here is;' and so the king made it to be put upon her; and forthwith she fell down dead, and nevermore spake word after, and was brent to coals.

Here, in a sample as little out of the common way as possible, you may see the easy run of rhythm, the presence of a certain not excessive balance, tempered by lengthening and shortening of clauses, the breaking and knitting again of the cadence-thread; and even (which is really surprising in so early a writer) the selection, instinctive no doubt, but not the less wonderful, of an emphatic monosyllable to close the incident and paragraph. If a more picked example be wanted, nothing better need be sought than the often-quoted passage of the Chapel Perilous. While one of the best of all, though perhaps too long to quote, is that where Lancelot, after the great battle with Turquine (the exact locality of which, by the way, is given in the old histories of Manchester), comes to the Giant's Castle of the Bridge, and slays the bridgeward, but riding into the castle yard, is greeted by 'much people in doors and windows that said, "Fair Knight: thou art unhappy,"' for a close to the chapter.

The dominant of Malory's rhythm, as might indeed be expected in work so much based on French prose and verse and English verse, is mainly iambic, though he does not neglect the precious inheritance of the trochaic or amphibrachic ending, nor the infusion of the trochaic run elsewhere. His sentences, though sometimes of fair length, are rarely periodic enough, or elaborately descriptive enough, to need four-syllable and five-syllable feet: and you may resolve sentence after sentence, as in the last passage noted, into iambs pure, iambs extended by a precedent short into anapaests and iambs, or curling over with a short suffix into amphibrachs, and so getting in the trochee.

Aňd sō | Sïr Lān | cĕlŏt aňd | tĥe dāmsĕl | dĕpārted.[3]

Yet, in some mysterious way, he resists, as has been said, the tendency to drop into poetry.

> Now hast thou ‖ thy payment that thou hast so long deserved

is, as a matter of fact, an unexceptionable blank-verse line, preceded by an unexceptionable fragment in a fashion to be found all over Shakespeare, in Milton, and sometimes in all their better followers as well. Yet you would never dream of reading it in prose with any blank-verse rhythm, though the division at 'payment' gives a fraction of further blank verse, which Shakespeare in his latest days, or Beaumont and Fletcher at any time, would have unhesitatingly written.

I had thought of giving a few more rhythmical fragments in the way of a *bonne bouche*. But on going through the book (no unpleasant concession to duty) for I suppose nearer the fiftieth than the twentieth time, I found that, to do justice, *mere* fragments would hardly suffice. Quintilian, I suppose, would hardly have appreciated Malory's matter; but he must have admitted that the style was not of that 'complexion sprinked with spots, bright, if you like, but too many and too different,' which the sober Roman hated. Every now and then, indeed, there comes a wonderful symphonic arrangement, as in the close of the story of Balin: 'Thus endeth the tale of Balin and Balan, ‖ two brothers born in Northumberland, ‖ good knights,' ‖ where I have put the double division to mark what we may almost call the prose-line making a prose-stanza with no trace of verse in it. More complicated and more wonderful still is the rhythm of the dialogue between the sorceress Hellawes, damsel of the Chapel Perilous, and Sir Lancelot; while the Graal part is crowded with such things. But Malory never seems to put himself out of the way for them; they surge up suddenly in the clear flood of his narrative, and add life and flesh to it for a moment—and the flood goes on.

It must, however, be observed that this prose of Malory's, extraordinarily beautiful as it is, was a sort of half-accidental result of the combination of hour and man, and could never be repeated, save as the result of deliberate literary craftsmanship of the imitative, though of the best imitative, kind. As such it has been achieved in our own days; and in the proper place I may point out that the denigration of Mr. Morris's prose as 'Wardour Street' and the like is short-sighted and unworthy. It is then a product of the man directly, but not (or only in an indirect and sophisticated way) of the hour. In Malory's days there was a great body of verse-romance in English, with a half-conventional phraseology, which was not yet in any sense insincere or artificial. This phraselogy lent itself directly to the treatment of Malory's subject; while the forms in which it was primarily arranged lent themselves in the same way, though less obviously, and after a fashion requiring more of the essence of the right man, to a simple but extremely beautiful and by no means monotonous prose rhythm, constantly introducing fragments of verse-cadence, but never allowing them to arrange themselves in anything like verse-sequence or metre. That the great popularity of the book—which is attested by such outbursts against it as that of Ascham from the mere prosaic-Protestant-Philistine point of view, almost as well as by its eight black-letter editions between 1485 (Caxton's) and 1634 (Stansby's)—was to any large, to even any appreciable, extent due to conscious delight in this beauty of prose, it would be idle to pretend. Milton may have seen its beauty when those younger feet of his were wandering in romance, and had not yet deserted it for Philistia and Puritania; when he forgathered with Lancelot, and Pelleas, and Pellinore, instead of with the constituents of 'Smectymnuus,' and the creatures of Cromwell. Spenser can hardly have failed to do so earlier, for though he has, with an almost whimsical perversity of independence, refused to know anything of Malory's Arthurian *matter*, the whole atmosphere and ordonnance of the *Faerie Queene* are Malorian. But that this popularity did influence Elizabethan prose few competent students of English literature have ever failed to recognise....

SELECTED NOTES

1 The fit reader will not have forgotten this vivid Johnsonism (which for the moment puzzled two such not blunt wits as Hester Thrale's and Frances Burney's), dismissing all that was dramatic of a dialogue printed as between '*Ti*granes' and '*Tiri*bazus.'

2 It has been urged that he owes this also to 'the French book.' Not in this quarter will any one meet depreciation of the prose Arthurian romances.

But I think my often-repeated caution as to translation applies here.

3 'And so | Sir Lan | celot and | the *maid* | departed' would, of course, be pure blank verse, and very difficult to smuggle off in prose. But the little extra short of 'dām | sĕl' saves the whole situation, and abolishes the blank-verse tendency.

402

Index

THE CRITICAL HERITAGE SERIES

GENERAL EDITOR: B. C. SOUTHAM

Volumes published and forthcoming